The Lives of

Danny Kaye

Also by Martin Gottfried

Sondheim

More Broadway Musicals

All His Jazz: The Life and Death of Bob Fosse

In Person: The Great Entertainers

Jed Harris: The Curse of Genius

Broadway Musicals

Opening Nights

A Theater Divided

Martin Gottfried

NOBODY'S FOOL

SIMON & SCHUSTER
New York   London   Toronto   Sydney   Tokyo   Singapore

Simon & Schuster
Rockefeller Center
1230 Avenue of the Americas
New York, NY 10020

Simon & Schuster and colophon are registered trademarks of Simon & Schuster, Inc.
Designed by Hyun Joo Kim
Manufactured in the United States of America

10 9 8 7 6 5 4 3 2 1

Library of Congress Cataloging-In-Publication Data

Gottfried, Martin.
Nobody's fool: the lives of Danny Kaye/ Martin Gottfried.
      p.   cm.
              1.   Kaye, Danny.
  2. Comedians—United States—Biography.
  3. Entertainers—United States—Biography.   I. Title.
        PN2287.K3G68   1994
        792.7´028   ´092—dc20
[B]   94-28185

            CIP
      ISBN: 0-7432-4476-1

Acknowledgments

A biography is only as good as its research, and its research begins with sources—those who knew and worked with the subject. They provide not only incidents and specific dialogue; they lend a sense of the biographee's presence, and, finally, they give the most important of all qualities to a work of nonfiction, its sense of truth, of proof, of eyewitness. Nearly a thousand hours went into the interviewing of sources for this book before even a concept was formulated. Gracious, forthcoming, detailed, and careful in their recollections, they provided a sense of David Kaminski and Danny Kaye, from his boyhood until his old age, from his radiance to his difficultness and griefs. I can only begin to thank these people for their cooperation—Murray Goldberg, Ben Gould, Isidore Skolnick, Joanna Simon, John Weiner, Blanche Ganz, Betty Hutton, Louis and Sylvia Eisen, Kitty Carlisle, Elaine Steinbeck, Benay Venuta, Imogene Coca, Herman Pollack, Richard Diamond, Dr. Isadore Rosenfeld, Rose Kaye, Mike Burstyn, Lillian Lux, Mary Lasker, Bronya Galef, Linda Palmer, Michael Jackson, Larry Gelbart, Henny Backus, Steve Wallace, Angela Lansbury, Cesar Romero, Perry Lafferty, Hal Kanter, Mel Tolkin, Lovelady Powell, Alan King, Martin

Charnin, Radie Harris, Walter Willison, Joan Copeland, Joe Layton, Julie Andrews, Warren Cowan, Victor Navasky, Arthur Rankin, Burton Lane, Josh Mostel, Tony Randall, Anthony Newley, Lord Lew Grade, Anton Mosimann, Bryan Forbes, Anthony Holden, Colin Romoff, Georgia Gibbs, Jule Styne, Michael Korda, Buzz Miller, Buddy Hackett, Ethel Martin, Farley Granger, Fred W. Friendly, Dr. Michael Ellis De Bakey, Marlene Sorosky, Jonathan Schwartz, and David and Nancy Sureck. There is not a word of dialogue or any incident in this book that was not directly witnessed by at least one of these sources or another participant whose account appeared in print.

I was especially helped by Dina Consolini at the Museum of Television and Radio and relied heavily, as usual, on the forthcoming staff and deep resources of the Theater Collection at the Library for the Performing Arts in Lincoln Center. I am also indebted to Ann King for helping to gather research materials. Gene Young proved to be, yet again, my meanest, most unrelenting, least sympathetic, and most stimulating critic. Finally, I am grateful to my dear Barrie Brett for her early, supportive, yet tough-minded reading.

If writing is the loneliest of efforts, it is not so solitary as to permit self-sufficiency. There is always a team behind a book and my team was the best, starting with Susanne Jaffe, the editor who supported the project from the outset. Chuck Adams finished the editing with equal enthusiasm and involvement. Carol O'Brien gave me advice and support from the London office of Simon & Schuster; my legal neck was saved by Leslie Jones, a publisher's counselor with a literary sensibility. I am grateful to them all.

For my darling brothers, Elliot and Stuart,
and all of us kids from Brooklyn.

Part I

Becoming
Danny Kaye

I wasn't born a fool. It took work to get this way.

THE THEATER DID NOT HAVE THE PLUSHNESS OF BROADWAY, THE LUSH WOOL CARPETING AND SOFT VELVET UPHOLSTERY. RATHER, IT had the sharp and arousing scent of a cedar linen closet. Its open rafters, wood walls, and bare floor gave the place a feeling of country, and it was as plain as the folding chairs, as plain as the audience and the sturdy women in their bright print dresses, the businesslike men wearing crisply creased white duck pants, as plain as the animation and the informal chattering that this was a theater at a resort hotel.

The stage lights went down, and with that, the country playhouse hushed. When the lights came up again, a different setting was on the stage, a simple backdrop with a hearth, and in front of the hearth was a bench. A rabbi sat on it.

This was a change in tone for a Saturday night show in 1932 at the White Roe resort, high in New York's Catskill Mountains. Unlike Fishel Goldfarb's opening monologue ("Fisheloonies"), Dave and Kathleen's ballroom dancing, and Blanche Felder's impressions of Maurice Chevalier and other stars of the day, this moment was serious.

The dark-bearded man onstage wore the purple-satin coat and the long side curls of a Hasidic Jew. At his feet were two youngsters, recognized by some in the audience as Sammy and Sonny Siegel, who lived in the nearby town of Livingston Manor. The seven-piece band took its cue from conductor Hi Frank and, with a high-pitched, squawking clarinet in the lead, croaked the Middle Eastern wails of Jewish klezmer music. Then the rabbi began to sing.

> *Oyfn pripetshik*
> *Brent a fayerl*
> *Unt in shtub iz haiss.*
> *Unt der rebbe lehrent*
> *Kley-ne kinder-lech*
> *Dem alef, beyz*

An audible sigh of familiarity slipped through the audience. Some of them leaned sideways, whispering translations, and that prompted hushes, for few in that audience could not understand Yiddish, and very few had not heard this lullaby. It lay at the heart of Jewish family life.

> In the hearth
> Burns a fire
> And it's hot in the house
> And the rabbi teaches
> The little children
> The A, B, C's

The atmosphere was nostalgic, inspired by the familiar song, by its heartrending dissonances and the gentle syncopation of the ethnic music. In the program the piece was identified as "*Malamud in Cheder*"—the Hebrew schoolteacher—but nearly everyone knew it as "*Oyfn Pripetshik*," and the rabbi sang those opening words in a light baritone that captured the little lullaby's sentiments.

When he was through, he patted the boys lightly on the backs of their heads and pinched their cheeks. Then the lights went down, and the audience applauded warmly.

When the stage lights came up again, the red-velvet curtains had been drawn shut, with "White Roe" embroidered at either end in bold white lettering. Stepping between them, the actor who had played the rabbi reappeared, bowing to acknowledge the renewed applause. Then he took off his yarmulke, slipped out of his coat, and peeled off the beard and wig. He was not even twenty. His hair was as red as a new penny, and his skinny young face was scrubbed and beaming. He was confident on that stage and self-conscious only about his nose. *"Keef off don do nasele!"* ("Look at the nose!"), he had scrawled in Yiddish on a picture given to the hotel owner.

The audience was already giggling, for he was their darling. Only the night before, they had watched him act in George S. Kaufman and Moss Hart's comedy *Once in a Lifetime.* All week he had been up and down the place, at lakeside in the afternoons and joking on the porch after supper, and those who had been at White Roe in previous summers knew him from other Saturday night shows. Now, out of the rabbi costume, wearing dark trousers and a neat white short-sleeved shirt, he began to sing in a strong, clear, good-natured voice. This song was quite a departure from *"Oyfn Pripetshik."* Its music was a wailing jazz melody with a strong drumbeat, actually rather like a burlesque bump. And yet, to tell the truth, it was not so different from klezmer music.

> Once there was a gal named "Minnie the Moocher,"
> She was a low-down hoochie coocher,
> She was the roughest and the toughest frail,
> But Minnie had a heart as big as a whale.

The audience rocked and cheered. "Minnie the Moocher" (or "Hi-De-Hi," as it was listed in the program) was a White Roe favorite, and the young man sang it at almost every show. Even if Cab Calloway had introduced the number in Harlem, Danny Kaye had made it his own at these Saturday night shows, and his audience knew their role. They were ready to sing along; to repeat each line after him.

> Oh, hi-de-hi-de-hi (Oh, hi-de-hi-de-hi)
> Oh, ho-de-ho-de-ho (Oh, ho-de-ho-de-ho)
> Oh, hee-dee-hee-dee-hee (Oh, hee-dee-hee-dee-hee)

There was something about him that an audience could not resist. Years later, the son of the hotel's owner would recall the contrast between *"Oyfn Pripetshik"* and "Minnie the Moocher" and say, "There wasn't anyone who saw him who didn't understand that this man would be one of the great stars of all time. It was obvious from the very beginning."

. . .

HOW MANY MOTHERS, LIKE DANNY KAYE'S, WERE CURATORS OF THE Jewish culture? Like primeval creatures with a sense of biological mission, they had crossed the ocean to the New World, carrying with them the tokens and rituals of Jewish life. They transported the style of the Friday night Sabbath ceremony—the way of draping the head with a shawl, how to enclose the candles within the arms, to cover the eyes with the palms. They brought with them the traditional recipes for tzimmes and potato latkes, a taste for bread and shmaltz with *gribbenetz*, their knowledge of the proportions for hot milk and honey, the correct approach for bringing a disrespectful child to his senses, and the complete notebook of sarcasm. They brought, as well, lullabies like *"Oyfn Pripetshik"*; indeed, they brought the Yiddish language itself. These were far grander than the pathetic few possessions they could carry—the pots and candlesticks and hair combs.

It was in a small upstairs bedroom of a modest, two-story, pale yellow wood-frame house at 350 Bradford Street, between Sutter Avenue and Belmont in the East New York section of Brooklyn that Clara Kaminski crooned *"Oyfn Pripetshik"* to Duvidelleh—David Daniel, her baby. Clara's other boys, four- and five-year-old Larry and Mack, had been born in the old country. Even though they were now in America, they all spoke Yiddish at home. Thus, it was the first language heard by David, born in Brooklyn on January 18, 1913, the only native-born American in the Kaminski family.

The prospect of his becoming an international star was surely inconceivable to his family, as unimaginable as the change in Jacob and Clara Kaminski's world when they traveled from Ekaterinoslav in the Ukraine to Philadelphia in 1910. Jacob had to work for two years to pay off those steamer tickets for Clara, Larry, Mack, and himself. Then he moved the family to Brooklyn.

Jacob was a little fellow (five feet six inches) with a real potbelly, and he tied his belt above it, closer to the chest than the waist. Walking with one shoulder hitched slightly higher than the other and wearing steel-rimmed glasses hooked on his prominent ears, he presented a look that was inevitably described as cute.

He had been a horse dealer in Kiev, but Brooklyn's limited horse population had forced him to reconsider his career options. Since some horses were to be found on the farms just beyond Bradford

Street, he started out sewing saddlebags. That led to corsets, and sewing them was what he finally chose to do as a specialty. So he took the subway from the nearby New Lots Avenue station to Manhattan's Garment District, where he had a job in a corset workshop. He didn't have to learn English to work there, and he never would speak it very well.

Clara doted on her Duvidelleh—too much, in Jacob's opinion. "His mother, *aaah*, she used to hold him close like he was a baby. She used to learn him songs from Russia and to dance."

"I used to teach him songs in Jewish, too," the father said, having been a cantor in the synagogue in the old country. "But dancing I didn't teach him. This is the mother."

Young David showed early signs of responding to his mother's encouragement. At four, when Clara brought him into a shoe store, he startled everyone there by bursting into song. She was probably not herself surprised. When there was company at home, she would encourage him to sing, crying *Mach vie* ["make like"] and naming some star of the day.

Given these circumstances, it is difficult to draw a conclusion about the source of artistic talent and whether it is genetic or psychological in origin. Clara Kaminski certainly encouraged David to perform, but while that might have given him the idea and strengthened his bravado, it did not produce the ability to perform well, the creativity to find a unique way to entertain, or the drive to persist in the face of discouragement and rejection. Perhaps, then, his relationships with his parents were more directly related to his emotional development—this unusually doting and physically demonstrative mother encouraging a little boy to perform; this father possibly not so approving. When Jacob said, "Danny was always a good boy," he would add, "When he used to make funny, he didn't do it by home. He did it by friends." Here, perhaps, were the seeds of a future extrovertedness in public, an introvertedness in private.

A year later, David made his stage debut in the P.S. 149 school auditorium, appearing with practically everyone else in his kindergarten class in a blackface minstrel show called *The Watermelon Fantasy*. Offensive as that might seem, it was not a matter of conscious racism. Race did not exist in the East New York section of Brooklyn because this little world was exclusively white and Jewish. The world was only as big as the neighborhood.

However, even the most homogeneous groups will find minorities, as if they are needed. In *The Watermelon Fantasy*, among the dozens of kindergartners playing the seeds in a big slice of watermelon, David Kaminski was the only redhead.

The psychological effects of being red-haired have not been studied as much as, for instance, those of being left-handed or short or fat, but many redheads speak of an early awareness of being peculiar and of being laughed at. This is not only because of their unusual hair color but also because of the heavily freckled skin pigmentation that frequently accompanies it. They are called "Red." They are often expected to be funny. Not uncommonly, redheads have feelings of loneliness because of their differentness and identify with other redheads when they find them.

For Kaye, the red hair might have been one source for what he became—a cause as well as a symbol of his difference.

The budding entertainer began his lifelong quest for laughs by making funny faces in the school yard. That was where he made friends with young Louis Eisen, who lived a block away on Miller Avenue. Louis was himself a performer, singing in public for who knows what reasons and accompanying himself on a ukulele he had taught himself to play. The boys began to sing together, and probably all of these factors were necessary to the incubation of David Kaminski's simple talent for making faces and singing songs and his eagerness to do so in public. For Jacob was setting the example of going his own way, Clara was urging him to make like Shirley Temple, and Louis Eisen was keeping him from feeling peculiar and alone. Perhaps, then, he was not so different from everyone else.

But, of course, he was. Most people did not want, need, or like to perform.

When David was twelve, he tried to contribute to the family income by finding an after-school job assisting Dr. Samuel Fine, a dentist whose office and home were directly across the street. But when Dr. Fine discovered him using a dental drill to carve designs in a block of wood, the boy was dismissed. The $1.25-a-week income would have ended, anyway, for Fine moved his office, his wife, Bessie, and their children, Robert, Rhoda, and Sylvia, to Flatbush, a fancier part of Brooklyn. David would not remember meeting Sylvia, the dentist's older daughter, but the precocious eleven-year-old girl would never forget the day.

Clara Kaminski died soon after David's bar mitzvah, and his grandmother moved in to take care of him. Jewish grandmothers were traditionally called "Ba," "Baba," or the affectionate "Ba-belleh." David's grandmother was a "Ba," and a couple of cousins moved in with her. His father paid little attention to any of them. Jacob also lost his interest in cooking. Something seemed to have gone out of "Pop" with the death of Clara. When she had been alive, he had enjoyed making Russian stews and soups like borscht or schav. Now he lived on a diet of potatoes and whiskey, both of which he kept in the icebox.

It was from Jacob that David inherited an interest in cooking, and it was from Jacob, too, that he learned to keep his emotional distance. He loved his father very much, and like his father, he went his own way. "I didn't have family restrictions imposed on me as much as other kids in my neighborhood," he would remember. "I didn't have my sense of curiosity stifled," and for a fourteen-year-old, he led quite a separate life with his partner. They already called each other Dave and Lou, the way men do, and, Eisen would remember, "We had nothing to do but eat, laugh, and live."

They already considered themselves a full-fledged *harmony* team like Reese and Dunn, a vaudeville team they had seen at the Premier Theatre on Sutter Avenue, just around the corner. Dubbing their act "Red and Blackie," they would spend the afternoons practicing songs and comedy. They even adopted Reese and Dunn's popular "Sweet Jenny Lee" and sang it on the Brooklyn radio station WBBC.

Dave and Lou remained classmates when they entered Thomas Jefferson High School in 1927. The full-block building on Dumont Avenue had only recently been completed, replacing a Gypsy encampment that had once brought an exotic danger to the neighborhood. The school was in walking distance, yet that was far enough away to make it foreign territory. To an urban adolescent, the entire world was reckoned in terms of adjacent city blocks.

The daily walk to school took the boys across the trolley tracks, past the Linden Boulevard swamps, and beyond the farms around Hendricks Street and New Lots Avenue. This was open land, with goats, horses, and the boys' favorites—cows. Eager for rides, they would leap on the poor creatures' backs and teeter a few yards before sliding off.

Lou and Dave, then, were growing up. They had already progressed from knickers to long pants. Now their world was expanding as they met boys and girls from the streets beyond their immediate neighborhood; from the apartment houses on Pennsylvania Avenue and above the stores on Sutter Avenue. Still, it was a parochial world. Almost everyone was a first-generation Jewish American, with parents from the old country and Yiddish the home language. Mothers kept kosher kitchens, boys were given bar mitzvahs, and they all followed the boxing matches. Baseball's popularity would come later, with radio, although Larry and Mack had already taken Dave to Ebbets Field, buying nickel bleacher seats to see the Brooklyn Dodgers play.

The boys' street games were stickball, stoopball, and punchball, at which Dave was especially good. He could punch a ball farther than a half block, a distance of "one and a half sewers," measuring by street landmarks, as city kids did. He was good at most sports, being tall, skinny, and fast. He played basketball for the high school junior varsity, and that was an achievement, because Jefferson High already had a reputation for superior athletes. It also had a superior academic reputation, which may have been why Sylvia Fine's parents enrolled her there instead of in Erasmus Hall, which was her district high school. Sylvia had to take two subway lines to get to Jefferson High, but Sam and Bessie Fine were more interested in the quality of education than traveling convenience or the status of a school in the fancier section of Flatbush.

The Fines lived in a neighborhood of brick houses with lawns and driveways and tree-lined streets. In socially inferior East New York, there were few trees and no driveways or lawns, certainly not on Bradford Street, where the Kaminskis lived, unless the ten-foot-square patch of grass in front of the house could be considered a lawn. The street might have been clean enough, wide enough, and light enough—certainly respectable enough—but the identical frame houses that lined either side of it were modest affairs. The families living there were only a step above the greenhorns fresh from the boats, packed into the tenements on the Lower East Side.

Sylvia was such a good student that by the time Dave entered Thomas Jefferson, she was already a junior, even though he was seven months older. (Her birthday was August 29, 1913.) And while he was an undistinguished freshman, she was a junior who played an active part in school life. She exercised her presence despite being a candidate for rejection as a brainy-and-she-knows-it girl who was unattractive in the bargain, being short, disproportionately bosomy, with protruding ears and a very long nose. But Sylvia Fine was a spunky girl, an achiever, and her wonderful eyes revealed her intelligence—big, dark, bright eyes. She became the president of her class and the assistant editor of the school newspaper, the *Liberty Bell*, for which she wrote a weekly humor column.

She was also a musician. She had discovered the piano at three, and her lessons began at six. By the time she was ten, she was studying harmony and theory, but her first recital prompted a painful case of stage fright, and she never again tried to play before a large audience. She preferred the more casual atmosphere of dance class or the company of playing with the school octet. She was also developing an interest in writing songs for the school shows. These were all group activities and might have been her way of making friends.

She came from a richer and better-educated family than most of her classmates, which couldn't have helped her social life, either. Ben Gould, her editor on the school newspaper, remembered, "There was a difference in her type of dress, the way she spoke. . . . Many parents couldn't speak English. Sylvia, on the other hand, had a father who was a college graduate." Because of that, according to Gould, "she was aloof. She seemed to be on a higher strata." Yet even though he considered her a snob, he admired her. Working together twice a week in the Press Club where they put out the *Liberty Bell*, he attributed much of her distance to shyness. "She was a bookworm, and she also had a better-looking sister [Rhoda]." But there was no mistaking her abilities. "Her writing," Gould said, "was incredible for a high school student," and she was clever, using her column to write doggerel and political satire.

Bright as she was, though, there was little she could do to make herself more attractive. Even wearing lipstick or rouge was against the school rules, and if a girl were caught at it, she would be given a "pink card"—a demerit. And so Sylvia Fine could only slip behind her desk, with its wrought-iron base screwed into the floor, slide her books under the lift-up lid, dip her pen into its inkwell, sit up as straight as her A's, and do her best, which was academic.

Dave's friend Lou Eisen would get to know her, remembering Sylvia as "the brightest of the group," but by then Kaminski was gone. He had survived the freshman academic rigors—algebra, biology, and a foreign language. He had even managed to get passing grades in a sophomore year of geometry and chemistry, but he was mischievous, and slogging through the snow one morning, he had been inspired by the piles of manure on the farms along Pennsylvania Avenue. Soon the halls of Jefferson High were echoing with laughter as word was passed that some of that manure had turned up in the lap of the statue of Thomas Jefferson in the school entrance hall. There were arguments about whether it was horse manure or cow manure, but whatever the primary source, there was no question about the secondary one. Everyone knew it had been Dave Kaminski.

He was summoned to the office of the assistant principal, Samuel Muldorf. In later years, school lore would have it that Kaminski could be heard through the door to Muldorf's office, mimicking the assistant principal to his face; sounding more like Muldorf than Muldorf did. The truth was that rather than accept punishment, the youngster had quit high school.

It was hardly possible to get a job. The stock market had crashed less than six months earlier, and even grown men with education and experience were out of work. Dave, idle when everyone else was in class, spent the evenings with Lou Eisen, going to the movies on Miller Avenue or the burlesque house on Pitkin Avenue. His father let him be. The only place that was off limits was the pool parlor at the corner of Sutter and Elton. That was where the Murder, Inc. crowd hung out. Red and Blackie were now hiring themselves out to sing at social affairs, and they even performed at one of Murder, Inc.'s parties.

One Christmas, with the bravado available only to adolescents, they ran away, hitchhiking all the way to Miami Beach. Their idea was to get work as entertainers. "He comes back," Jacob Kaminski remembered, "in nine, ten days. He's all black. He says, I stay here now." Whether "all black" meant dirty or suntanned, from then on, Dave had a case on Miami Beach.

Between engagements—when they were "at liberty," as it was put in vaudeville—they sang on the corner in front of the candy store. That was a social center, as it was in many such neighborhoods, and the reason was simple: Few homes had private telephones. Access to a candy store's phone booths was a personal and business necessity. For years Dave would take his calls at the corner candy store.

One evening, a young man named Nat Lichtman was heading for the telephone booths to conduct his business when he noticed Red and Blackie doing their act out in front. Lichtman didn't live in the neighborhood; he lived in New Jersey and was visiting his mother, but that was fortuitous, because Nat Lichtman ran the entertainment program of a resort hotel called White Roe Lake House in Livingston Manor, New York. After he had watched the boys singing duets, he invited them to join his summer staff. So, after all, there was something that Dave could do, and he was going to do it.

2

I used to fall into a pool fully dressed. I would do anything
for a laugh. I ran the gamut from A to double X.

WHITE ROE LAKE WAS, AND STILL IS, NESTLED DEEP IN THE CATS-
KILL MOUNTAINS, 112 MILES FROM NEW YORK CITY AND THREE AND
a half miles from Route 17. At that time the route was called the
Liberty Highway, because it ran through the town of Liberty,
the heart of the "borscht belt" of Jewish summer resort hotels in the
Catskills. The village of Livingston Manor was the farthest notch
along that belt. It was part of a farming community, with a population of roughly a thousand people.

Livingston's first Jew, a man named Schwartz, had arrived with
his nine children early in the 1900s and was greeted with a $500 offer
to leave town, which was a fair amount of money at the time. It
wasn't enough, and Schwartz turned it down. He stuck things out,
assimilating to the extent of becoming not only a volunteer fireman
but a Rotarian. Soon more Jews arrived—Meyer Weiner and his
family, buying a farm and running it so profitably that in 1919 he
was able to acquire 750 acres on the face of White Roe Mountain,
sloping gently down to the town lake. Weiner had a notion—a novel
one at the time—to create a summer place for young Jewish single
people—"no families, no children, nobody under eighteen, nobody

over thirty-five. Lots of athletics, all kinds of activities and all the food you can eat."

He opened for business with fifteen rooms. The second summer, he added thirty tents, each sleeping four. Within ten years, White Roe Lake House sat proudly on a beautiful site twenty-four hundred feet above sea level. The hotel had new and elaborate facilities, with accommodations for four hundred people, albeit five and six to a room. All of those guests were single. As for "all the food you could eat," it added up to six meals a day, beginning with two breakfasts, the regular one and then "late breakfast" for anyone who had missed it or was still hungry. After lunch, tea was served in midafternoon, and after dinner the kitchen was left open. Any guest could come in at any time to get anything to eat that he wanted. Finally, for the survivors, a midnight supper was served; like all the food, it was Jewish in style—white fish, herring, lox, and bagels.

White Roe, as everyone called the hotel, advertised "Elaborate social hall overlooking lake. Stage complete with modern effects. Staff of 30 pleasant personalities. Stage shows with Broadway talent. Eight piece dance and concert orchestra." That was 1929, Dave Kaminski's first year as a professional entertainer and his first summer at White Roe.

To get there, he and Lou embarked on a heady voyage. It started with the Forty-second Street ferry across the Hudson River to Weehawken, New Jersey. There they connected with the Ontario and Western Railroad. After a four-and-a-half-hour ride to Livingston Manor, they were picked up at the station by Irving Kahn, who was White Roe's official driver. Putting them in the backseat of the old wood station wagon, he took them the last three bouncing, twisting miles along a dirt road up White Roe Mountain to the hotel.

THE SUMMER OF 1929 WAS A GALA ONE AT WHITE ROE. A NEW CASINO had just been christened, and it was as grand as any in the Catskills. A "casino" was not a gambling room but a hotel's social center, and this one was an imposing edifice, a three-story gabled affair with brown shingles and white trim. Porches swept entirely around on two levels, offering panoramic views of the Catskills, and there was a recreation hall on the main floor. There was also a nightclub below, but it would not fully function until the repeal of Prohibition in 1933.

Inside, on the main floor, high, arched windows and French doors were spaced along the perimeter of the recreation hall. Above the fifty-foot-wide stage, the proscenium arch rose twenty feet to the ceiling, facing an auditorium whose folding chairs could seat five hundred in a pinch. The facility was as well equipped as any on Broadway, having wings and fly space, drops, dimmers, and full lighting. All of this was by design of Nat Lichtman.

Lichtman was the resident genius. When he had arrived at White Roe several seasons earlier as a director/designer, he had found a handful of old props and a load of ancient equipment. That was hardly adequate for a young man inspired by Gordon Craig, the pioneering designer-director of the 20th Century Theatre. But Lichtman was young enough (twenty-four) and visionary enough to consider imagination more important than equipment. Railing against "hackneyed trends," he aspired to combine "realistic objectivity with pure abstraction." That was the way idealistic young theater people talked at the time.

As today, a summer resort's season began on the last weekend in May and ended on the first weekend in September. Because Lou and Dave were only sixteen, instead of sleeping in a tent like everyone else on the staff, they were put up in a room in town with the parents of Herman (Hy) Pollack, who played saxophone in the hotel band. Lou had already decided on the stage name "Lou Reed." Dave had announced his intention to use his middle name, Daniel, and shorten Kaminski to "Kamin," as his brother Mack had already done, becoming "Max Kamin." But when Larry, the middle Kaminski boy, came home from the army and changed his name to "Kaye," David decided to go with that, and so instead of becoming Danny Kamin, he became Danny Kaye.

He and Lou had been hired as "tummlers," and their job was to tummle. The word has been spelled many ways, from "toomle" (in England) to "tumule" (in *Time* magazine), and has been traced to "tumult" and "tumble." But any spelling or meaning is only an approximation of the Yiddish, and there is no correct version. Whatever the origins of the word, the idea was to keep things moving, to be jesters and entertain the guests whenever they were idle lest the worst happen and a vacationer was actually forced to amuse himself.

A tummler's duties were broadly defined. Lou and Danny, besides being a harmony team in the Saturday night musical shows, were expected to participate in each night's entertainment. And there was something scheduled every night. On Sunday nights, there were concerts by the house band (drums, two violins, trumpet, three saxophones, and a piano), which at the time was Lew Sandow and his Columbia Captivators. Weeknights there were masquerades, campfires, or games—anything as long as it was something. Guests would even ask the owner what was scheduled between the end of dinner and the start of the entertainment.

On Friday nights there were plays; in fact, the first play that Danny Kaye ever saw, he was in. One of the cast recalled: "They had to push him into doing lines. He was unaware of all the things he was capable of doing." But its director, Dick Diamond, who was Lichtman's assistant, compared him to "a freak in arithmetic, an idiot savant. No matter what you wanted him to do and no matter how well you told him, he would do it better."

That first play was Frederich Wolf's *Mother's Day*, which the hotel newsletter (the *White Roe-Stir*) described to its liberal constituency as dealing "with the vital problem of birth control and abortion in a manner that gripped the spectators." The newsletter also gave David Kaminski his first review—"Danny Kaye played with fidelity and dramatic sense." It can only be conjectured how objective the critic was, since he was a member of the hotel staff, writing for the house organ.

Danny and Lou were expected to tummle not only at night but also by daylight, down by the lakefront or—in rainy weather—on the porch ("porch sessions"). There were also play readings after lunch, and these were not necessarily light entertainments. When there was a reading of Eugene O'Neill's *Emperor Jones*, Danny and Lou read all the smaller parts, while John Weiner, the owner's son, sat on the grass playing a tom-tom for atmosphere. In any weather, the two young tummlers stirred the listless and the bored, and when they were idle, the owner, old man Meyer Weiner, would find them and cry, "Boys! Pep up the people!"

For this they were given room, board, and seventy-five dollars each for the summer.

AS MEMBERS OF THE ENTERTAINMENT STAFF, THEY WERE PERMITTED to eat in the dining room rather than in the kitchen with the rest of the help so that they might tummle while they ate. Their immediate boss was the social director, Fishel Goldfarb. Like most everyone else who worked at White Roe, Goldfarb did it as an avocation. Many of the others, predictably, were schoolteachers who had long summer vacations, but Goldfarb was able to take the time off because he had his own business—novelties. It would ultimately make him a wealthy man. He would also become Kaye's lifelong friend.

Fishel, or "Phil," Goldfarb was in his middle twenties, a slender fellow at 128 pounds, but then they were all young and skinny. (Danny weighed almost 140, but he was tall—five feet eleven inches.) Goldfarb slicked down his black hair and had a dandy's taste for close-fitting, checked, double-breasted suits under which he invariably wore a short-sleeved shirt with suspenders. His polka-dot tie would be secured with a gold clasp halfway up his chest, and there was always a handkerchief flowing from his breast pocket. Although he might remove his coat on a warm day, he would never wear short pants, not even in stifling heat. Men did not wear them. Even when Goldfarb played handball he did not wear short pants, and he was a nationally ranked ace at the city sport. Handball was a favorite in Jewish circles, played with a solid black rubber ball so hard that leather gloves were needed for protection. Goldfarb also rode horses, and these various expected and unexpected sides of his personality evidently made him endearing and special to young Danny Kaye.

From all accounts, Phil Goldfarb was funny enough to have been a professional comedian. He patterned his act on Frank Fay and Jack Benny, who were at the pinnacle of their profession. Like them, he shunned the low comedy and pratfalls of the old-timers, preferring to tell jokes and anecdotes in a suave and well-modulated voice. His stage manner, like Fay's and Benny's, was that of a gentleman, with the coat buttoned and one hand thrust in a pocket of his trousers. Inevitably, a cigarette was in the other hand. Everybody smoked.

Fishel's well-modulated, pseudo-British style of speaking was peppered with Yiddish expressions, which were used for comic effect. Just a few years earlier, the cartoonist Milt Gross had published the immensely popular *Nize Baby*, with its Yiddish-inflected versions of common English expressions. Goldfarb was still influenced by it. He would tickle Danny with Yiddish-like descriptions of horseback riding ("dot noble beast, dot marwellos stelyun, dot fency steed") or of his novelty business. Young Kaye was smitten with Goldfarb's style as a person and as a performer and promptly learned to mimic

Fishel's readings of "comeback balls, whistles, squawkers, balloons, all sorts of novelties" as "comebeck balls, wheestles, squawkiss, balloonis, all sorts of nowelties."

But he would not be influenced by Goldfarb as a performer. Perhaps Fishel's anecdotal monologues were the way of the new comedians, and perhaps the visual style of the low comics was past, but Kaye seemed to have not thought about joining either school. He didn't seem to ever have considered being either a clown or a storyteller, and he never, ever, used a Yiddish expression onstage once he was out of the Catskill Mountains. He would have his own style. Whatever he was, he was.

AT THE END OF THAT FIRST SEASON OF BEING DANNY KAYE, EVERYONE else returned to real life. Dick Diamond went back to teaching, Fishel Goldfarb resumed his novelty business, and Lou Reed once more became Louis Eisen at Jefferson High. "I was from the old school," he said. "You had to be something before you could go for something else." He never would go into show business—go for that "something else." He would instead "be something." He would be a chiropodist.

Nat Lichtman was going for that something else, but he was lucky to have a wife—Etta—who not only supported his ambition and idealism; she had a job to do it with, a job with the WPA Theater to help pay for his unsteady career. That freed Nat to spend the winter dreaming up ideas for the next summer or going with Fishel to see heroes like the Marx Brothers, scribbling down their lines in the dark to steal them.

Danny would come along, too. He had nothing else to do. White Roe had convinced him that he had to spend his life in show business, that he was already a professional. Had not Meyer Weiner given him a hundred-dollar bonus and invited him back for the next summer? "I knew," he would remember, "that I had to get into show business some way." Unfortunately, Broadway's talent agents and managers were not eagerly awaiting a sixteen-year-old comedian/singer/actor.

He found a job behind a soda fountain, but it did not last. "The family didn't know it," he would remember, "but every week or so my father would come into my bedroom and put five or ten bucks under my pillow. There was never a comment that my brothers felt

I should be working, but they both had jobs, and I know what they must have been thinking."

When the next summer finally arrived, he was moved up to being Fishel Goldfarb's stooge, or comedy foil. That was a promotion, and stooging for Fishel Goldfarb provided sound experience. Fishel treated him like a protégé, teaching him the craft of comedy. Their sketches included "The External Triangle," "Lucid Hallucinations," and "The Hillbillies," which reached its comedic high point when Danny declared, "Mah brother was the most impohtent man in Georgia." Fishel retorted, "He's also the most impotent man on the hill!"

It wasn't Molière.

At the same time, Nat Lichtman coached Kaye in the more artistic aspects of performance. Danny Kaye's identity as an entertainer would result from this unique combination of low comedy and high aspirations. It was Lichtman who suggested that he sing the rabbinical lullaby *"Oyfn Pripetshik."* On the other hand, it would be Fishel's catchphrase "gagina richina" that would inspire an invention of Danny's. The phrase would be used anytime, anywhere, for instance, while Fishel was singing Eddie Cantor's "Making Whoopee":

> Another bride, another June,
> Another sunny honeymoon,
> Another season, another reason
> For making gagina richina
> Tippada, snippada
> Hetsada, petsada
> Pee!

Many comedians had signature catchphrases. Joe Penner's was "Wanna buy a duck?" Bert Lahr's was "Nnnga-nnnga." Jack Benny's was simply "Well!," and Fishel Goldfarb's was "gagina richina." He had been inspired by the mile-a-minute double-talk in Aaron Lebedoff's popular Yiddish song "Rumania, Rumania," which in turn derived from the cantors, the ritual singers, who improvised during synagogue services. Whenever Fishel said, "Gagina richina," the audience would roar, and soon Danny was himself singing "Making Whoopee," complete with "gagina richina" and with Fishel's blessings. Of course, Kaye had grown up learning Yiddish songs, and his father had even brought him to synagogue to sing with the cantor. So all of this was culturally familiar to him, and probably cozy.

Nat Lichtman suggested he interpolate that catchphrase when singing "Hi-De-Hi" ("Minnie the Moocher"). Danny would always get a laugh when he asked the audience to repeat the "gagina rich-ina" lines after him, and soon he was able to invent variations on it at indefinite length. When asked, he would say, "It isn't double-talk; it's a kind of gibberish."

Lichtman was also teaching him how to use his body, his face, even his hands, and to be precise about it. As Dick Diamond, the dramatics director, remembered, Nat taught Kaye "the importance of practice, repetition, and discipline. Take 'Hi-De-Hi,' for instance. Nat would work on it with him, to bring him out. Then he would have Danny practice his mugging in front of the dressing-room mirror."

Lichtman even taught his young protégé how to conduct classical music, or at least how to *seem* to conduct it, and Danny took to that at once. One Sunday evening, Nat even gave him the chance to conduct the house band in a couple of semiclassical selections.

Kaye became friends with all of these men as well as with Kathleen Young and Dave Mack, who were the ballroom dance team. (They preferred to be called adagio dancers.) Mack and Young were an elegant couple. They looked like the celebrated Vernon and Irene Castle. Kathleen was a slender and stylish marcelled blonde, gorgeously Gentile to Jewish eyes like Dick Diamond's, "like a sophisticated Vermont farm girl—tall, slender, blond, blue-eyed, small nose, small lips." Dave, her partner, was six feet tall and debonair. They were the only Christians outside the White Roe kitchen, and Kathleen became an early romance of Danny's, probably his first *shiksa*.

But all was not happy. As he learned more about the craft of stage performance, the endless tummling began to get him down, and he showed early signs of depression. "One night there was a show," he remembered with enduring resentment. "The next night there was a campfire. They used to wake me up and say, 'It's a rainy morning, go cheer up the crows.' If a waiter didn't show up, I waited on tables. . . . It was my job to see that all those lonely, pining ladies had a good time. In the daytime I took them rowing; in the evenings I had to dance with them."

The dancing sometimes led to after-hours tummling—what, at

the time, he called the "double ex" part of the job. He enjoyed the girlfriends but not the older women, who had to be tended to. "It was," he said, "a tough way to earn a living."

His winters remained idle and discouraging. As one of the other performers recalled, "Danny would be king for the summer, and then he'd come home and be nobody." Kaye, who was already prone to depression, would remember, "I tried to live on what I made in the summer." This was hopeless. Even as his salary grew to a stupendous $350 for a season, it was hardly enough to stretch past September. For a brief and disastrous time, he took a job with an insurance company as an appraiser of damaged cars, but after making a $36,000 accounting error, he barely escaped criminal charges. The best he could do in winter jobs was as an usher in the big Fabian Fox movie theater in downtown Brooklyn. Obviously, he was not suited for a traditional occupation, and the more time he spent as an entertainer, the less he had in common with workaday people. As Fishel Goldfarb said, "He seems to have been born for the show business, eats, sleeps, and thinks show business."

If his life had been nothing but summers, he would have been doing fine, because there, in the Catskills, his progress was steady. Within a couple of years he was Fishel Goldfarb's coheadliner at White Roe. He was also acting in a range of dramatic repertory that included *Private Lives, The Guardsman, Reunion in Vienna, Death Takes a Holiday,* and *The Play's the Thing.* As the director of these Friday night productions, Dick Diamond was "astounded by this young, inexperienced boy playing the roles of Alfred Lunt, Philip Merivale, Noel Coward—the great names in the theater—and playing them convincingly. And when it began, he had never even seen a play!"

But the audience of vacationers demanded his zanier side, and he himself seemed to prefer the instant gratification of laughter to the more subtle satisfactions of a well-crafted acting performance. Besides, the casino's stage was not big enough to contain his performing spirits. It was never surprising to hear him cry, "Okay—let's go out to the lake!" as he roused the disinclined for a dash to the waterfront. During some mealtimes, he would rip out of the kitchen and into the crowded dining room, a chef's toque on his head. The room would be noisy with young single people, eight at each big, round table, and suddenly Kaye was skittering about the dance floor, brandishing a ladle or a butcher's cleaver. He would leap onto the bandstand, "tripping" on the way to the bandleader's spot. The faked stumble was an old piece of vaudeville business, but the diners would roar, and then he would get the musicians' attention with a piercing whistle made by putting two fingers in his mouth. He would examine the imaginary musical score, bending ever closer until his nose was pressed up against it, and then he would turn the score right side up. Finally, he would "conduct." Decades later, most of this business would turn up in his symphonic conducting.

The more artistic side of him blossomed under Nat Lichtman, who encouraged him to express himself with his entire body, most strikingly with his hands. As for dancing, aside from the basic tap steps that every vaudevillian had to master, "he had a natural grace," one of the other performers remembered. "It was always balletic gestures, rhythms, movement. He had a marvelous body."

He would use that body and his hands to underscore monologues as well as music, and his songs showed the taste of an instinctual musician. Besides "Hi-De-Hi," he sang a more serious Cab Calloway piece, "St. James Infirmary," as well as Duke Ellington's bluesy "Sophisticated Lady" and Cole Porter's romantic "Night and Day." He also teamed up with one of the girls for a duet of "You're an Old Smoothie." Lichtman suggested the Depression classic "Brother, Can You Spare a Dime?" by E. Y. Harburg and Jay Gorney. Nat even painted a backdrop just for this number—an elaborate abstraction suggesting an under-the-elevated-train huddling place for the homeless. As several extras mimed warming their hands over coal fires, Kaye sang the great song about America's productive energies being reduced to panhandling.

> Once I built a railroad, made it run,
> Made it race against time.
> Once I built a railroad, now it's done,
> Brother, can you spare a dime?

His voice was steady and true, a youthfully light baritone. The words were clearly enunciated, acted out with irony and commitment. His eyes were fixed on the audience, as if in accusation.

Offstage he was a ladies' man. Instead of looking like the class clown, with pale skin, big ears, and red hair—the only blackface child with red hair—he now looked attractive. What had been a perhaps peculiar and even funny look was transformed into a unique look, his own. That is what can be accomplished with confidence, fulfillment, and finding a purpose. He let his hair grow full, piling and shaping its waves into a pompadour. He was practically handsome, and one of the actresses boasted, "I was just about the only one on the staff who wasn't a girlfriend."

As the summer of 1933 pushed toward September, Kathleen Young, who *was* a girlfriend, and her partner, Dave Mack, suggested to Danny that rather than spend another winter idling in New York, he team up with them. Concentrating on dance must have made sense to him, since he seemed to be on the wrong track as a singing clown. "I didn't know my left foot from my right as a dancer," he admitted, "but we made up a routine [called *"Amoris Dementia"*] and tried it out."

It was among the guests that he found his first serious girlfriend. Her name, by coincidence, was also Kaye, Rose Kaye, and she was dazzled by the exuberant young star. Offstage, she found him serious-minded, talkative, and curious about everything. But he was also a moody young man who could be quiet for an entire evening and then burst into anger. She had patience for all of it. "We were very young," she would remember sixty years later. "I had a tremendous crush on him, and he liked me."

Rosie Kaye was a bright, vivacious girl with dark, curly red hair, a sunny, freckled face, and a trim figure. One member of the White Roe staff gave her highest honors—"She was a mensch." Two years younger than Danny, she had first laid eyes on him when she was fifteen. At eighteen, she was still living with her parents in a tenement at 637 East Fifth Street on the Lower East Side of Manhattan. Those were teeming streets, and that was a typical immigrant apartment, with a big kitchen sink that was used for both dishes and baths. A communal toilet was down the hall.

Danny had little money to entertain Rosie, but they could spend an evening simply sitting in a cafeteria and speaking Yiddish. "Just," she remembered, "to keep in touch with it." He took her home to Brooklyn to meet his family, and like everyone else, she thought that his father, Jacob, was "the cutest little guy."

But just as they were getting started, he left town. He and Kathleen and Dave felt good enough about *"Amoris Dementia"* for Mack and Young to become the Three Terpsichoreans.

3

I tried to see people and I couldn't get past the door . . . the
same people who are now fawning all over me.

WHILE DANNY HAD BEEN CLOWNING HIS WAY THROUGH THE SUM-
MERS AND DRUMMING HIS FINGERS THROUGH THE WINTERS, SYLVIA
Fine was finishing her education. She completed Jefferson High at
fifteen, topping off her senior year by writing skits for Class Night.
She enrolled in Hunter College, the academically respected
women's school in Manhattan, but after her sophomore year she
transferred to the school's Brooklyn branch. It had a superior music
faculty and a busier theater department. The fact that Hunter's
Brooklyn branch (which would later become the independent
Brooklyn College) was in walking distance from her home could
hardly have mattered to a girl who used to take two different subway
lines to get to high school.

Sylvia began to write for the stage, providing both the music
and the lyrics for a college version of Shaw's *Arms and the Man*. The
libretto was written by her cousin, the novelist Irwin Shaw. Their
title, *Legs and the Lady*, was collegiate, but after all, they were in
college.

She was also writing for the college paper's humor column,
inspired by the likes of Dorothy Parker and Ogden Nash.

> The great American tragedy
> Is to have no date on Sagedy!

After graduation, she taught piano and worked for nothing at Keit-Engle, a music publishing house where she wrote songs and got none of them published. She was now pulling her black hair straight back, which was not a flattering look, but it did set off her big, dark, intelligent eyes. Comfort might have been her prime concern, because she didn't seem to care about conventional goals like boyfriends or marriage. Her consuming interest was show business, just like Danny's.

But she was a writer, while he was a performer, and he hit the road with the Three Terpsichoreans, starting out painfully on a stage floor in Utica, New York. For halfway through *"Amoris Dementia"* he took a bad spill and found himself sprawled on his backside. Worse, he had split the seat of his pants, and the audience was roaring. Twenty years old and hardly a stage professional, he froze with embarrassment, but Dave was immediately at his side.

"Wait for your laugh," his partner whispered, and Danny took the advice. Only when the laughter subsided did he get up, and that night they all agreed to include the business at the next booking, which was in a Syracuse vaudeville house. After that, they set out for Detroit and the Midwest.

To get there, they bought a used car, figuring that it would be cheaper than train fare for three. The trouble with owning this old Buick was that none of them could drive. They got Herman Pollack, the saxophonist from White Roe, to be their driver. He was not only stagestruck but lovesick over Kathleen. Since his parents had commanded him to enter New York University, the closest he could get to paradise was driving her to Detroit, if necessary with Danny and Dave.

One night, a promoter came backstage after the show and asked them, "How would you like to go to China?" The man's name was A. B. (Abe) Marcus, and as Kaye remembered it, he wasn't really a promoter at all. "Marcus was running a cleaning establishment in New England, and he got stuck with a lot of stage costumes because a traveling unit couldn't pay its bill. He decided the only thing to do was to go out and get the costumes filled, and that's how come he went into show business."

Perhaps so, but Kaye also had reason to be nasty about Marcus.

The man was impressed with Dave and Kathleen, but turning to Kaye, he had said, "You I don't want." Danny would omit that part of the Marcus story every time he told it. However, the Three Terpsichoreans, like their French predecessors, were all for one, and the other two stood firm. When Dave and Kathleen offered to divide their sixty-dollars-per-week salary three ways, it was a deal.

The Marcus show was called *La Vie Paree* and had a huge company of seventy-five. Playing two performances a day, the two-and-a-half-hour vaudeville wandered westward for five months. Kaye remembered: "We played every theater and outhouse—forty-one one-night stands" before winding up in San Francisco, from which they sailed, on February 8, 1934, for the Far East.

The tour began in Tokio, as it was then spelled, and on the first night, local demonstrators interrupted the performance, protesting the presence of American entertainers. Nevertheless, *La Vie Paree* played out its scheduled nine-week engagement, and by the end, Kaye was in it. At first, Marcus had refused to let him go on, but when some of the cast got sick, the producer had no choice. By the time the show moved south, Kaye was in sixteen of the twenty-one numbers.

One stormy night in Osaka, while waiting to go on, he stood in the wings, watching "the Silver Lady." She was a virtually nude dancer, her body covered with silver paint. As the applause ended, he strolled onstage to begin his song, only to almost literally be drowned out by a tremendous roar. The raging winds that could be heard outside and the torrential rain that was pelting the theater were part of a typhoon that was devastating Osaka. In a moment, the theater was thrown into darkness.

The audience started to panic. Kaye shouted into the orchestra pit for a flashlight, and after two were handed to him, he turned them on his face. The beams attracted attention, being the only light in the house. Then "I sat on the stage," he would remember, "and let my legs dangle into the pit, and I sang all the songs I knew." Gradually, the panic subsided, and the frightened audience quieted.

The tour proceeded along its exotic itinerary, from Osaka to Shanghai, then to Hong Kong and the Philippines. Unable to speak the languages, Kaye was forced to communicate through mime and foolish faces. No matter where, audiences laughed at his "gagina richina" double-talk, and that was when he came up with the notion of his own double-talk. It began with a simple nonsense phrase:

>Git-gat-giddle
>With a geet-ga-zay

He extended it, and soon he was able to improvise at length, singing the babble as he made it up. And the audiences roared. Nonsense seemed to be funny in any language.

He also capitalized on a wonderful ear for accents by singing or talking in mock German, Italian, French, or Russian. This, too, seemed to get laughs in any culture. There evidently was something intrinsically funny in the combination of an assumed accent and nonsense words. His Asian audiences didn't have a clue as to what he was saying, but they could tell when he was just making funny sounds, and they laughed when those funny sounds were made in one accent or another. Thus, his comedy was a kind of verbal slapstick. It was not based on anecdotes or ideas. That was why it would have no language boundaries.

There were many romanceable young women in the company, and a dancer named Holly Fine succeeded Kathleen Young as Danny's girlfriend while the tour pressed on to Siam, down the Malay Peninsula, across the Malay straits, and through the Indonesian islands. It gave the twenty-one-year-old Kaye an enduring taste for both travel and Oriental food. The show was also booked into Australia, but that engagement was aborted when Mrs. Marcus learned that her little dog Vita would not be admitted because of health regulations.

It was an appropriate time to come home, anyway. The company had been away for a year and a half, and the Japanese were beginning to make the Far East politically unstable. If an American vaudeville troupe was an anomaly in the South Pacific, it was all the more so in a troubled South Pacific. Dave Mack decided that war would not break out and remained there, paying for his poor guess by winding up in a Japanese concentration camp. Kathleen went home to Chicago, where she quit show business. Marcus, who was no more impressed with Kaye at the end of the tour than he had been at the start, did not renew the young man's contract.

That left him with nothing to do but, as he put it, "a starvation routine." It was 1935 and the middle of the Great Depression, which was not so bad for some show people, because a whole country needed cheering up. But it was no better than any other time for unconventional show people, and Danny was back where he had started: out of work and unable to get it for the same old reason. He fit no niche. The Three Terpsichoreans notwithstanding, he was not a dancer. He was also neither a comedian nor a singer. "I came back home," he remembered, "and proceeded to knock my brains out at the New York offices. [When] they'd say, 'What do you do?' I was finished. They'd say, 'Do you sing?' and I'd say yes, and they'd say, 'Do you do comedy?' and I'd say yes—and I was finished."

HE RETURNED TO WHITE ROE, FROM WHICH HE HAD SUPPOSEDLY graduated. His $1,000 was the most the Weiner family had ever paid an entertainer. At least his old pal Fishel Goldfarb was still there.

Rooming together in the attic of the lakeside cottage, Phil and Danny worked out a comedy sketch called "Rusty and the Doctor." It was all but lifted from the Smith and Dale classic "Dr. Kronkeit." With Danny playing Rusty (more subtle than "Red"), he was no longer Fishel's stooge. In fact, it was now *he* who got the laughs, between baby talk and punch lines.

DOCTOR:	Come here.
RUSTY:	I don't wanna.
DOCTOR:	Born?
RUSTY:	What do you think?

Kaye the entertainer was, in fact, being born here, and it was at a historic moment. The low clowns of burlesque and the elegant monologists of vaudeville—all of them flesh-and-blood performers—were being replaced by the cooler, more remote entertainers of radio and the movies. Transmission through a medium, electronic or film, would soon drain the entertainer's blood, his live, physical presence; it would chill and distance the style of performance as well. Kaye, like a genetic accident, was being conceived on a show-business grid that overlapped eras and styles—the low clowning of Bert Lahr, Willie Howard, and Ed Wynn; the musical babble of the Jewish entertainers; the burlesque flapping of Bobby Clark; the bawdy verbalism of W. C. Fields; the wise-guy antics of Groucho Marx; the suave anecdotalism of Jack Benny and Frank Fay. Ahead lay Bob Hope and the wisecracking stand-up comedians, those relentless pacers of the nightclub floors. Kaye would never have any part of that. He would be a show-business mutation, belonging to no school and somehow being a contemporary model of the classic line.

Fishel Goldfarb and Nat Lichtman had fortuitously, and not

unmiraculously, combined to father this ballet clown, shaping his talents and launching him in the direction of artistry.

DOCTOR: Where were you born?
RUSTY: In the hospital.
DOCTOR: Why?
RUSTY: I wanted to be near my mother.

His first and best medium would be the stage. All his life he would prefer live audiences.

DOCTOR: Did you ever have a nightmare?
RUSTY: Did you? Tell me yours first, Doc.
DOCTOR: Come on, now.
RUSTY: Yes, Doc. I walked in my sleep, and I met a pansy.
DOCTOR: Oh, that's nothing.
RUSTY: You don't know this pansy.

Such homosexual abuse, like racist material, was acceptable in the insulated world of a Jewish resort hotel.

He resumed his romance with Rosie Kaye, whose parents were still bringing her to White Roe. "I was in love with him," she would remember long afterward, "but we were kids." He probably was less concerned with love than with becoming a professional entertainer. This was a maddening aspiration, for there is no methodical way to approach it the way a career in business or law or medicine can be planned. What young Kaye surely did realize was that if he kept returning to White Roe he would become, like the rest of the social staff, a summertime performer and a dilettante. So in the summer of 1936 he accepted an offer from the President Hotel in nearby Swan Lake, if only for the change. His pay soared to $100 a week. This was almost progress.

While the aim at White Roe had been for the artistic, at the President the emphasis was on Jewish entertainment. The social director was Alexander ("Shula") Olshanetsky, a successful composer of such Yiddish songs as "Mein Shtetl Belz," and he installed the twenty-three-year-old Kaye as the President's master of ceremonies. Olshanetsky also teamed him up with a pretty young actress named Lillian Lux, and they sang Yiddish duets. "Diddle-dee," went their song, "diddle-dee-diddle-dee-dai-dai." And Danny was good at that kind of thing, for it was so like his own "Git-gat-giddle /

With a geet-ga-zay." He could rattle off streams of words, whether real or nonsensical, and he could make every syllable clear, if not meaningful.

The President Hotel had a policy of importing guest stars for the Saturday night musicals; not star-stars but performers like Benay Venuta. The writer Larry Gelbart would say he always thought her name was a show-business synagogue, but the truth was, she was Italian Swiss, and her real name was Benvenuta Scalmanini. Benay Venuta had begun in show business as a fifteen-year-old chorus girl. She had succeeded Ethel Merman in *Anything Goes* and had lived to survive the comparison. Now she had her own singing show on CBS radio.

She first met Kaye in the President Hotel's casino, when they were rehearsing. The next time she would see him, only a few months later, they would both be on the same bill in a New York nightclub, for he finally landed a city job. This engagement, at Billy Rose's Casa Mañana, was professional show business at last. It did not matter that he went from the top of the program at White Roe to less than an asterisk at the Casa Mañana. It only mattered that he had gone from the mountains to the city.

Jimmy Durante and Pat Rooney, Jr., were the headliners at the club, which loftily advertised itself as a "theater/restaurant," offering dinner, dancing, and a show for $1.50 a person. Benay Venuta was the singer on the bill, the band was conducted by Vincent Lopez, and the opening act was a comedian/dancer named Nick Long. Unbilled was Danny Kaye, making his big-city debut as Nick Long's stooge. His responsibilities ran to dashing through the audience with an empty coat hanger, shouting to Nick, "Your clothes just came back from the cleaners!"

One night, he invited his father to come see the show and afterward took the old man backstage to meet Benay. "Pop," he said in Yiddish, "she's so *goyishe* she can't even say 'knish' right," and translating that for Venuta, he added, "You're not supposed to pronounce it 'nyish.' It's 'ka-*nish!*' "

He would often relax in her dressing room auditioning new material. One idea was a musical joke, an off-key rendition of "Begin the Beguine." After the deadpan performance, he asked, "Well? What do you think? Is it funny?" It certainly was, she told him, and it showed an emerging sense of quirky humor.

His romantic interest at the President Hotel had been his singing partner, Lillian Lux. When they had come back after Labor Day, she tagged along as he shopped for clothes. He had decided to blow his entire summer's pay on a camel-hair coat with a belt and a scarf. "He used to swagger around in that tan polo coat," Lillian would remember, "looking like a million dollars. You'd never know he wasn't working."

And after the engagement at the Casa Mañana, he wasn't working once again. Lillian was doing better. She landed a part in a Yiddish revue that was being assembled by the President Hotel's social director. She even suggested Danny for the show, and he was hired to play opposite her. Had the financing not fallen through, Danny Kaye might well have wound up on the Yiddish stage.

But the financing did fall through, and Lillian signed on with another Yiddish company, the Clinton Street Theatre on the Lower East Side. Danny, having little else to do, would watch her rehearse, "sitting a few rows back," Lillian remembered, "and cracking pistachio nuts." That would infuriate the director, Pesach Burstyn, and something else that crazed Burstyn was Danny's imitation of his whistling. That was Pesach's specialty, whistling between the choruses of a song, and he was not finding Danny's mockery amusing. Last and certainly at the root of all this hostility, Pesach was himself smitten with Lillian.

But after rehearsals she would go out with Danny—very often to the other Yiddish theaters, the National, for instance, where they watched the legendary Samuel Goldenberg, or the great Second Avenue Theatre, where Maurice Schwartz and Jacob P. Adler reigned. The romance ended when Pesach Burstyn invited Lillian to join his company on a South American tour. On the day they were sailing for Argentina, Danny came to see her off. "Pesach," he blurted out, "please take me with you." Needless to say, there wasn't a chance.

If it seemed to young Kaye that things were as bad as ever, and possibly worse, in retrospect he was beginning to move up the professional ladder. In November 1937 there was the briefest of items in the *New York Herald Tribune*:

Vaudeville Comic Signed
Danny Kaye has been signed by Educational Pictures to
be featured in two-reel comedies.

4

When he walked across the room he seemed to dance, and his every movement had a flash and a flair to it.

—Sylvia Fine

K

AYE MADE THREE TWO-REEL MOVIES IN 1937, AND THEY WERE ALL FILMED IN TWO DAYS IN AN ASTORIA, NEW YORK, STUDIO. MOVIE theaters showed such "short subjects" (or "shorts") between the two feature films, along with the news and the coming attractions.

He was an extra in *Cupid Takes a Holiday* and *Money or Your Life* and then played the lead in *Getting an Eyeful.* In that one, he used some of the foreign accents he had developed on the tour through the Far East. All three were released by 20th Century-Fox and went unnoticed. Kaye would later say, "I'd rather forget about them."

Even so, the basic fact of doing such work meant his career was beginning to gather momentum. From that point of view, these were the best years so far, although in the thick of them that did not always seem the case. One particular disaster was a seven-week booking in the nightclub of a London hotel, the Dorchester Lounge. Danny was again stooging for Nick Long. The act, billed as Nick Long & Co., had played acceptably enough at the Casa Mañana in New York. It did not, however, travel well, especially Danny's songs.

These were new to the act. Long had given him a break,

allowing him to come in from stooge limbo and sing. Kaye's songs included "Hi-De-Hi" ("Minnie the Moocher") and something new that he had worked up, "Dinah (Is There Anyone Finer?)." He sang it straightforwardly except that the title and its rhymes were pronounced as "ee," making the song into "Deenah, is there anyone feener." This was similar to the oddball humor of his off-key "Begin the Beguine," only less funny. To compensate for the somewhat limited comic possibilities in assorted rhymes for "Deenah," he sang the song's second chorus in high-speed double-talk.

"Deenah" mystified the British audiences, and the remainder of Kaye's material left them hostile. That was not a winning combination, and after three weeks, the Dorchester's entertainment manager, Henry Sherek, canceled the "Co." half of Nick Long & Co. Kaye came home in shock. (Years later he described the engagement as "disastrous.") To make the homecoming complete, he also learned that Rosie was getting married. If he had any emotional responses to these events, however, he did not show them. His only overt feelings seemed to be elation when he was onstage and depression offstage, which some took as a kind of cold anger.

Rosie Kaye was still living with her parents. After finishing high school, she had gotten a job in the Seventh Avenue dress market. She had not heard from Danny while he had been away, but she never considered a future with him, anyhow, or so she later claimed. "I could never be married to him," she said. "He was an actor and was moody even as a young man. He would get very quiet—sullen. He had no patience, and he was so short-tempered."

She had been going out with a stockbroker named Martin Goldman, a fellow whose interests were not limited to Wall Street. He was even a member of the Friars Club—the show-business fraternity —and she accepted his marriage proposal.

Danny heard about the imminent wedding from Victor Sack, the short, sandy-haired fellow who had been a stage manager at White Roe and had stayed friendly with Rosie over the years. Danny promptly told Sack that he was going to the ceremony, and "I don't care if I wasn't invited."

The February 4, 1939, wedding wasn't a formal affair, and Rosie didn't wear a gown. She didn't even wear the traditional virginal white, but a light blue dress—"powder" blue, as she recalled. The wedding was in her sister's apartment, "a beautiful building," she remembered, at Second Avenue and Twentieth Street in the Gramercy Park section of Manhattan.

It was an orthodox Jewish ceremony, complete with a *huppah* —a cloth canopy that four of the men held with sticks over the heads of the bride and groom. Rosie didn't even know that Danny was in the room until, in the midst of the ceremony, she saw him standing alongside Victor, just behind her, holding one of the sticks.

With the stamping of the linen-wrapped glass under Martin's foot, the ceremony was complete, and Danny broke into song— *"Chazin de luv Shabbes"* ("A Cantor for the Sabbath"). When he was finished, he kissed Rosie and whispered to Martin, "You've got her now, but I'll get her later."

WITH SPRING, NAT LICHTMAN CAME TO HIS AID YET AGAIN. NAT WAS designing the sets and lighting for *The Sunday Night Varieties*, a little revue that was going to be produced at the Keynote Theatre on Fifty-second Street in Manhattan. The director of the show was a young Viennese émigré named Max Liebman, who had been nurturing the revue form at the most sophisticated of summer resort theaters, Camp Tamiment.

Kaye was all dolled up for the audition, in a tight-fitting suit and a shirt with a high collar, over which curled his theatrically long hair. Climbing the flight of stairs above a Chinese restaurant and stepping into the Keynote Theatre, he was introduced to a small, dark, and intense young woman seated at the piano. Already signed to write the songs for the show, she was playing for the auditions as well. Her name was Sylvia Fine, which meant nothing to Danny. She, however, remembered him from her father's dental office on Bradford Street in Brooklyn. She never forgot that: "my heart did a flip, my hands became wet and cold, and I stammered out an 'I know you!' "

Those days, Sylvia worked in a grocery store, demonstrating soup mixes. She simply had to make money for her family, with the Depression persisting and her father's dental practice faltering. She spent the rest of her time writing songs for shows that weren't produced, so this was an industrious and undiscourageable young woman. Max Liebman described her as "grimly serious and painfully shy." But, he added, "she bristled with ideas for musical-comedy numbers," and they were just what he liked: sharp, smart, witty, and political material like her own audition piece for him, the Nazi satire, "Sing a song of Blackshirts / A pocketful of lies."

Kaye's routines were not quite so serious-minded. He wanted to entertain, not educate. As Fishel Goldfarb said, he ate, slept, and thought show business. His audition piece, to say the least, was less topical than Sylvia's. After they agreed on his musical key, he first offered a sample of his double-talk, the "git-gat-giddle" that he had perfected on the Far East tour. Then he told a joke in a Japanese accent. Dialect humor had worked for him in Asia, it had worked for him in the short movie, and it worked for him now. He got the job, and he got Sylvia as well. "He wasn't the most attractive man I'd ever met," she remembered. "In fact, he was rather ridiculous . . . in that tight suit that pinched into wrinkles at the waist. What's this guy got for me, I thought—except everything! I was mad about him."

The Sunday Night Varieties was not destined to be a ticket to fame for Danny, Sylvia, or Max. Devastatingly reviewed, it closed after a single performance, but Liebman was sufficiently impressed with Sylvia's contributions to hire her for Tamiment the following summer, and she already had a number in mind. When he went for it, she went to work on her vest-pocket Yiddish version of Gilbert and Sullivan's *Mikado.*

She also went to work on Danny Kaye. As a brainy romantic, she had perceived something special for her in this young man. As a show-business aficionado, she had grasped the originality in his style. She urged Liebman to hire him, and when Tamiment lost Jules Munshin, who was its leading comic, she succeeded. But even as Danny was being hired, Sylvia was further along on his case than Max Liebman could imagine. She had, in fact, conceived the Yiddish *Mikado* with Kaye in mind. Years later, he would himself point out a similarity between his git-gat-giddle routines and the patter songs in the Savoyard operettas. It was the connection Sylvia made as she began writing material for the young man who had the faces, the gestures, and the accents but not the words. "And that," Tamiment's Imogene Coca remembered, "was sort of the beginning of things for Danny."

It was sort of the beginning of things for Danny and Sylvia as well. She was simply smitten with him, but how could she, so shy and unattractive, ever capture such a butterfly? Only, it may have seemed to Sylvia, with her dazzling mind. She would give him his material; a performer cannot exist without that. She would give him his act; she would give him *himself*—his stage persona, his career. She would also give up the core of herself—her own ambitions to be a Broadway composer and lyricist. In return, she would achieve not only her prince but the medium through which she could express herself. She would express herself through *him*, and like any medium, all he would have to be was passive. The emotionally remote Danny Kaye would have no problem with that.

SYLVIA WAS NOT JEALOUS OF ROSIE KAYE, PERHAPS BECAUSE THAT had never been a supercharged sexual affair, but it didn't mean she could not be competitive or strategic. She sought out Blanche Ganz, one of the few White Roe actresses Danny had not romanced. "Sylvia was very clever," Blanche remembered, "an intellectual. They were very different, but she was wild about him from the start and would ask questions about the women in his life because I knew him for so many years. A lot of women were crazy about him, and he was very accommodating in every sense of the word." Sylvia was particularly concerned about Holly Fine, the girlfriend on the Marcus tour, and Blanche was almost brutally candid, telling her that "Holly was blond, very attractive, and they were very serious." But Sylvia could not be deterred.

Perhaps it didn't matter then, as Blanche said, that "Danny was never very crazy about her to begin with. For him, it was a matter of professional convenience."

CAMP TAMIMENT WAS LOCATED IN STROUDSBURG, PENNSYLVANIA, deep in the Pocono Mountains. It was called a "camp" because, rather than offering full hotel services, it provided cottages with kitchens. The entertainers were put up in a low, barrackslike building. There they were housed along a corridor of spartan rooms, each having two cots, a sink and a closet, but no door. Just a cloth curtain.

For the mostly Jewish, mostly leftist vacationers, the place offered entertainment that was close to professional. Such stars-to-be as Alfred Drake and Imogene Coca were in the company that year, and Jerome Robbins was the choreographer.

Like most of the summer resorts, this one offered a variety show every week, but unlike the others, the variety show was not the highlight of the week. At Tamiment, the variety show was given on Friday nights, while the big event was the Saturday night revue. Revue was a cut above variety, aspiring to the legitimate theater. A variety show was based on vaudeville; in fact, most of the resorts, like White Roe, were basically presenting vaudeville material.

A vaudeville show is a bill of entertainment. It is always made up of eight acts, either jugglers or magicians or acrobats as well as singers, comedians, and "flash" acts (elaborate numbers). These acts are set in a ritual order (an opening novelty turn, a second-act comedian, a third-act group routine, and so on).

A revue, too, is a series of comedy and musical numbers, but it has no variety acts. Moreover, whereas a vaudeville entertainer brings his routine with him, a revue's material is created especially for the revue. Finally, there is a difference in tone. Born of honky-tonk, vaudeville was working man's theater, but revues aspired to sophistication. No jugglers or dog acts there; the pride of the revue was the smart comedy sketch. Indeed, revues established sketch comedy as we have come to know it.

What made Tamiment different from the usual Catskills resort, then, was the Saturday night revue, and that was the work of Max Liebman, who held Tamiment to the Broadway standard.

Danny Kaye, with his arrival, left tummling behind forever. Tamiment was too classy for tummlers. Its actors were above rainy-day porch sessions, dining-room antics, and romancing lonely guests. Nor were there any "Rusty and the Doctor" skits. Danny Kaye was about to have his act refined.

SYLVIA'S JOB WAS TO WRITE NEW NUMBERS FOR EACH OF THE TEN weekly revues. Almost all of her work took off on theatrical subjects, as if she had learned a lesson in show-business realities. Having been fiercely political, she was now writing only the occasional piece with social relevance, such as "The Wolf of Wall Street," which was about a man who takes over the pumpernickel market. Considering that the Depression was not entirely over, it was a kid-gloves treatment of Wall Street. But it must have been obvious that Danny's gifts were not best displayed in a political showcase.

From the outset, Sylvia's material for him inclined to a kind of fey humor that brought him across as sexually ambiguous, such as the double role of "The Masked Gondolier," who is actually "Danny Davenport of the U.S. Secret Service." Or "Pavlowa," the ballet travesty that he performed in drag. Perhaps Sylvia perceived an androgyny in him. Maybe she was tailoring him to her own sexual timidity. Of course, she could also have simply thought these were funny ideas.

In terms of work, the most significant piece she wrote for him that Tamiment summer was "Stanislavsky," which once and for all lent a stamp to his performing personality. It would be the model for the material that would eventually catapult him to stardom.

Naturally, "Stanislavsky" is in Russian dialect ("naturally," because it is about a Russian, and Sylvia catered to Danny's gift for dialect). It is a satire of the Moscow Art Theater director's acting theories. Although its satirical bite is superficial, "Be a tree, be a sled / Be a purple spool of thread" does anticipate "Nothing" in *A Chorus Line* some thirty years later.

Sylvia accompanied every performance at the piano, and in playing for Danny, she not only accompanied him but partnered him like a dancer, following or leading as the situation required. His confidence was growing, stimulated by the professionalism around him, but he was not yet a professional, and sometimes his behavior betrayed that. At rehearsal one day, he and Imogene Coca were working on a new number, a satire of an overarranged and overdirected musical scene. In the midst of rehearsal, Kaye interrupted her.

"Wait a minute, Imogene," he said. "I don't think you should do what you were doing just now."

She looked up in surprise. She was not only an intelligent young woman; she was a sensitive and proper one, and her sense of decorum was particularly refined in the realm of stage manners. She had learned them from her father, who was a vaudeville pit conductor, and she did not fancy Kaye's criticism.

"You know something?" she asked with a smile of pure ice. "There's a director." She said it as if Kaye might not be aware of it. "Max Liebman is sitting right there in the first row." Then she paused. "Now," she said, taking a measured breath before continuing, "in the theater, you ask the director if the other person is doing something wrong. Then, in turn, the director might say, 'By God, you're right—I hadn't noticed it.' And then"—she smiled sweetly at Kaye—"*he'll* come to me.

"Now . . ." She paused, but only momentarily, not giving him a chance to interrupt. She pointed into the house. "*There's* Max Liebman."

She took a deep breath, somewhat impressed with her own audacity. ("I wasn't mean about it. I had made a very clear statement, and I had amazed myself.")

Kaye stared at her ("as if I had eight heads," she recalled).

"And if you have to make a comment," she quietly concluded, "wait until the number's finished."

AT SEASON'S END, LIEBMAN TOLD HIS LITTLE STOCK COMPANY THAT he was going to make one big show out of the best of the summer material and he was going to take that show to Broadway. As a precondition, each of them would have to assign to him 10 percent of all their earnings for the *next four years*. Kaye agreed. This was the kind of thing that would teach Sylvia to henceforth be tough-minded in business. She certainly would be.

Liebman called his show *The Straw Hat Revue*, and it opened on Broadway in a modest production at the Ambassador Theatre on September 29, 1939. He had written the sketches; Sylvia wrote the music and lyrics. The program included Kaye, Coca, and Alfred Drake in "The Great Chandelier," a Viennese operetta satire; Imogene, as Carmen Miranda in a banana-topped turban, rolling her eyes; Kaye as "The Masked Gondolier" who is really "Danny Davenport of the U.S. Secret Service." Other sketches were "The Three Hicks" and "The Wolf of Wall Street."

As if a Broadway opening night were not terrifying enough, Max and Sylvia amateurishly decided to add last-minute revisions to their operetta spoof "The Great Chandelier." Danny grabbed the sheet of new lyrics and pinned it to one of the curtains in the wings. He planned on making a final check of the revisions before going on with the number. Then the curtain shot upward, taking the lyrics with it.

Nevertheless, the performance went smoothly, and the reviews were good—but not good enough. The chord they struck in common was condescending. Typically, Brooks Atkinson of the *New York Times* considered *The Straw Hat Revue* "too slight," although, he wrote, "most of it is written, acted and staged with skill and relish." Danny Kaye, he added, "knows how to drop irony into burlesque without overdoing it." Even better for Kaye, personally, the *New York Sun*'s man wrote, "He had the customers laughing so hard that the tears streamed from their eyes." But Robert Coleman probably summed up the reaction to *The Straw Hat Revue* when he wrote in the *Mirror* that while it was a "youthful and fresh little show, at a $2.20 top we would be inclined to recommend it but at $3.30 we honestly cannot."

The revue eked out an eleven-week run, and after it closed, Danny and Max Liebman took a train to Florida, hoping to wind down over the Christmas–New Year holidays.

On Danny's arrival in Miami Beach, he telephoned Rosie Kaye, now Rosie Goldman, who had moved to nearby Fort Lauderdale with her husband. She invited him and Liebman to visit, and she and Danny had some time to themselves. Martin could handle that, being, she remembered, "secure and unjealous." Anyhow, she said, there was nothing to be jealous about. She and Danny "had become very good friends."

When they were alone, he told her that he was going to marry Sylvia Fine; he was going to propose to her, and he was sure she would accept. Rosie listened without comment and would dryly recall that "he didn't say he was crazy about her." Then he and Max drove back to Miami Beach, he called Sylvia, and he did indeed ask her to marry him. She came down to Florida, and on January 3, 1940, they drove to Fort Lauderdale, where they were wed in a civil ceremony. Danny was broke, Sylvia had thirty dollars she had saved from demonstrating soup, and Max was the best man.

Sylvia, fearing her parents' reaction to a civil ceremony, telephoned and told them only that she was engaged. Danny gave Rosie a picture of the wedding.

5

One time I went to Florida and I was lonely, so I called her

up and said I wanted to marry somebody, and she said who /

And I said you.

—mock Kaye interview written by Sylvia

SINCE DANNY'S STUDIO APARTMENT WAS TOO SMALL FOR TWO ("WHEN I SMILED MY CHEEKS TOUCHED BOTH WALLS"), HE AND SYLVIA honeymooned by looking for a bigger place. As a fancy girl from Flatbush, her taste ran to better than that, anyway. She found a small but duplex penthouse in the stylish neighborhood of Sutton Place, at 414 East Fifty-second Street. Considering that they had less than a hundred dollars between them, the move was bold, but Sylvia was just that.

Their wedding seemed to have accomplished what a wedding is supposed to: It made them into a single entity. But this was a show-business entity, a dual "Danny Kaye," a performer and his material. The needs they filled for each other went beyond the emotional, to their core impulses, their life drives. The most important thing in Danny's life was to succeed as an entertainer, and for that he lacked not just material but a performing identity. Sylvia, as a writer, needed a medium. In Danny, she found more than that. She found a purpose, almost a maternal one: to use her gift to conceive and nurture the man of her dreams; to give birth to Danny Kaye.

The first step in this marriage was not setting up housekeeping but getting an agent. His name was Harry Bestry, and he acted quickly, as agents do for new clients. Bestry got Danny an engagement at Dario's La Martinique. It was for only a week, but it was a beginning, and at an astounding $250 for the week. That was where Kaye would have his big-city debut—"make his bone," as it was said in show business (an expression borrowed from the gangster world, where it referred to a first murder).

The Martinique was a basement nightclub—face it, a cellar—at 57 West Fifty-seventh Street. It was called Dario's to distinguish it from a previous incarnation as Dario and Ramón's La Martinique. With Ramón's departure went most of the Latin decor, along with the old policy of continental entertainment. Ramón had wanted the carriage trade, but the carriage trade had bridled at a minimum charge of $1.50 ($2.50 on weekends). Dario instituted a less pretentious approach to prices ("Superb Dinners from $1.50") as well as entertainment.

Kaye's early show played to a tepid reaction and left him despairing in his tiny dressing room. The club's press agent, Eddie Dukoff, vainly tried to shore up the young man's stricken spirits. There was, after all, a late show to get through. Meanwhile, Sylvia was rewriting furiously. Then she joined the pep talk.

Neither she nor Dukoff mentioned anything about the audience at the midnight show, which was bound to be even tougher. That was when the opening-nighters came, and the gossip columnists who reviewed the new acts.

The twelve-minute act had been written by Sylvia and Max Liebman, but he does not seem to have been there that first night. Possibly there was already friction over his taking a percentage of Danny's earnings. How much authorship credit he deserved is uncertain, since people who worked with them say that while Sylvia alone wrote the words and music, many of the ideas for the numbers were Max's.

Some was old material from Tamiment, like "Stanislavsky" and "Pavlowa." Other pieces, like the travesty of a Russian tenor ("*Otchi Tchorniya*"), had been written especially for this engagement and were untested. That number, which was inspired by if not stolen outright from a routine of the Ritz Brothers, included a lot of sneezing that capitalized on the word "gesundheit."

His second show did not merely go better than the first; this time, Danny received a standing ovation, and the laughter was still resounding through the cellar room as he came back for more bows. But the audience would not let him leave. He glanced over his shoulder at Sylvia—she was sitting at the piano in white opera gloves and tears. They had to do something; the audience was demanding more. She launched into one of the old numbers they hadn't used, and the applause subsided, but when he finished, the yelling and stomping only intensified. So she had to dredge up something else from the past. He sang "Minnie the Moocher"; he even conducted the band. More than an hour later, after everything else had been tried, Danny was inspired by something that caught his eye onstage —a remnant of the Martinique's old Caribbean decor.

He began to intone in Spanish-accented gibberish. His face was as solemn as his voice. Abruptly, he turned to the bandleader, Fausto Corbelo, and shouted at the top of his voice, "Conga!"

The effect, a columnist would write the next morning, was "electrifying." Young Kaye started to dance the conga, chugging to the one, two, three—kick. He sang in Spanish-accented double-talk. The audience began to stand up at their seats and join behind him on the conga line. Like the tummler who is leading a group of reluctant vacationers at White Roe down to the lakefront, Kaye wove between the tables, tossing his red hair and waving his elbows—all the while swiveling his hips to the dance step.

Pushing through the restaurant, he sang out, "One, two, three —kick!," now in different accents. The band's second percussionist added to the conga beat, shaking maracas. Those in the audience who weren't dancing were pounding silverware and glasses, and as the energy level built in the darkened club and the line of dancers followed Kaye's lead, the atmosphere grew to almost a frenzy.

To end it, Kaye "fainted." Two waiters rushed to his rescue. They lifted him high in the air and carried him away to the delirious and unbelievable applause and cheers.

The next day, he was the rage of New York.

LATER THAT WEEK, ON FEBRUARY 22, 1940, DANNY AND SYLVIA WERE remarried in a synagogue to please Dr. and Mrs. Fine.

At the Martinique, the one-week engagement was extended indefinitely. His $250 a week salary was first doubled and then tripled. It seemed as if everyone had to see him. Robert Taylor came with Barbara Stanwyck. Ginger Rogers was there, and Robert Young and

Greta Garbo. Orson Welles took time off from the final editing of *Citizen Kane* to bring Dolores Del Rio.

But of all, the most important in those audiences would prove to be the playwright Moss Hart, who was coauthor with George S. Kaufman of the current Broadway hit *The Man Who Came to Dinner*. Ironically, at White Roe, Danny Kaye had virtually learned to act in Hart and Kaufman's *Once in a Lifetime*.

Like Danny, Moss Hart had come from a lower-middle-class Jewish background and had fast become adroit at escaping it. He had quit school after the seventh grade—even earlier than Kaye— but successfully educated himself. He was even more successful at being not only a playwright but a sophisticate, and he suited himself to the part, draping stylish clothes on his tall and slender frame —even a mink-lined overcoat—and speaking in a vaguely British accent.

The company Moss Hart kept was smart, the Cole Porter/Noel Coward set. He had to be practically dragged to the Martinique by his producer, Max Gordon, who had come for a second time. Gordon was now urging Hart to write Danny Kaye into his next Broadway show, while the playwright insisted that he wasn't looking for a "borscht-belt comic." Perhaps that was because, once upon a time, Moss Hart had himself been the social director of a borscht-belt hotel, the Flagler, in not so swank South Fallsburg, New York. Possibly, being a graduate of the Catskills, he did not care to be reminded of it. There is no snob like a former peasant.

After the show, Max Gordon invited Kaye to join him and Hart at their table; of course, Danny brought Sylvia along. When Hart congratulated her on the songs, Danny somewhat ungenerously grinned and said, "We'd pay you a lot for a number." He already had a sense of what could nick Sylvia's ego, as in this suggestion that Moss Hart write the material that she lived to write.

"Well, if I ever write another revue," Hart coyly replied, "it would only be because you could be in it." There were whispers that the thirty-five-year-old and still-unmarried Hart might be homosexual. This could have been a subtle flirtation with Kaye, and even if not, there are wiles of allure and sly games that men will play for power or ambition or mere sport.

Only a few days later, as Sylvia recalled, the playwright telephoned to ask whether Danny might indeed be interested in something he was writing, but it was not a revue; it was a Broadway musical. This wasn't a sure thing, Hart said, and Kaye's would be far from a starring role, but he was creating the part with Danny in mind, and since he would be codirecting the show with Hassard Short, he would have a voice in its casting.

Was Danny interested? He and Sylvia would spend the next few months trying to find out if, whether, when, and how it might happen.

Meanwhile, the Martinique engagement was repeatedly extended, ultimately to thirteen weeks, and by then Danny Kaye's fundamental nature and identity as a performer had been set. In the first place, he was an act, which is a curious locution—an action. Being an act meant that he could *do* something in front of an audience, even if that "something" was vague. Being an act also meant that his stage presence was an established quality, charismatic and communicable to a live audience. Moreover, he was the act. People would talk, or write, about his material, which in fact was Sylvia's or Max's material, but it was his personality that they floundered to describe. "Impish," "crazy," and most frequently, "zany"—but the right word is always hard to find when confronted with an original.

Above all, he had proved himself a solo entertainer capable of dominating and bewitching a confrontational audience.

His movements were unique. His hands fluttered like a brace of birds, and his face had a glow that was at once angelic and devilish. That was a clue to him, a tension drawn between babelike joy and corrupt sophistication. It was a tension that set his performing gravity in balance, making for a knowing gaiety. This whimsy, these giggles, were laced with a deadly urbanity.

That was a promise of his evolving personality. Like many bright people, particularly those whose cleverness becomes the reason for their success, he developed a nasty edge. It did not belie a good nature; it was, rather, the underbelly of his character.

Sylvia's first love had always been the musical theater, but there was no sense in sitting still and waiting for Moss Hart to come through with a Broadway show. That musical might never happen. Taking on the role of his manager—Harry Bestry notwithstanding —and concentrating on Danny's nightclub career, she hired the Martinique's press agent, Eddie Dukoff, to handle his publicity. It would prove a stunning choice. This tall, thirty-one-year-old, vaguely disheveled fellow with dark curly hair, a slight paunch, a wayward tie, and a perpetually loosened shirt collar would reinvent publicity.

Eddie Dukoff would also become devoted to this one client; devoted, some felt, beneath his dignity. His admiration would turn obsequious, but Dukoff's ingenuity as a press agent, his energy and originality, would never flag. He would eventually ignite a blaze of publicity for Kaye, an unprecedented and continuous storm of favorable and fame-creating articles.

In the meantime, Bestry booked Danny into a string of top nightclubs, from the glittering Riviera in Fort Lee, New Jersey, to the elegant Chez Paree in Chicago. There, by coincidence, he was on a bill with Kitty Carlisle, the beautiful and stylish young singer/actress who was dating Moss Hart. She was headlining the floor show, which, besides herself and Kaye, included a chorus line, the dance team of Yolanda and Velez, Jack Cole and his Balinese Dancers, and the Emil Coleman Orchestra. In those times, most programs ran longer than they would in later years, whether they were concerts, Broadway plays, or nightclub floor shows. This revue, Carlisle remembered with a laugh, "lasted, I don't know, forever."

At the run-through for cues and timing, Sylvia introduced herself to Kitty as "Danny Kaye's accompanist," even though she was quite a bit more than that, including his wife. Carlisle was sympathetic when she realized that Sylvia didn't have a dressing room. "I hardly had one myself," she recalled. "Just a cubicle with chairs, but I invited her to share it." Since there were three shows a night, starting at eight and ending at two in the morning, there was a lot of time that would be spent at the club. Much of it was spent in that little dressing room, and so these two strong, bright women got to know each other. It was the start of a lifelong friendship.

"We had two subjects of conversation," Carlisle remembered. "One was: 'Do I think Moss Hart will really put Danny Kaye in his new musical?' The other was: 'Do you think I should marry that third secretary at the Brazilian embassy?' "

She would marry Hart, notwithstanding the homosexual whispers. Such rumors were heard about almost everyone in the theater. In Hart's case, they were inevitable, given his affectations of speech and manner, his slender fashionableness, his advanced stage of bachelorhood, and his friendships with Cole Porter, Monty Woolley, and Noel Coward. He even went on long working holidays—ocean voyages to the South Seas—with that crowd, so rumors were to be expected, but of course nobody knew.

Nothing about anyone's private life seemed to surprise Kitty Carlisle. She was too worldly wise, and yet she was no cynic. She was simply and truly sophisticated, and she was immediately aware of how crazy Sylvia was about Danny.

The two women would "cook up ways," Carlisle remembered, "to make Danny do new numbers." He was always reluctant to try untested material, and Sylvia was proud of "Anatole of Paris," which she had just finished. This send-up of the French couture mixed dialect humor with satire. There was nothing special about the music; it was a simple melody with unsurprising harmonies, carried along on sprightly rhythms. The wit was in the lyrics, which were clever and carefully rhymed, sometimes niftily so. That was usually the case with revue material—the music existing just as a medium for lyrics—and this was real revue material, arch in tone and a "set piece," freestanding and unrelated to a plot.

Although, to be sure, "Anatole of Paris" was a very smart number, with it Sylvia was once again creating effeminate material for Danny. It was, after all, a song about a fey fashion designer who "shrieks with chic." Once more, she was either responding to an androgynous quality in his manner or inspiring it, but that is a question for a psychologist. To be fair to the song, there is legitimate humor in its sudden jumps from archness to argot ("Voilà, a chapeau / At sixty bucks a throw"). No mistake should be made, there is a real cleverness about "Anatole of Paris."

However, afraid of risking his performing neck with unproven material, Kaye refused to sing it. One night, Sylvia said to Kitty, "Tonight I want him to do 'Anatole.' He won't break it in, so you announce that he's going to do it, and then he'll do it."

He did, and the audience just loved it. Sylvia and Kitty were so thrilled with the response that after the late show they took Danny out for silver dollar–sized pancakes at Rickett's Restaurant. Then they all drove out to watch the sun rise over Lake Michigan.

From then on, "Anatole of Paris" was a staple of Kaye's act.

Was Sylvia indeed his Svengali? The creative genius behind him? Had she invented Danny Kaye? "Everything," Kitty thought. "I mean, the talent was there. He had a natural physical grace that she couldn't have given him. And his hand gestures—she couldn't have given him that. [But] she certainly wrote all his material. He was extraordinarily talented and very intelligent, but the material and the performing—that was hers."

The question of how much of Danny Kaye was invented by Sylvia Fine was going to become a central issue in his career and their marriage.

· · ·

IN THOSE DAYS, MOST TRANSCONTINENTAL TRAVEL PASSED THROUGH Chicago, and just as Danny had become the must-see in New York, so he now became de rigueur for the coast-to-coast set riding into Chicago to connect with or from the New York–based Twentieth Century Limited. During the three-week engagement at the Chez Paree, Kitty Carlisle remembered, "the word spread like wildfire. Show people like Jack Benny would stop over to see him . . . just because they had heard about this extraordinary young performer. There was this aura of hot success about him."

And when he came home, he was indeed offered the part in Moss Hart's show *Lady in the Dark*.

Its authors were strange bedfellows. Hart was a product of commercial Broadway, a hugely successful collaborator of George S. Kaufman's, although he had not yet succeeded on his own. The lyricist, Ira Gershwin, had not written for the stage since his brother George's death in 1937, except for a few *Ziegfeld Follies* songs with Vernon Duke. The composer, Kurt Weill, was a refugee from the Nazis. A classical musician, he had an arty European reputation as Bertolt Brecht's collaborator, but he hadn't yet found his American voice.

What sort of musical comedy could such a trio produce? Would it be *very Broadway* like Hart? Vigorously American like Gershwin? Or acid, intellectual, and European like Weill?

Hart's libretto was based on an unproduced play of his. The central character is Liza Elliott, a fashion-magazine editor who is indecisive about everything, from cover photographs to men. With the help of her psychoanalyst, she comes to grips with this "neurosis" by exploring her dreams, and those dreams are musicalized. It was, after all, a musical.

Hart's play had been inspired by his own four years of psychoanalysis, which had been dealing, intimates said, with his difficulty sustaining a romantic relationship with a woman. The role that Danny had inspired Hart to create was an effeminate fashion photographer with such self-ridiculing speeches as "Girls! He's godlike, absolutely godlike. I mean, I have photographed beautiful men before, but he is the end, the absolute end. He's got a face that would melt in your mouth. He is heaven, absolute heaven."

Perhaps Hart wrote this gushing role for Kaye as part of a conscious or subconscious homosexual communication. Perhaps Hart did see an epicene quality in Kaye (a quality some noticed in Hart himself) that he then exaggerated. It is not likely that Moss Hart merely invented the "swishy" (Kaye's word) character for the sake of a laugh. While stereotypical humor was commonplace in those years, it was not commonplace among sophisticates.

The star of *Lady in the Dark* (although Kaye was actually signed first) was the fabulous Gertrude Lawrence. The small and slender darling of the London stage was associated with Noel Coward through his plays *(Private Lives)* and revues *(Tonight at 8:30)*. She had been successfully transplanted to Broadway, where she introduced "Someone to Watch Over Me" in the Gershwins' *Oh, Kay!* Snaring her for *Lady in the Dark* was a real coup, and Hart made sure that she would be supported by solid actors. Her admirers in this show would be played by Macdonald Carey and Victor Mature, both destined for successful movie careers.

As rehearsals began, Kaye became aware of his own inexperience. "I wasn't good," he admitted. "They were disappointed in me." His most challenging scene was "The Circus Dream." There the fashion photographer Russell Paxton is imagined by the heroine Liza Elliott (Gertrude Lawrence) to be a circus ringmaster. In that setting, she is tried for the crime of being indecisive.

Kaye had to announce, with three-ring grandeur, "a galaxy of clowns and neuroses in a modern miracle of melodramatic buffoonery and mental tightrope walking." The satire was heavy-handed, and the lines would have been difficult for even an experienced stage comedian to read. Then the chorus moved in, singing, "Ta-ra-ra-zing-zing-zing" as they musically set the scene:

> The Greatest Show on Earth!
> It's Full of Thrills and Mirth!
> You Get Your Money's Worth!
> Come One, Come All!

Ringmaster Kaye opens the trial with recitative-like lines:

> Ladies and Gentlemen, I Take Pride in Introducing
> The Greatest Show on Earth!
> Liza Elliott's Gargantuan Three-Ring Circus
> Featuring for the First Time
> The Captivating and Tantalizing Liza Elliott . . .
> The Woman Who Cannot Make Up Her Mind!

This material, although perhaps written by Hart and Ira Gershwin with Danny Kaye in mind, was not tailored to the same talents that Sylvia grasped. But a Broadway musical is not a nightclub floor show, and the idea was for Kaye to play the ringmaster, not himself. He simply was not yet equipped to act on the Broadway level, and that was where Moss Hart was smart enough to reverse himself, remembering exactly what Danny *was* able to do. Only days later, Kaye remembered, "along came Ira Gershwin and asked me if I could learn a new song in a hurry. I said I could, and I did. It was that song."

"That song" was "Tschaikowsky" (as it was then spelled), not even a *song* but a routine set to a recurring beat, a list of Russian composers, rattled off as quickly as possible. It was revue material, entirely irrelevant to the plot, but it was Danny's specialty.

"Tschaikowsky (and Other Russians)" was his only song in the show, but it was going to be a showstopper, and that was so obvious that upon hearing it rehearsed, Gertie Lawrence promptly demanded a big, flashy number as well—and she wanted it to come right after "Tschaikowsky." This is the basic definition of "star clout." She was not going to let a newcomer take the spotlight away from her. Gershwin and Weill promptly wrote "The Saga of Jenny," a bluesy, vamping number that in its own way was just as good as "Tschaikowsky."

Jenny made her mind up when she was three
She, herself, was going to trim the Christmas tree.
Christmas Eve she lit the candles—tossed the taper away
Little Jenny was an orphan on Christmas Day.

As *Lady in the Dark* shipped out to Boston for its trial run, the creators knew only that thirty minutes had to be cut from its four-hour length. Otherwise, the $105,000 musical was an unknown quantity.

On the opening night at the Colonial Theatre, the audience started to erupt even before Danny had finished singing "Tschaikowsky." Gertrude Lawrence, knowing that there was about to be an ovation, realized, "I was up against it. My song had to be good, as good as I could possibly make it if I was going to meet the challenge of Danny's ability and personality. It was an intoxicating feeling. There is nothing more fun than meeting an audience when they are feeling on top of the world—and Danny Kaye had certainly put them there."

She was being sly. As a star—as the star of this show—she had to protect herself. No matter how good Kaye was, she had to top him. She stood grimly behind him as he was milking "Tschaikowsky" for all it was worth. A stage wait is the only thing that stars loathe more than dogs and child actors, and she was onstage throughout his song.

Kaye remembered, "I was still bowing and smiling when the awful realization hit me! The great Gertrude Lawrence was onstage waiting to sing a number called 'Jenny.' And I knew that when a star is waiting, the worst crime in show business is to delay her entrance."

When he was finally finished, she pulled her sensational talents and energies into full battle array. With the start of "The Saga of Jenny," she unbuttoned the business suit she was wearing and revealed the sequined gown beneath. Then she began to work the mock striptease number back and forth with the chorus, eying them devilishly as they sang:

> Poor Jenny! Bright as a penny!
> Her equal would be hard to find.

And then she retorted:

> She lost one dad and mother,
> A sister and a brother
> But she wouldn't make up her mind.

Kaye had to admit it. That night, Gertie "sang 'Jenny' as I have never heard her sing before. She used every trick known to show business and kept the audience in the palm of her hand. . . . She met my success by winning greater triumph from those people who sat out front. That night, she tore the house down!"

Nobody disagreed with that. Witnesses describe Lawrence as belting out "The Saga of Jenny" while bumping and grinding like a burlesque stripper. Kaye might have tried to sound admiring when he said, "She walked majestically to center stage, threw me a wondrous and gracious smile, and sang," but Gertie was hardly in a gracious mood. To her, Danny Kaye was a nervy upstart, and as an opening-night gift to Moss Hart's friend who was playing a "swishy" photographer, she bitchily gave him an earring. He smiled and asked for the other one.

6

If you are in a profession that allows you to meet people who are intelligent . . . if you come from a very intellectually limited neighborhood in Brooklyn and you don't reach for something better, you're silly.

—Kitty Carlisle

*L*ADY IN THE DARK OPENED TO EXCELLENT REVIEWS IN BOSTON AND PLAYED TO SOLD-OUT HOUSES. THE NECESSARY ADJUSTMENTS were made, notwithstanding the vanity cutups of the star and the newcomer, whose battle was waged at every performance, all the way to the Broadway premiere, January 23, 1941, at the Alvin Theatre.

The Alvin Theatre was so-called because of its owners' names, Alex Aarons and Vinton Freedley, and they, of course, had the best seats in their house. But that night, Freedley was not seated with his girlfriend, the gossip columnist Radie Harris. She was holding the nervous hand of Kitty Carlisle, whose romance with Moss Hart had become serious.

During the second act, the "Circus Dream" sequence was proceeding through its Gilbert and Sullivan–like exchanges among the ringmaster, judge, lawyers, and jury. This was arch material, but Kaye had finally mastered its peculiar tone as well as Weill's difficult music. As the scene progressed, there was a choral outburst from the jury, and he beamed in response, resplendent in his shiny gold circus-ringmaster costume, with its epaulets, jodhpurs, and riding boots.

"Charming, charming," he declared. "Who wrote that music?"

"Tschaikowsky," replied the chorus.

"Tschaikowsky! I love Russian composers," he cried, and with that, he launched into the meaningless, irrelevant, and utterly wonderful number that Ira Gershwin had concocted for him.

> There's Malichevsky, Rubinstein, Arenstein and
>   Tschaikowsky,
> Sapelnikoff, Dimitrieff, Tscherepnin, Kryjanowsky,
> Godowsky, Arteiboucheff, Moniuszko, Akimenko,
> Solovieff, Prokofieff, Tiomkin, Korestchenko,
> There's Glinka, Winkler, Bortniansky, Rebikoff, Ilyinsky;
> There's Medtner, Balakireff, Zolotareff and Kvoschinsky,
> And Sokoloff and Kopyloff, Dukelsky and Klenofsky,
> And Shostakovitsch, Borodine, Gliere and Nowakofski;
> There's Liadoff and Karganoff, Markievitch, Pantschenko,
> And Dargomyzski, Stchertbatcheff, Scriabine, Vassilenko,
> Stravinsky, Rymskykorsakoff, Mussorgsky and
>   Gretchaninoff;
> And Glazounoff and Caesar Cui, Kalinikoff, Rachmaninoff.

"Godowsky" and "Dukelsky" were Ira Gershwin's inside jokes. His sister Frances was married to Leopold Godowsky, Jr., and Vladimir Dukelsky was the real name of Ira's friend, the songwriter Vernon Duke. The remaining forty-seven were legitimate Russian composers, and when Kaye finished rattling off their names, the audience went wild.

Gertrude Lawrence did not. As she stood upstage behind him, just barely enduring the stage wait, Radie Harris leaned over to Kitty Carlisle and whispered, "He'll be killed for that. Gertie's not going to let him get away with it."

She didn't. Just as she had done on that Boston opening night, she turned to her audience, stepped downstage toward it, and plunged into "The Saga of Jenny" like a princess in a brothel, complete unto every regal bump and grind.

The next morning, the critics were ecstatic—for *Lady in the Dark*, for Gertie, and for the newest discovery on Broadway, Danny Kaye.

The show's competition had been substantial. Broadway's stages were exploding with the likes of Al Jolson, Ethel Waters, Ed Wynn, and Ethel Barrymore. Only the previous week, Gene Kelly had opened in *Pal Joey*.

Moreover, and it was only the midpoint of the season, there had already been such arrivals as *My Sister Eileen*, *Arsenic and Old Lace*, *Life with Father*, *Cabin in the Sky*, *Tobacco Road*, and Irving Berlin's *Louisiana Purchase*. Yet even in such company, *Lady in the Dark* got special notice. Writing in the *New York Times*, Brooks Atkinson began: "All things considered, the American stage may as well take a bow this morning," and he went on from there as if Moss Hart had written the review himself. As for Danny Kaye, according to Atkinson the young man was "infectiously exuberant."

In the *Journal-American*, John Anderson found him "hilarious," while Louis Kronenberger *(PM)*, John Mason Brown *(Post)*, and Richard B. Watts, Jr. *(Herald Tribune)*, all agreed that he had stopped the show with "Tschaikowsky." As Kaye later said in one of his special moods of splendidly terse and tight-lipped insight, the size of his part was not the issue. "Never measure anything by quantity. I was on eleven minutes. Actually, thirty-eight seconds of it [the duration of 'Tschaikowsky'] made my career."

Gertie and Danny did not stop their zinging just because *Lady in the Dark* was a hit. In fact, the battle had just begun. Lawrence was using every weapon in her theatrical arsenal to maintain the stature it had taken her so long to achieve. She certainly had the high ground to begin with, for she had the leading role and the evening focused on her. Young Kaye had only "Tschaikowsky" to make his mark, but for Lawrence it was as if the loss of full audience focus for even a moment would mean the end of her recognition altogether.

It eventually settled into a duel of stage "business"—any kind of movement while the other was singing. An audience's attention is always drawn to movement, because in the theater the visual has greater impact than the vocal. Once, while Kaye was performing "Tschaikowsky," Gertie put a cigarette in a long holder and lit a match, holding it until it nearly burned her fingers. Then, as he continued singing, she lit a second match.

On another occasion, she wore a bracelet that had little bells on it. Not content with the visual distraction of its glitter, she actually shook the bracelet while he was singing.

Kaye, meanwhile, was developing his own hand movements. "Tschaikowsky" was a static number that had him simply standing

there, rattling off the names. Drawing on the gestures that Nat Lichtman had helped him develop at White Roe, he worked out a series
of expressive gestures while he sang the piece, gestures that had no
relevance to the words—what relevance could there be to Russian
names? His gestures, rather, were a kind of manual dance, his arms,
elbows, wrists, and fingers moving in continuous, bending, and swiveling combinations. It was novel, it was ingenious, it was mesmerizing, and, incidentally, it drew the audience's eyes back to Kaye from
whatever Gertie Lawrence, behind him, was doing to distract them.

Vivian Vance (later to be on the *I Love Lucy* television series)
was in the chorus of *Lady in the Dark*, standing onstage throughout
the number. The members of the chorus had been reminded of the
old stage rule about not moving on someone else's lines, let alone
during a song, and that protection was afforded Kaye as well as
Lawrence. The chorus had been specifically directed to remain mo-
tionless during "Tschaikowsky," but, Vance remembered, "Gertie
would do anything to upstage Kaye when he was singing." Even
Danny privately admitted that the jousting was getting to be "a strain
on our nerves." He told friends, "One night while I was singing
'Tschaikowsky,' the audience's attention wandered. . . . Glancing
over my shoulder, I saw Miss Lawrence nonchalantly waving a red
scarf. I plotted my revenge. While she was singing ["Jenny"], she
was startled by an unexpected laugh, because I . . . was mugging in
the background. The lovely Miss Lawrence turned around and
raised an arched eyebrow at me. I received the subtle reprimand
with a slight bow."

Offstage they did not bother with this grandness. Offstage they
were not even speaking. "But she's still a wonderful woman," Danny
would say with a sly grin.

Probably little of this mattered to him, for he was taking the first
heady breaths of fame. Newspaper interviews provided the world
with essential information about his taste in expensive suits and ties;
his favorite cologne (Tweed); parties he and his wife went to, Danny
entertaining while Sylvia accompanied him at the piano. There was
also a movie offer from M-G-M, the most prestigious of the Hollywood studios. It involved a lot of money, $3,000 a week, but Sylvia
turned it down. The studio, she said, only wanted him to do specialty
numbers, and she had character roles in mind. Translated, that probably meant M-G-M refused to give her approval of his assignments.

The rejected movie offer caused no financial regrets. He was
already making $2,000 a week, for only days after *Lady in the Dark*

had opened, he began doubling at La Martinique, where he was paid $1,000 a week and a percentage of the receipts. That was just for playing the late show. After curtain calls at the Alvin, he would scrub off his makeup, Sylvia would have a cab waiting at the stage door, and they would speed across town from Fifty-second Street and Eighth Avenue to Fifty-seventh Street and Fifth.

He had top billing at the nightclub now, or at least he shared it. The other headliner was another discovery of that theater season, the energetic singer-dancer Betty Hutton. Like Danny, she, too, was doubling after appearing in a Broadway musical—Cole Porter's *Panama Hattie.*

The nineteen-year-old blonde was described in *Variety*, the show-business trade paper, as "one of the pioneer jitterbugs in the jive tradition, doing her scat and hi-de-ho songs." It sounded like Kaye's act, and the similarity between their performing styles would not make for oceans of affection. Then again, they weren't strangers. A few years earlier they had worked on the same bill at the Casa Mañana, when Danny had been stooging for Nick Long and was still living with his father in Brooklyn. Some nights after the late show, rather than taking the long subway ride home, "he stayed with us," Betty remembered. "My mother, my sister Marion [a singer with the Glenn Miller Orchestra], and I lived in a sixty-five-dollar-a-month walk-up, and Danny would sleep on the floor."

Betty was used to unpleasant conditions at home. Back in Battle Creek, Michigan, her mother, Mabel, had run a "speaky" (speak-easy) called the Blind Pig. Mabel Hutton had been a drinker then, and she was a drunk now. The walk-up apartment she shared with her daughters was dark, small, and crowded enough; Danny's addition must have made it delightful. Still, they had once taken him in, and now he acted as if it had never happened and, worse, as if Betty were beneath him. "He didn't hang out with show people," she would recall with enduring resentment. "It was all society people like Moss Hart and Kitty Carlisle. He went high-hat."

At the Martinique, Danny and Betty argued about almost everything, from who had which dressing room to who went on first. "He didn't want to open," she said, "and he didn't want to close. I didn't care. I just said he had to follow or go before me, but it just had to be one or the other!"

Kaye was surely distracted by still more new material that Sylvia and Max Liebman were giving him for this return engagement. The situation was no different than it had been in Chicago when he first sang "Anatole of Paris." Then he was nervous about the audience's reaction to the new number, and he was nervous now, and he always would be, even at the peak of his career. Most performers are. Introducing new material is like driving an untested car.

One of the new numbers was "Rhythm," in which, to a jazz beat, he did his double-talk in the style of different personality types —a bashful person singing "Git-gat-giddle / With a geet-ga-zay," an angry person, and so on. The popularity of the double-talk was beginning to bother him, he said, but he was seduced by its surefire way with audiences.

At the piano, Sylvia was trying her best to look like a performer. Unfortunately, she had neither the physical equipment nor the taste for it, between her long white opera gloves and, Benay Venuta remembered, "those awful silver shoes." But her life was about her work, not her looks, and all of the material worked. The best-received number by far was "Anatole of Paris," and it helped Kaye win more rave reviews.

He responded to approval as actors usually do—by giving even more of himself. Rare, now, was the show that ran under an hour, and rare was the night that the Kayes went to bed before four in the morning.

"He has arrived now," *Variety* reported. "This is his hour. He is a full fledged star." And there was even a report that Billy Rose, the producer, had offered him $500,000 a year for a lifetime contract. That might have been press-agent hyperbole. Then again, Eddie Dukoff was more than just a press agent. Of course, he did not overlook such basics as interviews and newspaper pictures; in March 1941 he even had Gertrude Lawrence photographed watching Danny's show at the Martinique. Moss Hart and Kitty Carlisle had brought her there to settle the feud, and she showed up with Noel Coward.

But Dukoff was also disseminating what would in later times be called an "image," showcasing a quality of Kaye's that was beginning to emerge with success—a quality of personal class. Interviewers depicted him as not just a unique entertainer but an artist, one who was charming and even elegant. In one such interview he was not spoken *with* but *about.*

> [Kaye] drinks a mix of cream and ginger ale to keep his weight up . . . lives on an allowance. Loves bow ties. Hates hats with veils and earrings. He makes the potato pancakes.

Hates milk. "If there's a window to be closed in the middle of the night," says wife Sylvia, "we toss for it. If we go driving for the week-end he does the driving and I keep my mouth shut—and he plays tennis while I go swimming. He hasn't the vaguest idea about his bank balance. When he's worried he can't be effusive. He rarely complains, he's always late for dinner and punctual for rehearsals. He is an odd combination of confidence and diffidence and will take criticism graciously from anyone for whom he has respect."

The note about driving referred to Danny's brand-new 1941 gray Cadillac convertible with a black top and red leather seats. He and Sylvia had treated themselves to success gifts. Hers was a mink coat.

That spring of 1941, Rosie Kaye, now Rosie Goldman, took the train to New York from Fort Lauderdale, ostensibly to visit her parents but really, she had to admit, to see Danny in *Lady in the Dark*. The morning after, she was roused by a racket in the street below her window. It was unusually loud for early on a Sunday morning, even on the Lower East Side, whose raucous pushcart peddlers considered Sunday the busiest day of the week. Leaning out her window and looking down through the bars of the fire escape, she saw a beautiful, expensive open car on East Fifth Street below. Behind its steering wheel, beeping the horn and beaming up at her with his red, red hair was Broadway's latest discovery.

She dressed, hurried downstairs, and he took her for a spin. He always would be a fast driver, and they went for a long drive to Brown Hills, New Jersey. There they visited Nat Lichtman, who had been the resident genius at White Roe. Nat was only thirty, but his once-robust good looks had turned pale. With sunken cheeks and thin black hair, he had the classically wan, gaunt, and hollow look of a consumptive.

Visiting with Nat in the tuberculosis sanatorium, Rosie did not know that Fishel Goldfarb, Dick Diamond, and the old gang of White Roe friends had been contributing money to help Etta Lichtman with the expense of the blood transfusions. "We were all going broke from it," Diamond remembered. They had sent Danny a telegram at the Alvin Theatre, explaining the problem and asking for help, but, Kaye later told Diamond, Sylvia didn't show him the wire. "With her grim exterior," an unforgiving Diamond remembered decades later, "she was a son of a bitch."

. . .

SYLVIA'S PLACE IN THE BACKGROUND WAS MOVING UP TO THE FORE-ground. She was beginning to get public recognition. As Danny wearied of interviewers, Eddie Dukoff discovered that Sylvia was as articulate when talking as when writing. So she began to give some of the interviews for Danny, and such things added to the public impression of the Kayes. They became a husband-and-wife team unique in show business.

"It is she who writes all his material," read an item about Danny in the *New York Sun*, "words and music, and who works with him, coaches him and accompanies him at the piano at each perfor-mance. She doesn't take any bows but Kaye takes them for her and he is the first to give her full credit for his meteoric rise."

Sylvia would redirect the spotlight his way, insisting that she measured her success in terms of Danny's. Given the chance to contribute an article in the *New York Times*, she wrote, "Danny is a natural performer with an instinctive sense of comedy and what I think is an uncanny sense of timing. The written word is as nothing to him. He has to take the words in his mouth, eyes and hands. He must play them, bend them, stretch them and cajole them—and, most important, bounce them against an audience before he can truly evaluate them."

She was not only being clever; she was being smart. She knew how to make herself seem wifely and modest; how to lend her man-child just a touch of adolescent inadequacy; how to pepper her ob-ject of adoration and maternity, her perfect creation, with charming flaws.

Was she making a case for his needing her, or did he actually depend on her? The article of hers continued: "There's one place where his memory fails him and it drives Max [Liebman] and me to distraction. He'll improvise hundreds of swell pieces of business—and the next day remember only two or three."

The line between maternalism and insidious undermining is a thin one.

Along with Danny's marvelous reviews for *Lady in the Dark* came a rave notice in *Variety* for his cabaret act:

> A big, breezy, refreshing personality with a unique style of
> general kidding that should carry him along in good style.
> [The material includes] his travesty on a Carnegie Hall

singer, with "Dark Eyes" and a sneezing routine. He does a
hokum conga routine that's a natural in a Latin nitery like
La Martinique. Another highlight are some weird hat mon-
strosities as "created" by a fashionable modiste wherein Kaye
uses the musicians as pseudo-models of the goshawful cha-
peaux. . . . Comic is a self-assured worker on the floor and
his general al fresco style commends him for class or mass
appeal.

Whatever was meant by "al fresco style," the "sneezing routine" was
a reference to an emerging Kaye-Fine tradition of gesundheit jokes,
and this review came from no less than Abel—the trade journal's
editor, Abel Green.

Six weeks into Danny's success, his streak of perfect publicity
stuttered just a little bit. There was a cartoon in the *New York Herald
Tribune* depicting him as effeminate in *Lady in the Dark*. And there
was an effusive tribute to Sylvia, written by Louis Sobol, the enter-
tainment/gossip columnist for the *New York Journal-American*.
Sobol was hardly as powerful as Walter Winchell of the *Mirror* or
even Ed Sullivan of the *News* or Leonard Lyons of the *Post*, but
he was nevertheless influential. Sobol seemed to feel that he had discovered a woman-behind-the-man angle. It would appear that his
only possible source was Sylvia herself.

The quiet, expressive-faced young woman . . . sat at the
piano, a dark haired, smiling-eyed girl. Before Danny started
any number, he looked inquiringly at her, waited for either a
nod of approval or disapproval. Even as she played the piano
she never let her eyes leave him—they followed every movement. Occasionally her lips silently formed the words he was
singing or speaking.

An amazing young woman. If there ever were a Svengali
and Trilby in benign reverse, this is an instance, for she not
only makes his arrangements, writes most of his material,
but also it is she who rehearses him until she is satisfied
with his gesturing and posturing, his enunciation, his facial
expressions, etc. Mrs. Danny Kaye, always modestly behind
the scenes, is easily more than half the show.

A month later, Kaye stunned Sam Harris, the producer of *Lady
in the Dark*. Barely a half year into the musical's run, he announced
that he was quitting the show.

7

*You will never forget the movement of his hands, a shrug of
his shoulders, his look of innocence, his voice and a kind of
impishness which is his alone.*

—*New York Herald Tribune*

VINTON FREEDLEY, THE CO-OWNER OF THE ALVIN THEATRE, STOLE
DANNY OUT FROM UNDER HIS OWN TENANTS. A CARELESS SAM HAR-
ris, the producer of *Lady in the Dark,* had overlooked signing Kaye
to a run-of-the-show contract, as he had done with Gertrude Lawrence, Victor Mature, and Macdonald Carey. Because of that oversight, a brief half year into the run he was losing the sensation of the
season. The headline in the *New York Daily News* of June 27, 1941,
read "Danny Kaye Deserts 'Lady in the Dark' for New Porter Musical," and everyone involved was furious, most of all, Moss Hart.
Having written Danny into *Lady in the Dark,* he took the abrupt
departure as a personal betrayal and accused him of ingratitude.

But Kaye could hardly have refused the opportunity he had just
been handed. A year out of the Catskills, he was being offered a lead
part in a new Cole Porter show opening in just a matter of months.
A seeming lifetime of frustration and delay was suddenly behind
him, as if it had been but a moment. Moreover, success, when it
came, not only meant the kind of opportunity that he could never
have dreamed of; it also meant that he could demand to be well
compensated for it. And so, while Vinton Freedley had Kaye for his

next production, he had to pay for the privilege. Like most Broadway producers, his intelligence was compromised by a fan mentality, and he even boasted about overpaying his star. Kaye's contract, the producer said, "virtually makes him a partner." The contract, in fact, called for a salary of $1,000 a week in addition to 15 percent of everything over $20,000 gross at the box office. That would come to $2,900 a week for most of the run, as compared to the $550 a week that Kaye had been earning in *Lady in the Dark*.

Sylvia could not have anticipated this at all. She must have expected that *Lady in the Dark* would occupy Danny for some time, because she was finally working on her own musical. The libretto was by Max Liebman, and they had even found a producer. A Broadway opening was being projected for the fall of that year, 1941.

No more. Danny's leap from *Lady in the Dark* to a starring role in *Let's Face It!* (as the new Cole Porter musical was called) marked the end of Sylvia's show. A newspaper interviewer observed that "she has submerged herself without question for what she considers the greater career of her husband." Whether or not she explored the psychological resonances of that, her approval of this move to the Porter musical must have occasioned a long, hard look in the mirror for Sylvia Fine. It was the end of any independent career for her. She daringly sounded out the estimable Mr. Porter on the possibility of contributing several of her own songs to the show. She had no shame and she had no choice, for now her fulfillment rested utterly with her husband's.

She was now giving as many interviews as Danny, and the more she spoke for the two of them, the more they became a marital team in the public eye.

There have been husband-and-wife teams in and out of show business, but the teams usually are cooperators—men and women who do the same thing. There was too much need here, too much dependency, and whether professional or personal, dependency complicates a relationship. It breeds resentment.

Sometimes her interviews took a patronizing, even a condescending, tone toward him. "Danny is the worst judge of material I've ever known," she told a reporter who visited her in the East Fifty-second Street penthouse. "He's always one hundred percent wrong. We have to argue him into using skits that later prove tremendous hits at the club." The interviewer left with the impression that "Sylvia Fine writes every skit that Danny Kaye uses. She struggles for hours, days even, to give the proper lilt to a single line."

With a fine double edge, Danny had to joke, "Sylvia has a fine head on my shoulders."

HE SEEMED TO PREFER TO DO RATHER THAN TALK, AS IF HE WERE most alive when performing. A bare nine days after leaving *Lady in the Dark*, he opened a five-week engagement at the Paramount Theater in Times Square. This was a "presentation house," a term coined in the last days of vaudeville for theaters that presented movies as well as variety entertainment. Abbreviated vaudeville bills were offered between the pictures in an effort to please all audiences. (The movie at the Paramount was *Caught in the Draft*, with Bob Hope and Dorothy Lamour.) Although the performers played five shows a day instead of vaudeville's two, they got more money— Danny was being paid $3,500 a week—but money wasn't everything. This kind of entertainment would never have the cozy atmosphere or the audience give-and-take of a vaudeville show. The photographic detachment of the movie image seemed to affect the onstage performers. When, at movie's end, the screen proclaimed, "And Now—Live and in Person," the performers in the stage show did not seem to be either live or in person. They seemed to continue as celluloid. They needed time to warm up—both themselves and their audiences. They seldom got the time. Moreover, it was hard to create the intimacy of vaudeville in these enormous movie palaces.

The Paramount was not even the biggest presentation house in New York City. Radio City Music Hall was, but the Paramount had four thousand seats and three balconies, and that was big enough to make it the biggest house that Kaye had ever played. "When you're going to tell the audience a joke," he told an interviewer, "you must make sure that everybody, right up to the last row of the balcony, hears every syllable you say and understands it. If some of them don't catch on till after the rest, they laugh in the wrong place, and that spoils the timing. I see to it that the last row hears me even if I whisper. It isn't the volume. It's the way you project the sound."

That was a focused and professional way of discussing his craft. Having learned about theatrical projection while performing *Lady in the Dark*, he was applying the lessons at the Paramount.

"Maybe I'm all wrong," he continued, "but it seems to me that

a voice has a trajectory just like a bullet. It travels in a sort of curve
—up, over, and down—so you aim for the place you want it to land.
You don't just talk to the first few rows. You talk over them, to the
rest of the house, and the front rows hear your voice as it goes past."

LET'S FACE IT! WAS GOING TO BE A TRADITIONAL MUSICAL COMEDY.
Despite the recent ambitions of *Pal Joey* and *Lady in the Dark*,
Broadway musicals in 1941 remained lightweight affairs. Audiences
looked to them for chorus girls and comedians. *Oklahoma!* was but
a couple of years away, poised to exterminate such fluff as *Let's
Face It!* Frivolity, alas, would be lost in the transaction. Progress is
demanding, it is necessary, and it is wonderful, but it has no heart.
Ironically, although Cole Porter was Broadway's most sophisticated
songwriter, he was not serious-minded about his shows. His music
could be ambitious, and his lyrics were ingenious, but he showed
little interest in the dramatic vehicles they served. *Let's Face It!* was
a typical musical comedy for him, an adaptation by Herbert and
Dorothy Fields of *The Cradle Snatchers*, a 1925 farce by Russell
Medcraft and Norma Mitchell. The play had been a rickety business
about three society wives who, suspicious of their husbands' ab-
sences, engage three bachelors in the cause of jealousy. It remained
rickety in the Fieldses' adaptation, which was updated to make soldiers of the bachelors. The Japanese attack on Pearl Harbor still lay
ahead, but war was in the air. It was raging in Europe, and selective
service had already begun.

Two of the wives were played by Eve Arden and Vivian Vance,
and while none in the cast was given star billing, Cole Porter gener-
ously agreed to let Sylvia and Max Liebman interpolate special musical material for Danny. That was a considerable acknowledgment of
Kaye's importance, and writing the songs was the closest Sylvia
would ever come to her own Broadway show.

The Fine/Liebman interpolations were "A Fairy Tale," which,
as "A Modern Fairy Tale," had already been done at the Martinique,
and a new number called "Melody in Four F." That one, subtitled
"Local Board Makes Good," could not have been thought up without Danny Kaye having been thought up first. Sylvia and Max created it by feeding Danny a story line and having him improvise mime
and prattle to illustrate it. As she explained to a *New York Times*
interviewer, "We told Danny he was to do a draftee from the time

he gets his questionnaire, through his session with an Army doctor, his troubles with a drilling sergeant, and his final winning of honors in maneuvers. This," she said, "is to be done in pantomime [and] scat-singing, with occasional words to point the action."

Sylvia was borrowing "scat singing" from jazz to dignify what Danny had always called "gibberish." There were similarities; there were instances in which he was virtually scatting with the sprint and skill of a jazz singer. But in jazz the purpose is to improvise like an instrumentalist; with Kaye, the purpose was to be funny, and the nonsense syllables were the whole point. He wasn't discomfited by that, and he wasn't ashamed to call it gibberish, but he was becoming saddled with the routine, and he made it plain that he was. He had so many gifts—singing, dancing, dialects. He could clown, tell funny stories and serious stories, he could act. Beyond all these talents, he had an offbeat sense of humor and a charismatic warmth. He was, in brief, unique, but instead, he was doing *this*. Sylvia would alternately defend it as jazz—"This double-talk, or gibberish," she said, "is really a series of hot licks that worked its way up from New Orleans"—or she would minimize it as being "a source of great perplexity to us that this trick of the tongue should be regarded by so many people as Danny's claim to fame. We think it's a pretty happy facet," she would say diplomatically, "but nothing on which to base a career."

The main point was that audiences loved the git-gat-giddle, and so Danny continued to do it. He, Sylvia, and Max apparently agreed on that, and so although Sylvia had boldly announced, "I won't have Danny just march down to the footlights and grin and say, 'Here I go.' That's too much like a nightclub," that is more or less what she and Max were going to have him do in the Cole Porter show.

The five weeks of rehearsal began in New York in August 1941, and the producer was already worried about Kaye. Each day, two hours before the one o'clock rehearsal, Danny would run through "A Fairy Tale" at home with Sylvia. Then they would practice his double-talk, hand gestures, and mugging for "Melody in Four F." But when he showed up at the theater, even Sylvia conceded, "he walked through his numbers." She and Max were assuring producer Freedley "that it would be all right on 'the night' [the opening]" in Boston, but their assurances, she remembered, "were met with great false heartiness from poor Vinton Freedley, who could see no evidence of the brilliant performer he had thought he had."

After the final dress rehearsal, with Kaye still *marking* rather than playing with full energy, "five o'clock of the morning before opening," Sylvia recalled, "the worried producer could stand it no longer. Prefaced by many soothing phrases, he asked us to please understand that if 'Fairy Tale' didn't have an unexpected effect on the audience, it would have to come out of the show."

She and Max Liebman smiled at each other. They knew that Danny needed energy from an audience. The problem, "we knew," she would later tell a reporter, was "that Danny felt as though he were in the mental nude when faced with an empty house." Now she was using his material. It was he who had said, "Every time I closed my eyes, I saw myself standing nude on an empty stage before an empty house."

She assured the producer that when Danny played to an audience, "protected and warm with fifteen hundred pairs of eyes, he would blossom forth." To Freedley's relief, her assurances were borne out by the Boston critics—but not to Kaye's relief. "I knew Danny needed reassurance," Sylvia said. "He was in the channel of worry, gloom, and despair," and he would never completely emerge from it. That "channel" would deepen in the course of his life— pathological depression, worry about his performances, and a gloom fed by Sylvia's love, her maternalism, her grim determination to keep him.

BROADWAY WAS WAITING ON OCTOBER 29, 1941, AT THE IMPERIAL Theatre. The gossip columnist Radie Harris was at this premiere, too, now seated with her Mr. Freedley. She remembered Cole Porter, dapper as usual in his tuxedo, a traditional red carnation in the lapel. Only a cane and a limp betrayed the continuing effects of his awful horse-riding accident several years earlier.

The show's score was not among his best, although Porter did tailor a couple of clever songs for Danny. Sylvia's music could hardly compare, since Cole Porter was an inspired and schooled musician. His lyrics were also fresher as well as craftier than Max's and hers. "Farming" was droll in its satire of socialites with weekend farm homes in places like Bucks County, Pennsylvania, and there was an understated freshness to its music. Kaye performed the song with great charm, and his other Porter number, "Let's Not Talk About Love," was witty and sophisticated:

Let's check on the veracity of Barrymore's bibacity
And why his drink capacity should get so much publacity
Let's even have a huddle over Ha'vard Univassity
But let's not talk about love.

On the other hand, Sylvia and Max's "Melody in Four F" was not far above the level of Camp Tamiment, but Broadway audiences seek the level of what is onstage. Just like an audience at Tamiment or even White Roe, they responded to Danny and his double-talk.

Sylvia, whose strength, it was increasingly apparent, lay in words rather than music, set "Melody in Four F" to a simple, alternating musical phrase on a fast, steady beat. Kaye opened the number with his "Git-gat-giddle / With a geet-ga-zay," extending it with other babble syllables. He held his elbows high and gracefully swiveled his arms, twisted his hands, setting them almost to dance while he tilted his head, grinning and grimacing like a ventriloquist's dummy.

Abruptly, he whistled and cried, "The mailman!" Then he continued his git-gat-giddle while miming the opening of an envelope and a reading of the contents. "Questionnaire!" he shouts, and weeps before resuming his "Git-gat-giddle / With a geet-ga-zay."

He announces, "Report to doctor!," and strolls across stage, swinging his arms. "Hiya, Doc!" he cries, and then, in a lower register, he has the doctor speaking in "Git-gat-giddle / With a geet-ga-zay." "Fine specimen," says the doctor before continuing in double-talk. "Oh, no!" responds the inductee, and so it goes, from the medical examination through the medical report and the pronouncement that he is fit for the draft. ("One-A!")

Following a military fanfare, with double-talk throughout, he begins his basic training, marching with the drill sergeant and soldiering from dawn until nightfall, git-gat-giddling until he falls into bed, still singing in double-talk. Then, with reveille, the recruit is off to war, and the git-gat-giddle accompanies Kaye's clownish miming of flying a plane, shooting a machine gun, tossing a hand grenade, and, finally, stumbling offstage to exit—and wild applause.

The reviews went to this ninety-second showcasing of Kaye's zaniness and the git-gat-giddle he so despised. In fact, the critics made *Let's Face It!* Danny's show. "Mr. Kaye conquered every ermine in the house," exulted Brooks Atkinson in the *Times*, while Louis Kronenberger (*PM*) wrote, "Kaye gave a good routine musical the lift, the oomph, the special cachet that should enable it to live long . . . all evening he indulged in a slew of antics, his personality shone, but at least twice during the evening, it dazzled. . . ."

The twice, of course, were "A Fairy Tale" and "Melody in Four F," and within a week he was given star billing. He was living every actor's fantasy. In the program his name was reset above the title. Outside the theater, it appeared in lights over the marquee.

Everything was going swimmingly. Eddie Dukoff placed his name and face everywhere. On December 14, just four days after he signed the lease on a big duplex apartment at 230 Central Park West, Danny found himself, full face and in color, on the front page of the rotogravure section of the *New York Sunday Mirror*.

He was pictured with the show's featured actress, Eve Arden. By then they were in love.

8

When Danny's great I know the reason why. When he doesn't quite come off as well as he should, I know the real reasons, too.

—Sylvia Fine

IF SYLVIA KNEW ABOUT THE EVE ARDEN AFFAIR, SHE DID NOT BE-
TRAY IT. FRIENDS MAY HAVE HEARD ABOUT IT FROM THE RUMOR MILL
but not from her. Danny's old girlfriend Rosie, however, observed it
for herself. Once again, she had come up from Florida to see him in
a show, this time *Let's Face It!*, and from the moment he introduced
her to Eve backstage at the Imperial Theatre, Rosie knew that something was going on. "I knew through gossip, and I could see for
myself even if he didn't put an arm around her."

She was not surprised; from the outset, he had painted a revers-
ible picture of his marriage. Sylvia "adored him, she was mad for
him," Rose said, while Danny "loved her and he respected her, but
these were different kinds of love."

Rosie told herself she wasn't personally jealous of Eve Arden,
although at Lindy's restaurant, later that evening, when Danny said,
"I'm crazy about her," Rosie snapped, "She's old enough to be your
mother," which was neither fair nor true. Tall (five feet nine), blond,
leggy Eve Arden was only nine months older than Kaye, having
been born on April 30, 1912, in Mill Valley, California. By the time
she turned sixteen, she was a professional actress. Her real name

was Eunice Quedens, and she made a couple of movies under that name before taking "Arden," as she put it, "off a cold cream jar." Since then, she had appeared on Broadway in the 1934 *Ziegfeld Follies* and worked regularly in Hollywood. Some of her movies, *Manpower*, for example, were playing while *Let's Face It!* was in rehearsal.

She was also married—to an insurance agent named Edward Bergen—but "Ned," as she called him, had enlisted right after Pearl Harbor. Her best girlfriend was Henrietta Backus, married to the actor Jim Backus, and Henny sympathized with Eve's ardor for Kaye. "I knew her since the War of the Roses," Henny said, remembering her friend as gentle, modest, and quiet, even boring. She found the actress's acerbic image amusing. Atkinson of the *Times* had reviewed her in *Let's Face It!* as "a lovely and rangy clown with a droll style," but Eve Arden was hardly the dry, wisecracking woman she portrayed. Perhaps she could seem remote to some people. Benay Venuta, for instance, wrote her off as "a very cold broad," but Henny Backus just thought "Eve was a square," adding matter-of-factly, "She had no sense of humor. She was just a lovely, warm, nice lady."

But Henny could also sympathize with Sylvia. Watching the Kayes perform at the Martinique, she had been struck by "how in love these two people must be. She's playing piano, he's singing, they're together, they're working together, they love each other."

So much for girlish fantasies; now she knew better. Even had Eve not confided in her, Henny was someone who did read the gossip columns.

But although there were items about a marital rift, they made no mention of an extramarital romance. Danny's dressing-room door was always closed, figuratively as well as literally, and in those days, the press was more respectful of privacy than it would become in later times. Anyone who wanted to maintain his privacy could. There would never be any printed mention of the Eve Arden–Danny Kaye romance.

Sylvia acted as if she hadn't even noticed the rift items. She continued to come to every performance of *Let's Face It!* critiquing his work and giving notes. Describing her remarks, he could sound like a boy talking about his mother. "I was lousy last night," he said. "Sylvia came in and gave me an awful bawling out. Said I was letting down. She was right. She always is."

. . .

HE SETTLED INTO THE ROUTINE OF A LONG RUN, PLAYING EIGHT PER-
formances a week, with six evening shows and two matinees. He
would often kill afternoons with long lunches in Lindy's. The Times
Square restaurant was a show-business hangout. Its legend encom-
passed Jewish food, pushy waiters, and a front table reserved for the
great funny men. The fashion in comics those days ran to radio's
monologists, like Bob Hope and Fred Allen. Kaye preferred the low
clowns of an earlier era, particularly Ed Wynn and Bert Lahr. Still,
it was considered a mark of status to be accepted at Lindy's front
table, and he was not above enjoying the recognition of established
stars. After Eddie Cantor invited him to sit down at the table, he
boasted of it—and so did Leo Lindy, rushing from table to table,
pointing to Cantor and Kaye, and whispering, "Look! For free!"

The gossip columnists would check in at Lindy's looking for
material, the way they checked out "21" and the Stork Club, for
these were the celebrities' haunts. Much as Kaye found reporters
tiresome and troublesome, he seemed to realize that the loftier ones,
the columnists, were more important. He would even socialize with
them and told one, "I think Moss and George S. Kaufman have
more theater sense than anybody I know. Moss and I are pals again,
and everything's patched up about my leaving *Lady in the Dark*. He
knew I was going and said, 'So long,' before I quit."

It was to Lindy's, too, that he took Rosie after she had seen *Let's
Face It!* They sat with the gossip columnist Leonard Lyons, and she
watched the two men settle into a long, laughing Yiddish conversation. In an inside breast pocket, the small, slight Lyons kept an
elegant notebook in a silver case. From time to time, he would take
out the notebook along with a matching silver mechanical pencil
and jot down something funny that Danny had said to use in his
column the next day. Lyons invariably got his celebrities' stories
wrong, leaving readers mystified, but that was somehow endearing,
for it reflected on the humanity of this columnist, who never printed
scurrilous gossip.

Remembering Lyons and Kaye chatting in Yiddish, Rosie
seemed touched by a lingering warmth. The memory reminded her
of the early days of romance with Danny, when they used to spend
whole evenings talking in Yiddish. She doted on his love of *Yiddish-
keit*—Jewishness. Comfortable with Lyons, he would even tell jokes

in Yiddish dialect, as in the old days with Fishel Goldfarb. He would break himself up saying, "Yess, ah vent for an 'airgut but vass too big a negst." ("Yes, I went for a haircut, but it was too big a next!"— too long a line.)

Aside from such personal moments, Kaye was not dealing with Yiddish very much; in fact, his speech was growing positively pristine, utterly without accent and almost southernly soft. His physical moves, too, and the way he dressed were taking on a stylishness, even an elegance. People who didn't like him began to accuse him of being phony, pretentious, and even ashamed of being Jewish. That might have been their problem. Or not.

A long-running show can become constricting for an entertainer accustomed to the volatility of a nightclub floor. In February 1942, four months into the run of *Let's Face It!*, a restless Danny Kaye paid a call on Eddie Cantor, who was then starring in *Banjo Eyes* at the old Hollywood Theater. In fact, Kaye dropped in while Cantor was in the midst of a performance.

At the time, the slight, dark-haired, goggle-eyed comedian was doing an army number while, behind him, a group of chorus boys performed a comic military drill. Suddenly, Cantor became unsettled. The audience was laughing when it wasn't supposed to. Looking around, he noticed nothing untoward and continued the number, but the laughter persisted. Out of the corner of his eye, he spied one of the chorus boys munching a banana.

Cantor stepped forward, raising his arms to silence the orchestra and the audience. "Ladies and gentlemen," he announced, "we have a guest star at this performance." And with that he introduced the "chorus boy." Kaye grinned, stepped forward, shrugged his shoulders, gulped down the banana, and took his bow.

Such antics were expected of a zany. Zaniness is justified madness, a psychological git-gat-giddle that blows off the nerves. Danny Kaye's antics might have been a healthy outlet for whatever was raging behind his closed psychological door. But if so, at this time they did not provide release enough, because this master jester and court fool abruptly came down with what his physician, Dr. Milton Somach, called "nervous exhaustion."

Kaye did not seem to be overworking himself. It was not so long ago that he had worked fifteen-hour days in the Catskills. Then he had doubled between *Lady in the Dark* and the Martinique. His energy seemed inexhaustible. Perhaps the so-called nervous exhaustion was a minibreakdown over his romance with Eve. He might have been terrified by the possibility of breaking up with Sylvia. Was her current trip to California about nothing more than movie negotiations? Whether any of these speculations are valid or not, two facts were incontrovertible: first, that Sylvia—who had gone to every performance of *Let's Face It!*—was now three thousand miles away and, second, that Dr. Somach had ordered Danny into Mt. Sinai Hospital for at least a week.

Kaye wisecracked to an inquiring reporter, "Look, we must be a success. Only successful people are told to get a rest." But "we," for the moment, were separated, and when Kaye returned to the show, a friend asked about that. She was another old girlfriend from the Catskills and was visiting backstage—Lillian Lux, back from her European theater tour. She had always been straightforward with Danny. Now she asked about the marital troubles she had been reading about.

The reason Sylvia was in California, he said icily, was that she was "negotiating a movie deal."

Lillian's surmise—not necessarily a correct one—was that (a) Danny and Sylvia, if not actually separated, were starting to spend time apart and (b) they had an actual legal agreement giving Sylvia negotiating power. Whether or not these surmises were correct, the Kaye-Arden romance was indeed continuing, and whatever effect it had on Danny's feelings, Sylvia was not letting it alter her life, her marriage, or her role in Danny's career. And it was a dominating role. He had become a client of the William Morris Agency, but it was her idea, for instance, to keep the rights to the songs that she and Liebman had written for *Let's Face It!* The Kaye-Fine attorney, Louis Mandel, registered "Melody in Four F" and "A Fairy Tale" with the copyright office. Thus, when the movie rights to *Let's Face It!* were sold to Paramount Pictures, the two songs were not. Paramount was buying the property for Bob Hope, but Sylvia had other plans for the songs.

That would prove typical of her business acumen. Another example was the postponement of any movie contract for Danny until 1943, when Liebman's 10 percent interest in Kaye's earnings would lapse, and there now was very serious movie interest. The only problem was Danny's looks, about which every studio executive seemed to express concern. Their concern had sociological implications, for in worrying about his red hair and long, thin nose, these executives were afraid that he looked too Jewish. They had every reason to believe they knew what "Jewish" looked like, since most of them were Jewish themselves. And so theirs was a kind of self-disliking attitude, which—being spineless to the marrow—they expressed only through euphemism. As Harry Cohn, the tyrannical head of Columbia Pictures, put it, Kaye "looks like a [Catskills] mountains comic."

The Danny Kaye nose concerned Samuel Goldwyn, too, but when Sylvia returned from California to a Danny who had recovered from whatever it was that had exhausted his nerves, she had a movie offer in her pocketbook. It was not an offer that they promptly accepted. Some thought they were holding out for better terms, but more likely the reason was the few months that remained until the lapse of Max Liebman's agreement. Meanwhile, there was the small matter of the Second World War, now in its second year. Kaye had just turned twenty-nine. He and Sylvia had no children. He had never been seriously ill. By all accounts, he was in excellent health, "nervous exhaustion" notwithstanding. As a married man he was classified 3-A, which meant fit for service but deferred as long as single men were available. He could have enlisted, but he didn't. As the war continued, married men were being reclassified to 1-A, or draftable. Curiously, for the times, he was not in the armed forces.

Nobody was asking why, at least not yet. Like many entertainers who were not serving, he was active in the war-bond effort. Eddie Dukoff made certain that this was publicized, getting it into the press that Kaye had sold a million dollars' worth of bonds in six months. That was accomplished in a single night, at a gala war-bond show that Danny cohosted with the Broadway dancer Ray Bolger, and Dukoff thought up that idea as well.

The benefit was given in the famous bargain basement of Gimbel's, the Thirty-fourth Street department store. A ticket cost $753 —the price of a thousand-dollar war bond—and nearly a thousand people paid it. The extra three dollars was for a midnight supper of popcorn, peanuts, hot dogs, hamburgers, and coffee, a meal that was eaten army style, at long mess-hall tables.

The doors weren't opened until Danny was finished in *Let's Face It!* and Bolger was finished in Rodgers and Hart's *By Jupiter*. It was two o'clock in the morning by the time the show started, with an overture conducted by Meyer Davis, the society bandleader. Mr. Davis then read a telegram of appreciation that had been sent by

Secretary of the Treasury Henry Morgenthau, Jr. With that, Kaye strolled onto the temporary stage that had been set up in the store and launched into "Melody in Four F." He followed it with "Minnie the Moocher."

After Bolger's turn, the bond sales began—the two stars acting as auctioneers. The centerpiece was Jack Benny's violin—a seventy-five-dollar imitation of an Amati—and it brought $750,000, which meant a million-dollar war bond. Danny suggested that for a $10,000 bond, he and Bolger would do "a 1931 vaudeville act, the kind that played in Passaic [New Jersey]."

In all, the two stars raised $2,750,000 and that was wonderful public relations.

UNABLE TO HOLD SAM GOLDWYN OFF ANY LONGER, SYLVIA GOT MAX Liebman to release Danny from what time remained in their agreement. Perhaps Liebman was paid off, although the only evidence of that was his cowriting the songs for Kaye's first picture. That would be the last time Max Liebman ever worked for Danny Kaye.

On February 27, 1943, he played his last performance in *Let's Face It!*, and the understudy, José Ferrer, took over. But the show could not run without Kaye; in fact, the closing notice was already posted. Two days later, on March 1, Danny signed a five-year movie contract with Goldwyn, and it was only then that he legally changed his name to Danny Kaye. Being in the movies meant rebirth and transformation.

With the closing of the show, Eve Arden returned to California, and the romance was put to rest, at least for the time being. Danny would not go west until movie rehearsals began, and while the studio prepared his first production, he intensified his participation in "the war effort," as it was called. He began performing for the USO. He promised unfacetiously, "When my movie is finished, I'm either going into the army, or I'll go overseas to entertain the troops." The movie, it seemed, came first. He also vowed "not to return to Broadway until the war is over," but as he had just signed a five-year movie contract, that was a foregone conclusion. For the present, restless as usual and as usual in love with live performance, he would play the Roxy Theater. It was New York's biggest presentation house other than Radio City Music Hall, which did not book comedians.

The Roxy was going to pay him the then huge sum of $12,500 a week.

That was when he finally heard from the Selective Service System.

Dukoff was uncharacteristically dishonest in his handling of it. "Danny Kaye," he notified the press, "is being inducted by the Army on (October 30), but before he goes into uniform three weeks later (November 20), he will take his place as one of the top salaried personalities in show business. Opening today at the Roxy." In fact, there was no induction date or any time for Kaye to put on a uniform. It was apparently an attempt to sidestep potential criticism of a draft-age entertainer making so much money in a time of war.

In the midst of the engagement, he took three days off and went to Governors Island for his army physical examination. At its completion he was classified 4-F—medically unacceptable for military service. Dukoff issued a press release stating that "among the salients which deferred him was a congenitally bad back," but Kaye would never complain of back trouble for the rest of his life.

He promptly announced that he was volunteering to go overseas and entertain the troops.

His notion was to work up an act with Leo Durocher, the manager of the Brooklyn Dodgers. Kaye had been a fan of the team since his childhood. Durocher was likewise a fan of show business. (In a few years he would marry the movie actress Laraine Day.) Kaye envisioned himself and Durocher as a couple of song-and-dance men, working in straw hats and blazers, doing "practically all the jokes you ever heard." He had a notion for a baseball routine in Shakespearean language: "To bunt or not to bunt, that is the question." He never would be very good at writing his own material, and reconsidering the line, he allowed, "Maybe it doesn't sound like much, but I think the crowd will like it."

The crowd did, and after the routine he let Durocher tell baseball anecdotes to the servicemen. Then he sang "Melody in Four F," which excused it all, anyway. They took the act to the troops stationed in the South Pacific, and Warren Cowan kept them company.

Cowan was new on the Kaye scene, an additional publicity person for the West Coast. He was a modern corporate type, a "public relations" man rather than a lowly press agent. Certainly he was smoother than a rumpled, zealous, old-fashioned flack like Eddie

Dukoff. He concentrated on protecting clients rather than promoting them. The one thing that Cowan and Dukoff did have in common was the adulation factor. Cowan was especially impressed when Danny strode out on a stage that had been set up on the flight deck of an aircraft carrier. After scanning the first few rows of his audience and noting that they all were officers, Kaye stopped the show and asked if it might be possible for the brass to be moved to the rear. Then he suggested that the enlisted men be moved up front.

It was a decent gesture and a showmanly one. Cowan couldn't get over it himself.

When they got home from the USO tour, Danny reported to the Goldwyn studio to start work on his first movie. Sylvia had already rented a house from the actor Chester Morris. It had a patio and a swimming pool, and Danny even took up golf. They were Californians.

The screen tests continued because Goldwyn was still troubled by the Kaye hair. In fact, there was no final go-ahead until, as A. Scott Berg points out in his fine biography of Samuel Goldwyn, the producer had an inspiration and exultantly called his studio makeup department. "I've got it! I've got it! Expect Kaye in ten minutes. He's having his hair dyed blond!"

Newspapers were told it was done "to fit the demands of the Technicolor cameras" but whether or not Danny Kaye consequently looked less Jewish or more photogenic, the overriding effect was that he became Danny Kaye in total. Red Kaminski's transformation was complete. The redheaded frog was now a fair-haired prince, and he was going to be in the movies.

Part II

Being Danny Kaye

It is not fun to be different. It is more comfortable to fit in. People don't choose to be misfits; they are chosen by nature and then expelled, unless they are creative, in which case they are called "artists."

Because artists come by what they do instinctually, and because their creations are simply the way they express themselves, they are often surprised by the esteem in which they and their work are held. They are prone to suffer from a fear of being unmasked and revealed as frauds. It is a terrible fear, for if that were to happen, they would not exist anymore, as they tend to feel that they are what they do.

9

In every picture I've done with Danny we've managed to work in a "gesundheit" joke. It's sort of an inside gag with us to see how many variations we can come up with.

—Sylvia Fine

IF THE FINE ARTS REPRESENT US AT OUR LOFTIEST, SETTING THE SENSE OF OUR TIMES ACROSS A GREAT CANVAS OF PERSPECTIVE, THEN the popular arts are snapshots of the moment, recording us at our most mundane. Popular songs, commercial fiction, and perhaps most of all, the movies preserve our passing fashions with precision and a clarity that can sometimes be embarrassing.

Danny Kaye's first movie, *Up in Arms*, was made in 1943 for release early in 1944. It vividly captures the American mentality at the time of the Second World War. Its world is uncomplicatedly white and middle class. Its morality is certain, its patriotism righteous. The movie's propaganda is as subtle as a comic strip. As a commercial entertainment, it is painfully naive. But such were the ways of Hollywood and America at the time.

There are other aspects of *Up in Arms*, however, that, when filtered through a modern sensibility, are surprising and even disquieting. Movies are frightfully revealing, even of so private and covered a person as Danny Kaye.

The screenplay by Don Hartman, Allen Boretz, and Robert Pirosh is loosely based on a 1925 Broadway comedy, *The Nervous*

Wreck, written by a Pulitzer Prize–winning playwright, Owen Davis. *The Nervous Wreck* had been the basis for an Eddie Cantor stage vehicle called *Whoopee!*, and Samuel Goldwyn's choice of this material apparently reflected his wish to make Danny Kaye into another Cantor. (It was said that Goldwyn even called him "Eddie" from time to time.) Ultimately, however, the Kaye version would retain little more than the title character, for as Bosley Crowther quite accurately pointed out in his *New York Times* review, "The whole picture . . . is little more than a blunt enlargement upon . . . 'Melody in Four F.'"

The hypochondriacal Kaye character, Danny Weems, eager to be near doctors, runs an elevator in a medical building. There, too, as a nurse, works Dinah Shore, who was also making her movie debut in *Up in Arms*. She is attracted to Weems, but he is smitten with another (Constance Dowling), who makes a date with him and then suggests it be a double one. He brings along his roommate (Dana Andrews) for the Dinah Shore character, but the roommate has an instant chemistry with Kaye's girl.

Despite Weems's insistence that he is medically unfit for service, he is inducted along with his roommate, who, in more manly fashion, has been begging the draft board to take him. They are both shipped to the Pacific, while the two women receive instant WAC commissions and are sneaked aboard the troop ship. The romances continue all the way to the war zone, where Kaye wanders into enemy hands and accidentally becomes a hero.

Ordinarily, the role being played by Kaye would have been the hero's sidekick, cast with a second banana like (in those days) Phil Silvers. Then it would not be so noticeable that the character is passive, sissified, and all but sexless. But when the character is moved into the lead, these qualities emerge more boldly. Moreover, they are underlined by Elliott Nugent's directing, and Kaye plays to them. Although he winds up with the charming and beautifully built Dinah Shore, there is no physical contact, and she is the aggressor throughout, a strong mother figure not unlike Sylvia Fine. Interestingly enough, Sylvia took credit for transforming Danny's character from the nebbish (her word) that Cantor played into this, for her, acceptable character; this "eager beaver."

One other thing that is curious, even strange, about *Up in Arms* is a barracks scene in which Weems is taunted, tormented, victimized, and even physically abused by a mindlessly macho bully who grabs him by the scruff of the neck and the seat of his pants. This fellow pours all of the hypochondriac's medicines into a single bottle and forces him to drink it. It is no great stretch to view this nasty scene as being resonant with homosexual implications—for not only the victim and the bully but also Kaye's manly roommate, who comes to his rescue and threatens to punch the bully in the nose.

While these details contribute to the curious sexuality, or lack of it, that Kaye projected in his first movie—and which was perhaps created or perceived by his wife—this is not the greater substance of *Up in Arms*. It was, after all, an entertainment, one that successfully introduced Danny Kaye to the American public. No small part in that success was played by the musical numbers contributed by Sylvia and Max Liebman. While it is inconceivable that the wimpy character being played by Kaye would be singing such clever revue material, movies of the period allowed for such inconsistencies.

The first of the Liebman/Fine songs is "The Lobby Number," which Kaye begins while impatiently waiting on a movie line with Dana Andrews and their dates. He tells them—and everyone else on line—exactly what awaits them. His example is "Hello, Fresno, Hello," which, he says, was "produced by Manic and directed by Depressive." The Fine-Liebman song then satirizes the number and types of opening credits, going for laughs with funny names and funny sounds and concluding with "Terpsichore by Dickery, and Dickery by Dock."

This is revue material, wittier and more sophisticated than the character who is singing it, but movie logic is loose, and at the time, movie audiences were easy. It is a tour de force for the nightclub side of Kaye as he dashes up and down the lobby stairs, moving as gracefully as a whippet while making a manual ballet of his arms and hands. As he relentlessly mugs, assorted dialects spin dizzily from his tongue. His diction is flawless, his glow and energy radiant. The number is not only staged like a floor-show routine but in fact concludes with Kaye shouting, "Conga!" just as he had in the early days at La Martinique. With that, he slips into a Spanish dialect as well as his old conga number, carrying on until he is dragged away, lunging, lurching, and twitching. Thus, the youthful exuberance of the Danny Kaye who first delighted New York on the stage of a cellar joint is forever captured on film.

"The Lobby Number" is a tribute to Liebman and Sylvia and to her part in making the most of Danny's first movie opportunity. As she had surely intended, the screen radiates with everything she so admired in him. Even when performing in facsimile, he is unique and exhilarating. Nor did the sophistication implicit in his eyes and his readings make him too fancy for the mass market. He could appeal to children and adults, the general public and the smart set.

He was considered a comedian but was as unclassifiable as ever, all the more so because of the talents that were *not* shown in this movie. What was clear, at least, was that he was different. Given that, classification was beside the point. He was a purveyor of charm. He captivated. He was a Danny Kaye, elfin and warm, this remote (and getting remoter) man.

By the second of his numbers, he owned audiences in movie theaters across the United States, for that number was "Melody in Four F"—the *Let's Face It!* showstopper, exactly as performed on Broadway. Git-gat-giddle played as well in Wichita, Seattle, or San Diego as it did in the Catskills, the Martinique, and on Broadway. Now Kaye had the whole country demanding it. By the time the movie's finale rolled around, "Melody in Four F" had obliterated everything else he did, which was a pity, because the closing "Jive Number" features a zoot-suited Kaye and a hepcat Dinah Shore doing a smashing Broadway-style finale in front of a chorus of period swingers. Danny Kaye would move beautifully in many of his movies and dance comically in a few of them, but he would never again do a Broadway musical dance number like this one.

However, the public demanded his double-talk and his zaniness. The movies, the most whorish of the popular arts, would cater to that demand. Kaye's most popular films, the series he was now beginning for Samuel Goldwyn, would capitalize on this limited aspect of his talent.

Up in Arms opened in February 1944 at America's premier movie theater, Radio City Music Hall. The critics, like their stage colleagues, found Kaye irresistible, and it is no exaggeration to say that the entire country fell in love with him. The picture, although indifferently reviewed except for him, was a personal and commercial triumph, ringing in $3.34 million at the box office, according to *Variety*.

Naturally, he was asked to help promote it. He could not shunt these interviews off on Sylvia, for this time he was on a national stage and she was not sitting at the piano in her opera gloves. He was a solo act.

He gave fascinating interviews as long as the questions were
fresh and tried to hide his impatience when they weren't. He did not
trade in the usual clichés of self-promotion. His responses had a ring
of intelligence and candor that, in the world of show business, was
not merely rare but practically exotic. He told an interviewer:

> Of course I found the [movie] medium altogether different
> from the stage. Usually they printed either "take" one or two.
> By the seventh, I wasn't giving any kind of a performance.
> I'm never any good at stage rehearsals, and the constantly
> repeated shooting bothered me at first. However, when I saw
> the day-to-day rushes, I was always thinking of some new
> twist I might have given the scene.

He could also emerge as quite sensitive, and at such times, the real
Danny Kaye would seem to be very human, a performer stripped of
ego defenses.

> Whenever I did make a little fuss, they threatened to show
> me some of the shorts I'd made in New York . . . those very
> sad short subjects.

On the other hand, he could startle an interviewer (for a Sunday
rotogravure, "PIC") who mentioned his overnight success.

> I played every tank town in America, beat my brains out
> all over the world, worked in cover charge cellars, benefits,
> summer camps, vaudeville and every other form of enter-
> tainment for twelve years before I became a movie star. If
> that's overnight, then the Punic Wars were just a skirmish.

The success of *Up in Arms* made Samuel Goldwyn eager for a
follow-up, but Kaye flew off to entertain the servicemen in the Japanese war zone. Naturally, waves of excitement preceded America's
newest movie star as he hopped from one military base to the next,
accompanied by his new, high-powered public relations man, Warren Cowan. Eddie Dukoff still worked for him, but Eddie was a little
too open-collared, a little too unpolished, a little too scruffy for the
national media.

It was at an army base on an island in the South Pacific that a
young man named Bobby Sarles had been boasting of his friendship
with Danny Kaye. There was some substance to the boast. Fifteen
years earlier, Sarles had gotten a summer job as a bellhop at the

White Roe resort hotel near his home in Livingston Manor, New York. That was when Danny was at his Catskills peak.

The staff had mixed democratically enough, although there was something of a caste system that separated a mere bellhop from a star tummler. But Bobby Sarles had certainly been on chatting terms with Danny Kaye and, ever after, he had boasted about the "friendship"—especially on this wartime Pacific atoll where it was pretty unexciting being a cook in the mess hall.

When it was announced that Kaye was coming to entertain with a USO show, Sarles suddenly seemed less excited about it than his comrades. They boisterously clapped him on the shoulder, reminding him of how marvelous it would be to rekindle his friendship with the movie star.

The day that Kaye's troupe arrived, Sarles remembered walking somewhat sheepishly along the company street with some of his army buddies. They were headed toward the island's little airstrip, where an impromptu stage had been set up on the tarmac. It was still early, still light, but the rush for good seats was on.

Suddenly, one of the fellows cried, "Look! There's Danny Kaye!" and it certainly was. He was striding toward them, wearing crisply starched army fatigues and flanked by officers. "Okay, Bobby!" one of the soldiers cried. "Show us! Introduce us to Danny!"

Sarles suddenly became downright shy, but his pals were shoving him toward Kaye. Before he even had a chance to explain anything, Danny caught sight of him and shouted, "Bobby! Bobby Sarles! What the hell are you doing here?" He opened his arms wide and gathered a thrilled but certainly startled Sarles into a big bear hug.

From then on, Sarles remembered, "I was the biggest thing on the base."

THE TITLE OF THE SECOND DANNY KAYE MOVIE, *WONDER MAN,* WAS so perfect for him that given his popularity, his mere presence was practically enough to assure its success. This was just as well considering the flimsiness of the affair. The screenplay was again written by Don Hartman, this time in collaboration with Melville (Mel) Shavelson. An original story, it gave Kaye a dual role involving twin brothers, one of them a shy and bookish version of the hypochondriac in *Up in Arms.* The other twin is a cocky nightclub performer who is slated to testify against a gangster. A few minutes into the movie he is murdered, and for the next hour and a half the ghostly twin slips in and out of the bookworm's body.

Kaye could have inspired the split-personality plot, for colleagues were beginning to wonder aloud who was hiding behind the curtain of privacy that he put up. Many people find ambiguity frustrating. Kaye defied classification as an individual the way he defied it as an entertainer. For the writers of *Wonder Man*, the suspected real Kaye, the suspected hidden Kaye, could well have been the inspiration for the meek twin in the story. Everyday psychology, after all, suggested that he was remote merely because he was shy.

In the screenplay, there is a different love interest for each twin, Vera-Ellen for the nightclub comic and Virginia Mayo for the bookworm. Vera-Ellen was easy enough to type; she was a dancer, and her acting was secondary to that. But Virginia Mayo was being groomed for stardom by Goldwyn.

She was a typical pinup girl of the period, a Betty Grable clone, with blue eyes, long, curly blond hair, farm-girl good looks, no communicated personality, humor, or intelligence, and a kitchen apron where her sexuality should be. These qualities made her the perfect wife. Kaye had met her years earlier when they were both working in provincial presentation houses. Mayo, then Virginia Jones, was the bimbo in a burlesque-style comedy act involving a couple of men inside a horse. That act had been on the same bill with Danny at the Hippodrome Theatre in Baltimore, and Virginia remembered him as "a lanky redheaded comedian; he knocked himself out five times a day, but the paying customers just sat on their hands. [I felt] very sorry for him, he was such a flop."

Now Samuel Goldwyn had great things in mind for her. He had already made her one of the Goldwyn Girls in *Up in Arms*, and starting with *Wonder Man*, she would be Kaye's romantic interest in the remaining Goldwyn pictures. Sylvia may have suspected a Mayo romance, because she seemed to go out of her way to demean the actress to A. Scott Berg for his Goldwyn biography. (Watching Mayo's screen tests, she claimed to remember "that poor girl talking to two guys in a horse costume.") But although Kaye flirted with many attractive women, there is no evidence of any romance with Virginia Mayo.

Vera-Ellen's role in *Wonder Man* is smaller than Mayo's, but she is partnered with Kaye in "Bali Boogie," an elaborate spoof of

Far Eastern choreography that again demonstrates his rather amazing dance abilities. In Balinese dance, the body is held rigid, facing the audience with the legs slightly apart, bent at the knees, the feet firmly planted. All moves are made sideways and in small leaps. Expressive use is made of the arms and hands, which are held rigidly at chest height, making right angles at the elbows and wrists. The head is moved from side to side, as if sliding along the neck.

Kaye's mockery of these moves is itself the work of a dancer, requiring the same skills, discipline, and physical risks. In fact, during the filming of "Bali Boogie" he was required to leap onto a drum and turned his ankle in the process. He had to finish the sequence two months later, and the movie reveals the physical conditioning the number required. Naked to the waist, he looks better than fit, not merely slender but muscular.

The music and lyrics are credited entirely to Sylvia Fine—Max Liebman was out—but the song is only incidental to the number. "Bali Boogie" is a dance routine, and there are few other entertainers who could have performed it.

Sylvia's other material for the movie included "Otchi Tchorniya," which, like the "Conga" in Up in Arms, was recycled from the Martinique days. The credits attribute it to Sylvia, but she wrote this number with Max Liebman.

As the Bali number spoofs Oriental dance, so "Otchi Tchorniya" pokes fun at concertizing. It starts with Kaye frustrating his accompanist by endlessly introducing the song. He then suffers a sneezing fit over the flowers on the piano. (Gesundheit remained the Sylvia-Danny inside joke.) The number then proceeds in a broad Russian accent and concludes with a series of spastic twitches and head jerks. It was comedy for the time, not the ages.

Kaye's final number in the movie is again musical—that is, it is about music. His character flees the gangsters onto the stage of an opera house. Sylvia's music mocks the clichés of Italian opera and gives Danny ample opportunity to work in dialect—perhaps too much opportunity, for it certainly grows tiresome. However, in both "Otchi Tchorniya" and "Opera Number," he is asked to sing with considerable vocal production, over a wide range and with projection. He is quite good at this, demonstrating a real musical gift. The clowning is something else. These numbers were hailed at the time as comedy classics, but popular humor is transient and a matter of fashion.

Wonder Man was released at school vacation time in 1945, and it did excellent business. More than confirming Kaye as a star and a box-office attraction, it showed him popular for something beyond his talent. It wasn't his clowning, his singing, or his dancing that brought on the stardom. He was popular—indeed, he would soon be the number-one box-office attraction in Hollywood—for another reason, for something else he was communicating. Perhaps he was not being used to advantage or being seen as he was onstage, but the essential Kaye, the Kaye of live performance, was somehow emerging through the celluloid of the motion picture. What was unclassifiable about him seemed to be coming into focus. He emanated in performance what he was unable to demonstrate in real life. He emanated *love*.

10

You're a regular Dr. Jekyll and Mr. Hyde, and the good side
of your nature is being destroyed by the bad that's in you.

—Virginia Mayo to Danny Kaye
in *The Kid from Brooklyn*

DANNY AND SYLVIA WERE NOW LIVING WELL ON BOTH COASTS. SHE HAD RENTED AN ELEVEN-ROOM HOUSE IN RITZY BEL-AIR FROM THE ex-wife of the prizefighter "Slapsy" Maxie Rosenbloom. In Manhattan, she found a cozy twelve-room apartment at 770 Park Avenue.

She seemed to have made up her mind to crash the social life in the California movie community, for she immediately began giving a series of dinner parties. She gave so many that Mrs. Rosenbloom took her and Danny to court and had them evicted for "wrecking" the house with their parties and causing $3,000 worth of damage. (Kaye wisecracked, "We just took the boxing ring out of the living room.") It took seven process servers to get them out. Danny told a reporter that "the house was a wreck when we moved in," but, like most people, he enjoyed parties up to a limit. When it was reached, he would go reluctantly, sometimes not at all.

Work was an available excuse. Although *Wonder Man* had just been released and he would be free for several months before starting *The Kid from Brooklyn*, he had been offered a radio program. That was a final confirmation of star status.

"The Danny Kaye Show," subtitled "Pabst Blue Ribbon Time" for its beer sponsor, was going to be a half-hour program. Beginning in January 1945, it would be carried by the CBS network and broadcast on Friday nights at ten o'clock in the East and seven o'clock in the West. Everything about it was to be top drawer, beginning with Kaye's then record salary of $16,000 a week (compared to the $100 apiece he had been paid for three minor CBS radio shows in 1940). The producer was Goodman Ace, radio's premier comedy writer, who had so estimable a reputation that even though the program would be broadcast from Los Angeles, he was able to insist on running it from New York. "I don't want to go to Hollywood," he joked, "because California is too close to Mary Livingstone," a reference to Jack Benny's wife, who seems to have been universally intimidating.

But if Goody Ace had found that Mary Livingstone was a star's wife to contend with when he wrote for Jack Benny, he was stepping up in class with Sylvia Fine. She was momentarily distracted by the search for a new house, but after she found the place that would be her lifelong home at 1103 San Ysidro Drive in Beverly Hills, she went to work on the show. Certainly she was going to write songs for it and perform them with Danny, but her running of his career—their career—had surpassed merely writing songs. She demanded and won the right to approve the show's writers. Ace had assembled a team that included Shelly Kellar, Tony Stemple, and Mel Tolkin. The last was an odd choice, as Tolkin himself was the first to admit, since he was a refugee, fresh from the Ukraine via Canada. His accent remained as thick as borscht, and he would shake his head in wonderment over the absurdity of a Russian émigré writing jokes for American comedians. (Neil Simon would later immortalize him in the play *Laughter on the 23rd Floor.*)

Mel Tolkin was also terrified of the Kayes. When he was sent to New York to pass muster with Sylvia, only one of his concerns was "writing for this number-one movie star, a personality who I had seen hold an entire audience in his grip." Approaching their Park Avenue building, he was also fearful of the reputation that preceded the star's wife. He was drenched in dread by the time he arrived at the "sumptuous" apartment. (It was the entire top floor, the seventeenth.)

He was ushered into the living room, which was darkened because Sylvia had taken to avoiding daylight. "Some curtains opened," Tolkin remembered, "and she was lying like an odalisque.

"She looked imperiously distant."

That did it for him. "I froze," he recalled, "and a few days later I quit."

Another of the scriptwriters remembered a pause in a telephone conversation with Sylvia. When she asked if he would explain the silence, he replied, "I was bowing."

Goodman Ace made the necessary sacrifice of going to Los Angeles for the premiere broadcast of "The Danny Kaye Show," and that night, its star strolled onto the studio stage to do the audience warm-up himself. He was wearing a brown tweed sport jacket and a pair of brown trousers, a combination that would become his uniform. With almost no exceptions, he would wear it ever after, whether on the radio or the stage. According to his old girlfriend Rosie Kaye, he had "a closetful" of that combination.

He spent forty minutes with the studio audience, then, as ever, enjoying live performance more than any other kind. He introduced the bandleader, Harry James. He brought Sylvia out to sit at the piano in her long white opera gloves. Finally, he introduced the cast members, and they took their places behind the microphones, placing their scripts on the lecterns. They included Lionel Stander and Jim ("Chuck," as everyone called him) Backus.

And Eve Arden. If there was anything that Sylvia could have done about her being a regular on Danny's radio program, it hadn't been done.

For the first broadcast, Abe Lastfogel, president of the William Morris Agency, arranged that a direct telephone line be kept open from backstage to his New York office. Kaye was now getting star treatment as a matter of course. Lastfogel wanted to be in constant communication with Goodman Ace during the show. He was afraid that Kaye's zany style would not translate to an unseeing radio audience. Kaye wasn't, after all, ha-ha funny the way a comedian is. Then again, he wasn't a "comedian," even though Lastfogel seemed to think he was. That was the old problem, the need to classify him—to make the unique understandable and manageable, in the process destroying its uniqueness.

"What can we do," Lastfogel asked Ace during a commercial break, "to make the radio audience realize what a funny guy Danny Kaye is?"

The writer replied, "I'm sorry, Abe. You'll have to speak louder. They're laughing too much."

They weren't laughing enough, and Lastfogel's concern was justified. Like a number of other visual performers, Kaye would be frustrated by his sightless radio audience. (As *Variety* put it in a review of the premiere show, "He can't stand without benefit of those physical antics and gyrations.") However, if "The Danny Kaye Show" wasn't as huge a hit as his movies, it would become popular enough to tie the "Jimmy Durante–Garry Moore Show" for fifth place in the 1945 *Radio Daily* popularity poll.

That first broadcast began with a monologue, which was not Kaye's strength. He would never be able to *just tell jokes*. The rest of the program—other than a song of Sylvia's—was situation comedy. Ace's approach was modeled on his successful program for Jack Benny: fictionalizing the show itself so that it was about the people on the program. For instance, there were a couple of running characters who were supposedly Kaye's comedy writers. They were always trying too hard to be funny, and whenever they met with Danny, they would get into arguments with each other.

In Ace's script for this first broadcast, one of the writers said, "My sister married an Irishman." The other asked, "Oh, really?" and the first replied, "No, O'Reilly."

When it got a hearty laugh from the studio audience, Ace decided that he would try it again. The next week he had one of the writers say, "The audience gave my stuff a great reception." The other responded, "Oh, really?" "No," rejoined the first, "ovation." More laughter convinced Ace that he had a running gag. It would continue for months, "Oh, really?" "No, Oklahoma," and so on. It would never be as funny as Goodman Ace thought it was.

The real problem facing him and Hal Kanter, who was the head writer on the West Coast staff, was to invent a personality for Kaye. On the stage he could evade this issue by running so fast and in so many directions that he could not be pinned down. Radio was more revealing. Radio brought the voice into the home, where listeners could rummage through their imaginations and make character associations with it. What character could they read into Danny Kaye's soft, unaccented, elegant speech? Of all the dialects he could do— Russian, Japanese, Italian, German, French—his own was the one he did best. Its fabrication, its distance from his true origins, were testimonials not merely to his creativity, but to his self-creativity.

As Kanter put it, "It was difficult for me to grasp the Kaye persona, because he wasn't quite sure what it was himself. From my point of view he wasn't quite sure who he was." But, he added, "that gave you tools to work with, because he could be anything you wanted him to be. I didn't have to hew to the character lines already laid out because there weren't any character lines laid out. When you are writing for someone like Jack Benny or George Burns, you have to think like them. You have to take their melody and try to figure out variations. But Kaye didn't have a melody."

Kanter and Goodman Ace concluded that their only option was to *invent* a melody for Danny Kaye, a personality based on his screen persona, which Kanter defined as "the unlikely victim."

One person who did not contribute to this process was Danny Kaye himself. He never would write any of his radio, movie, or television material. Sylvia seems to have convinced him early on that he was a poor judge of his own work and that only she knew what was good for him. When she did not write it herself, she demanded the authority to approve those who did.

And so she was very busy those days, fixing up the new house (and doing an elegant job of it, too, with the help of decorator Billy Haines) while writing or supervising the radio show. Increasingly alone at night, she would stay up past dawn and then sleep late into the afternoon. Then she would go down to the basement and swim in the indoor pool before settling in at the grand piano in the living room. Her cigarette cough was not a thing of beauty, but in those days everyone smoked—Danny, too—and so the cough was a sound of being awake.

The program did not restrict them to the West Coast, since it could and sometimes did originate from the CBS radio playhouse on West Thirty-ninth Street in New York. Six months into the show, Kaye had to broadcast from there for a three-week stretch because he had been asked to substitute for an indisposed Frank Sinatra at the Wedgewood Room of the Waldorf-Astoria Hotel. He hadn't played a nightclub in a dozen years, not since the old days at the Martinique. The Waldorf engagement reminded him of how much he enjoyed such work, and he told a reporter, "I don't hate movies. They're a great medium. But I have more personal fun playing to a live audience. Working the way I do, I work from audience reaction. New audiences—I give a practically new performance."

In fact, he did not give a "practically new performance" with each show, but he did perfect the illusion of improvisation. As a reporter for *Variety* noticed, he strolled out and acted "as if he didn't know what in the world he is going to do next." But he knew perfectly well. He just was not so foolish as to risk untested material.

While the Kayes were in New York, Eddie Dukoff was around to again create the kind of publicity that had contributed so much to the Danny Kaye phenomenon. To help promote the radio program, he arranged for Danny to talk to an audience of students from his alma mater, Thomas Jefferson High School. The site was the CBS radio playhouse.

The kids, some seven hundred of them, were, of course, excited about this famous semialumnus, and he was in fine form, responding to a question about whether he had finished high school by crying, "Usher!" Another question, about his hobbies, was more seriously taken. "I go to hospitals," he said, "to watch operations," and that was true. He was fascinated by them. "I'm a frustrated doctor," and as another hobby, he said, "I have fun." That was true as well. Kaye believed in fun, defining "fun" as adventure and the satisfaction of curiosity. He had fun whenever he wasn't depressed.

During that period in New York, Sylvia came down with a cold and was unable to play the piano for one of the broadcasts. Goodman Ace found a pianist named Sammy Prager to fill in, and after she listened to the program from her sickbed, she telephoned the producer for his reaction.

"How do you think it went, Goody?"

"It went fine," Ace told her.

"And Sammy Prager?" she asked. "How did he do?"

"He did particularly well," Ace said to the opera-glove pianist, "considering the fact that he plays bare-handed."

Prager was going to become Kaye's regular accompanist as Sylvia phased out of performance.

THAT WAS A HECTIC PERIOD, THE KIND THAT HAPPENS AT THE CRESTing of a career. Not only was Kaye constantly crossing the country while doing the show, but he managed to make *The Kid from Brooklyn* between flights—and he made sure that Eve Arden was in the picture. If Sylvia had anything to say about that, she did so behind closed doors. She may have simply let Danny do whatever he wanted to do in that department so long as he didn't make it a public department.

But it was difficult to keep such affairs private. At one big Hollywood party, the actor Zachary Scott and his wife, Elaine Anderson, were chatting animatedly with Kaye. Standing with her back to Danny was Eve Arden, one of Ms. Anderson's best pals, deep in conversation with another cluster of people. In a kind of silent drama, Kaye unconsciously withdrew a pack of cigarettes from his breast pocket, shook one out and then another. He put both cigarettes in his mouth—as Anderson put it, "Paul Henreid style" (a reference to Henreid's romantic scene with Bette Davis in *Now, Voyager*). Then, as she remembered, "almost absentmindedly, he lighted both and, without interrupting his conversation, handed one of them to Eve."

Elaine glanced around the room to see if anyone else had noticed. Being a romantic, she considered it a "telltale event," for she had immediately thought of it as a gesture so familiar that it suggested intimacy. Later, when she and Zachary Scott were driving home, she said that "this familiarity between Danny and Eve had to mean they were having an affair."

Her equally romantic husband agreed. "It was a dead giveaway."

There are, perhaps, stories older than that of a man struggling with his involvement in an extramarital affair, but there are few stories that are more trite. The peculiar stresses on all three parties have been chronicled so often that the situation has become tiresome and even comic. As Orson Welles said about jealousy, this being caught in a romantic triangle is "like seasickness—you think you're going to die of it, and everyone else thinks it's funny."

Danny Kaye's romance with Eve Arden was typical in its on-again, off-again melodramatics and the toll taken on all three involved. War's end only further complicated the matter. Not enough significance is ascribed to the dropping of the atomic bomb on Hiroshima. It marked not merely the end of military hostilities and the beginning of the atomic age. Those may have been events of some consequence, but the history books do not deal with the effect that peace must have had on wartime's extramarital lovers.

To many Americans, the end of the war meant only the start of domestic hostilities, and for many servicemen like Eve Arden's husband, Ned, it meant a special surprise at the welcome-home party.

11

Do you know what it's like to come out six, seven, perfor-
mances a day doing that "git-gat-giddle"?

—Georgia Gibbs

WHEN NED BERGEN CAME HOME FROM THE SERVICE, EVE ASKED
HIM FOR A DIVORCE. SHE SAID NOTHING TO HIM ABOUT ANYONE ELSE
in her life. Eve's closest pals were the actors Cesar ("Butch") Romero
and Henny Backus. She told Henny that she was leaving Ned because she was in love with Danny Kaye.

But Danny didn't leave Sylvia. As a matter of fact, he was in the
process of impregnating her.

On March 11, 1946, his picture was on the cover of *Time* magazine, and in those days there was no greater measure of fame.
Sylvia's picture was on the cover, too. There was no greater measure of their marriage. This was being Mrs. Danny Kaye with a
vengeance.

Sylvia Fine was on the cover of *Time* magazine with Danny
Kaye because she was the embodiment of a sentimental cliché, the
woman behind the man. In prefeminist America, that represented a
great attainment for a brainy but wifely woman. She was so wifely
that while helping him become a star, she was also conceiving his
child. It was almost as if the achievement and recognition symbolized by the *Time* cover were fulfilling her. The public—published—

consummation of the marriage to her golden prince had impregnated her.

In psychological terms, there might be other analyses. Sylvia could have been trying to become pregnant as a defense against the Eve Arden threat. An even greater threat was Danny's burgeoning success and the growing apprehension that he could perform very well without her words and music. If she was going to hold on to him, she was going to have to find some other way to do it. This would not have been the first pregnancy designed to sustain a marriage.

Then again, there might have been nothing to analyze. Sylvia might have simply become pregnant. Her brilliant capacity for getting things done was nowhere more evident than in keeping her marriage intact. That, and Danny's internalizing of emotion, convinced the writers and researchers of the *Time* cover story that there was nothing to the rumors of marital trouble. And so, despite the intensity of the Eve Arden affair (at least to Eve Arden), the magazine's research assistant sent a memorandum to her editor. "I think," she wrote, as a "personal observation," that "it would be grossly unfair if we as much as hinted that Danny and Sylvia have a professional arrangement rather than a marriage." And so the cover story did not even refer to the "rift" items that had been appearing in gossip columns.

Sylvia was spending a lot of time with that *Time* researcher. She provided the recipe for Danny's favorite eggs (four scrambled, with diced onions, sour cream, and caviar). She allowed that Danny had a minor interest in cooking. ("He is a whirlwind enthusiast but has very little technique.") She said nothing about being pregnant. Yet while the cover story would protect and even reinforce the myth of this most famous of all show-business marriages, the Fine-Kaye-Arden triangle would have to be dealt with sooner or later. Like most men in such situations, Kaye was opting for later.

The *Time* magazine cover story was headlined with the Kayes' old joke "Sylvia Has a Fine Head on My Shoulders," which sounded less funny than ever. (The editors originally planned to have her head literally on his shoulder in the cover art.) The article itself, which was written by James Agee, was effusive in its praise of Danny and did not once stab him in the back, as was the magazine's disposition in those days. The piece certainly was written in the *Time* tone of universal sophistication, but that was turned to Kaye's advantage.

Giants of culture legitimized him with testimonials to his artistic stature. The magazine quoted the pianist Arthur Rubinstein, for instance, as saying, "I feel most often about him what everyone else felt about Chaplin. I am not so much amused as moved." That was more plausible than the British movie producer Gabriel Pascal saying he wanted Kaye to play Macbeth—a suggestion that Danny and Sylvia were taking seriously. Edward Johnson, the director of the Metropolitan Opera, told the magazine that "Danny would be the perfect Figaro if he only had an operatic voice," a more than minor qualification.

Not all was adulatory. The cover story ran in the magazine's "Radio" section and did not celebrate the Kaye program. Starting kindly enough by calling it "a new kind of radio show," the piece concluded that Kaye is "better seen than heard . . . [he] flounders as he lugs the weight of dull dialogue." The magazine's writers preferred his zanier side. "Danny Kaye is never at his best on radio. Listeners miss the virility of his clowning, the humor of his mugging."

The clowning of "Red" Kaminski, the mugging that Nat Lichtman had told Kaye to practice in the dressing-room mirror at White Roe, the git-gat-giddle that Fishel Goldfarb had inspired, and the songs that Sylvia had written to showcase them were aspects of his anarchic talent that had been tamed and domesticated; boiled down and homogenized; made palatable and marketable for mass America. Unrecognized by *Time* because he remained as unclassifiable, almost as indescribable as ever, were the manifold gifts of Danny Kaye—his rangy, true, and rich singing voice, his immense physical grace, his athletic and lithe dancing ability, his natural talent for acting, his gifts of mimicry and dialect, his offbeat humor and whimsy, his energy and stage warmth, his effusive charisma, and perhaps the greatest of all his gifts, his dazzling sense of what was right for a particular audience at a given moment.

Rather, while Kaye was appearing at the Paramount Theater in New York, the magazine had the researcher painstakingly record the nonsense syllables of the double-talk with which he was saddled: "Git-gat-giddle, giddle-di-peep, giddle-de-tommy, riddle de biddle de roop, da-reep, fa-san, skeedle de woo-da, fiddle de wada, reep!"

The Paramount engagement was to be the start of a national tour of presentation houses, an escape from his year in a radio tube. It would be a return to the live audiences he loved, and timed, as it was, to promote the release of *The Kid from Brooklyn*, it was a lucrative as well as strategic notion. In fact, from the financial point of view, his career could be seen as a series of masterstrokes, with record earnings in every possible show-business venue and even a few new ones. Over the course of this tour, he would be paid $25,000 a week plus half the weekly grosses over $60,000. That would come to an average weekly take of $40,000—a lot of money at any time; in 1946 it was staggering. He would have to pay his coperformers out of it, but that would not even amount to $5,000 a week.

This was an early version of the "concert" approach that would become common decades later. Whoever had concocted it, Sylvia or the William Morris Agency, it typified the smart management that would ultimately make Kaye a wealthy man; smart management, yes, but not infallible management. The radio show, for instance, was clearly a mistake, but there was only a one-year contract for "Pabst Blue Ribbon Time." In radio, a year meant three renewable thirteen-week segments or thirty-nine programs. The Kaye series had only been marginally successful, and CBS, as part of a cost-cutting program, was just about to cancel it for being "too arty." The decision would not devastate Kaye. He might well have sensed that it was not showing him off to best effect. He certainly could afford to do without it, especially now that there was big money available for playing the presentation houses.

So, with *Time* magazine researching its cover story while Kaye played the Paramount, the William Morris Agency was concluding the arrangements for the rest of his tour. That was how it worked; the agency booked the theaters and engaged the other performers. Naturally, they were all William Morris clients—the dance team Tip, Tap and Toe and a "girl singer" named Georgia Gibbs, who had been in California doing the Jimmy Durante–Garry Moore radio show.

Since these tours involved entertainers whose acts were set, there was never any need for rehearsal. The performers simply presented their orchestrations and timings to the bandleader before the first show at each theater. The only practice session was before the first show of the first stop on the tour, and that was the engagement at the Paramount Theater in New York City.

Since the first show was performed at nine o'clock, the rehearsal was called for six in the morning, and in wintry New York it was still dark at that ghastly hour. It was even darker at five-thirty when

Georgia Gibbs stepped out of her taxi at the stage entrance, still weary from the ten-hour coast-to-coast flight the day before.

There was already a line of customers winding down the street, waiting for the box office to open, but they were there to see Danny Kaye, and none of them recognized the small and slender blond young woman as she trudged up the few steps, through the snow, to the stage door.

Hot coffee was waiting in the rehearsal room, and she introduced herself to Robert Weitman, who was the Paramount's managing director. "All of us were hungry and ashen," she remembered, "holding our cups of coffee to keep warm." She sat down on a folding chair and watched Tip, Tap and Toe move through their dance routine; synchronized tapping at six in the morning. Then she sang her songs, and while she was singing, Kaye arrived with his accompanist, Sammy Prager. The star took a cup of coffee and sat down, pulling his coat around himself for warmth. After Gibbs was through, Weitman said, "Georgia, this is Danny Kaye." She extended a hand, but Kaye didn't take it. "He just nodded. He was very remote."

Doing six shows a day between movies was going to be a new and arduous experience for the young singer, but she had already proved herself a survivor. Born in Worcester, Massachusetts, she had been placed in an orphanage at nineteen months and lived in one or another until she was eight years old—abused along the way. "All my precious years," she remembered, "were in a regimented orphanage situation. You don't come out of that with a great deal of ego or self-esteem, but you do come out with a great drive to survive, because you don't ever want to go back there again."

Her singing had started in those orphanages, and by the time she was in her teens, she was a professional. She was barely five feet one, and "people would tell me, you're not big enough, and you're not pretty enough, but you're a hell of a singer," and she certainly was. Within five years she would be nationally known as "Her Nibs, Miss Georgia Gibbs" and have a string of hit records.

At the first show, she stood in the wings alongside Eddie Dukoff and watched Danny work. He insisted that the press agent be at every performance. Eddie would go out for coffee, sandwiches, newspapers, and sometimes women. "Eddie was the pimp," Georgia remembered, using the term figuratively, for these were casual dates, not prostitutes. "He would bring the girls to Danny's dressing room. They'd practically be lined up outside; sometimes three or four in one day." What happened inside the dressing room could only be surmised.

Tip, Tap and Toe finished their precision tapping. Gibbs and Dukoff smiled and applauded as the three dancers came running into the wings, then stopped and hurried back onstage to take another bow. She was wearing a magenta velvet cocktail dress that she had made herself. It was tightly fitted at the waist and then widespread over her crinolines. Her shoes matched the dress, with heels as high as she could stand, and when Tip, Tap and Toe introduced her, she strolled out wearing as big a smile as she could muster at nine o'clock in the morning.

Her first number was "I saw you last night / And got that old feeling." She followed it with the up-tempo "Sing, You Sinners," then "Blue Skies." From that she settled into the sultry "More Than You Know" and concluded with the new hit from Broadway's *Call Me Mister*, "South America, Take It Away." She took her bows— curtsies—and then said her one line: "And now, ladies and gentlemen, the star of our show, Danny Kaye."

The audience applauded, the spotlight went out on her, and she walked offstage as Kaye strolled out in his brown tweed sport jacket and brown trousers.

Now the cheering turned to screams—and wails, the ecstatic sorrows of teenage girls. Kaye smiled into the cavernous darkness, and then the youngsters emerged from out of it, surging down the aisles and into the spill of the stage light. He nervously ran a hand through his golden locks, and one of the girls tossed a comb up to him. As the screaming and cheers continued, a candy bar landed at his feet. He picked it up, unwrapped it, and bit off a piece. The wails and shrieks grew louder.

It was all faked. Eddie Dukoff had rounded up the girls to put on this show of teenage hysteria, and for once in his life he had not been original. Although he was a fellow of special resourcefulness and invention, the screaming girls were the idea of Frank Sinatra's press agent, George Evans. The crooner's career had skyrocketed a few years earlier when he had played this very theater to an audience of hysterical teenagers. Those "bobby-soxers," as they were called, had been hired and instructed by Evans; he had even arranged that an ambulance be parked outside the Paramount so as to treat the supposed fainters at that "Columbus Day Riot," as the *New York Daily News* helpfully headlined.

Eddie Dukoff could not match what George Evans had done for Frank Sinatra, and he could not transform Danny Kaye—or any other comedian—into a sex symbol. Dukoff did get some publicity mileage out of his effort when *Time* magazine duly noted a youthful audience at Danny's first show, but while the houses were very good, Kaye's was generally a young adult crowd.

His stage befuddlement worked again, a feigned uncertainty that seemed real. Smiling nervously, he wondered aloud about what to do first. The audience chuckled over that, and then he chuckled and he turned to the bandleader, and the bandleader chuckled. He exchanged small talk with members of the band, all amplified so that the audience could listen in. He worked his way into the act, and before it might have been realized, he was singing "Deenah" and then "Anatole of Paris." He did a boxing routine from *The Kid from Brooklyn*, and now, physically active, conducted the band with his feet while lying on his back. He sang the old, off-key "Begin the Beguine," which he introduced as a great song being sung by a ham actor. Then he did "Ballin' the Jack" in a lovely and special way, for instead of singing it fast and jazzily, as it was usually done, he made it nice and easy. And not only did he sing it lightly and softly, but when he finished, he danced it in the same understated way. His arms were delicately spread, and his steps were small, circular, and sliding.

He closed with "Melody in Four F" and for an encore led the audience in a round of "Minnie the Moocher."

It was a thirty-five-minute stint, and he was off. Gibbs watched as his beaming smile shut off like a light the moment he hit the wings. His face quite somber, he trotted up the backstage stairs, stepped into his dressing room, and closed the door behind him, not to emerge until the next show.

Between performances, he took off all his clothes except his shoes and socks, putting on a dark silk Chinese robe. It was a short robe, and whenever the others caught a glimpse of him as he opened his door to admit a guest, they giggled over his skinny white legs covered with red hair.

In his dressing room there was a small red upright piano that Sylvia had requested, even though she was back in California. A jar of Albolene cream was on his makeup table, and a bottle of brandied peaches, which he preferred to candy bars. He had visitors throughout the day—people bringing food and a man to massage his feet, which always seemed to hurt. His guests were in and out of show business. They would stay with him in the dressing room while the movie was on, and when the show began, he arranged for them to be seated on folding chairs in the wings, a royal box so that they could be specially played to.

"It used to kill us," one of the other performers said. "We would see these great people like Jack Benny or Richard Rodgers and whisper to each other, 'Gee, these big stars are here,' and he would never introduce us. We just didn't exist. We were like second-class citizens."

The novelty of live performance did not last very long, and after three days and eighteen shows, Kaye started to get restless. "He seemed unhappy" to Gibbs, and she suspected that he was bored. "At least a singer," she said, "you can sing it faster or slower, but you sing it, and then you're off. But when you have to interplay with an audience and you're bored, you're going to bomb, my dear. I don't care who the hell you are."

And it was only the fourth day of a three-week stint; just the first engagement on the tour. "It was the git-gat-giddle," Gibbs believed, the routine of it all, doing the same business over and over. Kaye had probably confided in Weitman, the Paramount's managing director, because that evening the two of them talked to Georgia about it.

"Look, Danny," Weitman said. "Just to break up the monotony, why don't you sing a song with Georgia? Just kind of fool around onstage."

The singer was stunned by the suggestion.

"I've never been onstage with anyone but myself," she pleaded. "My job is to sing a song."

Weitman did not seem worried about that.

"Working with somebody else," she said, "involves *lines*—saying them, listening to them, answering back. I haven't had that much experience."

Kaye smiled and relieved her. He was simple and direct, and he had an idea about what they might do.

"Why don't we sing 'Sometimes I'm Happy'?" he said. "Do you know that?"

She started to sing the old standard.

"Just walk out," he said. "I'll tell you when, and you don't have to say anything. I'll start the song. You just sing the next line. Sammy [Prager] will give you your key."

"Sounds all right to me," she said without much conviction.

"We'll try it at a matinee," Kaye smiled, and that was a relief, for she knew that matinee audiences were predominantly women, sympathetic and forgiving of nervous girl singers who are inexperienced with lines.

At the performance that he chose to try it, the next afternoon, Georgia said her usual "And now, ladies and gentlemen, the star of our show, Danny Kaye." He strolled onstage, and as she walked off and into the wings, she broke into a trot. She raced upstairs to change her dress and freshen her makeup. Five minutes later, she was back and waiting.

The moment came, Kaye looked offstage at her, smiled, nodded, and she stepped out to work with somebody else for the first time, not knowing that Danny Kaye was also working with somebody else for the first time—at least since he had been a stooge for Nick Long that disastrous time in London.

She just walked up to him, and he began to sing "Sometimes I'm happy—"

She sang the next line, "Sometimes I'm blue."

He gave her a deadpan stare. She was lost. They hadn't rehearsed. She didn't know what to do next, but he already knew what that would be. He kept staring, and she simply broke up. "I may be small," she would later say, "but I happen to have a very big laugh" (or "lahff," as she put it in her New England accent). And when she roared, the audience roared, too. "Because Danny was completely breaking me up. They loved that."

He started the song again.

"Sometimes I'm happy—"

She responded again, "Sometimes I'm blue."

He stared again, and again she laughed; a big, out-loud laugh.

Again, the audience roared, and Georgia was getting to like this. Danny's was a quirky and disarming comic approach. He certainly knew what an audience would enjoy. She also liked getting a laugh.

He began yet a third time.

"Sometimes I'm happy—"

"Sometimes I'm blue."

This time, she grabbed at his jacket and clutched it to keep from laughing.

"Georgia," he said, "you're breaking the jacket."

Now she guffawed from the depths of her abdomen. It was a huge laugh, filled with gusto, and she realized then that her big laugh was also making the audience laugh. It was compounding the laugh. So they decided, Danny decided, to keep that in the act, too —her clutching his jacket.

By the time they concluded the Paramount engagement, he was enjoying work again; in fact, at the last show he was onstage for ninety minutes, and Gibbs was there for a lot of it.

But not for all of it. At the closing show he performed the complete Danny Kaye repertoire, from pantomime to mimicry and musical burlesque. He even brought people onstage from the audience, which was something he ordinarily avoided, and when it was over, the audience serenaded him, singing "Auld Lang Syne." He certainly knew how to make love to them. The question was whether he could make love to a person.

HIS ITINERARY WAS GOING TO TAKE HIM TO THE BIGGEST PRESENTA-tion houses in the country, from New York to Philadelphia, Boston, Chicago, Cincinnati, Detroit, and San Francisco. The New York engagement at the Paramount had run through March. *The Kid from Brooklyn* had its nationwide opening in April.

The reviews were lukewarm. The movie catered to a pubescent mentality. For the same reason, business was excellent. The movie-going public was made up of pubescents of all ages.

The picture is based on the Harold Lloyd movie *The Milky Way*, with Kaye once again cast as a weakling. This time he is a mousy milkman thrown into the boxing game by a crooked promoter. Several fights are fixed for him, and then he is matched with the champ.

The fight scenes give Kaye a chance to do some very funny footwork, and he has a hilarious scene with Fay Bainter, teaching the handsome matron how to do his dodge-and-twist style of boxing. In all, Kaye demonstrates very real physical coordination and proves himself an astute observer of Charlie Chaplin's classic prizefight sequences. "Nimble and complicated grace" was the nicely written notice he got from Bosley Crowther, the critic for the *New York Times*, who typified most in finding Kaye better than the picture.

Sylvia's special material did not fare as well. Her centerpiece was "Pavlowa," written for Danny almost a decade earlier at Tamiment. It was a broad number that relied on such juvenilia as pronouncing it "Pavlowa" to wobble the "w." There was no attempt to justify the number in the story, and there simply was no sense in

Kaye's boxing milkman singing it. While the numbers in *Up in Arms* had also been irrelevant, it was his first picture; he and his songs were novel. This was Danny's third movie, and novelty was no longer sufficient. It wasn't enough for Sylvia's songs, either. She would remain a talented amateur, never any better than "Anatole of Paris." She would continue to write material for the Danny Kaye she had first met, the Danny she had shaped, but her songs would only show how far past them he had gone and she had not. If she had not devoted herself to his career but worked for herself instead, she probably would have developed and polished her gifts, which were real enough. But her future was her sacrifice. She conceded her own fulfillment for the sake of his, and now the special material that Sylvia Fine wrote for Danny Kaye—instead of developing herself, maturing, and learning how to write for Broadway—was no longer essential to his career. What she now provided was drive and canny management, not those simple songs, but mothering this mutually created Danny Kaye was the greater venture—or such was her delusion. It probably was necessary to rationalize her sacrifice; it might have nurtured a deeper rage and a grimmer determination to control him.

His tour proceeded in bookings of two or three weeks, with sizable stretches between to allow for still another movie, *The Secret Life of Walter Mitty*. Such activity was not unusual; some actors made as many as three pictures a year. But Kaye's combination of touring and filming was an exhausting schedule.

The earnings of it all, about a half million dollars that year, were immense for 1946, but it would be unfair to infer that the work was motivated by the big payday. As a matter of fact, Kaye could be downright peculiar about money. He never discussed it, didn't even like to touch it. He chose not to deal with it or even know about it. He was not penurious; in fact, he was generous about picking up restaurant checks, but he preferred to have someone else do the actual peeling off of dollar bills, to deal with the whole subject of money—his wife, his manager, his accountant.

They were apparently responsible for the business aspect of this tour; as for himself, the tour was related to his enjoyment of live performance. The Waldorf appearance in Sinatra's stead had reminded him of what he had been missing. The media—movies, radio—had nearly drained the stage blood out of him, as they had been doing with so many vibrant performers, such as W. C. Fields,

Mae West, the Marx Brothers, Bob Hope, Bing Crosby, Gene Kelly, Lena Horne, and perhaps the greatest individual entertainer of the day, Judy Garland. Some of these wonderfully gifted people would reclaim their juices and return to live performance, but most took their success in radio or the movies as being a ticket out of live work. Kaye was the rare star who never stopped being a stage entertainer, and there was no bigger star. He was not about to forsake the response of an audience.

He would even find a way to live with being on the road through much of Sylvia's pregnancy.

Meanwhile, *The Kid from Brooklyn* had become a very popular picture. It was only his third movie, and Danny Kaye was already an American institution. As a matter of fact, from the show-business point of view, he was better than an institution; he was beloved, which meant that people were grateful to pay to love him. And that made him the number-one box-office attraction in the movies.

12

He would read the script through, and then he would turn to
Sylvia and ask her to read it, and she would make all the
suggestions.

— Jule Styne, composer, *The Kid from Brooklyn*

WHEN DANNY INTERRUPTED THE TOUR OF PRESENTATION HOUSES
TO COME HOME AND START WORK ON *THE SECRET LIFE OF Walter*
Mitty, he and Sylvia began seeing psychoanalysts five days a week.
Danny's man was a favorite of the movie community, Dr. Martin
Grotjohn. The formal analysis would continue for decades, but its
effectiveness was probably undercut by the peripatetic nature of his
work.

Since he traveled so much, Sylvia's involvement with his life
became, largely, her involvement with his life in Hollywood. At the
Goldwyn studio, at least, she was so much a part of the business of
being Danny Kaye that she sat in on production meetings. Supposedly, her absence from one of them because of an appointment with
her psychoanalyst prompted the Sam Goldwynism "Anyone who
goes to a psychiatrist ought to have his head examined."

As a girl, she had been aggressive at school but shy in personal
situations. When something could be accomplished through will,
ability, and hard work, she would make up her mind to do it, and
she would invariably succeed. She was what would later be called
"an achiever."

It was the same in her adulthood. She seemed more comfortable—more poised and more successful—at work than in her personal life. At work, she got things done, and she seemed to like the process. Now she became active in moviemaking, at least in the shaping of Danny's movies.

A year earlier, in 1945, and with Kaye in mind, Samuel Goldwyn had bought the celebrated James Thurber short story "The Secret Life of Walter Mitty." Ever since its 1939 publication in the *New Yorker*, the story about a henpecked husband's daydreams of derring-do had been considered a small classic. Ken Englund was assigned to collaborate with Thurber on the screenplay, but ultimately, Everett Freeman was brought in to help invent a plot that would support the daydreams. By the time it was done, the twenty-two-hundred-word story had become a $3 million vehicle for Kaye's by-now-settled screen persona—a schizophrenic who is passive, victimized, and meek except when he is singing the sophisticated songs of Sylvia Fine. At those times, he is confident, strong, and assertive.

As with the previous movies, Sylvia wrote some new numbers and added old ones from the backlist. A fresh piece was "A New Symphony for Unstrung Tongue." Then she dealt her six-year-old trump card, the best number she had ever written and ever would write, "Anatole of Paris."

Perhaps she had once given Danny the glibness and suavity he did not have—the words he could not think of. At one time, it did seem that David Kaminski could become Danny Kaye only when singing Sylvia Fine's songs. He might have been a ventriloquist's dummy then, with Sylvia in effect speaking for him. Pursuing that image, she might indeed have been the woman behind the man and not merely at the piano.

But he was proving on the tour of presentation houses that he could perform very nicely without her. He was not even doing much of her material: an occasional "Melody in Four F" and sometimes an "Anatole of Paris." The rest was pure Danny Kaye.

It was a different story in the movies. There the legend of Sylvia Fine and Danny Kaye was intact, the husband-and-wife team, the great entertainer and the little woman on and at his side. Star vehicles are always at the mercy of the stars, and she stepped into the screenwriting process to speak for the star of *The Secret Life of Walter Mitty*. A minor suggestion of hers was to work in one of the gesundheit jokes that meant so much to her as a Danny-Sylvia tradition. A major suggestion was a daydream in which Mitty imagines himself a fashion designer. The reason was transparent; it was to cue "Anatole of Paris."

Thus began not a daydream but one of Mr. Thurber's worst nightmares. In working on the script with Ken Englund, he had come up with such additional fantasies as a firing-squad scene and a courtroom sequence in which Mitty defends himself brilliantly. Sylvia actively opposed them. "Next to our new dream scenes," Thurber would later say, "the greatest worry of Mr. Englund and myself was the possibility that this movie might be spoiled by one or more of Mr. Kaye's and Miss Fine's famous, but to me deplorable, scat or git-gat-giddle songs." That worry was justified when Sylvia set "Anatole of Paris" as a dream within a dream in which Mitty imagines himself an ace in the Royal Air Force. Thurber derided the number as "an utterly horrifying, shockingly out of taste and mood piece of scat." Certainly the fey fashion designer had nothing to do with the RAF superhero.

The elegant and esteemed Thurber also loathed the melodramatic story that had been invented to carry (and ultimately overshadow) the secret life that was lived in Mitty's daydreams. Moreover, the writer blamed all of this corruption on Sylvia, describing Danny as "talented but obedient."

Of course, she could not have been playing such a role without Kaye's acquiescence; he had to let her do the dirty work, but rather than appearing saddled with it, she seemed fulfilled by the assignment. Thurber himself heard her talking about the prospective *Secret Life of Walter Mitty* on the radio program "We the People." "The movie," Sylvia confided to the audience, "is based on a story written by James Thurber." She then added, under her breath, "*Was.*"

The added plot had a bumbling Mitty involved with comic-book villains—a Danny Kaye version of Mitty who is dominated by his mother, his fiancée, her mother, and ultimately the supreme woman, an ethereal beauty who appears in his dreams and then surfaces in real life. A superficial similarity to the Kaye-Fine relationship can be perceived in this maternalism and obedience, but the psychology in the Danny-Sylvia dynamic was more complicated than a mother-son cliché.

Virginia Mayo was cast as this powerful woman. Experience (this was her third assignment opposite Kaye) had given the actress assurance, transforming her girlish prettiness into a womanly and even ravishing beauty. Ultimately, Mayo would stride through *The Secret Life of Walter Mitty* as an emancipated woman reminiscent of Bernard Shaw's intimidating superheroines.

But in the daydream sequences she is at Mitty's feet, which is a nice way of saying that only in his dreams could he be a real man. For in real life this fellow is impotent, at least socially—badgered by his boss and cowed by women. There is no mention of sex, this being 1946, but while the Mitty in the daydreams is macho and hot, the Mitty in real life is eunuchlike. In neither mode does Kaye have an on-screen kiss, which at least he'd had in *The Kid from Brooklyn*.

Between the melodramatic plot and Thurber's additional daydreams, the next-to-last draft ran an unwieldy 180 pages. Sylvia had the last word. According to Thurber (in a letter to *Life* magazine), "Almost everything I had written, suggested and fought for was dropped." He later told an interviewer that the only ones to blame for ruining his story were the groups of men who made movies "and their wives."

One of the daydreams he had invented for the movie was, in fact, filmed, the trial in which Mitty finds himself the defendant. The scene was cut before the movie was released, and it may well be buried in the Goldwyn vaults. A rediscovered Mitty sequence would make a wonderful addition to a reissued *Secret Life of Walter Mitty*.

The funniest of the daydreams, surviving from Thurber's original story, has Mitty imagining himself a supreme surgeon, but in fairness to Kaye, all the daydreams give him the freedom to release and exploit his exuberance. There is Mitty steering a vessel through a hurricane despite his injury ("It's nothing, only a broken arm"), and Mitty as a debonair riverboat gambler. In each instance he is extravagantly arrogant, outrageously masculine, and very funny. Perhaps Mitty is sexy only in his dreams, but perhaps that is true of many people. That might have been why Thurber's original story was so popular: because readers identified with its hero. Without any doubt, it was the movie's daydreams (linked by a running joke of the sound *pocketa-pocketa*) that made *The Secret Life of Walter Mitty* the best in Kaye's series for Goldwyn. In fact, a sequel, *The Adventures of Walter Mitty*, was announced. It never was made, but the original was so popular it made "living a life of Walter Mitty" a catchphrase for fantasy fulfillment.

Indeed, *The Secret Life of Walter Mitty* was good and popular despite Kaye's hair having been restored to its natural Jewish red.

The picture was made just after he had concluded performances at the Chicago Theatre. The comparative economics are interesting. Only a year earlier, Goldwyn had paid him $125,000, the same as for *Up in Arms*, to make *The Kid from Brooklyn*. In only two weeks in Chicago he made $79,000. Either movies did not make financial sense, or Kaye's contract with Goldwyn didn't.

The Chicago money was more than any American performer had ever made in a two-week period, and Kaye's tour was geared for making money. The previous stand, in Philadelphia, had been played at the cavernous Mastbaum Theater, which was reopened just for the engagement. According to *Variety*, Frank Sinatra alone was Danny Kaye's box-office equal, but not everyone thought Kaye was worth that much money. At one performance in Chicago the show started out well enough. The new dance trio (the Dunhills had replaced Tip, Tap and Toe) finished their ten-minute routine, and Georgia Gibbs sang her songs. Kaye had kept their little exchange in his act ever since its New York debut, and so, as usual, she hurried to her dressing room to change. When she returned in the fresh dress, she saw Fishel (Phil) Goldfarb watching from the wings. Goldfarb was one friend whom Danny did introduce to the other performers. The stage mentor from the old days at White Roe had made a great success of his novelty business and at forty-one was a man of wealth and leisure. He had been backstage frequently in New York and had flown to Chicago to keep Kaye company. He might have once been a semiprofessional comedian, but he now played straight man to his former stooge. Phil would even roar when someone asked, "Oh, really?," and Danny replied, "No, O'Reilly."

"It was pathetic," Gibbs remembered, "a grown man idolizing to that extent. He was there whenever Danny snapped his fingers." And when Kaye was tired of him, "he got lost."

That time in Chicago, with Goldfarb watching, Georgia could see that Danny was not enjoying the show. He seemed to be walking through the act, and an audience can sense that. Someone in the theater evidently did, because he threw a penny onstage. The microphone picked up the jingle of the coin. The spotlight caught some of its glitter. The audience gasped, and Kaye stopped in his tracks.

A tossed coin is an old form of heckling, suggesting that the performer is no better than a street entertainer who plays for loose change and is worth no more than that. Any professional performer has to deal with hecklers, they are part of show business, and when no rejoinders come to mind, there are standard squelches. In the case of a tossed coin, for instance, the heckled entertainer can always say, "There's only one kind of an animal that throws a scent."

But Kaye, instead of taking control of the situation and lightening the moment, let the situation control *him*. He stopped short in the middle of the act, revealing his wounded feelings, and acknowledged the heckler by first insulting him in a humorless way, and then lending him importance by not getting on with the act.

"What kind of a thing is that to do?" he snarled into the dark. "Where's your manners?"

Then he stalked off to uncomfortable silence and scattered boos. Scowling, he plunged into the wings, striding past the silent, staring performers and stagehands. Suddenly, Eve Arden materialized from out of the darkness, rushing to comfort him. She followed in his seething wake as he hurried up the stairs, both of them disappearing behind his dressing-room door.

Arden had been in Chicago throughout the engagement, watching most performances from the wings. Naturally, this caused a great deal of gossip. "The talk backstage," Georgia Gibbs remembered, "was that she had left her husband because Danny had proposed. She was just nuts about him."

That was just gossip; none of them knew. Danny didn't introduce her to them, but he did invite Georgia to join Eve and him for supper with a newspaper interviewer one night after a late show. That was the first time she heard about Sylvia's being pregnant. Perhaps Danny brought up the subject to quash any suspicions the interviewer might have had about Eve Arden's presence.

The fellow asked, "Have you and Sylvia decided on what you will name the child?"

" 'Christopher,' " Danny said, "if it's a boy and 'Stephanie' if it's a girl."

Then, in a bewildering non sequitur, he turned to Gibbs and started singing "Happy Birthday" to her. It was not her birthday. Kaye smiled at the singer's befuddlement and then nodded toward Eve. It was *her* birthday, April 30. Thus prompted, Gibbs sang "Happy Birthday" to Eve Arden, that thirty-fourth birthday of hers in Chicago.

The stage interplay between Danny and Georgia was going so well that he was letting it run longer, and in the middle of one show in Cincinnati, he asked whether she could dance. When she nodded with a giggling, girlish apprehensiveness, he turned to his accompanist, Sammy Prager. The classic vaudeville dance number, of course, is "Tea for Two" and when Prager began to play it, they danced an impromptu soft shoe. It, too, was added to the act.

"He moved beautifully," she would remember. "When we danced, it was like Rogers and Astaire."

But no matter how many shows they did, Kaye seemed to believe that Gibbs was losing her composure at every performance. "Now, I would have had to be somewhat retarded," she remembered, "to say the same things and do the same thing and hear the same thing six times a day for weeks and weeks and keep laughing. You would have to be mentally defective.

"But he just believed it."

That is the meaning of *performing ego*, and without it there is nothing but stage fright.

Friendliness on stage did not mean friendliness off. "He would walk off the stage kissing and grabbing me, and the moment we got off that stage he went up to his room, the door was closed, and that was it. When you're with somebody six shows a day," she said, "six days a week, from nine in the morning until twelve at night, you have to get to know them.

"None of us got to know him."

13

Danny: I've had it! I'm going. I can't live this way anymore.
Good-bye.

Sylvia: You're right. I'm going with you.

—Hollywood lore

ON DECEMBER 17, 1946, AFTER A COMPLICATED PREGNANCY, SYL-
VIA GAVE BIRTH TO WHAT WOULD BE HER ONLY CHILD, A BABY GIRL.
They named her not Stephanie but "Dena," after Danny's song, and
Kitty Carlisle was asked to be the godmother. She wasn't surprised.
"Sylvia," she said, "considered me one of her very best friends all
her life." The Fine family probably *was* surprised, for godparents are
not part of Jewish tradition.

Sylvia had stayed close to her family, especially to her pretty
younger sister Rhoda, who made regular visits to California. Danny
rarely saw his family, but he did offer to put both brothers in business. Larry and Mack found a site in the Cooper Square section of
lower Manhattan, on East Tenth Street near Fourth Avenue, and
Danny provided the capital. They opened a hardware store specializ-
ing in electrical supplies and called it the Shell Electric Company.

Old man Kaminski was out of business; Danny made sure of
that. There would be no more subway rides to the Seventh Avenue
workshop for "Pop," as Kaye called him. The previous winter, he
had treated his father to a Miami Beach vacation, and Jacob would
say, "I got a good son, Danny. He sends me to Florida in the winter

and in the summertime to the country" (the Catskill Mountains). Now, in the cold of January 1947, a winter holiday was again suggested, and this time the little fellow said to his three sons, "Boys, I think it's time I went in a *luftmachine.*"

It was only a year since National Airlines had begun scheduled flights from La Guardia Airport to Miami Beach. Jacob was an adventurer, but a *luftmachine* was still a nervy proposition. So it was with a certain trepidation that Danny, Larry, and Mack presented the old man with his air ticket to Florida.

Much as Jacob tried to appear casual, he could not conceal a certain apprehensiveness about his first flight. He had Larry and Mack deliver him to La Guardia two hours before the scheduled departure, and plopping down between his sons for protection, he seated himself in a waiting area that afforded a panoramic view of the airfield. From that vantage point he was able to observe not only the departing and arriving flights; he could also watch the departing and arriving passengers.

When a woman his age came reeling into sight, fresh off a DC-4 and not nearly recovered from the landing experience, he was visibly shaken. She staggered toward him and then collapsed into a nearby seat, moaning feverishly in Yiddish.

Old man Kaminski just stared at the ashen-faced woman. Finally, he asked her in Jewish-style rhetoric, "It was that bad?"

She looked up at him, her eyes rolling upward in their sockets. "Oyoyoyoy," she said. "Don't ask."

"Look, lady," Jacob whispered anxiously, "I'm Danny Kaye's father," and he paused momentously for that superstar relationship to make its impression. Then he asked hopefully, "I'll be sick, too?"

The story went from Mack and Larry into family lore. Danny loved retelling it to friends.

WITH THE RELEASE OF *THE SECRET LIFE OF WALTER MITTY* IN APRIL 1947, he resumed his tour, beginning with a return engagement at the Chicago Theatre. He was moodier than ever and didn't even mention the birth of his child to anyone in the show. But there was nothing wrong with his career. On the screen, *The Secret Life of Walter Mitty* may not have been his most profitable movie: it dropped to twenty-fifth among the year's releases as compared to fifteenth place for the previous year's *Kid from Brooklyn.* But *Mitty* received the best reviews of any Danny Kaye movie to date and would become one of the two movies that defined him for the general public, the other being *Hans Christian Andersen*. The pair established him as first elfin and second lovable. It was on these perceived characteristics that he would build his legend.

As for his stage show, business at the Chicago Theatre was excellent. Yet if, as many artists have said, a creative person is what he does, it was more difficult than ever to describe exactly what Danny Kaye was and what he did. Even in the *Mitty* movie, just as in the earlier *Wonder Man*, there were two distinct Kayes, the Milquetoast and the mimetic sophisticate.

In his personal stage appearances he was becoming ever more the artist. For instance, he had developed a new routine with his pianist, Sammy Prager. A spotlight would be thrown on the keyboard, and as Prager played, Kaye would watch with seemingly profound appreciation. Then a second light would close in on his own hands as they began to move to the music. The ballet of his elbows, wrists, and fingers had been noted before. Now he was showcasing it. His arms and wrists shifted and swept with fluid grace; his fingers curled and danced. "They began," a reviewer wrote, "to move and wriggle."

His double act with Georgia Gibbs was now running eighteen minutes, but that didn't mean he stinted on his solo appearance. The entire show, scheduled for thirty-five minutes, could sometimes go on for an hour. Gibbs was now so assured at falling apart with rollicking laughter that after one performance Alan King came backstage to see her. He had stayed for two shows. "I just had to see whether Danny was really breaking you up. I didn't think anyone could fool me. You were so hysterical."

"And?" she asked. In reply, the young comedian laughed. "Second time, there you were, laughing at the same shtick."

King was the rare comedian to be seen backstage at a Danny Kaye show. Gibbs worked with Danny Thomas and Milton Berle as well as with Kaye, and she noticed that they enjoyed visits from fellow comics. "They would fool around with each other. In the kind of rough-and-tumble business it was then, when everybody was with everybody, they bounced off each other . . . [but] Danny just moved away, moved away. That was why nobody could make head or tails of him."

She thought the others "found he was snobby" and sensed that "he didn't want to be a part of them." But she didn't think of him as a comic, anyhow, and that was really the point. Kaye was unique; he knew that he was unique, and uniqueness makes for solitude. If being different in his case meant being classier, then that was only the good part of being different. Loneliness came with it, too. Thus, being unclassifiable had hurt him and had helped him, and that is the way being special works, onstage or off.

VERY FEW THEATERS WERE AIR-CONDITIONED IN THAT SWELTERING summer of 1947, although many were "air cooled," with fans blowing over giant blocks of ice. Kaye took a break and used the time to make an album for Columbia Records. It would test his singing ability, which, on a record, would have to sustain itself without the support of funny faces and hand gestures.

The album of four 10-inch 78 rpm discs was, for the most part, arranged and conducted by the top-flight movie musician Johnny Green. It included two git-gat-giddle numbers, "Deenah" and "Minnie the Moocher," with the band members repeating Kaye's hi-de-hi. Symptomatic of the trouble between Danny and Sylvia, only one of her songs was included, "Anatole of Paris."

He sang an unusual version of George and Ira Gershwin's "Babbitt and the Bromide"—unusual because the brothers had written the piece as a duet and Kaye sang both parts. He did it in two different voices and sang the whole song quickly, making for dizzy switches between the voices. It is one of the best pieces in the album, although the tops are the two songs that Cole Porter wrote for Kaye to sing in *Let's Face It!*—"Let's Not Talk About Love" and "Farming."

Finally, he chose "Eileen," a Killarney-type ballad, to demonstrate that he could sing simply and beautifully. While the piece is little more than a series of shamrock clichés and Kaye's voice is a light baritone rather than an Irish tenor, the rendition is sweet and touching. It was a promise of the lovely singing to come in *Hans Christian Andersen*.

Then it was back to the performance houses. The tour resumed at the Fox Theater in Detroit, although it nearly didn't. Danny was nowhere to be seen as the first show began, and after twenty minutes, nerves were beginning to fray. Usually, he stayed locked in his dressing room. This time he was not even in the theater.

Then, just in time to make his change, he strode briskly through the stage door. He had gone to a hospital at the invitation of a surgeon. He had been watching an operation. Nobody could deny that it was an original excuse, and it was true. Watching operations was an interest he was going to pursue.

The Detroit engagement was the rare one when Sylvia visited Danny on one of his road trips. She arrived with Abe Lastfogel, the head of the William Morris Agency, and went straight to the Fox Theater. While the movie was on, they closeted themselves in Danny's dressing room, and when the door was opened, everyone was invited in—the three Dunhill dancers, Sammy Prager, and Georgia Gibbs.

As they crowded into the little room, Lastfogel congratulated them on the show and told them that they were doing great business. Then he nodded toward Kaye and said, "I've told Danny that I think he should go to London and play the Palladium."

One of the dancing Dunhills gasped. "The Palladium?"

It was the top of the line in London, the number-one variety house.

"It's after the war," Lastfogel said. "The people need comedy." And turning toward Kaye, he said, "Danny, you'll be great."

"Don't bet on it," Kaye said sourly, still hurting from his experience with "Nick Long & Co." in England. "I bombed in London in the thirties. I'm really not sure I want to work there again."

"Danny," Sylvia said urgently, "I think you should. And," she added, glancing around the crowded dressing room, "we have decided to take you with us—Sammy [Prager] and the boys [the Dunhills]—but . . . Georgia, we're not going to take you."

The little singer went blind for a moment. Then she turned and fled. "I was a young woman," she remembered. "I'd never been to Europe. Today it's just like a subway ride, but then it was just an extraordinary thing—*and they're going to leave me out.* I was devastated. I cried my eyes out. They never said one word of explanation to me, not Danny, not Sylvia, not Lastfogel."

That was when she thought, When you're brought up in an orphanage, show business is the worst business in the world to go into . . . it's a world of rejection. There's no honesty, no loyalty.

Later, calmer, she decided that Sylvia's reason for leaving her out was "what a wonderful foil I was for him. Sylvia didn't want anyone taking anything from him." If that was a rationalization, it assuaged her hurt until she thought about it. "How was I going to get in his way? He was a superstar. What the hell was I? I was a girl singer, I was nothing, I couldn't figure out why they should feel threatened by me."

Her sore feelings made the singer receptive to a piece of mischief that the three Dunhill dancers concocted.

"Why don't you try this just for the hell of it?" one of them said. "Danny really thinks he's breaking you up. So why don't you just go out there and not laugh?"

Gibbs stared at him. "*Not laugh?*"

"Not laugh," he repeated.

She laughed for real then and shook her head, smiling, knowing it was a terrible, wonderful idea.

"I hated to do it," she would later say, "because I really am a professional, but I was truly hurt about London." And so she agreed to the prank as long as it would be done at a matinee. ("I wouldn't do it at night.")

When it came time for Kaye to bring her onstage, she was ready. So were the others. "Everybody was in on the joke, even the stagehands. They were all standing in the wings."

"I was very nervous," she recalled, "but I kept thinking about how angry I was with him."

Then Kaye announced, "And here she is, Miss Georgia Gibbs."

The band played her entrance music. She strolled onstage.

By this time, their duet had been simplified. Instead of singing "Sometimes I'm Happy," Danny would just turn and look at her, deadpan. That alone was supposed to break her up. But this time she did not laugh as she was supposed to. Instead of guffawing, she simply stood there and stared back. The audience fell silent.

"You know," she later mused aloud, "ten seconds of quiet on the stage is a lifetime." Then, and it was the only time that Kaye ever talked to her privately onstage, he whispered, "What are you doing?"

She replied—evenly but quietly, even though it was still amplified by the microphone—"I'm out here to sing a song with you, Danny," and she beamed. "I'm ready!"

She continued to look at him with a wide-eyed smile. The audience remained silent. It was no more than a half minute, but it was long enough. Finally, she gave in, breaking up and roaring "and pulling his jacket and doing the whole shtick."

Afterward, Kaye said nothing about what had happened. "He had no sense of humor offstage," she said. Then again, perhaps he wasn't in the mood those days, for when he got back to Los Angeles, he told Sylvia that he was moving out. Eddie Dukoff announced to the press that it was "a trial separation, merely for a period of readjustment," but on the afternoon of September 5, 1947, Sylvia telephoned her sister Rhoda, and she didn't even say hello. She just said, "Danny walked out on me."

IT SEEMS FAIR TO PRESUME THAT DANNY LEFT SYLVIA BECAUSE OF Eve Arden, but why had there been an Eve Arden romance in the first place? Kaye was never a romantic, never a womanizer, never sexually driven. He does not seem to have been rapturously in love with Eve—he was not the type to fall rapturously in love with anyone. That had never happened to him, and never would, because he wasn't emotionally or sexually available.

He had to have left Sylvia for some other reason. Perhaps it was to get his manliness in order and finally disobey her. Perhaps he left her so as to find in Eve what he did not find in the marriage—emotional equality. For even though there was no lack of respect between Danny and Sylvia, the respect was based on mutual need, on dependency, on fear of abandonment and on hard facts. They respected each other for what each of them lacked. In simple show-business terms, Danny had the confidence. He could go out and perform, while the inhibited Sylvia had the brains and could write the words that failed him.

But that was professional need. On the emotional front, this was a mother-son relationship without either physical attraction or romance; a relationship with a warning; a relationship whipped by obedience. This was the relationship that Danny Kaye seemed to be fleeing.

BEFORE HE HAD A CHANCE TO MOVE HIS THINGS OUT, SYLVIA DID, taking her nine-month-old baby with her. She rented a house in the 500 block on Hillcrest Street. "A nasty little Spanish type house," Benay Venuta remembered. "Furnished. Sylvia didn't like it much." But, Benay said, "she stuck her nose up and entertained more than ever. And Danny missed the old crowd."

Kitty Carlisle, a lot closer to her than Venuta was, knew how "Sylvia suffered." But, Carlisle remembered, "she wasn't a weeper. She loved him so much . . . she hoped she could stick it out."

Determined as she was to hold on until her husband came to his senses, Sylvia Fine certainly was not going to let herself be used in the process. When the time came for his next picture, she refused to work on it. As a result, *A Song Is Born* would be a movie about musicians, with musicians (Louis Armstrong, Benny Goodman, Lionel Hampton), but with no songs from Sylvia Fine. And with no songs for Danny Kaye. He did not—he would not—find anyone else to write material for him.

Like so many Goldwyn pictures and all of Kaye's, this was a remake of an old movie (*Ball of Fire*, which had starred Gary Cooper and Barbara Stanwyck). In this incarnation, it was about a group of music professors who are studying jazz. Virginia Mayo again served as Danny's romantic interest, this time playing a jazz singer, and even she had a song.

During filming, Kaye was in an emotional free-fall, "a basket case," the picture's director, Howard Hawks, said, "stopping work to see a psychiatrist twice a day." Small wonder, then, that *A Song Is Born* was the slightest and the least successful of the Samuel Goldwyn movies that played so important a part in establishing Danny Kaye.

Friends rallied around the deserted wife, the abandoned mother. Benay Venuta kept her company for a few nights, but all Sylvia would say to her was: "You know, when you sleep, you sleep just like Danny. I always think you're dead. You never breathe."

Kitty Carlisle suggested the possibility of finding a boyfriend, or at least a date, but Sylvia said, "I can't do that. I love Danny." And that was the end of it.

Kaye's anxieties made it hard on Eve Arden, too, but if she was suffering, only her closest friends cared. The *other woman* is not a sympathetic figure. And Arden was not only the Kayes' home wrecker; she had walked out on a husband of her own. Sylvia's friends blamed the female. It was as if a woman is supposed to know better. And so, as far as caring about Eve's situation was concerned, as Kitty Carlisle put it: "Listen—any lady who takes a man who's just had a baby, with a wife in the same town—well she's just asking for it."

As the months passed, there were times when it was unavoidable that Sylvia deal with Danny, if only to let him see his infant daughter. "In the beginning," Carlisle said, "he just wouldn't come home." Now Sylvia "just waited."

After the release of A Song Is Born in the fall of 1948, the contract with the Goldwyn studio was not renewed. The box-office showing, a paltry $2.4 million (that put it in forty-fifth place among the year's releases), made it clear that Kaye's popularity was waning, at least in the movies. When the producer was asked if he had any idea "what the hell's wrong with Kaye's film career," Sam Goldwyn replied, "Nobody wants to fuck Danny Kaye."

From Danny's point of view, the failure of the movie was not only the failure of a movie but the first setback in what had been a continuum of success, and that setback would always be linked to his walking out on Sylvia and her consequent, punishing refusal to help him. Now, perhaps, he would find out whether he could get along without her—emotionally or professionally, and in the entertainer those lives are related. If he was dependent on Sylvia Fine, perhaps he would learn whether he had himself developed the need for a mother figure or she had mothered him into it.

14

The most sensationally successful single performer to appear in London in living memory.

—*Sunday Express* (London)

THE MANAGING DIRECTOR OF THE PALLADIUM WAS A TALL, BEEFY, RUDDY-COMPLEXIONED, SANDY-HAIRED FELLOW NAMED VAL PARNELL. People said he resembled Colonel Blimp, the stereotypical British colonialist, but rather than being an aristocrat, Val Parnell was a carnival spieler in Savile Row finery.

That was a familiar type in British show business. America's entertainment professionals are smoother. They cultivate a veneer of suavity to mask the shady dealings and flexible morality that pervade the world of sawdust and greasepaint. Val Parnell's tailoring was elegant, but it could not disguise the roughneck beneath. As one of the entertainers who worked for him said, "No monkey business with this guy; he ran that Palladium like a boxing club." But just like the cliché, Val Parnell was meek when around his wife, Helen, a petite ex-dancer.

He was going through a discouraging phase at the Palladium. Having been struck by the notion of booking American movie stars as vaudeville headliners, he was finding them to be weak box-office attractions for his London audience. Mickey Rooney had just been unenthusiastically received, and before him, Rita Hayworth had played a calamitous engagement.

But Parnell was a persistent man, and he had optimistically engaged Danny Kaye for six weeks, starting on February 2, 1948. The supporting bill had been put together by the Lew and Leslie Grade Agency, which booked most of the Palladium shows out of its Regent Street office. For reasons of taste, their own as well as the audience's, and entertainment-union regulations, they chose British singers, and that, rather than anything personal, was why Georgia Gibbs had not been invited.

The Grades had started out as a vaudeville dance team, and they were not only familiar with Danny Kaye; they had actually seen him play that catastrophic 1937 engagement at the Dorchester. At least they had liked him, or so they remembered.

For the Palladium, they put together a traditional vaudeville bill, including a violinist-comic named Ted Ray ("Fiddling and Fooling"), the acrobatic Great Alexander Troupe, a team of black eccentric dancers called—as was done in those times—the Three Chocolateers, and the female ventriloquist Bobbie Kimber. There was also an aerial team, billed as Dorothy Gray and Brother, and Zohra, the contortionist dancer.

For the second half of the show, the program simply listed "The Danny Kaye Hour with 'the Skyrockets' Orchestra conducted by Woolf Phillips." When the time came, the houselights were dimmed, and a hush settled over the place. A disembodied voice announced, ". . . and here is Danny Kaye!" A spotlight appeared at the side of the proscenium, and the audience took its cue, applauding—only there was no Danny Kaye.

It was certainly possible for an American star to be nervous about performing for a British audience, especially considering the recent experiences of Mickey Rooney and Rita Hayworth. Moreover, Kaye never forgot his debacle at the Dorchester Lounge—he stored away the bad times so that his depressions would have something to feed upon during the good times. But now, in this February of 1948, he was near the pinnacle of his career. He was one of the most popular performers in American show business. *A Song Is Born* notwithstanding, he was a major movie star. His stage appearances had been consistently successful. This delay surely could not mean fear.

Finally, according to Harold Hobson's first-night review for the *Sunday Times* (London), Kaye came out from the wings and headed toward center stage "with a long, easy stride . . . moving with utter nonchalance." Another of the British critics wrote, "It took just 95 seconds for [him] to establish himself as the greatest personal success in the history of the English music hall for the last 30 years."

The songs he sang were his signature songs: "Anatole of Paris," "Minnie the Moocher," "Deenah," and a British favorite in cockney style (actually an Australian song), "I've Got a Loverly Bunch of Coconuts." He conducted the orchestra, beginning as usual with the spotlight on his hands. This vanity was neatly cut with the clowned conducting, and then he did his soft-and-easy dance with "Ballin' the Jack." In all, it was the usual Danny Kaye except that nothing about it was usual to the British. They knew him only from his movies. They had never seen this Danny Kaye, the live entertainer, which, of course, was what had made Danny Kaye Danny Kaye.

And then something happened that really was unplanned. Just after he finished singing "Ballin' the Jack," he moved toward the front of the stage. There, at the apron, he impulsively sat down and dangled his long, skinny legs into the orchestra pit. A baby spotlight plucked him out from the darkness. He bummed a cigarette from a man in the front row, lit it, and inhaled while the crowd nestled in the darkness. He puffed on the cigarette and chatted so quietly that he might have been alone with a friend in a sitting room. He talked about the time he had been touring the Orient with a vaudeville troupe. He remembered when the hurricane had hit Osaka while he was onstage. He told the Palladium audience about that time when he had asked for a flashlight and then sat down at the stage apron, just like this, to calm the Japanese audience through the storm.

He drew on the cigarette, lingered a moment over the memory, and then went on chatting for some five minutes. He would later say, of this Palladium opening night, "After sprawling there on the stage apron and having a little visit with the folks until I felt refreshed and relaxed, I stood up and went on with the performance."

The man who stood up was different from the one who had sat down. In those several minutes of sprawling, he became who he had been destined to become ever since singing "*Oyfn Pripetshik*" in the casino at White Roe. Sitting on stage at the London Palladium, he found his place as an entertainer. The tummling was over; he had found his voice. Perhaps he could not be intimate with any individual, and perhaps he never would be, but he certainly could be with an audience.

There would never again be a struggle to describe what he did. He defined what he did. What he did was Danny Kaye.

It was right for the reserved British to be a part of his epiphany.

For them, his stage sprawl and the chat in the darkened theater represented a kind of informality that was warmly American without being brashly so. For them, by reputation a people as unemotional and cool as Kaye, it was a justification by identification. For Kaye, certainly, it was surcease from the spastics of zanyism.

He rose and finished the act, and after fifty-five minutes, his performance complete, he paused and looked through the tight, still silence of the theater. After a very long and very dramatic pause he said quietly and with every drop of his acting skill, "God Save the King."

It is the phrase that traditionally ends every show at the Palladium. It is followed by the rise of the audience as the anthem is sung, and it was sung resoundingly. The performance was not only triumphant; it had created a chemistry with his British audience that can only be compared to the dynamic some lovers experience upon first meeting. It was a chemical attraction, emotional and, in a way, sexual.

But there was nothing mysterious about the performance itself. It was what he had been developing over the course of fifteen years, singing, clowning, chuckling his way through the hour, all in a low-keyed, relaxed, and warm way. He had had a year of six shows a day to polish the act. It was now a summary of practice, refinement, experience, and repetition. There was nothing rash or improvised about it. Rather, his show was careful and professional, inspired by the energy of presence—which is a transmitted sense of extemporaneousness—that made him special as an entertainer and an artist. That opening night, he rose to the occasion; that night, he was electrifying. The following day, the *New York Times* reported:

> Danny Kaye, making his first personal appearance in London last night as the star attraction in the vaudeville bill at the Palladium, scored the greatest success seen in the British music hall in many years. . . . On the stage for nearly an hour, he held the audience for every second of his act with something vital and entertaining. The London drama critics were taken completely by this "superb artist," as the *Daily Herald* critic called him.

Kaye gave the British a good review, too. "People who don't know Englishmen," he said, "think they have a torpid sense of humor. That impression is a caricature. It's as much of a canard as the lie that the British are emotionally unresponsive. I know that's nonsense from my own personal experience."

Hobson, in the *Sunday Times*, captured the exhilaration of that first night. By the very tone of his review, the critic communicated the delight and surprise of the British—not only about Kaye but about *themselves*. Despite their reputation for reserve, they had allowed themselves to fall in love with him.

Hobson realized the work that went into such a performance and was a good enough critic not to let that awareness diminish his own emotional response. He wrote in the *Sunday Times* that Kaye

> seems to be moving with utter nonchalance [and appears] to do nothing, with absolute ease and yet in reality with such precision and finesse that even the way you put your foot down on the floor is a vivid pleasure to the audience . . . his first night at the Palladium, the whole house was literally screaming and yelling in its uncontrolled delight. . . . At one point he has the spotlight thrown on pianist Sam Prager and at the same time he has a spotlight on his own hands, which begin . . . an intricate and complicated dance. . . . I should not be surprised if Mr. Kaye has not put into this brief, careless interlude as much thought and as much rehearsal as some music hall entertainers give to their entire act.
>
> He leaves no inch of the canvas undecorated. . . . When he has convinced the audience that the whole thing is just an improvisation, a thing tossed off carelessly on the spur of the moment, he has, of course, achieved his triumph.

Kaye became so much of a London obsession that one of the newspapers engaged a psychoanalyst to "watch him in action and write a report." The analysis was that "Danny . . . turns an adult audience into playful hysterical children because he himself captures the craziness and impishness of his childhood."

He became the country's darling. The second week of his engagement, on February 11, Princess Elizabeth and the duke of Edinburgh came to see him. The three-month newlyweds sat not in a royal box but with the commoners. After the show, the future queen and her consort visited Kaye's dressing room. They stayed for a half hour, chatting and sipping champagne.

Two nights later, he was at a private party, offering a toast to Sir Laurence Olivier and Vivien Leigh. It was the start of a friendship with the great actor. Some say they had met years before in Hollywood, but in his own memoirs Olivier first mentions seeing Kaye "in this fabulous one-man show at the Palladium."

The actor, at forty, was six years older than Kaye and had just been knighted. He was the youngest of his generation, if not the first, to be thus recognized. (Sir Ralph Richardson was the first.) It was an era of great British actors, but even in such company as Richardson, Alec Guinness, Paul Scofield, and Michael Redgrave, Laurence Olivier was a class apart, just like Kaye.

But as the greatest actor of his time, perhaps of all time, what could he possibly have had in common with an American tummler?

What they shared was the very apartness that comes with being above the crowd. Also, each was so withdrawn as to seem anonymous. Both men realized themselves most fully in performance, where they could bask in public attention. Such people cannot easily relate to individuals. That is close to the essence of the performing nature.

Neither of the two seems to have been a passionate man. Olivier admits as much in his autobiography, *Confessions of an Actor*, and as for Kaye, girlfriends describe him as being more compassionate than passionate. There would be more between him and Olivier in the coming years. For the present, they were becoming friends.

On February 26, Princess Elizabeth returned for a second show, and this time she brought her parents, King George VI and Queen Mary, as well as her sister, Princess Margaret. Although the king and queen had attended special command performances in the past, they had never seen a regularly scheduled show at the Palladium or any other variety theater. And they sat with the commoners. In fact, they sat in the very first row of commoners.

Kaye was presented to the royal family afterward, but in a way Princess Margaret already knew him. It was said that she had been smitten with the breezy American since his first movies. "She saw [them] so often," a magazine reported, "she mastered his intricate dance steps and executed them in the august salons of the Royal Palace." And so, after seeing him at the Palladium, the article continued, "for days she talked of little else than Danny Kaye, the American comedian who was like no other person she had ever seen."

The attractive princess wasn't the only one. All of England seemed smitten with him, but a princess was in a position to do something about it. A *Time* magazine correspondent reported in an interoffice memorandum that when she came a second time, they shared a bottle of champagne in his dressing room, and this time she came unescorted. That was, from the royal point of view, a bit forward. From the Danny Kaye point of view, it was a fair distance to have come from Bradford Street in Brooklyn.

Margaret was herself a performer, not just a cheerful dancer but an amateur musician with a special enthusiasm for Broadway show tunes. She would sing them at private parties, her voice a ladylike tea-dance soprano, and she accompanied herself on the piano—quite respectably, it was said. No less than Noel Coward described her singing as "surprisingly good. She has an impeccable ear. Her piano playing is simple but has perfect rhythm, and her method of singing is really very funny."

With such an affinity, the princess bore a curious resemblance to Kaye's estranged wife; she even looked like Sylvia. Perhaps Margaret was prettier, and she was certainly younger, but, like Sylvia, she was small, dark-haired, and busty. And, like Sylvia, she seemed to dote on Danny.

However, she was, after all, not a Jewish princess but a real one, and as attention from a real princess might suggest, the idea of being Danny Kaye had undergone an incremental change. With the Palladium appearance, he levitated to the international level. He had become, one could say, a world-class entertainer, in the same realm with Coward, Maurice Chevalier, Marlene Dietrich, and in his own way, Laurence Olivier. This elevation, and the epiphany that had been wrought in those moments of sitting on the stage, seemed to affect his personal style, his way of speaking, the way he carried himself and the way he believed in himself. He was a changed man.

But it was not so difficult to bring him down to earth, since he was prone to depression, anyway. London in 1948 could be an anti-Semitic place. People were still identified in newspapers as "Jew." In that regard, Kaye told a friend, "you think it's always so nice, so easy. It isn't always so nice or so easy." To some people, he shrank from his Jewishness. Val Parnell said, "I don't think Danny particularly likes being Jewish, especially here in London, where they don't like the Jews, anyway. He's trying," the Palladium director said, "to be a white one." Parnell would not be the only one to think so.

· · ·

HE WASN'T WITHOUT COMPANIONS. HE HAD EDDIE DUKOFF, AND DE-spite his treatment of the press agent as a flunky, the relationship was still strong enough for Danny to sign over to Eddie 7.5 percent of the profits from all future movies. Phil Goldfarb was in London, too, having flown over to see the show. He and Dukoff amounted to entourage, but Kaye was also surrounded by strangers. His thundering success was bringing all of London to his feet. His effigy was installed among the kings and murderers in the Madame Tussaud Wax Museum. He was unable to walk the streets without being mobbed. A car and driver had to be engaged for him. (It was hardly as common as today.) He could not leave the theater between shows, not even to have dinner. His brother Larry sent weekly shipments of Hebrew National salamis; the Jewish conductor brought food that his mother-in-law had prepared; the Irish cleaning women in the theater began bringing him corned beef and cabbage.

As in America, he enjoyed and encouraged backstage visitors. Among them was Winston Churchill, who feared, jokingly, that Kaye was considering a run against him. Such visitors, along with the royal, titled, and diplomatic set, must have made for a heady brew.

An entertainer's mingling with society usually ends in the dressing room, because show people have always been considered raffish. A backstage visit is usually the end of it, but Kaye moved into the salons. Sharman Douglas was his entrée. The tall, blond, vivacious nineteen-year-old was the daughter of Lewis W. Douglas, an Arizona mining millionaire whose political contributions paid off with an appointment as the ambassador to the Court of St. James's. Sharman left Vassar to go to London with him. She promptly won over the royals with her buoyancy and charmed the public with such spunky doings as getting herself invited for lunch at the mess of the royal grenadiers. The gossip columnist Elsa Maxwell reported in the New York Post that "Sharman is the first American girl invited to Windsor Castle" (except for Wallis Simpson, "but that was another era"), and the British tabloids promptly christened her "Charmin' Sharman."

She was especially winning with the princess in the palace. Margaret had festive energy that was being stifled, and Sharman Douglas was a girl who knew how to have fun. She loved parties, she loved nightclubs, she loved to dance, and she loved the glamour of Danny Kaye. It was she who first brought Princess Elizabeth to the Palladium, and now she became the perfect go-between for Kaye and the whole palace set, especially Princess Margaret.

As he neared the last performance of his six-week engagement, he had played to some 250,000 people. The closing night was bound to be dramatic, and Kaye had a special guest at the show. The William Morris Agency had urged him to invite Georgia Gibbs to fly over, for "that at least," and after not much coaxing, the piqued singer accepted the invitation. The agency was probably seeking to assuage her so that she would rejoin Kaye when his touring resumed in America.

He invited her onstage for that closing show, and they did their whole routine, with her guffaws and the breaking up and even the soft-shoe dance. He performed for two hours and had all twenty-eight hundred in the house singing "Tip Toe Through the Tulips" in separate sections as he conducted the left side of the audience, the right one, and the people in the balcony. At evening's end, the entire theater serenaded him with "For He's a Jolly Good Fellow."

He came home a legend. He also came home to his wife, or as Sylvia put it, "One day, he just came home."

Kitty Carlisle believed that "in his own strange way he loved her, too. She was smart, she was interesting, and I'll tell you something else—she was very, very funny. And that is a very endearing quality in a marriage. She had a funny take on things; she was quick-witted, and she was an original.

"But it was difficult to love her."

Friends believed the couple had reached an "understanding," and one of them said, "It's hard to tell how Sylvia reacted to the terms of the reconciliation, but she undoubtedly found compensation in accepting the conditions. By continuing to be Mrs. Danny Kaye, she continues to be somebody. She remains in a social world that's exciting."

Georgia Gibbs, not surprisingly, sympathized with Eve Arden. "That was a terrible thing he did to her. Eve had left her husband for Danny, but when the moment of truth came, he couldn't do it. She was a terrific dame. He just killed her. She was devastated."

15

*No one will ever possess this guy. I sometimes get the feeling
that the only time in his life that he is completely dedicated
is when he gives himself away publicly and unashamedly.*

—Max Liebman

HE HAD COME HOME TRIUMPHANT, ALTHOUGH, IN A SENSE, HE
WOULD SEEM HOMELESS EVER AFTER, COMPULSIVELY PERIPATETIC, A
man of the world but of only the world. He had also returned with a
truly splendiferous date on his calendar. The palace had put it "at
the request of King George VI," but it sounded more like a command than a request. In fact, the event was called a royal command
performance. Scheduled for the following November, it marked the
first time that a monarch had ever requested, if not actually demanded, that a specific performer of any nationality appear at one
of these annual shows.

In the eight months before that date, Kaye embarked on a new,
five-picture agreement with Warner Brothers. A number of ambitious ideas were discussed, including *The Inspector General, Don
Quixote,* and even *Macbeth,* but they were discussed mainly by
Danny and Sylvia, because Jack Warner, the Warner brother in
charge of production, was pressing for something a little less arty; a
little more in line with what he perceived as the public's expectation
of Danny Kaye. Perhaps the Kayes would give a little on that score,
but they would have no more of the wimpy Danny of the Goldwyn
days. Sylvia wouldn't allow that, and the reconciliation meant that

she was once again running interference for him. Notwithstanding managers and agents, there was nobody you could trust like a relative. That is a truism of Jewish lore, and it seemed an almost paranoid one for the Kayes.

The arrangement with Warner Brothers took that very much into account. Besides writing special material for Danny, Sylvia was going to be the associate producer on his pictures. That merely formalized the basis of her power, which was nothing more complicated than being the star's wife and therefore able to guarantee or withhold his appearance. If, in the past, Sylvia's activity on Danny's behalf could seem the behavior allowed a dominating woman by a passive man, that was no longer exactly the case. The power balance had shifted, for he had demonstrated that he could not only survive without her but even thrive. She needed him as much as he needed her, and perhaps even more, now that she was drawing on a credit balance of guilt.

And so what had once been wielding behind-the-throne power evolved into something akin to doing the dirty work. For instance, Kaye could easily grow impatient with interviewers whose questions were seldom original and frequently inane. At one time he had needed them, but now they needed him, and he wasn't always generous with them. Depending on his mood, he would either accept the reality of the press or simply disappear. He once insisted that Sylvia tell a reporter that she was going to do the interview because "Danny prefers to play with his daughter, Dena, rather than answer stupid questions."

Perhaps that was just as well. When he did sit still for an interview, he might go on automatic pilot and spew out the same old answers; or, if the questions were interesting, he might be talkative and charming. But if an interviewer had the misfortune to arrive on one of Kaye's foul days, there could be trouble. One session began with the question "Mr. Kaye, you're known for your sophisticated humor . . . would you . . . ?"

The interviewer's head was almost bitten off as Kaye interrupted and snapped, "Yeah, I'm very sophisticated. You know I dress up in ladies' clothes. . . ."

THE KAYES AND THE WARNERS FINALLY AGREED THAT HIS FIRST movie for them would be a biography of Harry Lauder. If there was any precedent for what Danny Kaye did, it was what the Scottish entertainer used to do. Working just after the turn of the century, Lauder, like Kaye, had taken a friend-of-the-audience approach, telling anecdotes, confiding his personal feelings, impersonating oddballs, and reenacting incidents from his past. In the midst of the act he might slip into the guise of an old man and then, just as easily, become a child. He sang, but the songs were quirky. "We Parted on the Shore," for instance, was being sung by a sailor who had never been to sea. And Lauder's audience, like Kaye's, believed every word he said. When the Scotsman was described in *Variety* as never seeming to be "on the stage" during his act, the subject might have been Kaye. So a biographical movie was a good idea.

But Sylvia, a liberal since her teens, was having difficulties with Jack Warner's conservative politics. Both she and Danny had signed their names, the previous fall, to a petition directed at the notorious House Un-American Activities Committee (HUAC). The petition condemned "any investigation into the political beliefs of the individual," and the Kayes were among some five hundred movie people who had signed it, along with Humphrey Bogart, Judy Garland, and Gene Kelly.

Danny had also once joined an organization called the Hollywood Democrats Citizen Committee, which was now being labeled as leftist. Yet he was not particularly political. In contrast to Sylvia, he seemed not so much indignant about the thought control being practiced; rather, he seemed worried. "A couple of the members of the [Citizen] Committee," he said, "were somehow involved with communism and Christ, people thought we all were. It was a mess."

Jack Warner was helping to make the mess. Only a few months earlier, in the fall of 1947, he had volunteered to be the first friendly witness at the HUAC hearings. He brought with him a list of employees he boasted he had fired because of their Communist beliefs. This enraged Sylvia, and her animosity only intensified when the Harry Lauder project ran aground. The behavior of the Kayes mirrors the confusion and fear that Communist hunting caused in the Hollywood community. Just that November, Danny accepted an invitation to address an Indiana chapter of the American Veterans Committee. But when the time for the address came, he excused himself. He had a past to worry about. Only a year earlier *Time* magazine (not as an editorial remark but in the context of a news article) referred to him and Fredric March, Olivia de Havilland, and Edward G. Robinson—all members of a Hollywood Independent Citizens' Committee—as "swimming-pool pinks."

There were rumors that Kaye made a secret appearance before HUAC as part of a deal to spare him, but inquiries under the Freedom of Information Act result in no substantiation of that. Moreover, Kaye was quite flippant when asked about a California version of the committee (the State Senate Committee on Un-American Activities). He told a reporter that he had never heard of it and added that what they were saying "sounds to me like a lot of hooey."

The friction between the Kayes and Jack Warner eased when the studio agreed to one of the original titles that Sylvia and Danny had submitted, an adaptation of the Nikolai Gogol play *The Inspector General*. Even with all the delays, the picture—directed by Henry Koster and featuring Walter Slezak and Elsa Lanchester— would be completed in time to be Kaye's sixth in as many years.

Gogol's play is a semiclassic that still receives the occasional repertory-theater production. A satire of political corruption in czarist Russia, its locale was shifted to Napoleonic France by screenwriters Philip Rapp and Harry Kurnitz. It is tempting to suspect that Warner insisted on the shift away from Russia as an anti-Communist gesture, but there is no evidence to prove it. Ultimately, the script retained only the broad outlines of the Gogol original. In the play the hero is a petty rake; in the movie, a penniless vagabond. He is hapless in both, like the Danny Kaye of the Goldwyn movies, although not quite as childish or sexless.

As in Gogol's story, this unlikely fellow is mistaken for a government official and is fawned over by the corrupt politicians of a small town. Aside from the name Farfel, which, with dubious wit, the writers renamed him, they neatly enough accomplished the goals of the Warners and the Kayes: satisfying the public's perception of Danny Kaye without making his character a complete twit.

Kaye would accomplish more than that. After the family-oriented Goldwyn movies—family oriented being a euphemism for childish—not only would this be his first adult movie; it would at last display some of his myriad talents. In it he projects a personality of charm, brightness, and feeling. Costumed with particular dash, he is romantic and even sexy—fit, agile, and healthy. His smile is dazzling, with teeth and hair made perfect. In fact, his hair appears a little too perfect, not only tinted blond again but waved.

His performance is a model of acting ability, an instinctual gift developed with thought and tempered by discipline. It is the work of a stage comedian, an actor with comic timing. This is Kaye's first real dramatic challenge, and he meets it, inspired by having a char-

acter to play and freed of inhibition by the period setting and costumes, which invariably have a liberating effect on actors. His
performance is physical, too, for he is comfortable with his body and
uses it as an acting tool, moving with grace and agility. This creates
a real sense of energy and imbues the character with life as well as
humor.

As for Sylvia's songs, there are too many (five) for a nonmusical
film, and they are but variations on her familiar patter. They also
force Kaye to break character, for just as he establishes Farfel as a
fellow who is trying to be dishonest, not knowing the quality of his
own decency, he must burst into numbers that belong in Camp
Tamiment.

If Sylvia was not developing as a composer/lyricist, Danny Kaye
demonstrated in this film how much he was growing as a performer.
And although these songs should not have been in the movie, his
singing of them showed what made him the toast of London. For
instance, in "The Gypsy Drinking Song" he pretends to play the
violin with astonishing credibility, his fingerwork nimble and his
bowing assured. The soulful look on his rapt face is worth the number alone. This piece also incorporates his stage routine of subdivid-
ing an audience, assigning sounds to each section and then
conducting the different groups. It gives a good idea of the tummler
grace with which he enchanted thousands at the Palladium. Otherwise "The Gypsy Drinking Song" is juvenile. ("Drink to me only
with thine eyes / And I will drink with my nose.")

Another piece, "Soliloquy for Three Heads," is staged in a tech-
nically adventurous way. Kaye is simultaneously seen as four fellows, his own character plus a Russian, a German, and an
Englishman. That makes for four voices singing harmony in four
dialects. The trick anticipates the multiple recording techniques that
the record industry would not develop for several years. Kaye's musicianship, his flair, and his accents are on versatile display here.

Finally, Sylvia managed to slip in a sneezing routine, which she
happily revived as the family signature. It was an old joke, but it
meant the old team to her. Then, with the picture finished, he left
for London, and this time, she went along.

IN RESPONSE TO ITS ANNOUNCEMENT THAT MAIL ORDERS WERE BEING
accepted, the Palladium received some 100,000 requests for the

roughly twenty-eight hundred seats available for the single show. Much of London was still beneath rubble, and almost everything was scarce, yet the public was undaunted by the stunning price of tickets, 10 and 20 pounds ($42 and $84). Scalpers would ultimately resell them for five times as much.

By tradition, a royal command performance was made up of a major star supported by a bill of entertainers who had been of note or interest during the year. The show was a benefit for the Variety Artistes Benevolent Fund, and this one would have thirteen acts. That promised a long evening, one that was going to range from the great American tap dancers the Nicholas Brothers to the sugary orchestra the Melachrino Strings.

For weeks the newspapers had been fueling public excitement over Danny's return to the British Isles. It was as if he represented all the Yanks who had come to England's rescue during the war. For a people who had survived a decade of sacrifice and were still doing without, the night at the Palladium signified a sentimental and glamorous connection, a communion of the American jester and the beloved Crown.

His reception, for a jester, was a king's. The management of the Dorchester, remembering well that a decade earlier it had fired Kaye from Nick Long & Co., offered him its very finest suite, not only free but repainted in his choice of color. With no need for bitterness, he accepted. It was compensation.

On the day of the command performance, he was asked to give a press conference and pose for pictures with some of the others on the program. The youngest was an adolescent singer named Julie Andrews. The future star was being promoted as "a thirteen-year-old coloratura with the voice of an adult." She was appearing at the Starlight Roof of the Hippodrome Theatre, where the management was using an old gimmick for her. The youngster would sit in the audience, and when the master of ceremonies asked if anyone cared to sing, she would volunteer. The audience would be delighted, because, as she remembered, "nobody expected this big voice out of a little kid." At thirteen, Andrews wasn't so little, but she was dressed in "a white dress with a pink underlay—sort of chiffony or Georgette, with puffy shoulders. The whole idea," she remembered, "was to make me look younger than I was."

She was wearing jodhpurs when she arrived at the Danny Kaye press conference. She had not heard about the photo session until the day of the concert and had come straight from the country, where she had been riding. "I looked absolutely ridiculous," she remembered, "with this huge toothy smile. And they plunked me on his lap."

The photographers crowded around the two of them, and as the bulbs flashed, Kaye made small talk to relax the youngster and create a semblance of candid pictures.

"What are you going to be singing tonight at the command performance?" he asked.

"Oh," she said self-effacingly, "I don't think you would know it."

She really did believe it was "a rather obscure song."

Kaye smiled gently and urged her: "Tell me what it is."

"Well," she said hesitantly, "it's the 'Polonaise' from *Mignon*."

"Oh!" He beamed. "The one that goes da-da-DUM-da-da," and he hummed it through. "He knew it quite familiarly," she remembered, "and I was astounded. Terribly impressed. He was divine. He could not have been more gentle, more kind, more truly interested. I sort of instantly fell in love."

Then they all left to change costume, she into her little-girl dress and Kaye into his usual brown tweed sport jacket and dark brown trousers.

When he returned to the Palladium with Sylvia, their limousine was greeted by a throng of screaming young women—England's answer to America's bobby-soxers. The fans were called "hankie hatters" because they wore kerchiefs tied over their heads, and this time they were not organized by Eddie Dukoff.

The evening was already two hours long when Kaye strolled out to the ovation that the audience rose to greet him with. The royal party was in a special box—King George and Queen Mary, Princess Elizabeth and the duke of Edinburgh, and Princess Margaret. The "royal box" is not a permanently designated box but whichever one is used for the royals on a given evening. It does not even have to be a box. Any group of seats can be designated as "royal" and be simply squared off with garlands of flowers. A box is preferable, as it can be more easily made secure and can also be seen by everyone in the theater, but the royal party can as well be seated in the front row of the balcony.

Kaye bowed to them and then, much to the surprise of the entire hall, did not begin his performance with one of his comedy turns. Instead, he opened with the Harry Lauder classic "Just a Wee Deoch-an-Doruis."

It made for a *coup de théâtre*, and he then turned to the Sylvia Fine numbers that he had downplayed during their separation. As a result, most of the Kaye/Fine classics were new to the British. He followed with his easygoing dance number "Ballin' the Jack." Then he did the new routine, the one that had sent him over the top the last time, sprawling downstage with his feet in the orchestra pit while he rested and smoked and chatted.

After the breather, he sang the Londoners' favorite "I've Got a Loverly Bunch of Coconuts," followed by his conducting the orchestra.

He called out a team that had already performed—Bud Flanagan and Chesney Allen, who were a great audience favorite—and all three sang the cockney standard "Underneath the Arches." Kaye seemed incapable of doing wrong. With Flanagan and Allen remaining onstage, he brought out the whole company—all the acts that had already performed—to join him in singing "There's No Business Like Show Business."

With the Palladium in a euphoric state, Kaye, like a pilot at the controls of an airliner, eased up on the throttle and let the place settle down. Then, as the entire company remained onstage, he did what Al Jolson used to do. (Kaye once said that he aspired to be the pure entertainer that Jolson was.) Now he performed for the actors as well as the audience.

The song was "Minnie the Moocher," and beginning with the performers onstage, he got all the responsive singing he might have wished for. After bringing the audience into it, he invited the royal party to join in.

Soon the king of England himself was grinning as Danny sang, "Oh, hi-de-hi-de-hi."

And then the king repeated, "Oh, hi-de-hi-de-hi."

And Danny sang, "Oh, ho-de-ho-de-ho."

And the king repeated, "Oh, ho-de-ho-de-ho."

Who, indeed, was the fool?

When it was finished, Kaye looked solemnly toward the royal box and said, "God Save the King." The audience rose and sang the anthem. The show was over.

Afterward, Sylvia was presented to the royal family, and Princess Elizabeth asked her to "tell your husband how much we enjoyed seeing him again." Then Ambassador and Mrs. Lewis Douglas gave a private party for Danny, and that began a week of socializing in his honor. The events ranged from a show-business party at Val and

Helen Parnell's home in Marble Arch to a luncheon in his honor at the Savoy Hotel, where Sir George Aylwen, the lord mayor of London, offered the toast "I'd like to see every meeting of ministers preceded by a little turn of Danny Kaye. That might even have an effect on Mr. Vishinsky [Andrei Vishinsky, foreign minister] of the Soviet Union."

When the applause subsided and the glasses were emptied, the room's eyes turned toward Kaye. Taking the cue, he offered his own toast. "I think emotions are the same the world over. I think they are just covered by different veneers—all the people of the world are made up of the same sort of emotions that we have back home, the same likes, dislikes, loves, hates."

The toast made the local newspapers. *Life* magazine scoffed, "Even Danny Kaye's corniest platitudes are news in Britain," but if he wasn't a diplomat or a philosopher, he was certainly smooth. There weren't many show people who could read such lines convincingly offstage.

"I am proud to feel," Kaye concluded, still holding his glass aloft, "that I've been able to reach you and find the same warmth that I experience in my own country. I have discovered that we are one people."

Such fancy socializing, coming in the wake of the royal command performance, lifted him above the common show-business herd. He had levitated as if in a magic act; risen above stardom. He began to tell friends that he wouldn't be surprised if he were knighted.

Three weeks later, he was back on earth, onstage at the Roxy Theater in New York. His act was business as usual, including all the old routines with Georgia Gibbs as well as some accidental new ones. For instance, at one show, after he did the soft-shoe dance with her, one of Gibbs's false eyelashes came loose with perspiration. As she peeled it off, he held his hand out like a schoolteacher with a misbehaving student. Georgia handed over the guilty eyelash, and as the audience tittered, he pressed it onto his upper lip. Snapping his heels to attention, he shot his arm out and cried, *"Sieg heil!,"* launching into an imitation of Adolf Hitler at a giant rally.

At another performance, while they were doing the ad-libs and break-ups, a sharp and piercing voice came cracking through the cavernous theater. The cry rang all the way down from the balcony, and it was so peculiar a sound, so striking, that the whole audience laughed at it.

But a scream followed, and that stifled the laughter in an instant. Then the audience began laughing nervously at itself as Danny and Georgia resumed their routine. After the show, they were met in the wings by an Eddie Dukoff whose excitement was not to be contained.

"This is fantastic!" he cried. "This is going to make every paper in town!"

Gibbs and Kaye were bewildered.

"Did you hear that scream?" he asked. "Well, did you?"

"Of course we did," Georgia said. "Did somebody have a heart attack?"

"There was a pregnant woman in the balcony," Dukoff said breathlessly, "and she was laughing so hard she broke her water! She just gave birth in the first-aid station downstairs! Is this great? I can see it already: 'Kaye Makes Woman Laugh So Hard She Breaks Water.' "

But when he tried to get the woman's name for the newspapers, she refused to give it.

"She couldn't let the story out," a forlorn Dukoff later said, "because she wasn't married."

The 1949 release of *The Inspector General* brought Kaye his second consecutive box-office disappointment. The receipts of $2.2 million were even worse than those for *A Song Is Born*. Given the unpleasant Warner-Kaye relations, there was no resistance from the studio when Sylvia and Danny asked to be released from the contract. A week later, he had a new agreement with 20th Century-Fox. Then he turned around and went back to London for a second engagement at the Palladium, and this time, the entire six weeks were sold out in advance.

His bill included Peter Sellers, who was not yet an international movie star and, from the looks of his act as a stand-up comedian, would be lucky to play Liverpool. This journeyman comic did impressions of George Sanders, Peter Lorre, and, inevitably, Walter Huston singing "September Song."

Kaye made some slight changes in his act. He added the popular spiritual "Dem [Dry] Bones." Another new number, "Flamenco," gave him a chance to sing in Spanish dialect and do a comic takeoff on flamenco dancing. He also included Sylvia's "Gypsy Drinking Song" from *The Inspector General*. But he kept "Ballin' the Jack" and of course his traditional finale, "Minnie the Moocher."

Royalty at all levels seemed to consider him their private jester.

They wielded their special privilege for seats and socializing, although there was a complex and changing pattern as to who was catering, who was pampering, who was condescending, and who was pandering. Princess Marina, the duchess of Kent, came to his second show, on April 26. A Greek princess, she had married George, the youngest son of King George V. He had been killed in the Second World War.

The rumors about a Danny-Marina connection were not making the tabloids the way those about Danny and Margaret now were, but it was the likelier romance, and it would prove the more durable relationship. That night at the Palladium, the duchess brought her two children backstage after the performance. They all four went out for supper. Sylvia seemed to have learned, like Phil Goldfarb, when to get lost. Perhaps it was worth it to her to enjoy the social perquisites of his British celebrity. She was certainly becoming impressed with herself. When her friend Kitty Carlisle showed up, Sylvia said that she and Danny were "too busy with royalty" to see her. There were a couple of evenings with the titled that Sylvia described to Kitty as "very intimate" during which she and Kaye sang and she accompanied at the piano. They were still singing for their suppers, at least when she was in London, but she did not stay.

Going to dinner with the duchess of Kent was a challenge. All twenty-eight hundred of the Palladium audience seemed to be waiting for Danny outside the stage door. Traffic was jammed for blocks. The party had to be escorted from the theater by the police, and it would be a daily problem.

Whatever freedom from Sylvia he exercised, it was not necessarily of a sexual nature. Sex is a powerful force in many lives, but not every life. Danny Kaye's seems to have been overtaken by other forces, most notably that of stardom. It might have been heady enough and even climactic enough to displace his sexuality. There certainly is no evidence that he was sleeping with the duchess of Kent or anybody else. He was not demonstrative in public or, by all accounts, in private, either. He was only demonstrative about entertaining. One evening, while at the BBC studios for an interview, he peeked into a studio where a very proper and conservative businessman was looking extremely nervous. Upon inquiring, Kaye learned that this was Sir William Rootes, a veritable lion of British industry. Sir William was momentarily scheduled to go on the air with an interviewer. He was going over his prepared remarks, clearing his throat, pulling the microphone toward him, squaring off his manuscript, and being nervous in general.

Suddenly, he looked up in alarm. The studio door had burst open, and a maniacal Kaye had leapt in, screeching like a banshee. The program was to go on in ninety seconds, but Kaye grabbed Sir William's manuscript and tossed it in the air, babbling as the pages scattered and fluttered to the floor. Then he put a friendly hand on the shoulder of the appalled businessman. "You must relax, Sir William," he said. "You must just treat your manuscript as if you despised it, Sir William."

Rootes's interviewer, Beverley Nichols, called the effect "pandemonium, nightmare, torture. This, we all thought, is the end. We shall be publicly disgraced. We shall go on the air like gibbering idiots."

But with only fifteen seconds remaining until broadcast time, Kaye somehow reassembled the script, set the pages neatly before Rootes, and backed out the door through which he had so alarmingly and somewhat excitedly entered. Now he slipped into the control room, and from there he gazed through the big window, smiling serenely at those who had not welcomed his most recent visit. He beamed approvingly and mimed applause. Then he started to make faces, rolling his eyeballs and pulling at his hair. Finally, he dipped down and came up doing a handstand.

When the program was over, Beverley Nichols shook Danny's hand and chuckled with what sounded like relief rather than appreciation. Sir William cleared his throat and shook his head in bewilderment, mumbling "old fellow" a few times in Danny's direction. He seemed to need more time for a proper recovery.

Although England was beside itself with love for him and while he was the darling of British royalty and the social circles surrounding it, naturally, Kaye was more comfortable with show people. There were newspaper accounts about his joining parties at Notley Abbey, the weekend home of Laurence Olivier and Vivien Leigh, an hour's drive from London. His entrée was Noel Coward, whom he had gotten to know through Gertrude Lawrence during the *Lady in the Dark* days. John Cottrell writes in *Laurence Olivier* (Prentice-Hall, 1975) that whenever Danny and Sylvia were guests at the Notley parties, "Sir Laurence at once became Larry the vaudeville comic, slapping a cheesecake in his own face during lunch and afterward joining Kaye in uproarious singing duets."

Kaye also visited with George Bernard Shaw, and that was quite a step up for a tummler from Brooklyn. It happened through a tea invitation from Stephen Winsten, the author of *Days with Bernard Shaw*. Winsten was the famous playwright's neighbor in the village of Ayot St. Lawrence, but while he told Kaye there was a possibility of meeting Shaw, he made no arrangements. He merely showed Danny through his garden. Suddenly, without notice or warning, Shaw opened the low, latched garden gate. "He was coming in," Winsten remembered, "for a little chat under the trees."

He was a frail and ancient echo of the tall, lean, bearded, tremendously vital George Bernard Shaw—the most intellectual dramatist in the history of the English-speaking theater. His mustache, bushy eyebrows, and flowing beard that once were as red as Danny's hair were now a ghostly white. He wore dark glasses to protect his eyes from the not very bright sunlight.

"Mr. Shaw," Winsten said by way of simple introduction, "this is Mr. Kaye."

The playwright did not seem to recognize the name.

"This is Mr. Danny Kaye," Winsten said, adding with a tease, "your brother entertainer."

That prompted Shaw to ponder until he brightly recalled, "I saw your name in the paper." But then he scratched his head. "Tell me," he asked mischievously, "in what connection?"

"I do a little turn at the Palladium," Kaye said with a smile.

"Comedian?" Shaw asked.

"No, a busker."

A busker is an itinerant British entertainer.

"How long are you staying?" Shaw asked.

"As long as they will have me."

"Humph," the old man snorted. "They still take *me* at ninety-three!"

"After that," Kaye later remembered, "he entertained us with stories, one after another." Indeed, as Winsten recalled, Shaw told anecdotes, recited from Shakespeare, and even sang. Kaye was mesmerized. "I just listened," he said. "The garden virtually vibrated with Shaw's beautiful voice."

Finally, he saw in George Bernard Shaw what others—the Broadway director Jed Harris, for instance—had seen in the great man. Harris had observed that "Shaw was always 'on' as an actor" and applauded the playwright to his face because "he put on a whole performance for me." Danny Kaye reacted in much the same way. "I can see, Mr. Shaw," he said, "why you despise actors. It is because there is not one equal to you."

The old man barely concealed a grin within the bushes of mustache and beard, and he snorted, "I do *not* despise actors." He proceeded to do an impression of Henry Irving, the nineteenth-century thespian. "You may call him a ham," he said, "but I have never yet come across anyone like him."

Impressions were something Danny Kaye knew a thing or two about, and—as one redhead appreciating and enjoying another—he followed Shaw's imitation of Henry Irving with his own of Winston Churchill. When he mentioned that Churchill had visited him backstage, Shaw's interest was piqued.

"Was he smoking a cigar? I have always wanted to know whether or not it was a real cigar. I have heard that it is a stage prop."

"Some people," Kaye said, "think your beard and eyebrows are stage effects."

Shaw shot over a quick glance from one entertainer to another and moved the conversation along. "Have music halls changed much? I haven't been to one for many years."

Kaye then described his own act. He hoped, he said, to break through the wall between entertainer and audience. "When I am tired," he said, "I lie down flat on the stage, make myself comfortable, and talk about things in general. Tonight, for example, I'll talk about the peaceful English countryside." That was his way of telling Shaw that he would not make this visit part of his show. "I might walk off the stage among the people, to make them part of the act. I am all wound up when I come onto the stage, and as I unwind, I let go and give and give till I can go on forever."

After some three hours of this folderol under the trees, Shaw agreed to be filmed with Winsten's home-movie camera. The neighbor promised it would be just "for the entertainment of myself and my family." They decided to have Shaw enter the garden on tiptoe from behind Kaye, surprising him with a tap on the shoulder. When Danny turned around, the two would embrace. There was no dialogue, for it was a silent movie, and as Kaye later told a reporter for the *New York Times*, "The whole act was spontaneous and carried on in mime." As the reporter had heard it, "Danny sat on the lawn being whimsical, and GBS slapped his knee."

The neighbor, Stephen Winsten, remembered that during the

moviemaking, Shaw admired Kaye's brightness. "I really shouldn't like you, Danny," he said. "If you have your way, you'll do away with authors. You do whatever comes into your head."

Then, after hanging his head in mock modesty, Kaye looked up with a grin and said, "Mr. Shaw, you're a better actor than all of us."

All of this was heady stuff and if Kaye seemed even more of a snob to those who already considered him one, not everyone had the same opinion. For instance, Lillian Lux, a girlfriend from the tummler days, arrived in London with her husband's Yiddish theater company, and she visited Kaye backstage. He gave her as much time and attention as he did to any star or socialite. "We compared pictures of Danny's two-year-old and my four-year-old twins"—he was perfectly capable of being friends with a former lover—"and when he complained about not being able to go out and eat, I told my friend Becky Cohen. She had a small Jewish restaurant on the East End. We brought him a roasted duck and gefilte fish."

As Becky and Lillian were leaving, Danny asked if the restaurant served cabbage soup. A few days later, Becky brought it, and he was so entranced that soon afterward he slipped out of the Palladium between the early and late shows and visited the restaurant himself. It is fair to assume that he knew what such an appearance would do for her business.

Celebrity is a commodity that invites using, whether for business, social, or egotistical purposes. Everyone seemed to want a piece of Kaye, none more than Princess Margaret. She became a regular visitor to the Palladium, accompanied by Sharman Douglas, who would then escort the princess to Danny's dressing room after the show. They would all three go out for midnight supper, and inevitably, photographs of them began to show up in the tabloids. Much as these pictures implied that Sharman was with Danny, nobody was fooling the palace press corps.

Lloyd Moseley of the *Daily Express* was one who was certain there was a Margaret-Danny romance. Mixing his metaphors into a bitter brew, he wrote of Danny's return to London: "They brought out the fatted calf, roasted it and served it to Danny Kaye on a red carpet." Now he began to note Kaye's personal relationship with the royals and with Princess Margaret in particular. When, in collaboration with Charles Higham, he wrote *Elizabeth and Philip, the Untold Story,* he spoke unequivocally about a romance between Kaye and Princess Margaret.

Princess Margaret became romantically drawn to Kaye. She was fascinated by his copper hair, handsome face and lithe figure. At first the King and Queen were amused by the intimate friendship and charmed by it. But gradually, the extent of Margaret's very warm interest disturbed her parents. There was something grotesquely improbable in the thought that she might even want to marry him—and he was married. His wife, the gifted lyricist Sylvia Fine, was in and out of London.

This is an imaginative report. There is no way to know whether the romance was consummated, but it seems fair to respect the possibility that the relationship between the entertainer and the princess was romantic in nature. Certainly Margaret was spending a lot of time with Danny, and she was plainly enjoying it.

When Sharman convinced her father to give a masquerade party at the embassy, even Princess Elizabeth got into costume, arriving as a chambermaid, with the duke of Edinburgh as a butler. Surprisingly, Sharman didn't seem to bother with a costume, simply walking around with a picture frame and being a *Portrait of a Lady*.

The sensation of the evening was Princess Margaret, who arrived as Madame Butterfly, complete with a wig and a Japanese robe. She also brought a second costume, and late in the evening she changed into it, reappearing as Mademoiselle Fifi, with a shockingly short dancer's skirt. Then Sharman also emerged in a brief dancing costume, and they were joined by six other young women to dance the cancan in their frilly skirts and high-heeled shoes.

The idea was Danny's and Margaret's. He had staged and rehearsed the girls, and there were nervous giggles when the chorus line kicked and squealed, even though their abandon was decorous. And while it was reported that a pair of royal panties was in evidence, an eyewitness insisted that "a glimpse of regal thighs was restricted, since kicks went no higher than knee height."

Near the end of the Palladium engagement, Georgia Gibbs arrived for an engagement of her own. It was at a local supper club called the Colony Club. Finding the city still heady with "Danny Fever" she determined to see his closing performance. Finding that there were no tickets to be had at any price, she correctly assumed that Fishel Goldfarb was in London for the closing, but not even he could help. And so she tried Helen Parnell, the wife of the Palladium's managing director.

"I'd like a ticket," Gibbs pleaded. "Just one, for the closing show." The last show always had a special excitement about it.

"Well, Georgia," Helen Parnell said, "why don't you just come and sit with us in Val's box?"

The singer sensed the special excitement in the theater as soon as she entered the crowded lobby. Joining the Parnells, she glanced over to the adjacent box and saw the American comedian Red Skelton. He was booked into the Palladium to follow Danny.

Skelton was a tall man, six feet four inches, and of course red-haired like Kaye. Their performing styles were not dissimilar, although Skelton was more of a clown and goofier. Danny, despite the wimpy character he had been playing in the Goldwyn movies, never played the fool in his personal appearances, not even for a joke. That was wise, because his eyes would have given him away. They were the eyes of an observer.

Skelton had an innocence that Kaye lacked. When Kaye tried to be silly, there was a snideness about it, because it was disingenuous. But Skelton was a true naif. He was not afraid to play the fool; he did not consider himself above it. He worked within the confines of slapstick and sketch comedy and had fewer dimensions as an entertainer than Danny Kaye; he was not the inspired artist that Kaye was; in fact, he might well have been inspired *by* Kaye. Others were. Just that year, Dean Martin and Jerry Lewis were creating a sensation, with Lewis doing an outright imitation of Danny Kaye.

But Red Skelton had his own qualities as a funny man, and they were considerable. Moreover, he was beloved.

There was a tradition at the Palladium that the outgoing star introduced the incoming one from the stage. That performer would be seated in a box prominently draped with bunting. Skelton was seated in such a box, along with his wife, Georgia, his conductor, David Rose, his biographer, Gene Fowler, and a priest, who was along for good luck.

"Red was in a terrible spot," Gibbs felt, "because nobody would want to follow Danny Kaye. He was so popular he could have been king. Untouchable. And so Red was very nervous, naturally."

The big comic leaned forward throughout the show, his face cradled in his hands, his elbows on the box's brass rail, the stage light reflected in his hopeful face. But as Danny eased into his closing minutes, he began to do a drunk routine. Gibbs turned to Parnell's wife.

A sixteen-year-old David Daniel Kaminski in 1929, his first summer as a tummler at White Roe Lake House. *(Courtesy of Rose Kaye Goldman.)*

Dramatic acting came with startling ease to this twenty-year-old who had never even seen a play. *(New York Public Library at Lincoln Center, Billy Rose Theater Collection.)*

Young Mr. and Mrs. Kaminski in Brooklyn for their second wedding ceremony, the Jewish one. Danny had not yet legally changed his name. *(Courtesy of Rose Kaye Goldman.)*

The official wedding picture. *(Courtesy of Rose Kaye Goldman.)*

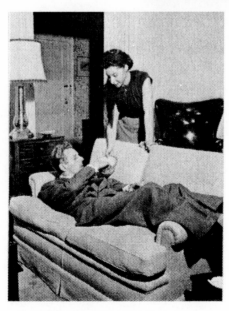

The couple at home for public-relations purposes. *(New York Public Library at Lincoln Center, Billy Rose Theater Collection.)*

With Gertrude Lawrence and Noel Coward.
(Courtesy of Rose Kaye Goldman.)

Card tricks with actor Clifton Webb at the Stork Club. *(New York Public Library at Lincoln Center, Billy Rose Theater Collection.)*

Jack Benny was Kaye's mentor as well as the model for his elegance of manner. *(Courtesy of Rose Kaye Goldman.)*

Let's Face It!, with Vivian Vance and then Eve Arden to Kaye's left. *(Courtesy of Rose Kaye Goldman.)*

Danny and Eve Arden were lovers when they appeared together on the cover of the *New York Sunday Mirror* magazine section on December 14, 1941. Arden stayed with the romance for five years, but when Sylvia gave birth to Dena, the triangle finally reached a crisis. Danny left for Eve, but in the end he could not break free of Sylvia. (*Courtesy of the Hearst Corporation.*)

Kaye enjoyed dugout visits with the Brooklyn Dodgers and remained faithful to the team when they moved to Los Angeles. *(Courtesy of Rose Kaye Goldman.)*

"The Lobby Number" from Kaye's first movie, *Up in Arms.* *(Copyright 1943 Samuel Goldwyn Pictures.)*

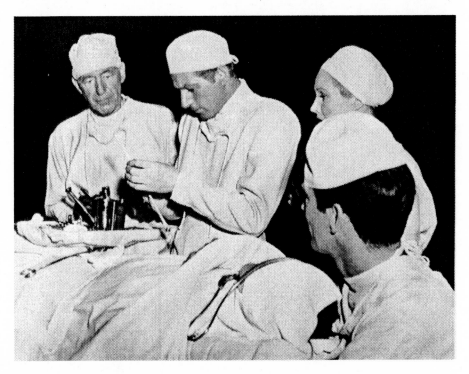

The classic operating-room sequence from *The Secret Life of Walter Mitty*. Virginia Mayo looks over Kaye's shoulder as he uses a fountain pen to fix a delicate surgical machine, restoring it to *pocketa* purr. (*Copyright 1946 Samuel Goldwyn Pictures.*)

Impersonating the nightclub singer Kay Thompson.
(Associated Press, Wide World Photos, Inc.)

With George Bernard Shaw and their host, the writer Stephen Winsten.
(Associated Press, Wide World Photos, Inc.)

These are the so-called drag outfits in which Kaye and Laurence Olivier as well as Vivien Leigh would sing "Triplets," here at a 1950 benefit in London. *(Courtesy of Paul Popper, Popperfoto.)*

There was a rare-for-Kaye sexual magnetism in this moment with Gwen Verdon *(left)* in *On the Riviera. (Copyright 1950 20th Century-Fox.)*

Georgia Gibbs, falling apart on cue as she did in hundreds of appearances with Kaye, here at the RKO Keith in Boston. (Stardom *magazine.*)

High stepping and prancing through "Tip Toe Through the Tulips."
Kaye's performing charm was unique, and no entertainer was ever more
ingratiating. (Stardom *magazine.*)

With his thirteen-year-old Dena.
(*Associated Press, Wide World Photos, Inc.*)

Kaye had only glancing contact with children on his final Unicef tour in 1975. It would be a public-relations disaster. *(New York Public Library at Lincoln Center, Billy Rose Theater Collection.)*

Despite his interest in medicine and health, Kaye aged prematurely. His haggard appearance reflected an assortment of operations as well as, perhaps, a lifetime of internalized emotions. *(New York Public Library at Lincoln Center, Billy Rose Theater Collection.)*

Unique beyond dispute and a very great performer. *(New York Public Library at Lincoln Center, Billy Rose Theater Collection.)*

"Helen," she whispered, "has Danny been doing this bit?"

The petite Mrs. Parnell turned in her seat. "No, Georgia. I've never seen this before. This is a new thing."

Puzzled at first, Gibbs then felt stunned—not because the routine was new to her. She was stunned because it was a drunk bit, and a drunk was one of Red Skelton's classic routines. In fact, Skelton's drunk was as important to him as "Minnie the Moocher" was to Kaye.

"Danny never did a drunk bit in his life," she would later say, and it was plain that Kaye's ego had grown to a vulnerable size. "What he was doing," Gibbs remembered with enduring shock and dismay, "was taking the edge off Red's 'Give me another gin' bit. *He was doing Red Skelton's act!*"

She glanced over to the adjacent box.

"Red was ashen," and she had an alarming thought. With Val Parnell roaming the theater, she turned to his wife. "Look, Helen, I think you'd better get Eddie Dukoff up here and remind him that Danny has to introduce Red Skelton."

"Georgia," the little ex-dancer said, "what on earth are you saying? That's our tradition. *Of course* he's going to."

"I'm telling you, Helen—"

Somewhat impatiently, Mrs. Parnell rose, walked to the rear of the box, and telephoned backstage. Moments later, Eddie Dukoff appeared, and Helen Parnell pointed toward Skelton in the adjacent box. "Tell Danny," she whispered to the press agent, "that—you know." She nodded toward Skelton. "Tell him not to forget to—"

As Dukoff later told Gibbs, he went back, stood in the wings, and attracted Danny's attention. "Don't forget!" he whispered. "Red Skelton!" And he pointed out toward the box with the draped flag. Kaye nodded.

With the drunk business concluded, Danny went into the windup of his act, singing "Minnie the Moocher" and getting the whole audience involved. Skelton knew that it was the last number in Kaye's act and straightened his tie. He extended his arms and pushed himself back from the velvet ledge of the box, half-rising in his seat. His lips were pressed together, and he was perspiring, but he ran a hand through his hair and smiled in anticipation of the spotlight, dimples breaking deeply into his full cheeks.

Kaye was below in his brown tweed jacket and brown trousers, "his blond hair," Gibbs remembered, "shining in the light."

With "Minnie the Moocher" finished and with the audience still cheering, he raised his arms for silence.

"Thank you, ladies and gentlemen," he said, and he paused and looked up toward the balcony. His eyes swept the house. "God Save the King."

Gibbs swore there was an audible gasp from the audience. The cue for the anthem meant that the show was over. The slur of Skelton was unmistakable—and terrible. Georgia Skelton began to cry. Helen Parnell whispered aloud, "What is the matter with that man? It's tradition! That's never been done!"

The Palladium audience had no choice but to rise and sing "God Save the King."

16

I am prepared to believe that the sense of romance in those of
our brothers and sisters who incline towards love of their own
sex is heightened to a more blazing pitch than in those who
think of themselves as "normal."

—Laurence Olivier, *Confessions of an Actor*

HE DID NOT GO DIRECTLY HOME AFTER THE PALLADIUM ENGAGE-
MENT; HE WENT TO SCOTLAND FOR A BOOKING IN GLASGOW. PRINCESS
Margaret also left England, even though it wasn't until September
that she was due in the Netherlands for the installation of Princess
Juliana as queen. Nevertheless, she set out months earlier for a long
stretch of traveling on the Continent. Some believed it was related
to her involvement with Kaye; that she was determined to put the
rumors to rest and would stay away until that was accomplished. In
their book, Moseley and Higham insist that the princess was agoniz-
ing over the situation. She "suffered from migraine headaches or,"
they add bitchily, "occasional hangovers, and frequently would take
to her bed. Her feelings for Kaye deepened daily."

This is not only melodramatic but no substantiation is given,
and nobody was going to get any more on the subject from Kaye.
When a friend asked him about a romance with the princess, as
usual in such matters, he smiled noncommittally and said nothing.
If there, in fact, was a romantic—not necessarily sexual—element
in their relationship, which seems probable, there was no hope for
it. Kaye was not only married, he was not only an entertainer, he

was Jewish. The realities of palace life are never dealt with in fairy tales; as far as Buckingham Palace was concerned, Sylvia Fine's prince was going to remain Princess Margaret's frog.

Kaye's reception in Glasgow was a repeat of London, and during the engagement he paid a visit to Sir Harry Lauder. There was a natural affinity between the old entertainer and the thirty-seven-year-old American who had once been cast to play him in a biographical movie. Lauder presented Kaye with one of his signature walking sticks, gnarled and crusty, and the gesture typified the treatment the younger man could expect as an international institution. On closing night, the Scottish audience serenaded him with the endearing air "Will Ye No' Come Back Again?"

They might have been singing about whether he would ever come back anywhere. He was almost always on the road. This time, he had been away for three months, and he nearly didn't make it back at all, because he was involved in two scares. The first occurred when he left Stephen Winsten's house after the visit with George Bernard Shaw. As Kaye stepped into the street, a car knocked him down. Luckily, he sustained only rib bruises, but they were painful enough to disrupt his next show, and he had to leave the stage midway through. After his chest was taped, he continued at the Palladium without missing a performance.

The second close call was on July 7, 1949, during the flight back to New York. His Pan American Airways plane, a Boeing Strato-cruiser, was flying at eighteen thousand feet, having taken off only hours earlier from the Shannon, Ireland, airport. Suddenly, the left outboard of its four engines lost all power. Then the faulty engine's propeller blew off, and a fire broke out in the wing.

The pilot swerved the plane to avoid its being hit by its own propeller and then dipped it into a speed dive in the hope of extinguishing the fire. The flight attendants instructed the passengers to put on their life jackets. The Atlantic Ocean was below.

Kaye was asleep in his berth when the emergency bells awakened him. He became active in those frightening moments, speaking to the other fifty-two passengers with stage command, indeed, instructing them to remain calm and even helping one of them into a life jacket. Meanwhile, the pilot's maneuver succeeded.

With safety restored and the plane regaining altitude, there was a natural relief and camaraderie among the passengers. Kaye himself strolled up and down the aisles taking drink orders as the airplane began the 640-mile limp back to Ireland. One of those who congratulated him was an elegant man named Maurice Pate, who invited him to sit down. Over a drink, Pate explained that he was the executive director of the United Nations International Children's Emergency Fund (Unicef). After it had been created by the UN General Assembly in 1946, he had successfully argued its merits before the U.S. Congress. Thus, more than being its director, Maurice Pate had committed his life to an organization dedicated "to the sad cause of endemic hunger and sickness among children in poor societies." He took the crusade personally. The children's needs were immediate, and he had no patience for regulations. He invariably chose the shortcut of personal contact over the official route of channels. He was allowed to do this at Unicef because he was subsidizing the organization out of his personal fortune. For the fact was that its funding from the United Nations was meager; without outside contributions it would have been impossible to fulfill Unicef's—and Pate's own—commitment to the millions of children in the developing world: Asia, Africa, the eastern Mediterranean, and Latin America.

So he ran the organization as a philanthropic fiefdom, and its work was what he chatted about with Danny Kaye as the Stratocruiser carefully crawled its way back to Shannon Airport.

By the time the passengers and baggage were reloaded onto a fresh craft, Pate and Kaye had exchanged telephone numbers. In the meantime, the American press had gotten word of the near accident, and there were front-page headlines about Danny Kaye's cool and helpful behavior. The mishap would have made some people wary of air travel, but it convinced Kaye to learn how to fly a plane himself, and when he was settled again in Los Angeles, he signed up for lessons.

The introduction to Maurice Pate was typical of how he was beginning to accumulate people, and as the numbers mounted, they would all consider themselves Danny Kaye's intimates. That is the way it is with many celebrities; only with Kaye it does not seem as if *any* of them were even friends.

On his return to California, he tried to make up for all the time away from his daughter. Over the past months, he had been calling Dena daily from London and Glasgow, but at that age, talking is not a very satisfactory form of communication for a parent. A child seems to grow before one's eyes, and Kaye tried to catch up on the parental rewards he had missed. One afternoon, he was having lunch with the two-year-old, but she was not eating. Instead, she looked at the plate and said, "I don't like that."

He touched her button nose and said, "Now, when you're older, I want you to remember that I tapped your nose when you said that."

And when she *was* old enough to understand and they were again eating together, he reminded her. "I tapped your nose once, and what that meant was, you can dislike anything, but *try it first.* Otherwise, you're going to stifle your sense of curiosity. And when you do that, you stifle your sense of growth. And to remain curious all your life is— Hey, you're gonna get your tail kicked, but by God, you will find a hell of a lot more to live for—and with—by meeting it than by ever turning your back on it."

This was a wonderful Danny Kaye. This was the essence of his best performing self. But away from the stage, this Danny Kaye seemed to reveal himself only to children. It was as if they were the only ones he trusted.

His first picture at 20th Century-Fox was set, *On the Riviera,* to be directed by Walter Lang. At the time, every movie studio was complete in itself. Each had its contract actors, directors, and cinematographers, and each had its imprimatur—a type of picture, a tone, a way of handling dramas or musicals, even a photographic quality with idiosyncratic lighting. A Columbia movie could be distinguished from a Paramount or Warner Brothers movie sometimes just by the style of its opening credits or the music, and certainly by the stars.

Because the fashion in stars at 20th Century-Fox ran to strictly defined genders—feminine sweater models like Betty Grable, June Haver, and Linda Darnell or the strictly manly Victor Mature, John Payne, and Mark Stevens—the new look for a Danny Kaye movie was going to include a refreshingly manly Kaye. Even his humor, which in the past could be not childlike but childish, is adult in this picture. In fact, his first line as a French air ace is a double entendre that was somehow slipped past the Hollywood censors. "Right now," the character says upon emerging from his airplane, "I am so tired, I would like to go to bed for a week." Then Kaye pauses, his timing impeccable. "Who will join me"—once more he pauses precisely before continuing—"in cheering my brave comrades?"

This Frenchman was, yet again, one of two roles for Kaye. The look-alike is a second-rate American impressionist who is about to be fired from a local cabaret. Realizing that he is a double for the French aviator, he keeps his job by suggesting that he do an impression of the ace. He does it in a major production number featuring an ensemble of cancan dancers led by a striking redhead with a fabulous body and tremendous dance energy. Billed in the movie as Gwyneth Verdon, she would change her name to Gwen Verdon when she went on the stage.

Concluding this dance number, she greets Kaye when he enters as the heroic aviator, stepping from a mock-up airplane. The camera moves in, their eyes meet, they nearly kiss, and the energy between them is unmistakable. In fact, a romance between Kaye and Verdon had already begun.

She was not only the lead dancer in *On the Riviera* but the assistant to Jack Cole, the choreographer assigned to the picture. Danny knew Cole since the days when they had both played the Chez Paree in Chicago. Jack Cole had already won a place in choreographic history for developing the basic vocabulary of jazz dancing—the kind of dancing done in nightclubs and Broadway musicals. He was also infamous for his disciplinary meanness, and it seemed to be focused on Gwen Verdon.

She had been telling her friends that she was in love with Cole, and they found it depressing. Not only was he a sadistic choreographer; Jack Cole had probably never known a heterosexual experience in his life.

Curiously, and perhaps coincidentally, at the same time that Verdon was emerging from the relationship with the homosexual Cole and beginning her romance with Kaye, Danny was himself becoming the subject of homosexual gossip. There were similar whispers about other actors in the movie community, but since, at the time, not even the tabloid press traded in such gossip, there was no forum for proof or denial.

The homosexual rumors about Kaye involved only one ostensible partner. That partner was Laurence Olivier, who, with his wife, Vivien Leigh, had moved to Los Angeles while he made *Carrie* and she, *A Streetcar Named Desire*. In fact, for a time they rented the house next door to Danny and Sylvia's place on San Ysidro Drive, and the two men saw each other often. They even traveled to the Caribbean together to visit Noel Coward at his Jamaica home. Vivien's presence notwithstanding, that was enough to start the gossip, even though nothing is known about the trip that substantiates homosexual behavior on Kaye's part. But between Coward's open homosexuality, the stories of a costume party in which Kaye performed in drag, and his sexless screen image, the Caribbean holiday did little to straighten his reputation. Small wonder, then, that Vivien was beginning to work up a real dislike for Danny Kaye.

He also showed up, dressed as a woman, to entertain at a Los Angeles benefit. Introduced as Kay Thompson, the cabaret singer, Danny strolled on wearing an evening gown. The resemblance was so striking, his mimicry so uncanny, that some in the audience actually believed he *was* Kay Thompson. Since there already was a mannish quality about her, it was an esoteric moment in the history of sexual ambiguity.

He frequently visited with Olivier in the house next door, and it is hardly surprising that there were whispers about them. Then again, Olivier was also friendly with Spencer Tracy—friendlier than he was with Danny Kaye—and there were no whispers about them. The explanation was simple: Tracy projected an unimpeachably masculine aura, while Kaye, if not effeminate, seemed asexual at least. When Samuel Goldwyn had said, "Nobody wants to fuck Danny Kaye," he had meant women, but he may have hit it on the button. And vice versa.

Sylvia wrote four songs for *On the Riviera*, and Danny did his standard "Ballin' the Jack"—which is wonderful to have on permanent record—but while he was well received personally, *On the Riviera* was only a passing success.

As for the Kaye-Verdon romance, in the dance community, where the gossip is often sexy, the talk about these two was that they were warm rather than hot. Of course, that was only talk, and it could have been based on her relationship with the homosexual Cole and the rumors about Danny. In any case, this was but the start of the Verdon romance and the homosexual rumors.

SYLVIA AND DANNY GOT IT INTO THEIR HEADS TO FORMALLY INTRO-duce the Oliviers to the Hollywood community, although the couple hardly needed an introduction. Larry had made *Wuthering Heights* years earlier, and, of course, Vivien had played Scarlett O'Hara in *Gone With the Wind*. Perhaps this was a way for the Kayes to advertise their special relationship with stage royalty, but whatever the explanation, "Introduce the Oliviers" was the theme of the party, and the invitations were strictly "A" list. The setting was the Crystal Room of the Beverly Hills Hotel, and the dress code was black tie. It was the event of the 1950 summer season for 170 of the biggest names in Hollywood.

They ranged from Humphrey Bogart and Lauren Bacall to Spencer Tracy and Groucho Marx. Errol Flynn was taken with a beautiful young actress at his table (Patrice Wymore, whom he would marry) and danced only with her, ignoring the almost unknown Marilyn Monroe at his side—which was just as well, as she was seated with her agent, Johnny Hyde, a man positively smitten with her. The rule was to separate husbands and wives, even those as close as the Herbert Marshalls and the Ronald Colmans. That was the idea suggested by the Beverly Hills Hotel's managing director, Hernando Cartwright, and everyone took his advice in such matters. As the gossip columnist Radie Harris said, "Hernando was very high class."

Sylvia was Larry's dinner partner, and at the other table of honor, Vivien sat between Danny and Elia Kazan, who was going to direct her in the movie of *A Streetcar Named Desire*. Kazan was not thrilled about the entire evening. The beautiful and spirited Leigh had just finished playing the London production of the Tennessee Williams play, and Kazan would have preferred that she conserve her energy instead of dancing until dawn. Blanche Du Bois is an exhausting role, and she was exhausted from playing it. She was a high-strung woman to begin with, and so she was especially distressed by the rumors about her husband and Kaye.

WHEN ROSIE KAYE VISITED DANNY IN CALIFORNIA, HE TOLD HER about his romance with Gwen Verdon. Rosie didn't approve of that any more than she had of Eve Arden.

"This isn't like it was with Eve," Danny said. "I'm not going to leave Sylvia for Gwen Verdon. I'm not going to leave Sylvia for anybody."

Rosie wasn't the only one he said that to. Like many men, he trusted such personal conversations to woman friends, and talking to another of them, he was "self-deprecating" about his behavior with Eve Arden. He spoke "as if admitting a weakness that he was never going to show again. . . . He said he would never divorce Sylvia because he felt so in debt to her."

That wasn't enough for Rosie Kaye, who told him, "I still don't like the way you treat her."

"What gives you the right to say that?" he snapped.

"You do." She smiled, adding, "Just don't be foolish about this. Don't do anything silly."

She couldn't tell him to stop, but she could tell him, "Don't make it public."

Nobody had to give Danny Kaye advice about privacy. The ability to withdraw was a tactical part of his system. Because of it, Eve Arden had given up on him entirely and was beginning to see an actor/artist named Brooks West. Now it was Gwen Verdon who was being seen waiting for Danny in the wings of one theater or another.

"I used to say exactly what I thought," Rosie remembered. Sylvia's sister Rhoda would sometimes observe this with amazement. "You're the only one," she said, "who gets away with what you get away with. He wouldn't let anyone else speak to him the way you do."

The closeness with Rosie Kaye was unique. "He wasn't the great Danny Kaye to me. I was just Rosie, and he was just Danny . . . even if he was the idol of England and even if he was talking to queens and princesses and presidents."

Talking to queens and princesses and presidents and being an international institution was by now his way of life, and it was a comfortable way of life. His career had been lucrative. His next movie—*Hans Christian Andersen*—was ready for production, and the fee of $200,000 was going to be his biggest yet. He could afford to turn down the huge sums being offered by the television networks. Perhaps his friend Jack Benny had gone into the new medium, but that made sense; Jack did not have the movie career that Danny had. To Kaye, and to most movie stars, television seemed a way station for a career in decline. Hollywood was contemptuous of the new medium, even though it was drastically affecting movie attendance. Such shortsightedness would cost it dearly, but for stars living in the moment, the big money was still the movie money. If anyone wanted to see Danny Kaye on television, they could watch Jerry Lewis or Sid Caesar.

Hans Christian Andersen was going to be Kaye's first outright movie musical, and its score was going to be written not by Sylvia Fine but by Frank Loesser. If that upset her, at least she was being displaced by a major songwriter. Loesser's *Guys and Dolls* was not only a smash hit on Broadway; it was already a theatrical landmark.

The movie brought Kaye back to the Samuel Goldwyn studio

in thoroughly first-class fashion. Its screenplay was written by Moss Hart. The ballets were going to be created by the French choreographer Roland Petit. The settings for those ballets, as well as for the picture's gingerbread Denmark, were going to be lavish, all of which was going to add up to a $4 million budget, the biggest for any movie that Goldwyn had yet produced.

Boosted by Danny's international triumphs, his royal connections, and now this prestigious movie, he and Sylvia ascended into the social ozone—so rarefied an atmosphere that not even Mary Livingstone reigned over it. The social arbiter here was Edie Goetz, who was the daughter of M-G-M's Louis B. Mayer and the wife of producer William Goetz. Her group was considered the "A" list of "A" lists, and it included Vincente Minnelli and Judy Garland, Desi Arnaz and Lucille Ball, David O. Selznick and Jennifer Jones, George and Gracie Burns, Frank and Nancy Sinatra, Frank and Lynn Loesser, Jack and Mary Benny, and the producer Armand Deutsch, who was married to Danny's old friend Benay Venuta.

This group was, or so the sharp and tough Venuta thought, a "deadly dull crowd." By and large, its men were the achievers, and the women belonged through marriage; they could express their power only in social leverage, which tended to manifest itself nastily. (For instance, Frank Loesser's wife, Lynn, was invariably referred to as "the evil of two Loessers.") As for the Kayes, Sylvia was still expected to play the piano after dinner. Only the public continued to think of her as the woman behind Danny Kaye. "She was invited," Venuta said, "as the proud wife. She played the piano."

Danny himself was not a party performer, although occasionally he would be in the mood. He once got into that mood with the movie producer Dore Schary when they were reminiscing about their youthful summers in the Catskill Mountains. Schary brought up Fishel Goldfarb, Danny's friend and tummling mentor, and that was how Danny got started one evening. The producer began an old Goldfarb routine: "I hear you're in business now."

Danny picked up on it with a thick Yiddish accent. "Dot's right."

"And tell me," Schary continued, "what is that business?"

"Nowelties," Kaye said. "I'm in nowelties."

"I don't know that business."

"The beesness"—Danny grinned—"iss mitt der comebeck ball."

"What does that mean," Schary asked in high-toned English, "a comeback ball?"

"Heet's a ball," Danny said, "ent it comes beck." Then, relishing Fishel's old routine, he finished it. "Ve heff all kinds nowelties . . . comebeck balls, wheestles, squawkiss, balloonis, all sorts of nowelties."

But Kaye would never be "on" at a party. Although the Hollywood "A" list included some of the country's most esteemed funnymen in Jack Benny, George Burns, and Danny Kaye, they saved their comedy for male company. That was an "A" list, too, only it was registered at the Hillcrest Country Club—the Hollywood golf club for Jews. In the Hillcrest dining room, first table on the right, which anyone could see but few could join, was the "roundtable"— never to be confused with its namesake at New York's Algonquin Hotel. These were not literary wits, but the top funnymen in Los Angeles—Jack Benny, George Burns, Milton Berle, and the funniest of all, by general consensus, George Jessel.

By chance and fate, Jessel's career had been sidetracked and shuttled off to limbo. Some felt that he had been cursed with too much talent, that he did too many things too well. As a singer he had been in a class with Jolson. As a monologist he had been a Palace headliner. It was said that he had let his private life destroy him, his weakness for women. Whatever the explanation, it had all gone awry, and he was now reduced to playing the fool on television talk shows and being a master of ceremonies for hire at weddings and bar mitzvahs. He might have been the funniest man at the Hillcrest roundtable, but the public would only know him, years later, as an occasional oddity on late-night television. The man played as a parody of himself.

The Hillcrest Country Club, like the Friars Club in New York, picked up his checks.

It was by a curious divination that a newcomer was accepted at the Hillcrest roundtable. As Buddy Hackett would describe it, "You weren't elected to this table. You just knew if you belonged." Anyone who was not sure of it did not belong. Of course, Danny Kaye belonged, but he joined this group only because of Benny. Otherwise, he kept at a distance from the mere mortals of show business, the *comedians* (a term that he loathed). It was for this reason that he never joined the Friars Club in New York.

Verbally jabbing each other, elbowing around the Hillcrest table like monkeys with cigarettes, the comedians vied for each other's approbation. Jessel would decide the worthiest. Danny was not as fast with jokes or repartee as some of these whizzes, but he could make Jack Benny laugh as no one else could. The two men shared an elegance, and Benny doted on Kaye's comic sensibility. The merest of Danny's glances could reduce Jack to tears.

"Watch," Danny whispered to Buddy Hackett at lunch one day. "I'll break Jack up."

Benny was deep in conversation with Milton Berle.

Kaye picked up a book of matches. Lighting one, he held it in the air, saying nothing and doing nothing. He just held the lighted match. Benny looked up, glanced over, his eyes met Kaye's, and he exploded with laughter.

It had been through Jack Benny's affection for Danny that Sylvia had cultivated a friendship with Jack's wife, Mary Livingstone. Mary led to Edie Goetz, and thus was Sylvia scaling the social heights. Ironically, she arrived there just as Danny was becoming less available for social events. For he was starting to stay in New York, while she was in California, and it was only when he was making movies that they were steadily together. Eve Arden was probably glad to be out of that sandwich—and that world. She had decided to marry Brooks West and did, at the end of the 1951 summer. The ceremony was performed on a New England farm, which was appropriate for this public sophisticate who was a Girl Scout in private.

But Danny's life was getting ever headier. While Eve was being married, he flew to London to appear in a special benefit at the Palladium. It was a midnight show to honor the legendary, late comedian Sid Fields and to benefit his three children. And while there has been many a "Night of Stars" in the exaggerated language of show business, this one fairly qualified. The cast ranged from Orson Welles and Douglas Fairbanks, Jr., to Judy Garland, while Kaye appeared with Laurence Olivier and the only-sometimes-angry Vivien Leigh.

The three strolled onstage dressed as Victorian children, wearing sailor outfits that were white, from the broad-brimmed, beribboned hats to the short skirts and patent-leather shoes. These, in fact, were the so-called drag costumes that prompted homosexual rumors after Leigh, Olivier, and Kaye wore them at Noel Coward's Caribbean house the previous year. The odd trio did the same song as then, too, "Triplets," which Arthur Schwartz and Howard Dietz had written for the Broadway revue *The Band Wagon*. In fact, they had written it to be sung just this way, by three adult performers dressed as children.

> We do everything alike.
> We look alike,
> We walk alike, we talk alike,
> We dress alike
> And what is more
> We hate each other very much!

Vivien, Larry, and Danny brought down the house. The show didn't end until five o'clock in the morning, and with tickets priced at £13 ($58), it raised $50,000.

Then, in the fall, Danny and the Oliviers were in New York, he in the opening-night audience and they onstage. The couple were repeating a double bill that they had done at Stratford-on-Avon, an alternating repertory of Cleopatra plays—Shakespeare's *Antony and Cleopatra* and Shaw's *Caesar and Cleopatra*. The Broadway crowd quickly christened the event "Two on the Nile," a wordplay on the 1950 revue *Two on the Aisle*.

This was an especially ambitious undertaking for Vivien Leigh, who was considered a lesser talent than Olivier by many in the British theater. Of course, virtually every actor who ever lived was a lesser talent than Laurence Olivier, but there was also a certain disrespect for women in the British theater. Some of it came from old-fashioned heterosexual bias against women, some from old-fashioned homosexual bias against women, and some of the criticism was even justifiable.

First couple of the international stage though they were, the Oliviers were foundering as a marriage. She was sexually frustrated, and the entire British stage seemed to know about it. In plain terms, Vivien was by reputation a lusty woman, while even Larry admitted (in his autobiography) to being less than hot-blooded. With her he had discovered "an attraction of the most perturbing nature I had ever encountered," but he was no longer perturbed. His enduring and prevailing passion seemed to be for the stage. Vivien's remained for the bed.

The Broadway opening night was a glamorous one. Even Danny showed up in black tie, joining an audience that included Richard Rodgers, Alfred Lunt and Lynn Fontanne, Cole Porter, John Steinbeck, Tyrone Power, Luise Rainer, Ruth Gordon, Sarah

Churchill, David O. Selznick, Margaret Truman, and Rosalind Russell.

The brilliant Kenneth Tynan, who was doing a guest stint as drama critic for the *New Yorker*, brought the dry and waspish sensibility of the British stage establishment to his review. In an erstwhile defense of Leigh, he cited several choice digs about her, using a ploy of "some have said" to repeat descriptions of her as "a galvanized waxwork," "calculating as a slot machine," with "businesslike wrists and ankles." He brought up her performance as Blanche Du Bois in the recently released movie of *A Streetcar Named Desire* just to dismiss it as a failure. She would merely win the Academy Award for that. Noting that some of his colleagues had already found her "great" in the two Cleopatra plays, he allowed that she was "sweet" and "pretty" before concluding with lyrics from Oscar Hammerstein's "Honey Bun" *(South Pacific)* to sum up his opinion of Vivien Leigh:

> Her figure is something to applaud;
> Where she's narrow she's as narrow as an arrow;
> And she's broad where a broad should be broad . . .

Sometimes it hardly made sense for a woman to even try.

17

I'm Hans Christian Andersen, Andersen, that's me!

KAYE'S RESTLESSNESS SEEMED COMPULSIVE, PERHAPS EVEN OR-
GANIC. IT MIGHT HAVE BEEN SYMPTOMATIC OF NERVES OR OF HIS PER-
vasive, unexplainable unhappiness. He didn't give excuses for the
sudden trips across the country or abroad, and when he was sure
enough of his flying, he would escape as smoothly as a cab ride to
the airport.

    With time to spare before the start of production on *Hans Chris-
tian Andersen,* he took off with Frank Sinatra to entertain the troops
in Korea. It was not an official tour; officially, there wasn't even a
war. Officially, American soldiers were in Korea as part of a police
action, and entertainers were discouraged from suggesting otherwise
by going. But nobody cared to turn down Sinatra or Kaye, and even
in the military, which did not have a reputation for free thinking,
there was the occasional independent mind. Gen. Matthew
Ridgway, for instance, told volunteering entertainers, "If you set it
up, I'll provide the transportation."

    On the Kaye-Sinatra trip there was no accompanying troupe,
just the two of them and a pianist. That was a matter of necessity,
for the helicopters were small, and so were the stage facilities; some

of the audiences were just a few units huddled together in a clearing. Then again, other performances played to mammoth crowds, eighteen thousand GIs once. Kaye always lingered to take the names and telephone numbers of relatives to be contacted, and he made those calls.

RETURNING TO START WORK ON *HANS CHRISTIAN ANDERSEN,* HE BEcame a remote figure on the set. When he did get involved with the cast, he was not always pleasant about it. The other leading players were Farley Granger and a French dancer named Renée ("Zizi") Jeanmaire, who had been hired when Moira Shearer, the ballet star of *The Red Shoes,* had decided against doing the picture. Farley Granger—his friends called him "Farfel"—was under contract to Goldwyn, and the producer had great hopes for this serious-minded and astonishingly handsome young man.

Granger had become friends with Zizi and was disturbed by Kaye's impatience with her uncertain English. On several occasions, Danny walked off the set, snapping at Charles Vidor, the film's director, "Call me when she understands what you're saying." The meek Vidor would accept that with a shrug.

Kaye also demanded for himself the song "No Two People," which Frank Loesser had written as a duet for Granger and Jeanmaire. That gave Danny every song in the picture, but he did not invent star ego, and so that was not especially surprising. More curious to Granger was Kaye's treatment of him, which was so inconsistent as to be bewildering. Danny could be solicitous or remote, the mood swings wide and unpredictable. At one point during the making of the movie, he became so petulant about the costumes that he wailed to Granger, "How come you get to wear all these beautiful clothes and I have to wear rags?"

Then, at a Hollywood party, he acted as if he barely recognized the young actor. Kaye's companion was Gwen Verdon, but it is not likely that he was uncomfortable about being seen with her. As with Eve Arden, when he felt that the circumstances were not compromising, he was willing to appear in public with a girlfriend. But the snubbing of Granger, like his dismissive treatment of supporting players, technicians, makeup people, and other noncelebrities, would give him a snobbish reputation among the working people of show business. It was a bad habit, and it would get worse.

Years later, Granger wondered whether Kaye's erratic treatment of him might have had a homosexual element about it; and guilt. Like so many, he was struck by Danny's remoteness and mystified by the sexual ambiguity that resulted from it. Searching for an explanation and unable to find one, he used almost the same words as Georgia Gibbs when confounded by Kaye. She had said, "There was something strange about him. We couldn't put our fingers on it." Farley Granger said, "There was just something strange about him; I never could pinpoint it."

HANS CHRISTIAN ANDERSEN STARTS IN ODENSE, DENMARK, WHERE the storyteller is introduced as a cobbler who makes up fairy tales and enraptures the children with them. This irritates their schoolmaster to such an extent that, somewhat overreacting, he threatens to quit if the storyteller is not expelled from the town.

An adolescent named Peter—an unexplained character who is Andersen's ward or friend—spares him the expulsion by suggesting that they leave Odense for an adventure in Copenhagen. The boy leads the cobbler around as if he were in some way retarded, which sometimes seems the case.

Arriving in the capital city, Andersen observes a lovers' quarrel between a ballerina (Jeanmaire) and her choreographer (Granger), who is in fact her husband, although the cobbler doesn't realize it. Smitten with a schoolboy crush on the beautiful dancer, he is inspired to write "The Little Mermaid," and when the pages accidentally blow through her window, she and her husband decide to make a ballet of the story.

After the ballet is staged, Andersen realizes the futility of his romantic fantasy and leaves Copenhagen, again with his young companion. That, Granger remembered, prompted a joke around the Hollywood community, describing the plot as "Boy meets girl, boy loses girl, boy gets boy."

The picture's odd story line might have been a reflection of screenwriter Moss Hart's own troubled relationships with women or of Samuel Goldwyn's determination to make family-style pictures, meaning sexless ones. Strangely enough, the likeliest explanation seems the unlikeliest—that Hart decided Hans Christian Andersen was homosexual, a theory that was more or less certified forty years later. The psychological ramifications of *that*, vis-à-vis Hart and

Kaye, are too exotic to pursue. It is enough that the sheer *eunuchness* of the Andersen character is distracting.

The screenplay is surprisingly graceless for a writer as experienced as Moss Hart, and betrays an uneasiness with fantasy—a problem that would recur in his libretto for the 1960 musical *Camelot*. Hart was the soul of urbanity, but a family movie about a writer of fairy tales needed a lighter touch. The stilted storytelling of *Hans Christian Andersen* is unconvincing, and its dialogue sounds disingenuous. ("But Hans's stories are good. The children learn from them. They are not foolish stories, burgomaster.")

Hart's most serious mistake, however, was not stylistic but editorial. It had to do with the movie's most valuable asset—Andersen's fairy tales. Instead of dramatizing them, the picture lets them be described in song lyrics. Composer Frank Loesser leaped at this opportunity to use the rich material, and as a result, his score is the best, and best-remembered, thing about the movie. Each song is a self-contained story, touched with the magic, the economy, and the simplicity of good children's fiction.

Thus, in the vernacular of musical theater, these are not "book" songs. They do not advance the plot, they are not sung in place of dialogue, and they do not explain character, which was what songs were doing in the period's more progressive Broadway musicals. Rather, they are "justified" songs, sung when people might in real life sing—in this case, to tell a story. For that reason (much like the movie *Cabaret*), *Hans Christian Andersen* does not come across as a "musical." Its reality is never violated by musical numbers.

In addition to the lyrics telling the stories, Loesser's music catches their spirit. As singable as nursery rhymes, these tuneful pieces are in turn antic ("The King Is in the Altogether"), melancholy ("Inchworm"), playful ("Thumbelina"), bittersweet ("The Ugly Duckling"), exuberant ("Wonderful Copenhagen"), and inspirational ("Anywhere I Wander"). A couple of the songs are even musically provocative, for example, the canonlike duet "No Two People" and the title song, with its shifting keys and dissonances.

Kaye sings them with immense musicianship, rapture, and brio. Moreover, just as Loesser composed the songs as children's stories, so they are sung to children by Kaye, and his on-screen relationship with the youngsters is warm, relaxed, and convincing. In real life, too, he seemed more comfortable with youngsters than with adults.

Delivering the songs without *selling* them, he makes this nearly pointless movie work. The key to its commercial success was the combination of Loesser's wonderful songs and Kaye's portrayal of Andersen. For the first time, he was really acting. And acting is a variable thing in the movies. For most film actors, especially American ones, are personalities rather than impersonators. They do not transform themselves into the characters they play but instead play themselves. Some of them do this with great magnetism. Cary Grant was such a personality actor to perfection, as were Gary Cooper, Henry Fonda, and James Stewart. Kaye cannot do that very effectively because he does not have a personality to project—or at least has hidden it behind enigma.

That gives him the anonymity a character actor needs but must be born with. Like the quintessential character actor, Laurence Olivier, who, without a doubt, was his inspiration, Kaye could not comfortably play himself. But he could play another. Even though the title role in *Hans Christian Andersen* does not offer much in the way of dramatic material, Kaye's playing of it is an example of real character acting.

The acting begins, like an Olivier characterization, with physical disguise. Kaye's red hair is cropped so close that it changes his basic look. For the first time in any of his films there is no attempt at making him handsome, and yet he does not resemble the nebbish of the early Danny Kaye movies, nor does he act like the satiric comedian who shows up in some of the later ones or the zany on the nightclub floors. As Andersen, he is childishly sweet, but it is an assumed characteristic, and Kaye adheres to it. When he believes that the choreographer is abusing the ballerina, he expresses his anger convincingly, even while mouthing Hart's banal dialogue. ("How could a girl like you marry a man like that?") When he insists that he has been able to imagine a ballet that was performed while he was locked in a closet, his conviction is compelling. This is creative acting, and Kaye stays within the bounds of his character.

While *Hans Christian Andersen* was still in production, the Danes began complaining about its portrayal of their national hero. At the end of filming in the summer of 1952, Goldwyn sent his star on a conciliatory trip. Upon arriving, Kaye paid a highly publicized, internationally reported visit to the storyteller's statue in central Copenhagen. He even climbed its pedestal to pose for pictures embracing the bronze figure.

If that made for good public relations, there were less successful events on the trip. Kaye's ego was giving him a not always trustworthy sense of when he was amusing. His last stop in Denmark was a visit to Andersen's birthplace in Odense—a house that was enshrined as an official landmark. There he sat at the great man's writing desk, then plunked himself down on the bed. The photograph in the next day's Danish newspapers showed him clowning in the Andersen shrine, sprawled on Andersen's bed, even holding an open umbrella. By then he was over the Atlantic and halfway home.

The Hans Christian Andersen Society publicly protested his "scandalous conduct" and addressed the complaint to the American embassy. Kaye was met at Idlewild Airport with aggressive questions from a crowd of waiting reporters. They might as well have been tossing pennies at him onstage. He never could handle hostility with finesse and was in a foul mood, anyway, because his father was dying. He was able to hold his temper to a scowl, and his answers were curt but temperate. He explained that he had intended no disrespect. "I was a guest of the Danish Newspaper Guild," he said. "One of the photographers asked me to sit on the bed and lean back for a photograph. The curator assented. That was the end of it."

To further soothe the Danes, a prefatory disclaimer was added to the movie: "This is not the story of [Andersen's] life, but a fairy tale about this great spinner of fairy tales." In the end, *Hans Christian Andersen* pleased not only the Danish but Sam Goldwyn, becoming a $6 million success, the sixth-biggest money-maker of the year, and the songs provided wonderful new material for Kaye's repertoire. It was his most popular film so far, and it had a prestigious aura that was worthy of an international star.

Ironically, the bed on which he had so undiplomatically reclined was not Hans Christian Andersen's at all. Some weeks after the incident, the director of the Andersen Museum in Odense sheepishly admitted that the real Andersen bed, painted yellow and two meters long, had been stored away years before.

THE PRESS HAD MISSPELLED THE FAMILY NAME IN SO MANY DIFFERENT ways (Kaminsky, Kominski, Kominsky) that Danny, a bit absurdly, took to telling interviewers he didn't remember which spelling was correct. Perhaps it no longer mattered, as he was no longer David Kaminski in any sense. As a gesture of pride, Jacob Kaminski changed his own name to Kaye in 1952, the year he died.

The old man never did see *Hans Christian Andersen*, a picture that would take Danny's career to yet a higher plateau and set in motion an American deification nearly equal to that of the British. Kaye would be forever elevated above the roiling ranks of show-business commoners. Such prestige was obviously important to him, and he was repeatedly accused of being obsessed with it, of being a show-business snob. But after a certain level of achievement is reached in any field, perhaps prestige is the only thing left.

A quality often found among the artistic is the need to be unique. When Kaye had been young and out of work, he had bemoaned his unclassifiability. Then nobody would hire an entertainer who couldn't be pigeonholed. Now he wanted to be unclassifiable. He was generally considered a comedian, which was a classification he despised. Comedians, he would contemptuously say, were synonymous with the borscht belt. Thus, Kaye now presented himself as *sui generis*, and it was time to demonstrate this for America, to show that what he was, essentially and exclusively, was Danny Kaye.

The American equivalent of the Palladium was the Palace Theater on Broadway. The onetime mecca of vaudeville had degenerated into a seedy movie house, but recently it had been restored for Judy Garland, and her career was reborn there. Betty Hutton followed Garland into the historic theater and broke the box-office records that Garland had just set. Now it was Kaye's turn to play the Palace.

But the engagement was not merely a matter of prestige; it was also a matter of money. The brilliance of Kaye's career management was in making prestige pay. Even before opening at the Palace in November—in the few months after the release of *Hans Christian Andersen*—he would play the Dallas State Fair, receiving $153,000 for one week. Not even Dean Martin and Jerry Lewis could match that, and at the time they were the hottest performers in show business.

The shakedown of the Palace act in San Francisco would itself be lucrative. Then the Palace engagement would introduce a new approach to personal appearances; a more profitable, more prestigious, and less toilsome setup than six shows a day between movies at a presentation house. The new approach, with two performances daily at reserved-seat prices, was one that *Variety* would call "Palladium-type shows."

As for prestige, "Playing the Palace" said it all. Once again it was the phrase that stood for the pinnacle of show business.

. . .

THE SAN FRANCISCO WARM-UP CALLED FOR TWENTY-ONE PERFOR-mances in September at the Curran Theater. The weekend before, in a typical burst of restlessness and perhaps a release of tension as well, Kaye flew to Miami Beach to visit Rosie Kaye and other friends in the area. The winter season was just beginning at the popular resort, and there were lots of celebrities there, whether entertaining at the hotels or simply vacationing like Kaye. So it was not surprising that Walter Winchell, the most powerful gossip columnist in the country, was writing a week's worth of columns from Miami Beach.

Hearing that Danny was in town, he telephoned with an invita-tion to see Georgia Gibbs, who was opening an engagement at a small nightspot in the city of Miami. She was testing a new act, which was why she was singing in a small club in Miami itself rather than at one of the big hotels in Miami Beach. If the act went well, there would be time enough to let Miami Beach and Walter Win-chell know about it.

By this time, Georgia was a recording star, with hits like "Kiss of Fire" and "Dance with Me, Henry," but she sang other songs too, including "Ballin' the Jack," a number she enjoyed because it let her show off the soft-shoe dancing she had learned with Danny. It was a song she could never sing when she worked with him, of course, since it was his number. But now she was free to do it.

Finishing the late show on her opening night, she strolled off the floor and was at her dressing room door when she was pulled up short by the manager, who caught her by the elbow.

"Do you know who was out there?" he asked.

"Who?"

"Danny Kaye and Walter Winchell."

She was still startled as she closed the door behind her and sat down in front of the mirror, dabbing a sponge into the jar of cold cream to scrub off her makeup. There was a tap at the door. It was her sister, who had come along for company and luck. Looking up in the mirror, Gibbs said, "I can't figure it out. When people you know are in the room, usually they send a little note. 'Hi, good luck, Georgia. I'm here.' That kind of thing. But there was nothing."

Her sister listened silently, a mysterious smile on her lips. "Georgia," she finally said. "You'll never believe what happened after you were finished."

Gibbs looked up.

"They announced that Danny Kaye was in the audience."

"Oh?"

"He got up and got on the floor."

"What?"

"And then he sang, 'Ballin' the Jack.' "

Gibbs was stunned. In her experience, Danny Kaye never got up in a nightclub. He would specifically ask that he not even be introduced. He would scowl if a spotlight was thrown on him.

"What the hell is he doing," she asked her sister, "in a cocka-mamy little club in Florida, getting up to sing 'Ballin' the Jack'?"

What he was doing was asserting his ownership of "Ballin' the Jack"—the easygoing rendition of the song and the soft-shoe dance to go with it. The old vaudeville dictum—*don't steal my material*—overcame even his aloofness. But where had the dictum been when he used Red Skelton's drunk routine at the Palladium?

Georgia Gibbs continued to stare at her sister in the mirror. Kaye never did stop by to congratulate her. He did not send a note. By the time she left her dressing room, he and Winchell were gone.

18

Mr. Kaye has been seduced into thinking that we love him for himself, whereas in truth we love him only for his talent.

—Kenneth Tynan

Like many Californians, Danny relished the drive along the coastal highway between Los Angeles and San Francisco. He drove it whenever he had reason to go north and sometimes when he had none. He liked to drive, and he was a fast driver.

In September 1952, he made the drive with Sylvia and Dena for the engagement at the Curran Theater, which was going to serve as a warm-up for the Palace in New York. The six-year-old had never seen her father perform in front of an audience. In fact, Dena had led an unusually sheltered existence. Friends of her parents noticed with some dismay that she was not even allowed to go to children's birthday parties in Hollywood—and there were plenty of them, since most of the movie stars were her parents' age. Although there are safety factors and psychological problems that are unique to the children of the famous, some of the Kayes' friends felt that Sylvia was being overprotective. One pointed out that Judy Garland and Vincente Minnelli let their Liza go to those parties, and she was only nine months older than Dena, while it always seemed that at party time somehow "either Dena was sick, or the nurse was."

The isolation contributed to her being an unusually timid,

overly dependent little girl who could become upset merely by watching her father get into trouble in a movie.

On the day she went to see him at the Curran Theater, she was scrubbed, starched, brushed, and shiny, from the ribbon in her hair to the patent-leather Mary Janes on her feet. Gripping her mother's hand, she took her aisle seat down front. Immediately behind was a local columnist with the imposing name of Stanton Delaplane, and he noticed the child's fright from the moment the applause greeted her father as he strolled onstage from the wings.

Kaye noticed it, too, and kept watch over his daughter as he performed. He added special children's material at that matinee. Like so many youngsters, Dena doted on the songs from *Hans Christian Andersen,* and he sang some of those, as well as, of course, "Deenah / Is there anyone feener / In the state of Caroleena?" As he recalled, "I watched Dena during the performance. She stared wide-eyed while I ran about, waving my arms and twitching my face."

But as the audience roared, the child covered her ears and burst into tears. Her father stopped the show. He walked toward the stage apron—the edge—and sat down sooner than usual. From there he could see his daughter, and as the theater hushed in the darkness, he spoke.

"My daughter Dena is in the audience this afternoon."

There was applause, but he shut a window on it.

"She has never seen me act like this before."

That provoked laughter, and he stopped that, too.

"Dena—are you out there, honey?"

In a shy voice, she peeped, "Yes."

"Do you like the show?"

That brought a tinier yes, and the audience laughed again, which only prompted another burst of little-girl tears.

Kaye later said, "She couldn't stand the laughter of the people. But if she only knew how much her daddy loves that laughter. . . ."

He finished the show and then waited in vain for mother and child to come backstage. There were the usual visitors, but no Dena and Sylvia. After everyone had gone, he dressed and walked through the abandoned backstage area, looking until finally he stepped onto the darkened stage. It was there that he found his daughter, sobbing in a bundle.

"They just shouldn't laugh at you," she said.

. . .

EVER SINCE THE NEWSPAPERS AND NATIONAL MAGAZINES HAD TRUM-
peted Kaye's triumphs in England and his intimacy with the royals,
the impending engagement at the aptly named Palace had begun to
take on the aspects of not merely an event but the challenge of
matching his London success. However, the London heroics lay not
only in having pleased a king but also in the luxuriously sly way he
had found to play the court jester. For something mysterious could
be perceived in this jester. It was something that the British, ordinarily masters of understatement, seemed to have missed. It was a
new underside of Danny Kaye. It was arrogance.

The premiere of *Danny Kaye at the Palace* on January 18, 1953,
was one of the most glittering opening nights in Broadway years.
The duke and duchess of Windsor led the British contingent, a unit
that included future Prime Minister Harold Wilson, Ambassador
Lewis Douglas, and Sir Gladwyn Jebb. Then there were the stars—
Marlene Dietrich, Jackie Gleason, Milton Berle. In keeping with
Kaye's transcendence of show business, there was a faction from
industry—Walter Chrysler, Paul Hoffman, Dorothy Schiff, and
Robert Sarnoff of RCA. There was also a group of famous couples,
as if in homage to the Danny-Sylvia phenomenon. These star marriages included the conductor Andre Kostelanetz and his wife, Lily
Pons; Peter Lind Hayes and Mary Healy; Tex McCrary and Jinx
Falkenberg; Skitch Henderson and Faye Emerson. The national fantasy of marriage as a working partnership and an enduring alliance
was increasingly becoming sustained only by such public duets, a
simulated reality.

The rest of the Palace audience was made up of assorted celebrities—Clifton Fadiman, Gertrude Berg, Jack Palance, Piper Laurie,
Irene Selznick, Billy Rose, Robert Q. Lewis, and of course Abe
Lastfogel, the head of the William Morris Agency. Finally, in that
audience, and seated with Sylvia, were Rosie Kaye and her husband,
Martin Goldman. Dena was there, too, and already getting used to
an audience laughing at not her father but his antics.

The first half of the show was vaudeville fare—a chimpanzee
act, a couple of jugglers, and a team of ballroom dancers. The Dunhills were still dancing for Kaye, but Fran Warren had replaced
Georgia Gibbs, who had become too successful to be second-billed.

After the intermission, Danny strolled out to a standing ovation, dressed as usual in his brown sport jacket and brown trousers. He began by reminiscing about his visit with Harry Lauder in Glasgow and asked for the gnarled and twisted cane that the Scottish entertainer had given him. When it was handed out from the wings, he leaned on it and sang Lauder's signature song, "Just a Wee Deoch-an-Doruis." This was the way he had begun the royal command performance, but now he embellished the moment with a Scottish medley that included Will Fyffe's "I Belong to Glasgow" and then "Will Ye No' Come Back Again?" with which the Scottish had serenaded him on closing night. These numbers allowed him to do the kind of dialect at which he excelled.

Sensing that the Palace was about to overdose on sentimentality, he burst into mock tears. That got the audience laughing, and he capitalized on it with the "Gypsy Drinking Song" from *The Inspector General*. He managed to move from that to his "Ballin' the Jack," with its easy lilt and gentle dance steps, and then, as if he had just thought of it and had never done such a thing, he sat down at the orchestra pit to relax and chat. It worked as magically as it had in London, Glasgow, and San Francisco, a spotlit performer enchanting the audience as the big theater was swallowed into darkness. His mere request for a cigarette set the house at ease, for it broke through the entertainer's wall. And there is such a wall in variety entertainment, too, not unlike the "fourth wall" of drama. This one is made of the entertainer's polish, his facade of professionalism and fakery, his preparation and material. By convincingly abandoning the paraphernalia of showtime, Kaye was able to meet the audience in present time and place, or at least to create the illusion of it. The warm and winning atmosphere he conjured up might have sent a show-business cynic into heart spasms, but new as it was to American audiences, it was charming. And it was indeed new, for it had taken Danny Kaye all these years—successful though they were—to distill the qualities that were unique and unclassifiable and take those, rather than one of the familiar categories (a comedian, a singer, a dancer), as his stage persona. In short, and at last, the man and his act had become one.

Thus, he came to capitalize on the very qualities that had made him undesirable as a young performer; his very differentness. That, he found, was the key to his success, and in the bargain, it brought him love, or at least made him beloved.

Rising to his feet, he went back to the business of entertaining. For a flamenco dance, he looked arrogantly over his shoulder, click-

ing his heels and snapping his fingers. His arms, hands, and fingers
were as airborne as ever, balletic and mesmerizing. Then he imper-
sonated an English balladeer who is giving his fifty-fourth encore
and a German singer relaxing after a Wagnerian program by singing
a lullaby.

Now the evening was his, and he slipped into his standard repertoire—the ham actor singing the off-key "Begin the Beguine," "Deenah," and, of course, "Melody in Four F." The audience of two
thousand was ecstatic. He quieted them by giving the orchestra a
break while, accompanied only by Sammy Prager at the piano, he
sang three songs from *Hans Christian Andersen*—"The Ugly Duckling," "The King Is in the Altogether," and "Thumbelina."

More was to come. He was giving a ninety-minute show. He
used material that even his truest fans hadn't heard—"Tom, Tom,
the Piper's Son," as sung in the various styles of a baritone, an overly
chic nightclub singer (that was his Kay Thompson impression, but
without the dress), and a Brazilian. Then, for his best accent, he did
the Russian "Play, Gypsy."

Opening-night audiences are paradoxical in that they are hard-
bitten pushovers, nonparticipant and yet demonstrative. Kaye's first-
night audience was not a blasé crowd of theater sophisticates, but it
certainly was a reserved and starchy group. Still, they had come for
him, and he soon had them roaring their approval. As if they were a
working-class audience at the Palladium, they obediently let themselves be separated into singing groups, making any silly sound he
requested. At the end, their cheers and cries for more of his making
fools of them threatened to resound until early morning.

Max Liebman, who had played so formative a role in Danny's
early development, saw this supreme entertainer as complete at last.
"When I first met Danny," he remembered, "he was more or less an
inarticulate man before an audience. Every word was rehearsed."
Sylvia had provided those words, and Liebman had pointed the direction for her. He taught her how to shape revue material and tailor
it so as to give form to Kaye's multiple but unintegrated talents. Now
Danny did not need anyone else to write material for him. "He
used to hide behind his characters," Liebman said after the Palace
premiere. "He doesn't have to anymore," because he realizes "he
can charm an audience by himself."

The charm that Kaye was purveying did not have universal sales
appeal. One of the few to resist was Kenneth Tynan, who was still
reviewing for the *New Yorker*. Tynan had once been Kaye's cham-

pion but that was when Danny was first being discovered by the British.

A critic's profession offers few rewards, and salary is not one of them. Nor does the job provide entrée into glamorous circles. The critic is an outsider, with his nose pressed against the window. Only his power has meaning, and because of that, the critic covets his power.

It rests in pronouncement, in defining, in revelation—in discovering and proclaiming success or failure. Thus, Kenneth Tynan, like any critic, needed to lead the way, not follow with the crowd, and Danny Kaye's praises needed no further singing. It was time for debunking.

There might also have been a scintilla of personal jealousy in Tynan's critique of Kaye. This critic moved in theatrical circles and in fact would soon abandon dramatic criticism to become the literary manager of Laurence Olivier's own National Theatre of Great Britain. Some observers felt that there was a homosexual element in his relationship with Olivier. Donald Spoto, in his biography of the actor, describes Tynan as "fascinated by homosexuality, which he denied so often and so vigorously that many were convinced of his secret experimentation." This sort of reverse circumstantial evidence only makes insinuation the more insidious. Then again, Spoto would not even bother to insinuate when categorically stating, also without citing substantiation, that "by this time [the time of the Palace engagement] Olivier and Danny Kaye were lovers."

Whatever grounds there might have been for such a speculation —and there are some—there is no evidence of and there are no witnesses to a Kaye-Olivier sexual relationship. But mere facts have never deterred gossip. Another Olivier biographer, the British journalist Anthony Holden (Olivier), had access to the same rumors about Kaye and Olivier as Spoto; in fact he told them to Spoto. But Holden did not consider them sufficient for any conclusive statement on a homosexual affair between Olivier and Kaye.

IT IS POSSIBLE THAT KENNETH TYNAN WAS SIMPLY JEALOUS OF OLIVier's friendship with Kaye. It is even conceivable, lunatic as this might seem, that Tynan's opinions about Danny Kaye's performances were not jealous at all but just honest opinion. And if that opinion can be disputed, the brilliance of his writing cannot.

When a clown pins his faith to incidentals he is lost. Pathos, for example, is a drug which has debilitated many fine comics; and so is charm, to which Mr. Kaye has surrendered himself. . . . Kaye demands that [the audience] snap their fingers and sing, among other things, "boing." Four years ago I would have boinged with the best of them, convinced that I was doing so at the bidding of an authorized maniac; this time, the experience of spending an hour in the palm of Mr. Kaye's hand grew slightly oppressive and I boinged not at all. . . . I cannot improve on the comment made by a woman behind me. "He's so natural," she whispered in awe. "No side at all. Just like an ordinary human being." The tribute might have been appropriate to royalty; but we had come to see a clown. . . . When there was an edge, he was magical. Where there was astringency, nothing remains but a mesmeric niceness and behind the hooded eyes a whimsical arrogance.

Most of the other reviews of Danny Kaye at the Palace were ecstatic, but good or bad, they didn't make much difference. Kaye had continued in the direction that England had sent him, and that was above reviews and beyond show business. He had become a phenomenon of the times. In New York, the original engagement was sold out, extended, and sold out once more. There was a limit to how long he could stay because of a movie commitment (*Knock on Wood*), but the press reacted as if Danny Kaye at the Palace were essential to life in New York. The *Daily Mirror* even ran an editorial about him.

To the readers: Please go see Danny Kaye at the Palace, 47th and Broadway. To the Palace Management: Please lift the limits of this limited engagement until all our readers have had a chance to see Danny. . . . We're not a drama critic. We'll describe the audience. We saw the creases go out of worried foreheads. We saw troubled men and women made over through the miracle of laughter—and the blessing of tears. We saw them leave happier, healthier, stronger.

Sentimentalism was endemic to tabloids like the *Mirror*, but there was also a germ of truth in the plea. Danny Kaye did have an extraordinary effect on his audiences. He enchanted them and made children of many adults. He could restore their innocence, at least for a while, and along with their innocence, a curiosity and a sense of wonder. He was indeed that magical tummler from the lawns of White Roe in the Catskills, rousing the inert vacationers and leading them down the hill to the water.

But perhaps, too, there was, in Kenneth Tynan's words, "a mesmeric niceness" about him "and behind the hooded eyes a whimsical arrogance."

AT THE SAME TIME AS KAYE WAS PLAYING THE PALACE, VIVIEN LEIGH was having a nervous breakdown. She was halfway around the world, on location in Ceylon making a movie called *Elephant Walk*. She had fallen in love with Peter Finch, her costar—or as Olivier wrote in Victorian prose (in his *Confessions of an Actor*): "The two of them were hopelessly lost in the floodtide of the all-consuming passion to which, for the first time, they were giving enthusiastic license."

While Danny's Palace engagement was being extended into the middle of March, Vivien's condition was worsening, and upon arriving in Los Angeles for interior photography on *Elephant Walk*, she again fell apart. So it was that Olivier, who was vacationing in Italy, began the long journey to California, flying first to London, where he was joined by his business manager and friend Cecil Tennant. The next stop was New York's Idlewild Airport, where—at least according to Donald Spoto in his Olivier biography—Kaye fooled Olivier by masquerading as a customs officer.

This is hard to believe for several reasons. Aside from showing an uncharacteristic insensitivity to a critical situation, Kaye presumably went unrecognized by a close friend and a master of stage disguise at point-blank range, wearing a "heavily powdered latex mask." In Spoto's imaginative description of an event not witnessed by himself (or, at least as far as he discloses, by anyone else), Kaye spoke to Olivier in "a nearly incomprehensible accent," insisting that the actor strip for a search, not so subtly put, "of every inch and crevice of his body." Only then, according to Spoto, did Danny remove his disguise and

They spent the night at the St. Regis Hotel before continuing to California the next morning.

Even had such a prank occurred, it might have been just that —a Danny Kaye prank, minus the homosexual suggestiveness. Indeed, he played similar pranks on other occasions, as when he disguised himself as a room-service waiter at the Stanford Court Hotel in San Francisco and served tea to Dame Margot Fonteyn. That time, he got as far as puffing up her pillows and pulling down the counterpane before the ballerina shrieked, "Oh, my God!" in recognition of him.

As for spending the night with Olivier, no other biography refers to that event, and the actor's own version of arriving with Tennant is utterly different:

> Danny Kaye met us [at Idlewild] and gave us the latest overall picture. He took us to the Sherry-Netherland, fed us, fixed us up with some rooms, and I had a massage and a sleep before taking off again to Los Angeles.

That makes more sense, staying not at the St. Regis, as Spoto writes, but at the Sherry-Netherland, since Kaye's own apartment was in the Sherry. Moreover, Kaye did not go to Los Angeles with Olivier as Spoto writes and could not have, since it was March 13 and he was in the midst of the Palace engagement, which did not end until early April.

Nor does Spoto's account mention the presence of Cecil Tennant or his whereabouts during the supposed airport interlude and the overnight stay. In fact, the manager and Olivier flew on to Los Angeles, where they were met at the airport by Sylvia. She was, Olivier writes, "the first person we saw. . . . Then," he adds, as far as Vivien Leigh was concerned, "it was the turn of the psychiatrists."

He didn't put much faith in psychiatrists but had no other recourse, and it was the Kayes' psychiatrist, Dr. Martin Grotjohn, who saw Vivien. Grotjohn was a sort of psychiatrist to the stars, and Olivier called him "the big chief" (the American version is "big cheese"). Grotjohn advised Olivier, making "one pronouncement in his mid-European accent (at which I nearly laughed out loud): 'She must go to her home. You must take her there immediately. . . . She wants her moo-ther!' "

Elizabeth Taylor was hurried in as a replacement in *Elephant Walk*, while Vivien Leigh—again sedated—was loaded onto an eastbound airplane on a stretcher. Olivier and Tennant walked alongside, shouting at the newspaper photographers, "Careful with those flashbulbs, she's a very sick woman!"

In New York to connect with the flight home to London, they were again met by Kaye. In describing this meeting, Anthony Holden, in *Olivier*, makes his own reference to a possible Kaye-Olivier homosexual relationship.

> [Kaye's] reunion with Olivier grew so intense that Vivien . . . had a jealous relapse. . . . Her sedation having worn off, she noisily refused to board the flight to London. Kaye made himself scarce.

Holden later said that he made this reference subtle because of uncertainty about the Olivier-Kaye rumors. In the autobiographical *Confessions of an Actor*, Olivier's version is not at odds with Holden's, but it is more detailed and more dramatic:

> If there was one thing of which Vivien was terrified it was needles, hypodermics of any sort, but the time came when she had to be put out and got onto the plane. Our new nurse appeared with what seemed to be an unusually large needle and a hefty container filled with liquid. Vivien saw them and made a desperate attempt to escape. To my horror I saw that the nurse was enjoying it; she was waggling the syringe in her hand and there was a glint in her eye. But there was no time for anything; Danny Kaye and I threw ourselves on top of Vivien and held her down. Vivien fought us with the utmost ferocity as the needle went in, biting and scratching Danny and me, screaming appalling abuse at both of us, with partic- ular attention to my erotic impulses. It seemed an eternity before she went limp and Danny and I were able to let go of her, both shattered and exhausted. That night, back in England, she was safe in Netherne Hospital.

Olivier privately told his editor, Michael Korda, that Vivien's "appalling abuse" about his "erotic impulses" included accusations of homosexuality. They were in part legitimate, for he had engaged in several homosexual affairs, but the actor decided to delete details from his manuscript and merely admitted to testing the homosexual waters. Although he never mentioned Danny Kaye as a sexual part- ner, Korda drew that inference, and so he told Donald Spoto in an interview. That may have been a (the?) basis for Spoto's assertions. But this is not proof, as Korda well knew, which is why he himself set the rumors, the whispers, the bits and pieces of fancy and fact into fictitious form in his novel *Curtain,* an extremely readable and theatrically knowledgeable *roman à clef* about the Oliviers and Kaye.

As for the airport incident, given the condition that Leigh was in, she might have said anything. In short, even though the prim Olivier did try homosexuality, there is no proof that a similarly repressed Kaye followed suit. They both seemed to sublimate their sexual drives into stage performance, but there the similarity may end. Danny Kaye's covert sexuality seems of a piece with his general emotional repression rather than being a signal of any alternate sexual activity.

KAYE CLOSED AT THE PALACE AFTER EXTENDING HIS ORIGINAL SIX-week engagement to fourteen, playing 140 performances to 250,000 theatergoers. The final box-office take was $744,692, of which he personally kept $456,036. The times were being very good to him. His career had been a financial bonanza, but that was as nothing compared to the payoff for the Palladium triumph and the royal association. Since then he had earned $25,000 for a week in Dublin, $117,600 during a five-week tour of the British provinces, and $185,250 for five weeks in San Francisco. That was only the beginning for Danny Kaye as an American institution. The business of *Danny Kaye at the Palace* was now going to be repeated across the country, as he played theaters rather than movie houses, and at theater prices with a $6 top ticket.

The initial engagement was at the Shubert Theater in Philadelphia. The first part of the show was the same as in New York except that Fran Warren had left. Like Georgia Gibbs before her, she had graduated to headlining. Coincidentally, while Danny's show was in town, she was opening an engagement in a Philadelphia nightclub called the Latin Casino. The three Dunhill dancers decided to see her late show and invited Danny to come along.

The opening act for Ms. Warren was Alan King, by his own description "a ragtag kid." It was one of his first big-city engagements, and, he remembered, "I was doing a kind of Milton Berlish act," by which he meant that his comedy routine was a string of unrelated anecdotes and one-liners. To make it worse, some of them were off-color and "pretty crude," King remembered.

Before he went onstage, he was told that Danny Kaye was in the audience. "That was as close to fright as I've ever had," he would remember, for he had long been an admirer. "If Danny Kaye could make it, then any Jewish kid from Brooklyn could make it. You could aspire to become Danny Kaye."

In fact, King so idolized Kaye that he had used "Melody in Four F" as an audition piece. "He was my first hero."

But there was also something about Kaye that Alan King found disturbing. "This is a Brooklyn Jew who played *Hans Christian Andersen*. He beat the Brooklyn out of himself with a vengeance, like Moss Hart. It's not that Danny denied being Jewish. It's just that, well, I never considered him what my mother called *unzer*—ours. Family. Even though he spoke Yiddish fluently, he didn't speak *mammalushen*—mother's tongue."

In short, the high polish that Alan King found so impressive in Danny Kaye onstage, he found snobbish and even phony in the man offstage. "When he became *Danny Kaye*, he carried himself in a standoffish way around other comedians. He had worked so hard on not being the *kid from Brooklyn*. He was elegant onstage, but offstage he was affected."

That time in Philadelphia, with Kaye in the audience at the Latin Casino, King was desperately anxious to impress. Striding onto the nightclub floor and grasping the microphone, as comedians always do, he "busted my balls out there. I did everything I knew," he remembered, "every trick. And I was a big hit."

When he was through and after he had introduced Fran Warren and when he was safely back in his dressing room, sipping a scotch and wiping off his makeup, there was a tap at the door. Danny, he was told, wanted to see him.

"Well!" he remembered feeling. "This is it! Danny Kaye was at his peak after his British triumphs and on the heels of the Palace. This had been my command performance for him!"

And so, freshened up and with Fran Warren having finished singing, the young comedian buttoned his tuxedo jacket, walked into the nightclub, and approached Danny Kaye's table. He was invited to sit down.

He waited to hear what Danny thought of his act. "But," King would remember, "he didn't say, 'You're terrific, kid.' Instead of saying that, he spent a half hour telling me about my Jewishness.

"He said he was embarrassed by Harry Ritz of the Ritz Brothers
—and in the early days *he was doing Harry Ritz.*

"He said that I was a 'Jew comic.' "

Forty years later, King was still shaking his head over that.

"I never forgave him for it. I was broken-hearted, stone frozen.

"Hurt? Forget about it."

Part III

Having Been
Danny Kaye

He would soon be billed as the "Pied Piper of the World's Children." He had always been called childlike; however, no adult can be childlike. As Kaye himself insisted, childhood is for children. But he did seem to grasp the Piper's meaning —to lead in order to follow so as to go where children go. Unfortunately, adults cannot go there without being discovered.

19

Danny, I've got an idea that would make great PR. How about, we get you to be the voice of Unicef?

—Eddie Dukoff

T HE PEAK OF A CAREER IS THE SUPREME RUN OF EVERYTHING GOING RIGHT, THE CROWNING STRETCH OF ACHIEVEMENT. LIKE ANY PEAK, IT is not only the highest point of ascent; it is also the beginning of decline. Sorry to say, this can only be perceived on the way down.

Danny Kaye began his peak years, as so many do, in early middle age. He was nearing forty, he had gone from the stage of the Palladium to the stage of the Palace Theater, and it was the spring of 1953. That was when he became a legend, and it was within the legend that he would be confined ever after.

Charity was an appropriate activity for a legend, and Kaye focused on two causes. The first was the musicians union. Like many, he had a profound sensitivity to music. His musical instincts had always been sound, as if he were a musician without portfolio, and music had been one of the bases of his communion with Sylvia. She had refined his taste and given him the gift of classical music. His friend Jack Benny had for some years been appearing at symphony-orchestra benefits as a comic violin soloist. By being *almost* able to play, by wanting to and trying to and failing in public—in white tie and tails, at that—Benny appeared modest and willing to laugh at himself. This was the grace of Jack Benny—vanity in the face of public humiliation.

Moreover, he educated as he amused, for even as an audience winced at his not quite making it across the strings, it learned to trust its instincts about classical music, and that—trusting one's own responses—is the start of understanding and enjoying good music. It was for such activities, carried out with style and generosity of character, that Jack Benny was considered an elegant entertainer.

There can be no question that Kaye recognized these qualities in his friend and mentor, and it is not a stretch to consider that he might even have been emulating them. He had always made conducting a staple of his act, and so it was simple enough to graduate from conducting house bands to leading symphony orchestras. He started with eight minutes in front of the Philadelphia Orchestra at the urging of its musical director, Eugene Ormandy. In time, Kaye would be conducting a full evening's program. It was funny and it was fun, and as a friend said, "When you get in front of a symphony orchestra with a hundred musicians and you're waving your arms, you feel pretty good. You are really in charge." Or, as Kaye put it, "There's no greater feeling of neurotic power in the world." He would say that to interviewers again and again, repeating the same phrase as he did a handful of other phrases and assorted anecdotes, which was inevitable when asked the same questions so often.

When he conducted the New York Philharmonic Symphony Orchestra in Carnegie Hall, he came on after the intermission. The first half of the concert had been a traditional program, led by the orchestra's musical director, Dimitri Mitropoulos. Then, according to the mischievously written program, the orchestra was to play "Under the Direction of Danny Kaye?" The question mark was followed by the warning "The management assumes no responsibility for this portion of the program."

Kaye had special advantages as he strode from the wings of the country's, and ultimately the world's, concert halls. One advantage was the zany reputation that preceded him, which had the audience giggling at the mere idea of his conducting. Another advantage was his long and wavy (rebleached) golden hair, which fit the image of a conductor. Nor did it hurt that he moved with the grace of a dancer and was supple and lithe in a full dress suit. An advantage, finally, was the brilliant and delicious glow that radiated from him onstage, to light upon any audience he faced.

If it might seem daunting to face an audience from the stage of a concert hall, it wasn't for Kaye. In the first place, he had been on stages all of his adult life—in auditoriums that were as big as these. He also had a dignity and a confidence that at least suggested he believed in his own legend. Finally, most concert halls are old and tend to be cozy for their size—wide and shallow with deep, thrusting balconies. It is easy, looking out from the conductor's podium, to see the eyes of the audience in the first couple of dozen rows and in the box seats and even the faces of the people in the balconies.

Just as he had done as a tummler at White Roe, he would "trip" on his stroll from the wings, nearly dropping the dozen batons that were jammed under his arm. His concert-hall audiences responded no differently than the Catskills vacationers of twenty years earlier. After they quieted down, he would step onto the conductor's podium and pile the batons on the music desk. Then he would step down again and shake hands with the concertmaster. Stepping back up, he would examine several of the batons, holding them in the air to see how straight they were, pinging their tips for sharpness.

Then he would step down to shake hands with the second violinist.

Thus, the concerts began, or didn't, as he went up and then down until he was wending his way through the orchestra, shaking hands with all the first desk men and kissing the females. (Times were different.) Finally, he settled on the podium, and as one reviewer wrote about the batons at a Carnegie Hall concert, "Selecting one—he flung the others away disdainfully—he launched into his first number, which consisted entirely of a single, simple B flat chord."

Only then did he open the musical score that was before him. He examined it so closely that his nose touched the paper, which he then turned right side up—more business from the Catskills days. Ready at last, he picked up not his baton but a fly swatter, and raising it above his head, he launched the orchestra into "The Flight of the Bumble Bee."

With the brief Rimsky-Korsakov piece finished, he would daintily set down the swatter, pick up a baton, and poise it in the air, preparing to cue the orchestra. Then, like a baseball pitcher, he wound up and threw the cue. He *literally* threw it, heaving the baton like a cue stick. With the blast of the orchestra, the stick went flying over the heads of the ducking musicians.

When calm was restored, he would choose another baton and

strike the note anew. Shaking his head disapprovingly, he would break off a piece of the wand so that the note might be played more quietly. Finally, he would launch into a frisky overture, such as Rossini's for "The Thieving Magpie."

In the midst of the piece, he would grow elated, crying, "Sing! Sing! Sing!" But when a passage met with his disapproval, he could roar in Brooklynese, "Get out-a here!"

Writing in the *New York Times*, music critic Harold C. Schonberg called him "the most appreciated amateur conductor in history . . . with a thousand faces and the ability to reduce an orchestra to a pitch of helplessness unparalleled since the invention of the printed note."

In time he would lead orchestras with real joy. "I'm so delighted that if I were any more delighted I would be in an institution."

He could not read music and, despite his claims of intellectual curiosity, never tried to learn, even though it is not a difficult thing to do. He could act becomingly frank about his ignorance or be boastful about it—"I know every entrance of every woodwind, every string, every brass. I can't say, offhand, 'Ladies and gentlemen, let's go to [measure] 178. I don't know where the hell that is. So I sing to them where I want them to start, and then somebody will say, 'Oh, that's bar 121.' I'll say, 'Fine, let's start two bars before that.' "

Yet he would take his conducting seriously. Developing friendships with such musicians as Zubin Mehta and Itzhak Perlman, he began to speak with a certain musical confidence. As one of the musicians he worked with said, "Danny got the idea that he was really a better conductor than he was." Ego being what it is, he took to quoting Dimitri Mitropoulos, who "told me I wasn't funny—I had a gift." (The gift for conducting good music would not keep him from buying the Muzak franchise in Cincinnati.)

Kaye did not presume to conduct long, serious works but concentrated on lighter pieces or jingles from commercials, such as Gillette's "To Look Sharp/To Be Sharp." There can be no denying that he raised a lot of money for the musicians' fund, that he brought a sense of fun to classical music, or that he attracted audiences who would not ordinarily have attended symphony concerts.

On occasion he would turn around and face them while he conducted so that they might see "what a conductor looks like to an orchestra." Then he would demonstrate how some conductors contort their faces, writhing, groaning, or even collapsing in musical

ecstasy. Describing this in the *New York Herald Tribune*, music critic
Jay S. Harrison wrote, "You know the Kaye sneer and leer—one eye
grimly closed and the mouth puckered up so as to suggest that his
hands tied behind him, he was blowing a bee from his nose."

Much of this mimicked the conducting manner of Leonard
Bernstein, who was beginning to become famous for conducting
with every part of his body, leaping on the podium and suffering
spasms of musical delirium. The more famous Bernstein became,
the more balletic and wriggly was Kaye's conducting. He never identified Bernstein—one of the premier musicians of the era—as the
object of his mimicry, but after becoming the director of the New
York Philharmonic, Bernstein was one of the few conductors who
never invited Danny Kaye to do a benefit concert. Of course, Bernstein had his own place in show business as a Broadway composer;
even off the podium, he was something of a performer, making
regular television appearances on the popular *Omnibus* series. He
probably had his own star ego when it came to sharing his concert
hall with Danny Kaye.

Amusing as Kaye was, he never made fun of the music. The
orchestra was always faithful to the printed score, and no matter
how often he conducted a benefit concert, he seemed to love every
minute of it. "I don't know about you," he told one of his audiences,
"and I couldn't care less, but I'm having the greatest time of my
life." They roared at that. They loved such candor, and his zest was
genuine. No longer searching for a niche as a comedian or a dancer,
a singer or an actor, it was himself he was exhibiting. The use in
show business of the noun "act" is taken from behavior or a deed
and relates to what a performer "does." Zest was Danny Kaye's
act. It was what he did. He was a depressive with a public capacity
for joy.

Kaye's informality with the conductors he mocked was sometimes mistaken by detractors as disrespectful. The musical world
takes itself very seriously, and a maestro is often treated as a high
priest. One of the music critics in Boston took Danny to task for
calling out, "Chuck!" in the middle of a concert with the Boston
Symphony. The cry was directed at the orchestra's dignified music
director, Dr. Charles Munch, who was looking down on the pro-
ceedings from a box seat. The stern-faced French conductor did not
respond to Kaye's shout, but after the concert, he dispatched the
first violinist, Harry Ellis Dickson (whose daughter Kitty would later

marry Massachusetts governor Michael Dukakis), to convey his feelings. Munch gave Dickson a gift to deliver to Kaye, a framed, signed photograph of himself. Its inscription read *"De Tout Mon Coeur"* ("With all my heart"), and it was signed "Chuck."

After that, whenever Kaye was in Boston, he would regularly attend Symphony Hall concerts and visit with Dickson. On one such occasion, the program featured Mozart's scintillating clarinet concerto. The last movement is written to be played at a heady tempo, and that represents quite a challenge to the soloist.

That evening, Maestro Munch took it at a frantic clip. Afterward, when Danny came backstage to visit Dickson, he asked if he might meet the fellow who had played it with such demonic speed and virtuosity. The instrumentalist's name was Gino Cioffi, and Kaye mischievously asked to be introduced by Dickson as "a famous British clarinetist." He added, "I'll take it from there."

Wearing a hat, glasses, and a false mustache, Kaye then complimented Cioffi on his performance, with the terribly British qualification "But about that last movement, old man. I think you were a bit slow."

The musician, totally exhausted from his performance, stared at the ostensible British clarinetist in disbelief. "You play this *faster?*"

"Oh, yes, indeed," Kaye said archly.

"When do you breathe?"

"One breath at the beginning," Danny said, barely able to suppress a giggle, "and one breath at the end."

OUTSIDE APPROVAL HAS HISTORICALLY IMPRESSED HOLLYWOOD, AND Kaye's ascension to the headier ranks of international show business was not lost on the studios. By the time the Palace engagement ended, he had clinched the movie deal of his career. It was between his own company, Dena Productions, and Paramount Pictures, and the first film, *Knock on Wood*, would be made in his beloved London.

But he needed a break. He had worked three long months of two performances a day, following that with more shows on the road. Being away from Sylvia meant being away from Dena, but when he was with his daughter, he seems to have been as good with her as with other people's children, which is not true of everyone. The eight-year-old came into the den once while he was preoccupied, and he said very straightforwardly, "I'm sorry, but I really do not have time for you now. I'll play with you later."

Not long afterward, "later" came, and he went to her room to play with her. Now it was Dena's turn, and she said to him, "I'm sorry, but I do not wish to play with you now. I want to be by myself. I will see you later."

That pleased Kaye. Years afterward, he would say, "It established a very honest relationship. Today I can see my daughter and tell her I need to be by myself, and she will understand. She can tell me exactly the same thing, and nobody feels hurt or rejected. It is an established practice. You don't have to demonstrate love for each other every second of your life."

Perhaps what he said was true, but it probably would have been easier for Dena to accept if he demonstrated the love with his presence a little more often. Instead, after being away for nearly half the year, he was preparing to leave for a Far East vacation. That was when he received a telephone call from Maurice Pate, the Unicef man he had met a year earlier on the nearly calamitous airplane flight out of Ireland. Pate was calling with an invitation for lunch with UN secretary-general Dag Hammarskjöld.

Such an invitation was probably impressive but not unusual for Kaye. In addition to his friendships with British royalty, he had performed at the White House for both Franklin D. Roosevelt and Harry Truman.

Besides Dag Hammarskjöld, Pate brought Mrs. Vijaya Lakshmi Pandit, the president of the UN General Assembly, and she supported the idea being proposed to Kaye—and, of course, there was a proposal. They were not at lunch simply to eat. They all hoped that Danny might be able to help Unicef. They weren't asking him to be involved with fund-raising. As David Sureck, who at the time was head of public relations for Unicef, recalled, "That would have been kind of tacky. The idea was for him to be a kind of spokesperson so that Unicef would be better known and the work it did would be better understood."

And so Hammarskjöld, Pandit, and Pate arrived at lunch armed with a notion of how that might be accomplished. The notion was, since Danny was already planning a trip to Asia, why couldn't he devote some of that time to visiting Unicef's health and nutrition projects in the Far East? The visits would attract publicity, and publicity could help raise money for the impoverished organization.

Kaye not only agreed; he suggested that a movie camera and crew be brought along, adding that since he had just signed a contract with Paramount Pictures, the studio might be willing to underwrite the cost of the crew and perhaps the whole trip. Then the documentary could be commercially released, with the profits going to Unicef.

It was a suggestion that Pate, Hammarskjöld, and Mrs. Pandit accepted before coffee was served.

Maurice Pate made Danny's association with Unicef a formal one through an official proclamation, which not only sounded like something out of a Disney movie or *Hans Christian Andersen* but in its way made Kaye *into* Hans Christian Andersen. Being a scroll, the proclamation even looked like a prop, and it certainly read like one. Pate unscrolled it at a UN press conference on the day of Kaye's departure for Asia. "The United Nations Children's Fund," went the announcement, "has the honor to appoint you its Ambassador-at-Large, charged with making known the needs of children throughout the world." Although this meant nothing, it would ultimately mean many millions of dollars for Unicef.

It would mean something even more valuable for Danny Kaye —something so valuable that its worth could not be calculated in dollars. It would make him the personification of Unicef for a worldwide constituency; it would identify him with the United Nations and with children, two powerful symbols, one for peace and the other for innocence.

Inevitably, there were cynics who viewed this as a calculated scheme for self-promotion. While it was true that public relations could get no better, it would be unfair to ascribe (as some in show business did) selfish motives to Danny Kaye's original association with Unicef. It was another ambiguity, a matter of both idealism and prestige. He was inspired by the cause of children, and yet it would be naive to think he was oblivious to its effect on his image.

He went directly from the press conference to Idlewild Airport, where, at four o'clock in the afternoon, on April 16, 1954, he took off for India. A few days later, Mrs. Pandit greeted him in New Delhi, and a style was set for his Unicef travels. The style combined the formality of official meetings with heads of state, which Kaye handled with a respectful aplomb, and observations of medical and social work, when he was convincingly serious-minded, with clowning for children, at which he was wonderful.

He was taken to a small village outside New Delhi, where a vaccination program was in progress. In Burma, he joined a malaria-control team that was working its way through the rice paddies.

When he traveled through Thailand, he befriended a youngster suffering from yaws, his body covered with frightful raspberry blotches.

Kaye went on to Rangoon and Manila before arriving in Japan, where he entertained some two hundred orphaned children who were regular recipients of Unicef milk. The camera crew filmed all of this, the rewarding and the painful.

The seven-week journey ultimately took him to eleven countries, not counting a stopover in South Africa, where he played a commercial engagement. The resulting twenty-minute documentary film was released by Paramount in 1954 and was shown in theaters as a supplement to the feature. Immediately afterward, Unicef collection cans were passed through the audiences, and this was an international campaign. The narration was translated into eighteen languages, including Arabic, Danish, Hindi, Japanese, Persian, and Tagalog (the principal Indonesian language of the Philippines).

Finally, *Assignment: Children* became a centerpiece in the campaign for a UN Declaration of the Rights of the Child as well as the UN General Assembly declaration that a Universal Children's Day should be celebrated in every country. Sporadically, over the next two years, Kaye traveled around the world with the picture, appearing at galas on behalf of Unicef fund-raising campaigns, and it was ultimately seen, according to the United Nations, by over 100 million people. Some in the organization even believed that it went beyond helping Unicef; that by identifying the United Nations with the cause of needy children, the documentary created an atmosphere of international goodwill in general and helped to relax Cold War tensions. It was not so far-fetched a notion.

Eventually, Kaye's lead would be followed by other performers, but none would be so identified with the organization. "He was 'Mr. Unicef,'" according to public relations director Sureck.

With Danny's travels organized by Unicef, Sylvia had a place to call whenever she wanted to locate her husband, and she called the New York office for information whether or not he was on tour for the organization. They were seldom together anymore except for formal occasions, and so she was Mrs. Danny Kaye more often in public than in private. But what satisfactions the marriage gave her in terms of celebrity and social standing were surely less important to her than Danny's presence would have been. It had been love at first sight forever for Sylvia Fine. "She just plain loved him with all her heart" was the way Kitty Carlisle put it. "There wasn't anything he could do to destroy it."

Indeed, Sylvia would rise at her dinner parties and hush the table to raise a glass and offer a sad and spooky toast to her absent husband.

She had always been the brains, Danny the beauty, and so it remained. She was not polished. She still had a trace of Brooklyn in her speech. She still wore silver shoes with black dresses and was still lumpish, while he was the willow. He seemed to become ever sprightlier and more elegant, and she never stopped doting on that. There are, occasionally, marriages in which a wife is so smitten with a husband, so adoring, that she pays more attention to him than to her children. That seems to have been the case here, only exacerbated by Danny's ultimate remoteness—he in fact was not there.

It put Dena in a complex psychological situation, competing with her mother for an unavailable father. Sylvia would even ask her to join in the toasts to the absent Danny—so sad and a little weird.

Small wonder that the little girl was having a hard time with this complex, bright, but difficult mother who was capable of publicly describing her as "intelligent, pretty, and graceful but so far she has no discernible talent." Sylvia would add, apologizing with a knife, "I'm not worried, though. Before she was seven she begged me to give her piano lessons. I gave in, but I warned her she'd get tired of it after two weeks.

"She did."

DENA PRODUCTIONS WAS ORGANIZED TO BE A COMPLETE MOVIEMAK-ing operation. Beside the Kayes, its equal partners were the director Norman Panama and the screenwriter Melvin Frank. *Knock on Wood* was to be the first production, and the arrangement with Paramount Pictures had the studio providing the financing, the offices, and salaries for Panama, Frank, and the Kayes. Paramount was also extending its studio facilities, soundstages, and personnel for their use. The film's profits would be equally divided between the studio and Dena Productions, and the Kayes' share was arranged in a way that was most advantageous under the capital-gains laws. As usual, then, Danny's business life was a model of financial planning. That, rather than writing his material—and by no means is this disparagingly suggested—may have been Sylvia's greatest practical contribution to his career.

The notion that movie audiences had never seen the real Danny Kaye was very much on the Dena Productions team's mind. When Panama, Frank, and Sylvia (but not Danny) held a press conference to publicly introduce the new company, they insisted that they were going to "prove that films can capture the quality of spontaneity that Kaye reveals onstage before an audience."

How would that be done? In the case, they said, of *Knock on Wood*, the script was going to be flexible enough for Danny to improvise. Moreover, director Norman Panama said, "the cast has been chosen carefully, with a view to getting as many actors with stage experience as possible so that they can give and take and, in many cases, add their own remarks."

Such an improvisational approach could not alter the fundamental, mechanical reality of a movie. But in any case, there would be few stage actors in *Knock on Wood*, and few ad-libs, which was just as well. Improvising actors are as dangerous as writers who try to act. Kaye himself knew the importance of polished material and was always reluctant to try anything new. These and similar pronouncements notwithstanding, he rarely improvised, even onstage. The ad-libs in *Knock on Wood* would be limited to a few words in the middle of a car-salesman routine about an "overhead, underslung oscillating compression decravinator."

Norman Panama also said, at the press conference, that "Danny's greatest shows are the ones touched with his own inspired insanity, and we want to capture some of that insanity in our picture." They succeeded only in a sequence in which Kaye is being pursued and flees into a theater, getting into costume and running onstage in the midst of a classical ballet. When he is forced to make a rather frightening leap, his dance begins, and it even includes partnering a ballerina (Diana Adams of the New York City Ballet). In the *New York Times*, the superlative dance critic John Martin wrote:

> Now Mr. Kaye is not a ballet dancer; has, in fact, never had a lesson, it seems. Yet he supports [ballerina Diana Adams] beautifully in her pirouettes and catches her with great skill when she leaps at his shoulders from time to time. It is a truly wonderful two-way comedy performance. . . . If Mr. Kaye had not had a remarkable muscular intelligence, Miss Adams would have suffered a broken bone or two. Mr. Kaye is something of a genius . . . he would have made a superb ballet dancer had he been so inclined.

Knock on Wood became, of his own movies, the Kaye favorite, "the funniest," he said, "and the best constructed," but he was wrong. Intended to capture his stage vitality, it did not succeed the way *The Inspector General* had or *The Court Jester* would. Either he was a poor judge of his own work, or, back in London after four years away, he confused enjoying the city with enjoying the picture.

Knock on Wood is about a ventriloquist whose mind wanders in the middle of a nightclub routine. He loses self-control and speaks disparagingly about his fiancée through the mouth of his dummy. It seems that this is the fifth time he has broken an engagement in such a way, and in a plot resembling Moss Hart's original version of *Lady in the Dark*, he decides to see a psychiatrist to find out why he cannot maintain a relationship with a woman. It gives Kaye's character an excuse to do a great deal of psychologizing, and it is a fair surmise that this reflected Danny's continuing, intense involvement in psychoanalysis.

Meanwhile, and unknown to this ventriloquist, a spy has stolen British war secrets and hidden them inside the heads of the dummies. One final point: The psychiatrist is played by the beautiful Mai Zetterling, providing the love interest and allowing Kaye's character, the patient, to analyze the analyst, much as Kaye himself liked to play doctor.

The plot complications are inevitable and unimaginative, and the screenplay is not much different from Kaye's pictures in the Goldwyn days. Caught up in the spies' efforts to recover the war secrets, he is mistaken for a murderer, which puts him to flight. Sylvia's songs are, yet again, revue material that intrude on an essentially nonmusical story.

The movie does try to be adult, and appeal to adults, by making Kaye an adult. He is a plausible lover to Ms. Zetterling and romances her while dancing and even singing a rare (but very ordinary) Sylvia Fine ballad. It is a nice scene, but it seems effortful. Danny Kaye could never be mistaken for a romantic leading man.

Returning from England, he unexpectedly went directly into another big movie, and it would be the most commercial he would ever make. The box-office gross of $12 million would in fact make *White Christmas* the most popular movie of 1954.

Paramount had planned it as a sequel to the popular *Holiday Inn* of more than a decade earlier. That was a picture whose personal and musical chemistry worked beautifully, as Bing Crosby costarred with Fred Astaire, singing the holiday songs of Irving Berlin. But when Astaire announced that he had grown too old to dance and his replacement, Donald O'Connor, became ill, Kaye was brought in to join Crosby, Rosemary Clooney, and Vera-Ellen.

Because *White Christmas* had not been conceived with Danny Kaye in mind, it had no room for him to be funny or do dialects, and certainly not to sing Sylvia Fine's special material—not with a score by Irving Berlin. He couldn't even act. His part was designed for a personality actor like Crosby, Astaire, or O'Connor. This presented a problem, as there was no Danny Kaye personality. As his radio writer Hal Kanter had put it, Danny "wasn't quite sure what [his persona] was himself . . . he wasn't quite sure who he was." As a result, he is bland in *White Christmas*.

The picture has little in common with *Holiday Inn* except the title song and a country-inn setting. The charm of the original movie, with its easy affinity between Crosby and Astaire, is lost in the distance between Crosby and Kaye, one that amounts to a gulf of ethnic difference. There weren't many singing voices better than Crosby's or personalities more in tune with the time, but he emanates so much pure *goyishness* that in his presence the Kaye elegance turns not Jewish—never Jewish—but elusive; something that was not Gentile. Crosby was cool and understated, but *he was that*. Kaye was the eternal question mark.

Their inability to relate as performers is nowhere so evident as when they dress up as females to lip-synch "Sisters," being sung by Vera-Ellen and Rosemary Clooney. Crosby was very uncomfortable with this, and Kaye had to talk him into doing the number. Even then, this dressing up as women amounted to no more than hitching up their trousers, slipping on a few accessories (tiaras, bracelets), and waving great feather fans. It is the one moment in the movie when the usually cool Crosby looks ill at ease, whereas Kaye is plainly relaxed with the camping.

Irving Berlin not only wrote mediocre songs for *White Christmas* ("Sisters," "Count Your Blessings"), but even his dance number is ordinary. Great dance songs like "Cheek to Cheek" and "Let's Face the Music and Dance" were the composer's specialty. His modest explanation for them was: "I just write about Fred Astaire dancing." Perhaps that was also the explanation for the weakness of "The Best Things Happen When You're Dancing." He didn't have Astaire to write it for.

However, Danny Kaye does do a complete, no-fooling dance number, partnering Vera-Ellen through a long series of spins, leaps, taps, flamenco stomps (with hands gripping the lapels, elbows out), and even a few twirls in the air around a pole. It is a formula dance number as choreographed by Robert Alton, but considering that Kaye was not a professional dancer, he performs this piece more than creditably. Every singer and comedian was expected to do a little dancing, but that merely meant a simple time step. This is an outright dance routine. It is his only outstanding moment in the movie, and with Crosby around, he was not even perceived as the star. That was a curious first.

White Christmas was fated to be Danny Kaye's last successful movie. While finishing it, he fired Eddie Dukoff, his press agent, friend, and flunky of fifteen years, and Dukoff had to sue for his 7.5 percent interest in the Dena movie receipts.

20

*You know how hard I worked for him. How many years. He
sent some little guy up to my office. The guy said, "Danny
Kaye says you're fired."*

—Eddie Dukoff

A SPECIAL ACADEMY AWARD WAS PRESENTED TO KAYE IN MARCH
1955, BUT WHILE *ASSIGNMENT: CHILDREN* SEEMED SURELY THE REA-
son for it, the documentary was not mentioned. Instead, the citation
referred to Kaye's "unique talents, his service to the Academy, the
motion picture industry and the American people." This was probably not an oversight but a sign of political intimidation. In the ongoing paranoia about Communist influence, even the United Nations
and its children's arm had come under suspicion.

Kaye took the Oscar and went to London for his first appearance
at the Palladium in four years. Friends (or erstwhile friends) said he
flatly told Sylvia to stay home. When he opened the engagement in
May, the tabloids were ready. They had found a dependable news
attraction in stories about the escapades of Princess Margaret. She
had been leading a merry nightlife, escorted by London's most eligible bachelors, including, according to one report published in classic
tabloid journalese, "tall and handsome Lord Plunkett, wisecracking
and 'fast' Mark Bonham-Carter, polo champion Billy Wallace . . .
Croesus-rich Robbie McEwen." Another suitor of Margaret's, who
was less eligible but more troubling (because the romance was more

serious and he was divorced as well as common), was the Mitty-like aviator Group Captain Peter Townsend.

Now the tabloids had Mitty himself to exploit. Picking up on those reports, an American sensationalist magazine called *Confidential* ran a cover story all but asserting that a Danny–Margaret love affair was in progress. This was before the era of irresponsible, bizarre, and even funny supermarket tabloids in the United States. It was a time when libel law was actually respected, not to mention privacy. Even the articles in *Confidential* could not be entirely fictitious.

This particular article described after-midnight arrivals at Buckingham Palace, with Kaye escorting Margaret Rose to a "secret little side door used by the British Royal Family for inconspicuous entrances and exits." On these late nights out, after Kaye's shows at the Palladium, it was reported that the couple traveled in a hansom cab, its curtains drawn. The story offers only innuendo, but because the palace denied the Kaye rumor instead of, as was its common practice, ignoring such questions, the gossip was encouraged. There was also a rumor that Margaret Rose was considering taking the veil, but given the sexy bathing suits that she was photographed in by the paparazzi and her obvious enjoyment of nightclubs and drinking, a romance with Danny Kaye seemed likelier than a trip to the convent.

More shocking to the British, it seemed, was Kaye's audacity in calling her "honey." That bit of daring happened one night at the Palladium when the princess unexpectedly turned up backstage after a performance. Danny was overheard saying, "Hello, honey, I didn't expect to see you here." At her station, the prescribed form of address was "Your Royal Highness" or, at the very least, "Ma'am." Even the princess, unconventional though she was, had the reputation of being a stickler for protocol. As a British journalist assigned to the palace said, "You don't call her 'honey.'"

The outrage was reported by a *Sunday Pictorial* gossip columnist named Rex North, who sniffed, "In America, any woman of any rank who has been met socially a few times is almost automatically a 'honey.'" When Kaye was asked about North's story, he snapped, "I'd like to spit in his eye. Ask him if he was there. Anyway, it's a pitifully poor way to fill a column, to hop on things like that."

He also renewed his friendship with Laurence Olivier, and if Vivien Leigh harbored any ill will toward him, she did not show it. She even joined the two of them in a reprise of their "Triplets" routine, this time at a benefit for the Actors Orphanage. Olivier was in high spirits that night, not only singing with his wife and Danny in the baby dresses but, later in the show, waltzing with Bob Hope. There were no subsequent rumors of Hope's being gay.

Kaye's Palladium shows were played, as before, on a two-a-day schedule—rather, two-a-night—with performances at six-fifteen and nine. His half of each evening was the usual, generous hour and ten minutes—and sometimes more when he was so inclined. It was amazing that he still enjoyed performing after doing the same material—"Melody in Four F," "Tschaikowsky," and all the rest—for fifteen years.

If twelve weekly performances of familiar material made him at all restless, the only symptom, as the engagement stretched into July, was the lengths to which he would go on his days off. He had always liked short escapes over long distances, and Paris was only a few hours away, so a flight across the English Channel on a day off was nothing peculiar. Some, however, might consider dinner with Maurice Chevalier and Marlene Dietrich in Paris an event on the order of special.

It was while the three were dining in Chevalier's home that the telephone rang with a call from Prince Rainier of Monaco. He was planning a gala to celebrate his engagement to Grace Kelly and asked for her preferred entertainer—not Maurice Chevalier or Marlene Dietrich but Danny Kaye.

This was but the latest attempt to engage Danny. For weeks in London, a Monacan courier had been personally delivering the prince's request, initially offering $10,000 for the single appearance, then $15,000. Now Prince Rainier was himself on the telephone, suggesting a $25,000 fee, and still Kaye refused. This time, his excuse was that "I am having too much fun in Paris to leave."

But on the night of the gala, he presented himself at the palace in Monaco uninvited. Recognized immediately, he was brought to Prince Rainier and then to the princess-to-be. Kaye proceeded to put on an hour-long show for her, but it was without a fee. He was not a court jester for hire.

THE STAY IN ENGLAND COULD NOT HAVE BEEN BETTER TIMED, FOR IT sharpened his sense of British stage acting. Perhaps the atmosphere in *Knock on Wood*, which had been filmed in London, is *terribly* British, but *The Court Jester*—made on the Paramount lot in Los

Angeles—was going to be positively Elizabethan, and as filming began, he was at the top of his British game.

It would be the best movie he ever made, the most stylish, the cleverest, the most smoothly and tightly written. While he is unmistakably its star (there is only one scene in which he is not the center of attention), this is not the mere star vehicle that his other movies were. In this picture, he works *with* the actors instead of *in front of them*. The cast included such seasoned players as Angela Lansbury, Basil Rathbone, Mildred Natwick, Glynis Johns, and Cecil Parker—all stage actors and all British except for Natwick. And so even though, as Lansbury would say, "Danny wasn't an ensemble player—he was the one around whom everyone danced, and we all dressed to him. [Nevertheless] he came as close to being an ensemble player as he ever did in *The Court Jester* because he was surrounded by ace farceurs.

"Including," she quite frankly added, "yours truly."

The movie required not only that he cavort while, to some extent, subverting his ego to the ensemble effort; he also had to be physically agile, handle literate dialogue, and engage in routines written in the language of vaudeville. In short, he was offered the chance to exploit his myriad talents as never before.

The basic idea of *The Court Jester* is to burlesque *Robin Hood* and similar swashbuckling movies set in medieval England. The look is traditional, with the usual castles, armor, and jousting. The characters are also traditional: a wicked king (Cecil Parker), his even more wicked minister (Basil Rathbone), and a roll call of "G" names, including Giacomo—"king of jesters and jester to kings"—the witch Griselda, Princess Gwendolyn, and her suitor, "the grimly, grizzly, gruesome Griswold."

Kaye plays a carnival entertainer who gets mixed up in castle intrigue through a plot line that is complicated, improbable, and strictly logical—all of which are required by the rules of farce. While he is impersonating the bad king's new jester in order to restore the good king to the throne, the princess (Lansbury) is smitten with him and commands her personal witch (Natwick) to help him. This is a rather beleaguered witch ("Take that witch out and burn her!"), and the princess regularly warns her, "If he dies, you die."

So Griselda hypnotizes Kaye into believing he is a swashbuckler, and in that conviction he swings on ropes, leaps across parapets, and engages in flashy swordplay. Unfortunately, this court jester can be brought in and out of the trance with a snap of the fingers, and fingers keep snapping, switching him instantly from derring-do to cowardice. When doing derring, Kaye is a model of physical grace and fancy. Lansbury said: "His use of his hands was inspired by commedia dell'arte, and in the way he moved, he was absolutely original—he was one off the mold." But when he plays the coward, he merely indulges his familiar movie role of twit.

Visually, the movie peaks with a close-order routine performed by a real drill team, a routine so precisely and speedily tuned that Kaye's participation, comic though it is, actually is a feat of fancy footwork. Yet the best of the movie is in its deadpan dialogue. When the king tells his harp-playing daughter, "Gwendolyn, will you stop plucking that thing," and commands her to marry for his political benefit, the young, blond, slender, and beautiful Angela Lansbury responds as if she has no idea that she is speaking in movie clichés. "Marriage with Griswold?" she cries. "Never! He is a brute and a lout."

This kind of material is beautifully underplayed, as the writer Norman Panama and the director Melvin Frank keep their tongues deftly in cheek. Often there is such meter and balance in the exchanges that rhythm alone seems to be getting the laughs. In such comedy, timing is everything, and that is especially evident in a routine that is a modern classic, comparable to the best of Jack Benny or Burns and Allen, S. J. Perelman's material for Bert Lahr, George S. Kaufman's for the Marx Brothers, or Abbott and Costello's "Who's on First?" The routine starts when a fearful Kaye, preparing to duel the imposing Griswold, is being reassured by Mildred Natwick, as the witch Griselda. While Kaye's love interest, Glynis Johns, looks on, Natwick explains the plan.

NATWICK: Griswold dies as he drinks the toast.
KAYE: What?
NATWICK: Listen—I put a pellet of poison in one of the vessels.
KAYE: Which one?
NATWICK: The one with the figure of a pestle.
KAYE: The vessel with the pestle.
NATWICK: Yes, but you don't want the vessel with the pestle. You want the chalice from the palace.
KAYE: I don't want the vessel with the pestle. I want the chalice from—the what?
JOHNS: The chalice from the palace.

KAYE: *Hmmm . . .*

NATWICK: It's a little crystal chalice with a figure of a palace.

KAYE: Does the chalice with the palace have the pellet with the poison?

NATWICK: No. The pellet with the poison's in the vessel with the pestle.

KAYE: The pestle with the vessel.

JOHNS: The vessel with the pestle.

KAYE: What about the palace from the chalice?

NATWICK: Not the palace from the chalice. The chalice from the palace.

KAYE: Where's the pellet with the poison?

NATWICK: In the vessel with the pestle.

JOHNS: Don't you see? The pellet with the poison's in the vessel with the pestle.

NATWICK: The chalice with the palace has the brew that is true.

JOHNS: It's easy. I can say it.

KAYE: Well, then, you fight him.

That is how Burns and Allen would have ended the routine, with "Well, then, you fight him"—a dry punch line in a different meter. Daringly, the exchange continues. Just as Kaye has got it right, Natwick tells him:

NATWICK: There's been a change. They broke the chalice from the palace.

KAYE: (with dismay) They broke the chalice from the palace?

NATWICK: And replaced it with a flagon.

KAYE: A flagon?

NATWICK: With a figure of a dragon.

KAYE: (wretchedly) A flagon with a dragon.

NATWICK: Right.

KAYE: And they put the pellet with the poison in the vessel with the pestle?

NATWICK: No, no. The pellet with the poison's in the flagon with the dragon. The vessel with the pestle has the brew that is true.

KAYE: The pellet with the poison's in the flagon with the dragon. The vessel with the pestle has the brew that is true.

NATWICK: Remember that.

KAYE: Yes, thank you very much.

Mildred Natwick was a supreme professional, and she delivers her lines with the timing of a top-flight comedian. Johns was likewise an experienced comedy player, and her interventions provide expert punctuation, but the routine is Kaye and Natwick's, and they are a study in synchronization. His overall performance is a generous one, crisply disciplined and yet shining with bravura. Not so young anymore at forty-two, he was in superb physical condition, moving through the picture's rigors with seeming effortlessness. His tights reveal a youthfully trim man, with good muscle tone (although he apparently didn't think so, wearing "symmetricals"—stockings padded with sponge rubber in order to fatten up spindly legs).

The versatility, then, that had once made David Kaminski unclassifiable and had made Danny Kaye's early career so frustrating and problematic was now precisely what *The Court Jester* celebrated. Nobody else could have done everything that he does in this movie, and it is as simple as that.

Artists and athletes seem to revel in exhaustion, the use of every last drop of resource. Perhaps that was why Kaye, so athletic in his artistry, seemed happy on this set in contrast to his dourness while making *Hans Christian Andersen*. "We never stopped laughing," Lansbury remembered. "There was none of that moodiness he could have elsewhere, that abruptness, ignoring people." And yet he remained complicated. "If something interested him, sparked him, he came alive," she remembered. "The minute that was over, he was closed for business—which I think is true of many of the great comic performers. They are constantly out to lunch. Where they are, I don't know."

He was given the star treatment. "In the 1950s, in Hollywood," Lansbury said, "all the great male stars were automatically treated like demigods because they were male and this was a male-dominated industry. Danny was a prince of Paramount like Bing Crosby and Bob Hope . . . prop men brought cigarettes, chairs, cars. He didn't throw his weight around, but he certainly got special treatment."

He wouldn't be a prince of Paramount for very long. At $4 million, *The Court Jester* was said to be the most expensive comedy ever filmed. It was also the biggest comedy flop, grossing $2.2 million.

With his movie popularity ebbing, Danny and Sylvia had to be thinking about television, his repeated disavowals notwithstanding. It had already replaced radio as the country's dominant entertainment medium. Most movie stars had come to accept that, and some already had their own shows. Television was even creating stars. Danny's ex, for instance, Eve Arden, had never been more than a supporting actress in the movies. Although she had originated "Our Miss Brooks" as a radio show, its televised version made her a major star. Now she was in her fourth year of the popular series.

Of those still holding out, Kaye was the most intransigent. Repeatedly asked why he refused to appear on the home screens, he would be evasive, but one of his explanations did make sense. "I can't say exactly what a live audience does for me. But I do know I get back a thousand times more than I give." As the question was repeatedly asked, he could be testy. "I still like to make pictures," he told another reporter. "I still love the theater, working to live audiences, and I intend to do more traveling for Unicef. This obviously wouldn't leave me enough time for television, to do justice to the medium and to myself." If there was a certain sophistry there, it was no match for Sylvia's pretentious "There's the question of which sponsors, Danny being identified so much with children."

Some simply saw snobbery in this superior attitude, but one fellow comedian said, "Danny talks a lot about ignoring television, which is like saying he doesn't believe in the telephone. The truth is, he's afraid to try it. He couldn't stand it if he got panned by the critics or if he were to draw low ratings."

That was unfair. Perhaps Kaye was being arrogant or resisting change, but as for pans and low ratings, if such possibilities worried him, he would have been no different from any other entertainer. The real difference between him and the crowd was made clear when he finally did agree to appear on television. Early in 1956, after turning down $250,000 for a single "special," as one-of-a-kind variety shows were called, he telephoned Fred W. Friendly, the executive producer of CBS's prestigious documentary series *See It Now*. They made an appointment, to which Danny came dressed, as was becoming usual, in a floppy hat, a sweater, slacks, and "space shoes" molded to his feet. The feet were bothering him, the shoes helped, and he would soon wear space shoes on all occasions, even formal ones.

Fred Friendly was a tall, athletic-looking man, very well dressed in the country-gentleman style, tending to corduroy trousers, tweed jackets, and cashmere sweaters. His office walls revealed him as a political creature. The photographs and citations stressed democracy and freedom in America, and several of them attested to his proudest moment. That had come the previous year when he and Edward R. Murrow had done a *See It Now* show that took on Sen. Joseph R. McCarthy and set his political decline in motion.

All of this actually did reflect Fred W. Friendly, a cultivated, charming, and very polished gentleman who took journalism and democracy seriously. He took television broadcasting perhaps too seriously, but that is the way of most professionals.

Kaye shook his extended hand, sat down, and announced, "I'm going on a trip for Unicef." It was to be a two-month tour of the organization's centers in Europe and the Middle East. The idea that he presented to Friendly was essentially the same as the one that had resulted in *Assignment: Children.*

"Would you send a cameraman with me?"

The producer was interested, but he said, "If we're going to do this, we wouldn't send a cameraman. We would send a crew."

"That's even better," said Kaye.

The producer picked up the telephone. "Get Ed Murrow and tell him I've got Danny Kaye here. Ask him to come in."

Murrow was the narrator and star of the *See It Now* series. As a radio correspondent during the Second World War, he had become a legend at CBS, and he remained one as a television journalist—a writer, a reader, and very much an actor. With his dashing manner, shiny black hair, and matinee-idol looks, he bore quite a resemblance to Humphrey Bogart.

Beyond even these attributes, Ed Murrow's portentous voice was a thing of broadcasting beauty, although its resonance might actually have been a warning sign of the throat cancer that would eventually kill him. Smoking was his sexy trademark, and it was while smoking and with that resonant voice that he greeted Kaye, shaking hands and settling into the chair opposite.

"Mr. Kaye is going on a trip around the world," Friendly said.

Danny explained that although his intent was to help raise

money for Unicef, he was not suggesting a sales pitch. The purpose, he said, was "to bring to the attention of the people of the world what Unicef is doing."

Friendly glanced at Murrow. "Why don't we send a couple of cameramen along and do an hour show about it?" He turned to Kaye. "That is, if Mr. Kaye'll buy it."

"Oh, I'll buy it," Danny said, "only there's one problem."

"What's that?" Murrow asked.

"I'm leaving on Monday."

This was Friday. "We'll be ready," Murrow and Friendly said in unison. They pointed out that this was going to be a documentary, not an entertainment show, and so there would be "no rehearsals and no retakes." That was fine with Danny. He would later say that he liked the air of impromptu. The only thing that even came close to a snag was a telephone call from Abe Lastfogel of the William Morris Agency, who tried to wangle a fee for Kaye. Friendly pointed out that *See It Now* didn't even have a sponsor and was so unenthusiastically carried by CBS that it had been moved out of prime time and into "the Sunday afternoon ghetto," which was televisionese for the pocket of low viewership time devoted to public information and cultural programs.

"We'll do it," Friendly told Lastfogel, "but we can't pay him."

For the next "hour or so," the producer remembered, "we had a little argument on the phone about that," but Lastfogel finally gave in. "All right," he said, as if handing over the keys to heaven. "If Danny wants to do it, let him do it," and he settled for the Kayes getting coproducer credit. Lastfogel may well have figured that once Danny broke the television ice, there would be bigger payoffs, but even that was shortsighted. Any fee that *See It Now* might have paid would have been trivial compared to the intangibles of image and prestige that would come from such exposure, under such auspices, in such a cause, to an audience of immeasurable millions.

Friendly definitely realized that a Danny Kaye show could help him get a sponsor, which, in fact, it did. ("If he wasn't salable, nobody was.") He would use the early film footage to sell Pan American World Airways on not only the Kaye program but on all nine *See It Now* shows that season.

When Kaye met with the press before setting out, one of them asked whether Sylvia was going along. Danny laughed and said, "Good Christ, no!" and with that he took off with Unicef's Willy

Myer and the CBS travel coordinator, Martin Sandburg. They traveled by plane and car, visiting, entertaining, and filming for seven weeks, although Kaye did take a break in the middle, "to make a living," playing a three-week engagement at the Carter Barron Theater in Washington, D.C.

As Friendly and Murrow had promised, there was no shooting schedule. They would let the program take form by itself as events unfolded. Thus, it would be a true documentary rather than a preplanned television show that was being made to look like a documentary. If Kaye was going to be shown as an entertainer, it would only be in the course of touring for Unicef. "Not only that," Kaye said, "but we never knew what we were going to shoot. . . . The camera was an onlooker, like the audience."

The thirty-two-thousand-mile itinerary was exhausting, taking him from Los Angeles to New York, Paris, Geneva, and then to Rome, where the technical teams were waiting—three cameramen, Leo Ross, Charles Mack, and William McClure, and a sound crew, including David Blumgart, Robert Huttenloch, and Maurice Reitberger. After shooting in Rome, they went to Ankara, Istanbul, Tel Aviv, Haifa, Jerusalem, back to Tel Aviv, then to Athens, Belgrade, Sarajevo, Novi Sad, back to Belgrade, then to Zurich, London, Cannes, London again, Coventry, Sheffield, Manchester, Glasgow, Edinburgh, London again, Cambridge, Portsmouth, London again, Barcelona, Madrid, Casablanca, Zagora, Rabat, Casablanca again, Algiers, Kano, Katzini, back to Kano, then to Rome, Paris, London, New York, and, Kaye concluded, "from New York to the Mayo Clinic."

The nature of each stop varied, sometimes involving excursions to Unicef stations, on-site observations in remote villages, visits with heads of state, or actual entertainment by Kaye before audiences —occasionally at fund-raising benefits but generally on location, whether an amphitheater on the Lake of Galilee, a village square in Nigeria, or a children's hospital in Athens.

"The camera," he said, "had nothing to do except show my relationship to the audience. This is something different from just 'entertainment.' I couldn't be that free if I was performing to a camera. I never thought of the camera."

As the film packs were processed in New York, Friendly found that "each one was better than the last." In the end, the three cameramen shot 240,000 feet of black-and-white film. (This was before videotape and color television.) "There was so much good footage," Friendly remembered, that instead of the usual hour-long *See It Now*, "we scheduled the show for ninety minutes."

They stopped editing when they had it cut down to 10,000 feet. Realizing what an audience attraction Danny Kaye would be, Friendly and Murrow capitalized on his name and one of his best-known movies by calling the show "The Secret Life of Danny Kaye." It was slotted as the series' season premiere and was aired from five to six-thirty on Sunday, December 2, 1956. As the saying goes, the program made television history.

It began with a montage of announcers from stations around the world (as it was, in fact, being broadcast), each introducing the show in his own language. The last was Murrow, deliciously baroque in tone and in language. "The secret life of Danny Kaye," he deeply intoned, "is an open covenant, openly arrived at," which sounded beautiful but hardly meant anything. He promised that the program ahead was going to include "several ugly ducklings, some lepers that jitterbug, a jazz band in the Balkans, and a small Italian boy who sings a song about a donkey named 'Ciu-Ciu Bella.' " With that, Kaye was seen at the Acropolis holding hands with a couple of children and surrounded by a dozen more singing "Thumbelina." This and Murrow's "Ugly Duckling" reference suggest the impact that *Hans Christian Andersen* had made for Kaye. The show proper then began, at a polio hospital near Rome. There is no question that Kaye had a brilliant way with children, and he was wonderful counting out the exercise numbers in Italian while the youngsters squealed with joy, especially when he intentionally got the numbers wrong ("*uno . . . quattro?*").

As the location changed to Africa, Murrow's narration turned spare. He was painfully learning that the spoken word, so essential and beloved in radio, was redundant in television. Thus, he merely asked, "How does Kaye beat the language barrier?" and left the rest to the pictures. The pictures showed Kaye amusing an audience of African children as he mimed a proper lady sipping a cup of tea, first by mincing girlishly and craning his neck like a bird, then pursing his lips, lifting a pinky, and finally chattering and giggling like a biddy. The children plainly adored it.

"Ed," Kaye said into the camera, "it's 120 degrees here on the fringe of the Sahara on the slope of the Atlas Mountains of Morocco. We're here, you might say, with a cast of thousands—you might even say with a cast of millions, because the story here is trachoma, the almost universal disease which eventually blinds millions of children in Africa as well as Asia and many parts of the Middle East."

Behind him was an awesome vista, a herd of robed tribesmen trundling down from a village perched high on the desert dunes. Once a month, Kaye said with a flatness that successfully framed the shock of it, the entire population of the village comes to be treated by Unicef medical teams, "because every single person in the town has trachoma."

He interviewed a French ophthalmologist about the disease and its cheap, effective cure (his interest in medicine was obvious), and then the show jumped to Festival Hall in London, where thirty-five hundred schoolchildren watched him conduct the London Philharmonic Orchestra—only there was no orchestra. He mimed the concert while describing it in a *veddy British* accent. A moment later, he was leading a real orchestra, the Israel Philharmonic in Tel Aviv. And through all of this, Kaye came through as good-natured and sensitive, mischievous but intelligent.

The entertainment sequences balanced out the informational ones, as Kaye explained (talking to France's president, René Coty) that every Unicef grant is not merely a matching one but that each country doubles it, or when he spoke about vaccinations and milk pasteurization. Even his generalizations were thoughtful, such as a remark about children who "not only look alike throughout the world but behave the same." Rather, it was Murrow whose remarks rang false, set in televisionese, and seeming to be written in the language of advertising copy. "In an atomic world where one out of every three children goes to bed hungry, where five hundred million kids suffer from malaria or trachoma or yaws disease, where Unicef supplies a quart of milk for less than a cent a day and a shot of penicillin for five cents, Danny Kaye, professional entertainer, one part Pied Piper, one part traveling ambassador, and one part Sir Lancelot, travels the world as the official delegate for Unicef and the unofficial goodwill ambassador for his own country."

In Madrid, before another benefit audience, Kaye introduced his old number "Tschaikowsky," explaining that in Barcelona recently he had rattled off the Russian composers' names in thirty-six seconds. He warned, "I am now trying for a new record." This "record" was a routine he would do at almost every benefit for the rest of his performing life.

The show moved with professional finesse to a dancing sequence, first in Belgrade, where he tiptoed through *Coppelia* with a company of youngsters—being careful not to upstage them—and then to Ankara, where, in rare-for-Kaye black tie, he watched a group of eleven-year-old dancers and then stripped off his shirt so as to do his version of what they did. Telling them that his favorite Turkish word was "halvah," he suggested they go to sleep to his lullaby and sang "My Bonnie Lies Over the Ocean" in Turkish.

Murrow noted that "in all, Ambassador Kaye traveled more than thirty thousand miles . . . did as many as five performances a day, flying as much as four thousand miles in between." In Israel, he did the one dialect that, as a premier dialectician, he assiduously avoided: Yiddish. His explanation, in private, was that in public it would demean Jewish people, but some felt that it was part of a general disassociation with Jewishness.

If there is any brief for this perception of a certain Jewish anti-Semitism in Danny Kaye, it does not relate to his dealings with Israel. On *See It Now* he visited with President David Ben-Gurion as part of a series of conversations with world leaders, including Pope Pius XII, the sultan of Morocco, Sir Anthony Eden, President Gronchi of Italy, the king and queen of Greece, and Yugoslavia's Marshal Tito, who not only smoked during the conversation but kept the cigarette in his mouth while talking. When chatting with President Coty, a charming Kaye tried out his high school French. Curiously enough, his accent was as clumsy as the rest of ours. The marvelous French accent of his comedy routines would seem to have been available only when he *pretended* to speak the language.

While television audiences and critics became enamored of an Italian boy unabashedly singing "Ciu-Ciu Bella" (so enamored that Kaye later recorded the song himself), the dramatic high point of "The Secret Life of Danny Kaye"—one that led off almost every published account—was the visit to a leper colony in Nigeria. Although the disease can kill if untreated, "leprosy," Murrow explained, "can be cured and is not contagious. Danny Kaye walked among them and danced with them. It was a long cry from when they were avoided as unclean and condemned to a leper colony for life."

In 1956, the word "leper" still carried a connotation of contagious mutilation and the shunned, so this was very dramatic footage of Kaye mingling with these infected people in their village square and learning native dances from them. When he introduced a medical authority on leprosy, he listened to the explanation of the disease with convincing absorption. His interest in the subject seemed unquestionable, his concern for the unfortunate compelling.

Without doubting this commitment, the public relations impact of pictures—televised to millions—of Danny Kaye walking among lepers, talking to heads of state, and representing the children of the world in the cause against disease; his emergence as the personification of Unicef; the references to him as "Ambassador Kaye," this was incalculable in terms of what would later be called "image." He came to symbolize the innocence of children and the hope, the peace, and the idealism of the United Nations. It was an achievement that no public relations man, not even a common flack, would have had the chutzpah to conceive—Eddie Dukoff realized the possibilities only after the ball had started rolling—and this image was to endure for the rest of Kaye's life. It influenced even the toughest, most sophisticated and cynical of people in show business and the press—to so great an extent that when coming in contact with him, they would henceforth judge him according to that image and be accordingly disappointed or even shocked when there was any human disparity.

The climax of the *See It Now* program was filmed outside UN headquarters in New York, and as the equipment for sound and lighting was being set up, Danny was briefed by Friendly and Murrow on the questions he would be asked. Ralph Bunche, who was Dag Hammarskjöld's chief troubleshooter, looked on with the crowd of Kaye watchers who were being held back by UN security guards. Bunche was perfectly aware of celebrity power. He had even taken phone calls from Prime Ministers David Ben-Gurion of Israel and Jawaharlal Nehru of India, asking to come to UN parties just to meet Danny Kaye.

At the end of the show as it was finally broadcast, Murrow asks, "Why do you do it?" and Kaye replies, "Because I believe implicitly in the kind of work that Unicef is doing for children throughout the world and because I had the greatest time I ever had in my whole life doing this."

There is no reason to doubt the sincerity of the remark, and it would be unfair to do so. But when Murrow and Friendly were preparing Kaye for this portion of the show, that was not the answer he came up with. Murrow had said, "Danny, I'm going to ask you, 'Why do you do this? It's so much work.' "

Kaye suggested that his reply be "I'm doing it for my kid. I'm doing it for my daughter Dena."

She was going to turn ten years old just two weeks after the broadcast. The trouble was that her dad had lots of time for all the children of the world but not very much for her.

Friendly looked at him. "I liked Danny," he would remember, "but I didn't want him to say he was doing it for his kid." The producer, himself a father, said to Kaye, "That doesn't help your daughter. If you want to do that, why don't you stay home more often?

"That's the way to do that."

21

The marriage? I don't think it was anything that Norman Rockwell would have painted.

—Kaye staff writer Hal Kanter

AFTER DANNY AND SYLVIA WATCHED "THE SECRET LIFE OF DANNY KAYE" AT THE NETWORK OFFICES, ED MURROW AND FRED Friendly hosted a party for them at Toots Shor. The restaurant, which catered to a show-business and sporting crowd, was just down Fifty-second Street from CBS headquarters, and it was especially opened for this Sunday evening party. Of course, William S. Paley, the president of CBS, was there, as well as Friendly's pal, the artist Ben Shahn, and Ralph Bunche from the United Nations. Eric Sevareid came from the old Ed Murrow crowd of radio correspondents, and there was an unlikely pair of previous *See It Now* subjects, the physicist J. Robert Oppenheimer and the poet Carl Sandburg.

Danny was in a merry mood. It had to be the absolute peak of his career, and he did impressions of Sevareid as well as Sandburg, Murrow, Paley, and Friendly. Sylvia was in equally high spirits. She had insisted on being a part of the editing process, which, naturally, Friendly "didn't think was much of an idea," but it was an idea that she pressed and an issue that, as usual, she won. She could not, or did not wish to, trust anyone else with control of a Danny Kaye situation.

Getting things accomplished means not only drive but technique; knowing not only how to get something done but also when to do it through aggressiveness and when through tact. In this case, Sylvia had been tactful, arriving at the editing sessions with lunch for everyone, a lot of good humor, and genuine brightness. Fred Friendly emerged from the experience with the opinion that "she was a kibitzer and a nice woman," and he was glad to see her at the party.

The atmosphere became so amiable that Carl Sandburg climbed up on top of the piano, and then, with Friendly harmonizing, they sang duets. The stragglers didn't leave until after two in the morning.

The next day was the best of all possible worlds, great ratings and great notices. Moreover, the critics reviewed Danny not merely as an entertainer; he had transcended that. He was now a major human being. In fact, they tended to see the program as being not about Unicef or Danny Kaye or the world's needy children but as a single entity: Unicef–needy children–Danny Kaye. No entertainer in the world could compete with that. His old problem of unclassifiability was permanently resolved. Caretaker to the world's children was now his act, and that was how he was reviewed.

In the *New York World-Telegram*, Harriet Van Horne called him "a man of great compassion and goodness," while in the more proletarian *Daily News*, Ben Gross found Danny "more lovable and effective than many of the stuffed shirts," meaning the various prime ministers and kings who were given their moments of glory on camera.

Befitting a critic for the *New York Times*, Jack Gould skipped the issue of sainthood and even expressed reservations about the show. "There was a great deal of repetition," he wrote, "in showing Mr. Kaye, the entertainer, at work and not enough penetrating information on his mission as the unpaid representative of Unicef." Then, writing like a student, the critic conceded, "On the show he did explain how Unicef provides medical treatment for whole towns and takes care of lepers."

The notice in *Time* magazine was more like it. "Possibly because Kaye relied on his instincts, something was generated between him and the children—an atmosphere, a holiday spirit—which shines through the whole film and lifts it to a level perhaps not reached on television before."

There was no denying that. A glow of benevolence had emanated from the screen, and because of its intensity, because of the worldwide exposure of such charming altruism, Danny Kaye was installed in a pantheon beyond show business. Established as the UN ambassador to children around the world, he let the identification speak for itself. He was modest on the subject. "The truth is that I have dealt with children most of my life and for a very simple reason: I somehow can communicate with children. I don't know how, but it hasn't been any work; it hasn't been any trial, and it has been a great source of pleasure, a source of enjoyment."

But in show business as in physics, every action has a reaction, and the adoration of Danny Kaye invited a skewering. The skewer was wielded by a New York television columnist, Marie Torre, whose article appeared on February 11, 1957, just three months after the broadcast.

She adopted an analytic tone, finding a clue to the Kaye psyche when he walked out on Sylvia. With no mention of Eve Arden, Torre suggested "mental anguish" as the reason for that breakup, and not merely the marital breakup. The same anguish, Ms. Torre wrote, led to a severing of "all professional ties in America," an unexplained remark that might have referred to the lapsing of the Samuel Goldwyn movie contract. As for Sylvia, the article suggested that she had "a strong professional hold on the 44 year old mophead —whenever he's at home, that is, which isn't very often." The article continued: "Along with maturity, colleagues say Kaye has cultivated a tremendous ego and an all-consuming ambition to maintain his status among the aristocracy of show business."

Torre also referred to the "spells of moodiness, which prompt him to shut himself off from everybody and sit in gloomy meditation . . . he's been known to strike a subacid pose within seconds after he'd been on a laughing binge." If that suggested the possibility of a manic-depressive pattern, in all his years of psychoanalysis, Kaye does not seem to have been diagnosed as suffering from it.

Implying that Sylvia had been a source of this information about moodiness, the columnist added, "Danny and his moods have been together a long time, as Mrs. Kaye can tell you." But in fairness, Torre credited him with being "sensitive to sham and [he] withdraws from people whom he feels are too free with compliments." She also conceded that he was intelligent, since (proof positive) "he is one of the few comedians who reads the newspapers."

And speaking of newspapers, all of this was considered important enough to be printed on the front page of the *New York Herald Tribune*.

Ms. Torre's dark account was the first signal that the *See It Now* broadcast marked that dreaded peak, the start of descent. She even implied why, in middle age, he had reached the end of everything going right in her references to "ego," "ambition," and "aristocracy." It seemed to be a classic case of hubris. Danny Kaye's absorption with his position in the show-business aristocracy took him past mere status; he considered himself above a television series and beyond, even, a television special. The only television show worthy of him was not with him, not starring him, but about him; a news special that treated Danny Kaye as a force of international goodwill, its host the most prestigious of all television journalists.

"I did a documentary with Ed Murrow," Kaye said, "and that's my idea of TV at its best for me."

The stretch of time that followed *See It Now* was filled with frantically empty activity, momentum without direction. Even though Kaye made three movies, bought a group of radio stations, conducted symphony orchestras, and watched countless operations (for which he was inducted as an honorary member of the American College of Physicians and Surgeons), he considered these years a period of "semiretirement."

The first of the three pictures was *Merry Andrew*, a strained lark about an English headmaster who gets mixed up with a small circus and its beautiful aerialist (Pier Angeli). Kaye had no illusions about the piece, saying, "We probably won't win any prizes at Cannes," and that kind of statement anticipates failure. With the movie's release, his box-office decline continued, and it was the last time audiences would see him play the tummler. That, at least, was a good sign, for an aging zany is a pathetic sight.

The director of *Merry Andrew* was the Broadway choreographer and director Michael Kidd, and afterward the two men remained friends. It was Kidd who took Kaye up in an airplane and convinced him to follow through on his decision to learn how to fly. Danny was not afraid of heights, but he wasn't crazy about them, either. Kidd's argument was that learning how to fly was the only way to deal with any kind of air fright. It would prove more challenging than the average hobby. Certification as a pilot would require classes in navigation and meteorology as well as taking a written exam. Kaye applied himself to all of that.

He also went into the media business, buying, in partnership with Frank Sinatra and a Seattle businessman named Les Smith, the Mount Rainier Radio and Television Broadcasting Corp. The company owned three radio stations—KXL in Portland, KNEW in Spokane, and KJR in Seattle. After the sale, the company was re-named Seattle, Portland and Spokane Radio. Kaye left the running of the business to Smith, but he liked the Pacific Northwest, and it became another of his havens.

While *Merry Andrew* was slipping off the country's screens, he went to work on his first dramatic movie, playing a Jew who is in flight from the Nazis. *Me and the Colonel* was based on *Jacobowsky and the Colonel*, a Broadway play that S. N. Behrman and Franz Werfel had derived from a Werfel story. It was about a middle-aged businessman who is trapped in Paris in 1940 as the German army is approaching. He buys a Rolls-Royce, even though he does not know how to operate it, and engages a vaguely anti-Semitic Polish colonel to drive him to safety.

If Kaye seemed to be succumbing to the cliché that every come-dian wants to play Hamlet, he denied it. "We who are fortunate to have been gifted with an ability to make people laugh," he told a reporter, "should be satisfied being comedians. I don't mean to boast, but there do not seem to be too many of us." He promptly contradicted himself by saying, "It opens up a new, dramatic facet for me." Then, in an irrelevant and positively peculiar aside, he added, "They'll probably rename it 'The Love of Jacobowsky and the Colonel One Night.'"

Me and the Colonel had slim commercial prospects, being a black-and-white movie about not the top four on a list of moviegoer interests—a Jew, a Pole, the Nazis, and compassion. With the pic-ture's failure, the Danny Kaye Hollywood career was all but over. He had been switching from one studio—M-G-M and *Merry Andrew* —to another—Columbia and *Me and the Colonel*. Now he returned to Paramount for *The Five Pennies*, a biography of the jazz musician Loring "Red" Nichols.

It was a peculiar movie, on the one hand casting him in a character role in which he performs quite capably but, on the other, requiring that he sing three Sylvia Fine songs—because it was a Dena Production and because she was "Associate to the Producer." Although this is the film biography of a jazz musician, Kaye spends more time singing than playing his cornet.

While Sylvia's songs are not nightclub turns that violate the film proper, they do muddle the tone and contribute to making this rather dour drama unconvincing. None of the songs are memorable, although "Lullaby in Ragtime" is a neat three-part counterpoint and Sylvia's lyrics for "When the Saints Go Marching In" do allow Danny to give a rather wonderful demonstration of scat singing. He sings this with Louis Armstrong as if they were on a television special. While the number has little to do with the picture, it is still an ingratiating reminder of how vastly charming an entertainer he (not to mention Armstrong) could be.

When *The Five Pennies* became his third straight Hollywood failure, Kaye decided, as do so many entertainers, that it was all his agent's fault. Quitting William Morris, he signed on with a small, dark haired, very smart, very aggressive, and very dapper forty-year-old named Ted Ashley. A partner in the Ashley-Steiner Agency, the smooth and elegant agent correctly analyzed the problem with Danny Kaye's career from a 1960 point of view. The problem was a disparity between his perception of himself as an aristocratic performer and the avenues for making money, which were a bit seedier. Ashley seemed to perceive this as a clash between old show business (vaudeville/movies) and new (Las Vegas/television). His job was to capitalize on the Kaye image without tarnishing it, and that was difficult when everything that paid well was considered degrading for an ambassador to the world's children who, according to his wife, could not be associated with certain advertisers.

From Ashley's point of view, then, the problem with Kaye's career was Sylvia's management of it. She was the snob, she was the representative of old show business, and—when you got right down to it—she was his competition. If Ted Ashley was going to have a free hand in running Danny's professional life, Sylvia Fine was going to have to be deposed, and that is precisely what happened. From all the evidence, it was a deposing with which Kaye concurred, even if not as an active participant. When it came to emotional war, he was a conscientious objector.

Thus, he finally achieved his independence of her. The price of that would be guilt and an inability to ever leave her in real life. But then, his professional life might well have seemed more real to him, more important than his personal life. After all, it gave him his identity. It made him Danny Kaye, and that was his act. He was his act—at least he was his best self while doing his act. And yet he could never be sure whether he really was Danny Kaye or whether it was only an act.

Maybe that was why he became depressed when not doing it.

Ted Ashley's options were obvious, and the agent moved quickly to exercise them, convincing Danny to work in precisely the areas he had been snubbing—Las Vegas and television. In the process, the agent ended Danny Kaye's days as a unique and inspired entertainer; ended the kind of performing that Kaye enjoyed, which was for live audiences in theaters. Danny had managed to make the most money out of what he loved to do. Now, in the modern world of Ted Ashley, he would make more money doing what he did not like to do.

It was surely pointed out to him that such fellow legends as Marlene Dietrich and Noel Coward were already accepting the extravagant salaries that were being paid by the Las Vegas gambling casinos. Jack Benny had been playing there for years. Ashley booked Kaye into the Desert Inn for four weeks, starting on August 9, 1960.

Even more money was available in television. The agent did not have to work overtime to change Kaye's opposition to it. The time had arrived, he had been worn down, and Ashley gave the three networks the opportunity to bid against each other for what *Variety* would call "the choice program plum of the fall season." As recalled by the agent's wife, the beautiful Linda Ashley, "Ted manipulated a fabulous, unprecedented television deal." CBS topped out the bidding, offering a million dollars apiece for three specials. That was merely four times the once-stunning $250,000 that Kaye had been offered for a single special only four years earlier. The network promptly recouped its money when General Motors signed on as the sponsor. In fact, board chairman Frederic Garrett Donner was so eager to have Danny Kaye do a special each fall to introduce the new car models that he involved himself personally in the negotiations; he even agreed to a no-cancellation clause, regardless of the ratings and reviews.

Danny, as if to compensate himself for these concessions to nightclubs and television, got his pilot's license just in time to be able to commute between Las Vegas and Los Angeles. The deals were worth millions, but the license may have been worth more to him. Perhaps he was losing his zest for performance. He would never before have said, "Entertaining is my business, but it's not my whole life." It had once been his whole life.

Inevitably, there were reporters who tossed the years of television resistance back in his face. Someone else might have finessed the gibes by taking this as good-natured ribbing, but just as Kaye had once exploded over a penny being tossed onstage, so he remained touchy around disapproval. "Why now?" he snapped at one interviewer. "Why not? Look, you want me to make up a fancy story about how I'm doing a TV show now because I feel this is the right psychological time for me, that I've spent years studying audiences and I feel they're now ready for me? That would be a lot of bunk. The fact is that there isn't any real reason. Five years ago, I didn't feel like doing a television show—now I do. It's as simple as that."

Turning away from the questioner, he snapped, "Most reporters only last twenty minutes with me."

If Danny Kaye had understood the reasons for this testiness, if he had been less self-absorbed and more self-aware, he might have been less cavalier about television and more wary of it. But the arrogance of his charm and his inexperience with the medium made him ignorant. Melvin Frank, who directed so many of his movies, expected that "the public will not buy him in television." As Frank told Hal Kanter, who was going to be one of the writers of the Kaye specials, "Much more than a motion picture camera, television really gets in and tells you the truth about a performer. And when the American public finds out the truth about Danny Kaye, about what a miserable prick he is, they will turn him off."

IF KAYE WAS BEGINNING TO LOSE HIS JOY IN WORK, HIS INSTINCTS AS A live entertainer remained unerring, and despite an audience of drinking gamblers, the monthlong engagement at the Desert Inn went well. Much like Jack Benny when he played Las Vegas, Danny did not let the brash and vulgar atmosphere corrupt his performance; rather, he made the crowd adjust to him. His act was what it had been for years, from "Melody in Four F" and "Deenah" to "Minnie the Moocher," "Ballin' the Jack," and dialect routines. He avoided the tuxedo that was standard issue for a Las Vegas comedian precisely because he refused to be such a comedian. Donning the brown tweed sport coat and brown trousers that had become his costume, he simply treated the Las Vegas audience like any other, and it responded like any other.

Variety's review was succinct: "Kaye is one of the most potent entertainers ever to play Vegas," and Hal Kanter agreed. The television writer, who was in Las Vegas for preproduction meetings, saw the show repeatedly and found it consistently "superb. He could play an audience like an instrument." Then, with the engagement concluded, work began on the first of the specials, "An Evening With Danny Kaye." It was to be televised on October 29, 1960, in the best of all time slots, eight to nine o'clock on a Sunday evening. That was not only the primest of time; it preempted the popular *Ed Sullivan Show*, thus inheriting one of the biggest audiences of the television week.

With Dena Productions doing the specials and herself as producer, Sylvia was in her favored position of power, and she engaged the kind of personnel appropriate to a million-dollar show. Norman Jewison was hired as the director and André Previn as the music supervisor, at least until she fired him. Sylvia considered herself a musician.

She also considered herself a writer as well as the ultimate authority on Danny Kaye. Perhaps Ashley had usurped her managerial role, but her reputation, her significance, her identity, her own myth, depended on being perceived as someone without whom Danny Kaye could not succeed. "There are a great many people who appreciate what Danny does," she said to Murray Shumach of the *New York Times*, "but they do not have the faintest idea of what makes it come out that way."

Except for some help from Kanter with the sketches, she told the reporter, the writing of the show was hers: She established its musical format, she set the balance of music as opposed to monologues, and she worked in the jokes. Shumach accepted what she said, for Sylvia Fine was as established as Danny Kaye, and talking to her was as good as talking to him.

> On this show, Miss Fine works, for the first time, as producer. She was reluctant to do so, she said, because she knows that a woman boss is often resented and in this case the possibility of friction would be increased because she is the star's wife.

Writing the television special, Hal Kanter realized that, like the old radio show, there was no Danny Kaye personality on which to hang material; no character for situation comedy. That was what made the creative period difficult, and Sylvia's dominating style did not help. "She would never raise her voice," the writer remembered. "She was very quiet. Even in a roomful of people she would speak quietly. And still," he said, "she forced her own ideas, rejected anyone else's, and in general was a spreader of insecurity. After a while you began to doubt yourself—is this funny or not?"

But Sylvia was not geared to care what anyone thought of her as long as she did what was best for Danny, and in the electronic environs of television, she seemed to be fighting for his very life as a performer. She had decided at the outset that the show would be videotaped, which was a new process, and that it would be performed without retakes, as though it were live. There would be an audience at the dress rehearsal as well as the actual show, and it would be a popular audience rather than one of professionals and friends. The idea, Sylvia said, was to "let Danny work for the kind of timing that comes only with a live audience.

"The miracle of tape," she added, "is that it looks live, and I believe in the magic of a live show. I want this to be like opening night at the theater." But that was impossible, for there is a contradiction in terms between a live show in the theater and a performance transmitted on television. The transistors and cathode-ray tubes do not carry blood.

The show was going to have just one guest star, Louis Armstrong. Otherwise, it would be all Kaye. He did "Minnie the Moocher," his flamenco routine, and a send-up of Edward R. Murrow, the humor of which ran to calling him "Egbert R. Murrow." But the only section of the show that would be well received was a routine about a recipe being exchanged among the great chefs of the world. As Kaye was seen in multiple images, talking to himself, he had the chance to do his Japanese, French, and British dialects.

The ratings were better than the reviews. A few notices were kind, such as Harriet Van Horne's in the *New York World-Telegram.* ("As specials go, this went uncommonly well.") But Jack Gould of the *New York Times* and Ben Gross of the *Daily News* found it disappointing. It was Jack O'Brien, however, the meanest and most neurotic but also the smartest, the most articulate, and cleverest of the local critics, who saw through to the core of the Kaye problem: Greatness had been supplanted by pride of greatness. "From an entertainer with delusions of Chaplin," O'Brien wrote, "plus self-aimed overtones of Harry Lauder and undertones of Al Jolson, the least expected should have been a brisk, imaginative, tightly produced hour. It was not a disaster; worse, it was ordinary. And too frequently, it was precious but, as the man said, not valuable."

Kaye's own assessment of the show was realistic. "Some of it was quite good. Some of it was only fair. Let's face it, I don't march down the street with a brass band, but I don't destroy myself, either."

He took the million and started filming another movie, *On the Double*. It was yet another dual role, described in the *New York Times* as "a melancholy dive into self-plagiarism." Perhaps the quality of his work was not that important anymore. These were occupational years, productive without being fertile, meaning that they were only about money. He could enjoy escape and perhaps enjoyed escape for its own sake. Whatever flying meant to him, he loved it.

The second television special was taped in color when CBS finally accepted the RCA/NBC color system as the industry standard. Bud Yorkin replaced Norman Jewison as the director, and he put the show's focus exclusively on Kaye. The ancient, off-key "Begin the Beguine" was hauled out, while Kanter and Yorkin wrote another dialect routine, a simple variation on the first special's French, Japanese, and British chefs. It couldn't have taken much imagination to come up with international golfers explaining how they managed to miss two foot putts—in French, Japanese, and British accents.

There was also a sketch about a Washington cocktail party, but Kaye, a lifelong solo act, always looked uncomfortable doing sketch comedy. It made no difference, because one piece of material showed how a single mistake can befoul an entire show. The mistake was a monologue entitled "I Am an Is."

Ever since the tummler days, when he did sketches like "Rusty and the Doctor," Kaye had got it into his head that baby talk was funny. He would screw his face up, and audiences giggled, and that sealed it for him. It came to be part of his treasure chest, as if dependable along with "Minnie the Moocher" and the rest of the old material. But one of the cruelest signs of an entertainer passing his prime is a burgeoning treasury of such security blankets. The old material betrays a congealing fear of audience judgment.

Kaye couldn't be weaned off his baby routines and the coy monologue "I Am an Is" was the result. When his second television special was broadcast on November 6, 1961, the contempt of the *New York Journal-American*'s Jack O'Brien was again unleashed. Smart and nasty as ever, the television critic described the Kaye of special number two as "a fiftyish comedian who leans a full sixty minute show on the thick, syrupy goo of cuteness." Relishing the juicy target of "I Am an Is," O'Brien described it as "a far fetched tangle of pretentious sermonizing simplicity full of arch little simperings and fears that 'I Am an Isn't'—all in a style loaded to the diapers with googoo and gaga and glug."

He summed up the show as "Kaye's cavalcade of the cutes," and nobody could blame it on Sylvia this time. For when Danny had asked Hal Kanter to work on the second show, the writer had replied, "Not with her."

"Don't worry," Danny said. "She's not going to be doing it."

"I won't work with Sylvia again," Kanter said.

"I told you," Kaye repeated. "She's not doing it."

Nor, as it turned out, would Kanter. In the midst of production, producer/director Yorkin brought in his own writer, his new partner, and set him up as a coauthor. "I'm sorry, Danny," Kanter said, "but I don't agree with anything this man wants to do." That man was Norman Lear.

Googoo, gaga, and glug notwithstanding, Danny took the second million and again ran, and this time he bought himself a real present. He had just qualified for a commercial pilot's license (one of twelve amateurs in the country to get a twin-engine license), and with it he promptly moved up to an eight-passenger Beechcraft Air Queen. He hired his own pilot—Bob Dorn—as "an insurance policy" and never went up without him. The radio equipment alone, Kaye boasted, cost $48,000, and the twin-engine, propeller-driven plane, which Dorn called "a small airliner," had a price tag that was estimated at the time to be in the $100,000–$150,000 range. That was a lot of money in 1961, when a new Chevrolet cost about $2,000. Flight meant that much to him.

22

*Whatever happened to Danny Kaye, that wonderfully versa-
tile comedian who used to play in lots of movies a few years
back?*

—New York Times *movie critic Bosley Crowther reviewing*
The Man from the Diner's Club

WHEN SYLVIA WAS REPLACED AS THE PRODUCER OF THE TELEVI-
SION SPECIALS, SHE TOLD FRIENDS THAT SHE WAS WORKING ON A
Broadway musical. The property was *The Scarlet Pimpernel*, and
she had already acquired the stage rights; she even claimed to have
cast the title role, at least in her mind. The Pimpernel, who was
portrayed by Leslie Howard in the movie version of the Baroness
Orczy novel, would be played in her musical by either Danny or
Laurence Olivier.

But this was only talk. It was as if she had made a Faustian pact
to sacrifice her professional future for the chance to be Mrs. Danny
Kaye and there was no going back on it. Her musical would never
be produced.

The Kaye movie career hit ground zero that year (1962) with
The Man from the Diner's Club. Written by William Blatty (later to
write the novel *The Exorcist*), the picture was shabby, from its cut-
rate production values to the commercial tie-ins. Worse, an overall
depression seemed to have overtaken Kaye's career. Despite Las
Vegas engagements and television specials, either he was in an artistic crisis or simply didn't care anymore, or he was in an artistic crisis
because he didn't care anymore.

He cared about his Beechcraft Air Queen. He flew it to visit friends in Florida, San Francisco, or Seattle; to check in on the Los Angeles Dodgers during spring training; to tour for Unicef. And the organization needed him more than ever, not just for help in raising money but with its own image problem. This time, however, his liberal past made him impotent, and being Jewish made him a hindrance.

Unicef's problems had to do with the anti-Communists, for superpatriotism had not gone out of business with McCarthy's fall or even his death in 1957. The United Nations had always been a target of reactionary groups, and the criticism of its children's affiliate was intensifying. The Daughters of the American Revolution passed a resolution condemning Unicef as being pro-Soviet, and the American Legion endorsed that resolution. An organization called Americans from Seattle issued a call to arms entitled "Red Influences in Unicef."

At the center of the trouble were Unicef's holiday cards, which some considered un-Christian because they were nondenominational. The "Greeting Cards Operation" brought in considerable, desperately needed funds, but just as the United Nations was seen by the extreme right as being pro-Communist because the Soviet bloc was included in it, these Christmastime cards were perceived as anti-Christian because they were not exclusively Christian. The DAR described them as "a Communist-inspired plan to destroy all religious beliefs." The John Birch Society attacked them as being anti-Christian and subversive.

Danny could only stand by and watch as President Kennedy's wife, Jacqueline, came to the rescue by announcing that she was herself a Unicef holiday-card customer. The endorsement by the popular and admired Mrs. Kennedy not only elevated Unicef above the attacks; it actually boosted card sales.

THE THIRD DANNY KAYE SPECIAL WAS THE BEST, AND LUCILLE BALL was the reason why. Besides being one of the most popular performers in the country, she was an accomplished clown, with star magnetism, and her personal class was in tune with Kaye's. He allowed her to share the stage with him, and she provided a sense of confidence and gala. Whether she was goofing around as a confused chorus dancer in the opening number or playing drunk with Danny in a sketch about an unsophisticated couple in a fancy French restaurant, she provided strength without competition. At the end, perched on bar stools in satire of so many television specials, the two of them took turns doing impressions. Lucy did Judy Garland, Marlene Dietrich, and Carol Channing, while Danny took off on Frank Sinatra, Dean Martin, and Perry Como. An audience responds to a sunny entertainer, and these two seemed to be having grand fun elbowing each other off the bar stools. It was Danny's show, but Lucy primed it for him.

TED ASHLEY CAPITALIZED ON THE SUCCESS OF THE NOVEMBER 1962 broadcast. The agent negotiated his client a weekly series with the network for the following season. The onetime television snob was going to do thirty-nine shows a year. It was one of Ashley's biggest contracts, and it was why a personal manager named Herb Bonis handled Danny's private business affairs, but Ashley made the deals.

In fact, Ashley seemed more interested in Kaye's work than Kaye himself. Piloting the Beechcraft began to possess him in the way that performing used to. This was also a solo act, and it could take him above everything that was tedious and common. On high, he could escape depression as if it were simply bad weather. Coast-to-coast flights became as everyday as his elbow-pumping morning walks down San Ysidro Drive.

In the midst of one transcontinental flight, he began to suffer sharp stabs of back pain. As the attack grew more severe, he turned the controls over to his copilot, Bob Dorn. The plane was conveniently soaring toward the northern Midwest, and Kaye told Dorn that he wanted to drop in on the Mayo Clinic.

Landing in Rochester, Minnesota, he went directly to the famous medical center, where he was given a bewildering diagnosis. The examining doctor told him that he had appendicitis. As a person who was fascinated with medicine (what some physicians call an AAD—also a doctor), Kaye found no logic in back pain being diagnosed as symptomatic of appendicitis, which, after all, concerns an organ near the abdomen. He was even more confounded by the suggestion that he should have an operation, "like in half an hour."

But after the surgery he had to concede, "I can usually diagnose myself pretty accurately. This time I goofed."

. . .

EXPLAINING WHY HE WAS DOING A WEEKLY SERIES AFTER ALL THE years of avoiding television entirely, he claimed restlessness. "It doesn't do much for creativity," he said, "being in semiretirement." Hardly semiretired, he had, in fact, been working a lot. But he had not been doing live performance, the kind of work he enjoyed, because his new agent, Ted Ashley, had found ways to make more money more easily. What Ashley did not seem to understand was that Kaye (and most performers) enjoyed work as long as it was the kind that had first attracted him. For Danny Kaye, it meant performing in front of an audience. Though that could be difficult, it wasn't work.

Thus, being "semiretired" meant being retired from satisfaction.

"I haven't been very active for the last five years," he insisted. "A picture here and a personal appearance there, but lots of time in between. But now I feel that a performer should perform."

Alas, a television series was not likely to fulfill his need to perform. Even with a studio audience, television is not an animated medium. As Kaye himself had said, "No TV camera can supply a performer with the energy transmitted from a live audience." There was another reason for concern. *The Danny Kaye Show* was scheduled for ten to eleven o'clock on Wednesday nights. That was late for an entertainer who was beginning to appeal to an early-to-bed audience of the older and the younger. But CBS and his sponsors, the Armstrong Rubber Company and American Motors, had decided on the time slot, and that was that.

A television series starts with a producer. The man assigned to the Kaye show by CBS was the forty-five-year-old Perry Lafferty, who cut a smoothly tailored, slender, graying, and crisp (almost military) figure. He had produced important network shows for Arthur Godfrey and Andy Williams, as well as *The Twilight Zone* and *The U.S. Steel Hour*, but he wasn't a broadcast-business android. Trained as a classical musician, he also enjoyed the lingering effects of a Yale education.

For the next two years, he and Danny would be together, as Lafferty put it, "every day, all day. I was his father, and I was his son. He would ask my advice and then turn around and talk to me as if I were a little boy."

Perry Lafferty, like many people who had grown up with *Up in*

Arms and *The Secret Life of Walter Mitty*, was a charter member of the Danny Kaye fan club. Now, as a professional in the entertainment business, he considered Kaye an entertainer in a league with legends. "Danny," Lafferty said, "was like Maurice Chevalier or Al Jolson—entertainers who could talk and sing and hold an audience in their hands for an hour and fifteen minutes. There are very few of those. His movie career was over, but he was an international star, and now he had a big television series. You don't find too many people that have conquered all three of those media."

Even so, he was surprised by the network's agreement to build a private apartment for Kaye on the top floor of Television City, the three-story West Coast headquarters building for CBS. After all, Judy Garland and Red Skelton also broadcast their weekly shows from this building, and they did not have their own apartments. Ted Ashley had negotiated it. The design and construction of the suite cost CBS some $50,000 and provided a private entrance to a living room, bedroom, powder room, large kitchen, and terrace.

Lafferty suspected that it "was all connected to the Sylvia thing. They were under the same roof sometimes, but not a lot of the time. If she was in Los Angeles, then Danny had a place where he could go." Otherwise, the producer said, there was no sense in it, for Kaye's home was only a ten-minute drive away.

The apartment was not for trysting; Danny was never known to bring a date up there, although he did bring women on several trips with Lafferty. That only made the producer more confounded by a question that was being repeatedly posed.

"People would ask me, 'Is he gay? Is he gay?' I never saw anything to substantiate that in all the time I was with him." But obviously, there was something about Kaye that suggested gay.

Before production began, Danny insisted that Perry watch him at work not only in Las Vegas but also at symphony-conducting appearances. The producer, who hardly needed to be sold on his star, was only the more impressed. Yet he anticipated certain problems with the series because Danny "didn't do monologues like Bob Hope—getting up and talking to the camera. 'Hello! Good evening! Welcome to the show, tonight we have a wonderful show for you' and all that."

Sid Caesar didn't, either. The solution was going to be the same. Instead of monologues and jokes, there would be sketches and special material.

Until now, special material for Danny Kaye meant special material by Sylvia Fine. But from the outset Perry Lafferty gathered from Ted Ashley that Sylvia was going to have nothing to do with this series. In fact, it was his understanding that "by contract she was not allowed to participate in the show. That," Lafferty said, "had to be by Danny's instigation, because the network would never have insisted on something like that." In fact, during the four years of the series, "she had nothing to do with the show, she was never consulted about the show, she never offered her opinions about the show, and she only came to see it once, toward the end."

Lafferty spent six months preparing for the inaugural season, and Larry Gelbart was the first person he engaged. Gelbart was not only a top-flight comedy writer. He had a gift for program concepts (some years later he would create the M*A*S*H series). He had been a member of the legendary Sid Caesar television writing team. He also had, at that very moment, a hit musical on Broadway (A Funny Thing Happened on the Way to the Forum, co-written with Burt Shevelove). He was available for only two months, but Lafferty considered him worth it, if only for four weeks of working on the form of the series and another four to "physically write" one or two shows with the rest of the staff. In television jargon, this process of actually writing and forming a show was called "working in the Room." The Room is wherever the writers happen to be, although it is usually a conference room because they can all brainstorm together and the refrigerator is there. "Television writers eat all the time," Lafferty said. "They never stop eating, from morning till night."

Larry Gelbart was another who had admired Kaye since the first Goldwyn movies and, like Lafferty, remained awed by "his technique, his difference." Gelbart admired Sylvia's talent, too. She had once suggested that they write a musical together (based on Shaw's Doctor's Dilemma). He declined but believed that "she sacrificed her career for Danny. I think we would have had three or four musicals by Sylvia, but I guess in that family there was room for only one gifted child."

Gelbart flew to New York for meetings at the new Kaye apartment in the Sherry-Netherland Hotel. Instead of the old, huge place, this smaller, one-bedroom suite made more sense, with their divided style of living.

"Being a smart man," Gelbart recalled, "Danny listened more

than he talked. He didn't know what he was about, and he was looking for people who had done shows like this." And so the show Kaye wanted was not, as Gelbart put it, "bespoke"—tailored to suit him. Rather, it would be "generic"—a show like other shows that already worked. It would be written not merely by people who had written similar series; they were the actual writers of *Caesar's Hour.*

"It was an open secret," Gelbart said, "that we were still writing the Sid Caesar show."

That was painfully ironic, first, because of Kaye's unique genius and, second, because the Caesar shows had been produced by Max Liebman, and it was Liebman who seemed to have consciously or subconsciously modeled Caesar on Kaye. Now the original was the clone.

While Perry Lafferty was casting "a talking woman," as Gelbart put it, to play opposite Kaye and be "his Imogene Coca" (who had played opposite Caesar) the newly hired writing staff went to Las Vegas to watch their subject open an engagement at the Desert Inn. "It was a kind of huge icebreaker," Gelbart recalled, and afterward Danny joined all of them for drinks and dinner. There his conversation turned to airplanes and his beloved twin-engine Beechcraft. He had already pounced on Lafferty when the producer had mentioned that he was afraid of flying. Now Perry was about to start lessons. When Gelbart also admitted to nervousness, Mel Tolkin, another of the writers, conceded similar fears.

"Your fear," Danny told them, "comes from ignorance. If you knew what a plane was about, you wouldn't be so frightened."

There were a lot of gags about that from the assembled comedy writers.

"We're going up tomorrow," Danny said, and two of the smiles vanished.

The next morning, Tolkin and Gelbart made an apprehensive pair as they inched across the McCarran Airport tarmac to the Beechcraft. Climbing aboard, Kaye slid into the pilot's seat. He told Gelbart to sit beside him, in the copilot's place. Tolkin sat behind them with the actual copilot, Bob Dorn.

Kaye beamed at Gelbart. "We'll get up," he said, "and you'll see, it's wonderful."

"And with that," the writer remembered, "he gunned it, sat back, and said, 'Take it!' "

Gelbart would later admit, "That scared the shit out of me. I grabbed onto whatever it's called—the wheel—and I actually took the plane up from the strip."

Kaye had his feet on the pedals. He could have taken the plane over at any point. "He was no fool," Gelbart said, "but I did fly. I got up there, and I was doing what you do. And it was thrilling. Scary in the best sense."

Then Danny turned around in his seat.

"Okay, Mel," he said, "now you take over."

And that, Gelbart recalled, "was when I really got scared. Because Mel Tolkin doesn't *walk* well. Suddenly he's my pilot."

MEL TOLKIN WAS A THINKER, AND A THINKER IS A WORRIER. HE WAS already concerned about the series. He smartly observed, "Danny had class—not always a plus in comedy. You have to be able to take a pie in the face." Gelbart understood that, saying, "We think of Danny as elegant, choreographed, but when you do television, you have to get down and dirty." Still, he continued to view Kaye as "this sort of artistic comedian."

He was not bothered by the tacit agreement to imitate the Caesar show or surprised by it. "What are you going to do on an hour show?" he asked. "You're going to do sketches, either original sketches or parodies. You're going to do monologues. You're going to do mime. You have straight men, straight women, this sketch, then that takeoff or movie satire."

Tolkin was not so pragmatic about it. He thought Danny Kaye was "a marvelous singer and a graceful dancer," but, unlike Gelbart, he hadn't grown up on Danny Kaye movies and didn't think of him as a unique artist. Also, he didn't like Danny personally, while Gelbart did not concern himself with liking, or being liked by, the comics he wrote for.

"The big difference between the two shows," Tolkin felt, "was . . . Danny lacked Sid's depth of humanity in his characterizations. Sid was able to capture the heart and soul of an Italian paisano, a Japanese samurai, a French baker, a German general, a parade of gangsters and show folk, satirizing these foreign and American stereotypes—all of it done as an amused observer, a commentator on the human condition. . . . What truly separated the two was the one quality Sid had in abundance and Danny lacked—a warmth, an empathy for the common middle class dealing with the vagaries of day-to-day existence."

Warmth was always a subject around Kaye, because he managed to exude it in public and exclude it in private. For instance, the comedienne who was finally hired as the female sketch partner for the show was a tall (five feet nine inches), slender, elegant thirty-three-year-old with the wonderful name of Lovelady Powell. She was discovered by Lafferty and Kaye while performing in a smart Manhattan revue, Julius Monk's *Plaza 9.*

Upon meeting Danny, "Lovie," as friends called her, responded to the famous charm that he was capable of turning on when it suited him. She found him engagingly unimpressed with himself, "a sweet, giddy person." After lavishing attention on her, along with some hugs and a few light kisses, she remembered, "He made a vague pass, but it was playing games. The flag didn't go up. That's why I knew it was just froth. It was as if he couldn't follow through.

"Perhaps he wanted to," she said, "but I don't know if he was able to."

Kaye flew back to California, but he called Lovie regularly and sent flowers. When she arrived in California to start work, he invited her to his home for dinner. As in the oldest of stories, what she anticipated as a dinner party turned out to be a table for two.

Everyone in America knew that Danny Kaye was married to Sylvia Fine, but as some women do, Lovelady made inquiries about that, "and had been told that the marriage was on the rocks. Anyhow, Sylvia certainly wasn't in residence."

That evening in Danny's home, however, seduction was not his intention. "He didn't throw me on the couch," she remembered; in fact, he became strangely chilly. "He wasn't as 'friendly' as he had been in New York." Baffled by the mysterious and mixed sexual signals, she finally decided, "He didn't make any demands on me, because I don't think he wanted that. I think that he just wanted you to think he did."

Her first day of work, she came into the studio and found Danny talking with Larry Gelbart in the rehearsal room. The writer's first impression of her was that she was "extremely attractive but flat-chested."

So as not to give Gelbart the impression that there was anything going on between her and Danny, she smiled, extended a hand, and said, "Hi, Danny, I'm Lovelady Powell."

He looked at her and said, "Where are your tits?"

. . .

WITH BOB SCHEERER HIRED TO BE THE DIRECTOR, TONY CHARMOLI as choreographer, the writing staff in place, and with Lovelady as Danny's female comedy foil and Harvey Korman, formerly Red Skelton's second banana, as the counterpart to Carl Reiner on *Caesar's Hour*, the toughest slots ought to have been filled. The music director would prove even tougher. "That," Lafferty sardonically remembered, "was because Danny fancied himself a fine and knowledgeable musician." Lafferty, who was himself a schooled musician, had to be patient with this. "I knew I had to get a fine conductor and arranger who Danny would like—and who would also take his interference in stride."

That slot was filled by Paul Weston, one of the most respected studio musicians in Hollywood. Forewarned, Weston was not surprised when, as he led the orchestra at the first rehearsal, Danny snatched the baton out of his hand and cried, "Oh, no! No! No! No!"

Kaye proceeded to conduct the orchestra and demonstrate exactly how he wanted the music to sound. The music director stood quietly alongside and smiled.

"That," Lafferty said, "was when I knew I'd made the right choice. A lot of conductors would say, 'Forget about it, I'm leaving.' But Danny would wave his arms for eight or sixteen bars, and then he would go away. Paul would resume and get the number straight. They got along fine, but you needed somebody with Weston's disposition, because if you went up against Kaye, there would be trouble."

Anticipating the backbreaking schedule required in taping thirty-nine weekly shows, Danny asked Lafferty whether there was any way to get ahead of things. The producer proposed taping five complete shows before the series began. Then they would work on a week-by-week schedule so that after each third show they would be able to drop in one that had been done earlier. "That way," Lafferty said, "Danny would get a full week off every four weeks."

They were ready to begin the first season.

23

*I had a feeling that he was either gay or bisexual. I think that
was evident in his work.*

—Lovelady Powell

EVERY WORK WEEK STARTED ON MONDAY, JUST LIKE A REGULAR
JOB. DANNY WOULD COME INTO "THE ROOM" TO SEE WHAT THE WRIT-
ers, all ten of them, were working on. (As with the radio show, he
did not write anything himself.) Shelly Kellar was the designated
demonstrator. He took down the material as the guys brainstormed,
and then he would audition it for Danny.

While Kellar demonstrated, the others fell apart over their own
jokes, but Danny was a tough sell. One idea for the first show,
for instance, was "Fractured Fairy Tales," which was supposed to
combine his talent for dialect with his Hans Christian Andersen
connection. The notion was to tell "Little Red Riding Hood" with a
Russian accent. If it worked, then other fairy tales could be told in
French, Japanese, or German accents.

Kaye was dubious about it. He was always wary of new material.
As Lafferty recalled (much as did Sylvia and Kitty Carlisle with "Anatole of Paris") the staff had to "bludgeon" him into trying it, but
"when the audience started laughing, Danny's expression turned to
amazement. He looked offstage at me, and I just urged him on." So
it became a feature of the show, yet his resistance was not foolish,

as he carefully explained. "You may be right about what you have in mind here, but never forget, *I'm* the one who has to stand up in front of thirty million people and do this."

And the producer did begin to understand. "That's what these big stars are saying. It isn't a matter of being spoiled. It's a matter of anxiety."

Rehearsals began on Tuesday and continued until Thursday lunch. Then there would be a dress rehearsal on Friday, and the show would be taped on Saturday, because it had to be shown in Canada first. Otherwise, those just across the border would be able to pick up the signal from the Wednesday night American broadcast, and that would hurt advertising sales in Canada.

The first show of the series went well, but a problem arose during the second. Danny and Lovelady were singing "Take Me Out to the Ballgame" as it might be done in *My Fair Lady* ("Why Can't a Woman Be More Like a Fan?"), *West Side Story* (a switchblade fight over an umpire's bad call), and *The Music Man*. In the midst of the *My Fair Lady* section, Lovelady "went up"—forgot her lines. That was it for her. She was let go, even though the mistake could be, and was, edited out of the tape. Naturally, she thought the firing was because of the goof, but Larry Gelbart knew otherwise: "She was too tall, too slender, and too sophisticated to be another Imogene Coca."

That was only the first change. Every new program has to make adjustments, but television is expensive, networks and sponsors are impatient, and audiences are fickle. There isn't always time for getting things right. By December, the new Jerry Lewis and Judy Garland shows were already canceled. Lafferty had decided to replace Lovelady Powell with a rotation of straight women, including Danny's former girlfriend Gwen Verdon (who had since become a Broadway star and married the director-choreographer Bob Fosse). At Christmastime *The Danny Kaye Show* checked in at thirty-seventh place in the ratings.

It was not impressive, but it was not bleak, and progress was being made. The production routine had found its rhythm. At Danny's request, and much as Sylvia had urged with the first special, the show was being done "almost live," meaning that it was taped without interruption. Kaye said he wanted "to go right through to the end, and I want the mistakes kept in." Except, presumably, for Lovelady's blown lines.

The nonstop taping was hardly a sign of impatience. He was always prepared, and his performances were crisp. There would be occasional disagreements, but Lafferty had learned, from watching Danny's personal manager, Herb Bonis, that handling this star was like handling a baby.

"Now, Danny," Perry would begin, "let's talk about this for a minute. Do you want to do this? Do you want to know what I think?"

A petulant Kaye would grumble, "No."

"Okay," the producer would shrug, "then forget it."

After a moment's silence, Danny would say, "Tell me what you think."

Despite such occasional star pampering, Kaye was a professional, and he knew what he wanted from the nonstop taping: an air of spontaneity. Lafferty translated that as "Danny wanted to be 'up' for the show."

But such onstage ups were counterpoised against serious off-camera downs. The depressions that so many had noticed throughout his life seemed to be coming around more often. It was as if there were a connection between a professional entertainer's public high spirits and a psychic payment for them; as if all the moodiness and anxieties were put on hold while the performer sang and danced and grinned and sold himself. The crash came later.

"He was capable of very black moods," Lafferty said, recalling a typical ten o'clock alarm one night, when Danny telephoned.

"Hey, Per," he whispered low. "What are you doing?"

"Nothing," Lafferty lied. "What's up?"

"Could you maybe come over?"

Lafferty dressed and got into his car for the fifteen-minute drive to 1103 San Ysidro. After the gate at the bottom of the driveway was opened for him, he drove up to the house, where the front door was ajar. He let himself into the darkened hallway, a light glimmering ahead in the living room. There he found Danny sitting in a corner armchair, staring into dead space. Plopping down opposite, the producer listened and chatted for an hour. Finally, Danny yawned, stretched, rose, and went upstairs to bed.

"It might have been that he didn't like a review that somebody wrote about the show." Lafferty didn't even remember the specific incident. It didn't matter. "It could have been something equally unimportant."

Unimportant, perhaps, to Lafferty, but reviews can make performers bleed and the Kaye show was being raked. In December, *Newsweek* ran a Danny Kaye cover story that cut some more.

> The flying feet, the magic hands, the rubber face, and the vaulting voice are generally put to work one at a time, and they have not yet gotten together . . . Too many of his comedy skits have been pointless. Sometimes he tends to peddle his own cuteness, which is inappropriate for a man of 50.

Although Melvin Frank had predicted that television would expose the "real," mean-spirited Danny Kaye, that had not happened because the real Danny Kaye was ambiguous. *Newsweek* did notice that off-camera

> Kaye can be hugely rude but most of the time he gets away with such behavior because he can muster a staggering amount of charm . . . [he] can be formidable when he meets someone he doesn't cotton to. He simply looks away from people or situations. His crew sometimes calls him "The Great Stone Face." You ask him a question he doesn't want to answer and he just looks at you.

As for the magazine's depiction of the marriage, Sylvia could have given politicians lessons in media management. While she could not stop *Newsweek* from noticing the separate lives she and Danny led, it not only came out as acceptable ("Their separation is largely one of careers"), but the story even certified her fantasy: "Sylvia is in New York working on a Broadway show."

Meanwhile, Lafferty stepped up the guest power. Louis Armstrong was one of Danny's favorites, and the two of them got together to sing a smashing version of "When the Saints Go Marching In." With both doing scat singing, it not only underlined Kaye's versatility; it served as a reminder that he no longer did the old git-gat-giddle except for the occasional "Minnie the Moocher."

On the show that Gene Kelly played, even Mel Tolkin had to admit, "They created theatrical magic. It was an hour that deserves a place of honor in television history."

What other comedian could sing and dance like this? The answer is that he was not a comedian.

By the end of that first (1963–64) television season, *The Danny Kaye Show* was still alive. It even won a couple of Emmy Awards, although Danny wasn't at the ceremony to receive them. He was working at the Desert Inn. Perry Lafferty accepted the prizes and then, carrying them in a paper bag, flew to Las Vegas to deliver them himself. He had just got his own pilot's license but wasn't arrogant about it. He took a commercial jet.

When Danny closed at the Desert Inn, the two of them left on a promotional trip to Amsterdam, Stockholm, London, and other European cities whose television stations had bought the rights to the show. The producer, although he liked to think of himself as a show-business sophisticate, was still star struck enough to be awed by the receptions accorded Kaye in those cities. "When the airplane would land, the doors would open, and you would look out there at the crowd waiting for him—now that is an international star. A hundred, two hundred, three hundred people at the foot of the ramp, whenever you landed. I mean he was a big star."

London was their last stop, and it was for pleasure as well as business. Danny was catching up with his British friends, while Perry was waiting for his wife to join him on a European holiday. As for Danny's wife, according to Benay Venuta, Sylvia was never again to be invited along. "All those years in England that Sylvia could never enjoy. He wouldn't let her go. She never went."

Danny and Perry both stayed at the Dorchester, which seemed to have become an English haven in deference and dedication to his youthful flop in its lounge. Late one morning, the producer was awakened by Danny on the telephone.

"Get your clothes on," he said. "We're invited to Kensington Palace for tea."

Perry Lafferty still thought of himself as an Iowa farm boy. He had been impressed when Danny took a call from Laurence Olivier and chatted away about *Othello* at the National Theatre. Tea at a palace with royalty, however, was beyond his imagination. He wasn't even sure what clothes to wear and considered renting a morning suit. He settled on a blazer.

Arriving with Danny at Kensington Palace, which is set along the perimeter of the lovely Kensington Gardens, he found it to be "a smaller palace, I guess for lesser members of the royal family to live in." A liveried butler admitted them to an interior that resembled the producer's fantasy of royal life. "Dark floors," he remembered, "and portraits on the walls and suits of armor—like everything you've ever seen about palaces."

They were led down a long corridor ("it seemed to me like ten minutes") and were ushered into a formal drawing room, "beautifully lit, beautifully appointed, beautifully furnished with flowers and chintz and silver."

Two attractive women were seated and in conversation. They looked up, rose, smiled, and one of them greeted Danny with an outstretched hand. This was his friend of fifteen years, the duchess of Kent. Now in her forties, the former Princess Marina was a handsome and stylish woman who had become a familiar figure in the courtside boxes at Wimbledon.

The other woman was presumably her secretary, although, for Perry, she might as well have been a princess or a duchess herself. "My chin was hanging down, and Danny was there, and they knew him. I didn't know how or what."

As he gaped, Danny chatted easily. "He didn't even call them 'ma'am.'"

In fact, to Lafferty's horrified amazement, Kaye began to speak with them "exactly the way he had teased the production assistants —with four-letter words all through the conversation. And they're roaring with laughter. They think this is the funniest thing they've ever heard.

"I'm dying, I'm so embarrassed. I can't believe my ears."

A team of servants arrived with tea carts, two men in black livery and a pair of maids. When Kaye and Lafferty were alone again with the women, Danny resumed his scatological conversation and Lafferty resumed his farm-boy gulp.

"I'm sitting in the corner, I'm an Iowa boy, and I don't know what's happening to me—I'm here with British royalty and Danny Kaye, and he's talking dirty."

Years later, he was able to reconsider it all. "There was this element of control," he concluded, "using this language that gets them a little off balance. He loved to test people. Whether it was a friend or an audience, he wanted to see how far he could go. And so he's in charge of the situation. But it was a very friendly, warm, fun afternoon that we were having.

"Ordinary people have medium ups and downs. His were extreme. He was up that day, and he loved it!"

THE SECOND SEASON OF *THE DANNY KAYE SHOW* BEGAN WITH A FEW handicaps. NBC started broadcasting big Hollywood movies at nine o'clock, and that was going to provide tough competition for Kaye at ten. CBS made his "feed," or lead-in program, a weak new series called *Cara Williams*.

Nevertheless, *The Danny Kaye Show* held its own in the all-important ratings, and the taping schedule continued as before, with several shows completed ahead of time to give Danny a regular week off. "He would often jump on a jet," Lafferty remembered, "and go to places like Hong Kong or Bangkok, and he'd come back and tell me about going in the back streets to all these little out-of-the-way restaurants."

He went to Oslo, for the presentation of the Nobel Peace Prize to Unicef, and to the Moscow International Film Festival. But he didn't need any excuses to travel. "He would fly off to Paris," Lafferty said. "He wouldn't sit around here. He had to keep moving."

SKETCH COMEDY CAN CURDLE FASTER THAN MILK, BUT THIRTY YEARS later, some of the skits from *The Danny Kaye Show* remain funny. For instance, one of the programs included a military satire featuring José Ferrer as an intelligence officer who keeps saying, "I don't know." Opposite him, Danny played a German prisoner who defies all torture and then cries, "Don't hit!" when Ferrer makes a conversational gesture.

But other sketches seem painfully stale, such as a primeval business in green leotards called "William Tell and Son." Of that, Kaye's former radio producer, Goodman Ace, said, "He likes to dress up like Robin Hood, so they do Robin Hood." But Ace had reason to be snide about Danny Kaye, having produced his failed radio show and now being the chief writer for a fading Sid Caesar.

As for Kaye's guest stars, they continued to be unstintingly drawn from the general variety-show lists, whether sizable stars like Robert Goulet and Bobby Darin, bigger stars like Dinah Shore and Mary Tyler Moore, or great stars like Harry Belafonte. A re-viewing of the Belafonte appearance on the show is a revelation, for in 1965 he was a bronze prince—a couple of inches taller than Kaye's six feet, broad-shouldered, narrow-hipped, with a sculpted face, smart eyes, and a musical laugh as rich as his buttermilk voice. In this guest appearance, he was dressed in black, with the shirt—as was his trademark—unbuttoned to the chest.

When Kaye strolled out for their duet, he was wearing the same outfit as Belafonte, with the same open shirt, which was immediately funny. He promptly mimicked the singer's sexy gyrations while joining in one of Belafonte's calypso hits, "Mama, Look a Boo-Boo." The two were plainly fond of each other—confident of their stardom, pleased with equals, and unafraid of competition. The number was delicious.

Kaye not only appeared friendly with black fellow entertainers; he seemed to make it a point to have them as guest stars and to show his appreciation of and affection for them on camera. There was a flap the night that Diahann Carroll was on the show because he spontaneously kissed her cheek. Lafferty heard from CBS network headquarters about that—"it caused something of an uproar"—and it had to be deleted from the tape.

More curious was a show with Art Carney, one of several that the actor did with Kaye. One of their sketches was set in a kitchen with a ringing telephone. Kaye was down front, facing the audience, and couldn't see Carney taking the call behind him. He couldn't see, either, that the actor/comedian dropped the phone.

Improvising to cover the accident, Carney invented a little comedy routine as he leaned over to pick up the telephone. It was based on business that had become his trademark when doing *The Honeymooners* with Jackie Gleason. Just as Ed Norton would prepare to sign his name by gesturing elaborately with his arms, making filigrees with his elbows and wrists, so Carney now made a series of great arcs with his arms and elbows before picking up the telephone. Then, when he finally did pick it up, he did the old vaudeville routine about getting the wire tangled under his arms and through his legs.

Lafferty, watching from the wings, remembered that "it wasn't very long, maybe five or ten seconds. But the audience was screaming with laughter.

"Now Danny can't see what's happening. But he knows that *he* didn't do anything funny. So I could see this veil go across his eyes, because he's right in the foreground of the shot."

And the producer groaned to himself, "Oh, boy!"

For he knew that while the audience was loving it, and while they may have been rollicking and guffawing, Danny Kaye was not pleased. The only thing worse than someone else getting a laugh on his business—and he was doing comedy business at that very moment—was not getting the joke himself. And he didn't know what the audience was laughing about.

The show continued, ending as usual with the stage being cleared, leaving an "infinity set." That, as Lafferty described it, "isn't anywhere"; it is a bare, completely white studio space, with a white floor and white walls and a white cyclorama in the background. Kaye would then come out and say, "Good night," and the orchestra would play the closing theme while he skipped around the stage like a youngster or an elf. And then he would skip his way upstage while the credits were rolling—finally skipping offstage.

After the Carney sketch, he not only skipped around the stage and then offstage; he skipped right out of the building and into the parking lot. He didn't bother scrubbing off his makeup or changing clothes. He got into his Mercedes and drove home, leaving Lafferty's "hands full, because Mr. Carney didn't mean to do anything. He was just reacting [to the dropped telephone] as a performer. He was terribly upset because Danny didn't say good night to him."

The producer knew that there was no sense in going home, because Danny was bound to call, and then he would just have to get up and drive over. So he drove directly to the Kaye house.

"And there he was in the corner of the living room."

Perry watched his glum star for a moment and then said, "Come on, Danny. The guy didn't mean it."

Kaye just stared. The producer knew it was going to be a couple of hours.

"If you were a psychiatrist, you could call him a manic-depressive, because he could be way up or else way down. If he gets a call to Kensington Palace for tea one afternoon, that makes him go up. If Art Carney does something with the telephone when he's not looking and gets laughs, he gets down."

Art Carney was never invited back on the show.

24

Kaye all but abandoned his talent the last third of a career. For some reason that has always troubled me, he walked away from his public and his huge gift. . . . The great ones leave too soon, the mediocre go on forever.

—Gerald Nachman, *San Francisco Chronicle*

THE PRESIDENT OF CBS WAS JAMES T. AUBREY, A MAN AFFECTIONATELY KNOWN IN BROADCASTING CIRCLES AS "THE SMILING COBRA." His vice president for West Coast operations was Hunt Stromberg, who had to carry out Aubrey's directives. Both of them were unhappy with Kaye's ratings, which had plummeted to eightieth place among network shows, and Stromberg was peppering Lafferty with suggestions. The producer passed them along to Kaye, "but," Perry said, "he would never go along with the ideas, and I was being blamed for that." In fact, in the spring of 1965, toward the end of the second season, with the ratings continuing to fall, Lafferty was fired.

Danny, at least, wasn't concerned. "Don't worry about it," he told his disconsolate friend. "They can't make me take another producer. I'll play their game, but I won't approve of anyone else." And Perry Lafferty trusted to that because he and Kaye were "so tight." But as chance had it, trust wasn't even necessary. Only two weeks later, a new management took over, Aubrey and Stromberg themselves were fired, and Lafferty was offered Stromberg's job as vice president of West Coast operations.

Instead of being pleased for him, "it was like Danny had been stabbed through the heart" and Perry knew why: because this also meant that he would no longer be personally producing the series.

"Hey," he told Kaye, "I was fired, remember?"

"Yeah," Danny replied, "but I told you I'd talk to all those guys and get you back."

"What am I supposed to do? I'm out of a job, and they come and offer me this *huge* job."

Kaye didn't care to grasp that, it seemed to Lafferty. "He scarcely spoke to me those last five weeks that I was producer of the show. He cut me off like *that*. It was this mood thing again.

"I'd walked out on him."

Danny would do two more years of the series for CBS, and Perry Lafferty was going to be the West Coast vice president for eleven years, and in all of that time, with only momentary and chilly exceptions, Lafferty would not hear from or speak to Danny Kaye. Still, he was on the team that renewed the show for a third season.

With that came a staff shake-up. Bob Scheerer, the director of the show, became the producer/director. After the writers were told, "Enough of the old Sid Caesar–type crap," they were all replaced. (Among the replacements was the future movie director Paul Mazursky.) Kaye's approval was needed for all of this, but considering the trouble his show was in, he couldn't be blamed for agreeing to the changes.

And so the third season of *The Danny Kaye Show* began on a none-too-happy note, but as Perry Lafferty himself said, "The greats have this sensitivity. It's a gift, and it can be awfully hard to handle, because they are so sensitive that the littlest things can set them off. And I don't think that among people with these gifts—well, I don't think a one of them was very happy."

IN NEW YORK, SYLVIA'S SOCIAL LIFE WAS A VERY *SOCIAL* SOCIAL LIFE. If the occasion was fancy, or just special, and Danny was in town, he might even escort her. On New Year's Eve, for instance, at the end of 1965, he went with her to a dinner party at the Manhattan home of Mary and Albert Lasker. Lasker was an advertising tycoon who had become a serious philanthropist.

Sylvia may not have been aware of it, but the Laskers knew Danny through Eve Arden, a woman Mary Lasker found "lovely, don't you think?" For the same reason, Mrs. Lasker didn't fancy Danny's general treatment of Sylvia. ("He made his wife miserable.")

The Laskers lived in a town house on Beekman Place, and that New Year's Eve, their guest list had a special medical contingent. It was because the centerpiece of Lasker's philanthropic activities was the Albert Lasker Award for Clinical Research.

Predictably, Kaye homed in on the doctors, beginning with Dr. Isadore Rosenfeld, who was Mary Lasker's personal physician. The cardiologist was thirty-nine years old, a tall, lean fellow who bore a striking resemblance to the actor Walter Matthau; he also sounded like Matthau. In fact, Rosenfeld was just the opposite of Kaye—he was a doctor who wanted to be a comedian.

The other subject of Danny's attention was the celebrated heart surgeon Michael Ellis De Bakey. A few years earlier, the soft-spoken sixty-seven-year-old Texan had received the Lasker Award for his pioneering work on mechanical-heart-pump implants. (He would later become famous for leading the way in heart transplants.)

Few could resist when Kaye chose to turn on the charm, and he was in good form that evening. Even Mrs. Lasker, who thought "he never took much trouble with other people because he was a big star," had to concede he was amusing that evening, although she had to add, "Even if it wasn't in good taste." Dr. Rosenfeld's appreciation was not as left-handed. For him, "it was the most exciting thing to meet this childhood idol," and although Rosenfeld enjoyed being in the spotlight himself, he said, "When you were in a group with Danny, he was the center. He was entitled to it."

Sylvia was in good form as well, although Mrs. Lasker, looking on with her usual disapproval, noticed that Kaye "said mean things to her, and he didn't seem to realize that she was very gifted herself." The view of her seemed to vary with the viewer. As Izzy Rosenfeld saw it, "Danny was very protective of Sylvia and never said a bad thing against her—how could he? For her, the sun rose and set on him. She absolutely adored him."

If that was the sense of many who knew them, there is no record of either Danny or Sylvia ever saying anything negative about the other, and that seems to have been a matter of dignity.

The next morning, Kaye called Izzy Rosenfeld just to prove he meant it when he said he wanted to keep in touch, and later in the spring they met for lunch. It was at Brownie's, a health-food restaurant on lower Fifth Avenue in Manhattan. Danny wasn't obsessed with health food, only with good food, and over a fried-egg sandwich and cranberry-apple juice, he talked medicine. "He knew more pop

medicine than many doctors know medicine. He kept up with research developments," Rosenfeld said. The trouble was, Rosenfeld
wanted to talk show business, especially television, as he had just
accepted an offer from the *CBS Morning News* to be the resident
medical authority.

Danny was more interested in the guest lectures that Izzy was
preparing to deliver at the Baylor College of Medicine in Houston.
The lectures were at the invitation of Dr. De Bakey, the surgeon
they had met at the Lasker party. The medical center at Baylor was
De Bakey's domain.

"If you're that interested in the lectures," Rosenfeld said to
Kaye, "why don't you come down to Houston with me and sit in on
them?"

"Are you serious?" Kaye asked.

"Of course I'm serious."

A week later, Kaye was in a merry mood as they boarded the
plane for Houston. Rosenfeld would notice his shifts in tempera-
ment soon enough. "He could sit there for a couple of hours and
not say a word." Although disinclined to be an amateur psychiatrist,
the doctor did have his opinion about these mood swings. "Danny
was moody because he felt unfulfilled. He was successful—he was
worshiped—but I don't think he ever felt he deserved it."

But that time on the way to Houston, he gaily strolled through
the airplane cabin taking drink orders from the first-class passengers.
It was an old routine, something he did when he was cheerful.

When they landed, they were not met by a limousine, as Dr.
Rosenfeld expected and to which he had become accustomed.
"When you're a cardiologist," he said, "they send a limo. When
you're Danny Kaye, they send a helicopter." And it flew them directly to the Fondren-Brown Building at Methodist Hospital in
Houston. Built specifically for, and partly designed by, De Bakey, it
was a cardiovascular center with its own operating rooms and teaching facilities. Like the hospital, it was a co-operation of the Methodist church and the Baylor College of Medicine.

While Kaye and Rosenfeld chatted with De Bakey in his office,
Danny asked whether, besides attending the lectures, he might
watch an operation. The next morning, he found himself in one
of the hospital's operating-room amphitheaters, seated among the
medical students, and they weren't the only ones agog at his presence. "He was a celebrity, of course," De Bakey remembered, "and

all the nurses and doctors were fascinated and sort of awe-struck when he walked in."

By afternoon, Kaye had moved from the seats to the side of the operating table, for De Bakey had suggested he "scrub up," which meant sterilizing himself and getting into surgical mufti. That was something no amateur doctor could refuse, De Bakey recalled: "Kaye came into the operating room with me in a sterile gown and gloves."

He also brought a camera to take pictures of the surgeons and nurses, the equipment, the procedure, and the operation itself. He joked around, making the *pocketa-pocketa* sound from *The Secret Life of Walter Mitty*, but as well, in De Bakey's opinion, "he made some of the most beautiful [operating room] photographs I've ever seen."

The next day, Dr. Rosenfeld joined Danny as an observer at the operation. This time there were no students in the amphitheater, and De Bakey did something rather startling.

"They were putting in an artificial valve," Rosenfeld noticed, "which is a very delicate thing. And he asked Danny, 'Would you like to make a stitch?' "

Kaye looked up and nodded.

Rosenfeld was stunned.

De Bakey himself recalled, without seeming to consider it odd, "I showed him what to do. And he actually put a stitch in. It was delicate, but it was in a situation in which I felt secure about it, so there was no chance of any harm coming."

That did not satisfy Rosenfeld, who would later say, "I frankly can't understand how a surgeon could do this."

In fact, De Bakey recalled, Kaye even tied the suture. And then he got his camera so that he might be photographed at the operating table.

This was not *The Secret Life of Walter Mitty* but an actual heart operation being performed on an actual patient. Rosenfeld, who usually saw things in a comic light, was not amused. "[De Bakey] told me the stitch Danny put in was more graceful and sophisticated than some of his four- or five-year residents," but that did not relieve the cardiologist of his sense of impropriety. Neither did De Bakey's insistence that Danny was "just a natural—he knew exactly the angle at which to do it."

The patient had never been asked whether, in his open-heart

surgery, he would appreciate a stitch being taken by an entertainer—even if it was one who, when it came to operations, was "a natural."

De Bakey said that the patient was told afterward. "I explained what it was and that it didn't have anything to do with the actual operation. It was sort of an extra stitch."

And, the surgeon claimed, "he was very pleased."

"From then on," Rosenfeld said, Danny "told everybody he was an open-heart surgeon."

Oftentimes he would open a briefcase and show the photograph of himself in the surgical mask and gown. He had a copy framed and hung it on the wall of his den in Los Angeles.

WITH PERRY LAFFERTY RUNNING THE CBS TELEVISION ACTIVITIES ON the West Coast and Bob Scheerer producing *The Danny Kaye Show* itself, the series headed unsteadily into the new television season. Notwithstanding the new production staff, the ratings continued their downward drift. For Kaye, a fast trip for Unicef might have seemed a good idea, a breather at a time of stress and a reminder of his former life as a flesh-and-blood entertainer.

A few years earlier, a group of youngsters attending a Sunday school class in New England had used Halloween as an occasion to raise money for Unicef. Instead of asking for candy, the children asked for contributions for needy children. Collecting seventeen dollars, they sent it to Unicef, along with a class letter. It was referred to the public relations department.

Paul Edwards, Unicef's director of information, now turned that notion into a promotional campaign, christening it "Trick or Treat for Unicef." Kaye was designated the "Unicef Trick or Treater." Flying his own plane, he took off on a whirlwind tour, making thirty stops in three days. He gave pep talks to school and church groups of youngsters while they were handed Unicef canisters and black-and-orange buttons labeled Help Children Help Children. The campaign was widely reported, and Trick or Treat for Unicef became an annual event, another public relations triumph for Kaye as well as Unicef.

But it didn't help his ratings, and neither did NBC's *Wednesday Night at the Movies*, which had become more than formidable competition. With the season just starting, there were already rumors about a Kaye cancellation; inevitably, the rumors surfaced in the gossip columns. Still, the show struggled through the season, and in the spring of 1966, Danny took a two-week trip to Vietnam to entertain the troops. Perhaps entertainers are encouraged to do such things as career boosts as well as good deeds, but for Kaye this particular trip did not prove to be an enjoyable experience. Soon after his arrival in Saigon, a bomb went off in a hotel that housed American officers. Then, as he began the troop shows, he found some of the outposts decimated. In the middle of one performance, Buddhists were immolating themselves in the street beyond, and on the day he left, the Vietcong destroyed the airport.

Upon his return to Los Angeles, he was met by a group of reporters whose treatment of him reflected the difference between this war and previous ones. Instead of rewarding the trouping entertainer with publicity pictures and patriotic praise, they challenged him self-righteously, even belligerently. Kaye was asked whether he had heard about a shortage of bombs and medical supplies. He was asked whether the soldiers he talked to seemed committed to the war. He was asked whether he personally approved of the American role in the war.

For once, he was deft in coping with hostility, answering some of the questions and finessing others. Finally, he said with a certain curtness that was armed with sense, "I was there fourteen days. I don't think that's enough time to get well informed."

As Peter Bart wrote in the New York Times, "If Danny Kaye, surrounded by his entourage, engaged some airmen in conversation, would the fliers really take that opportunity to complain about a shortage of bombs?"

Kaye himself concluded the press conference by saying, "For entertainers and soldiers alike, Vietnam has been a frustrating war."

He returned to ongoing rumors of cancellation. Bob Williams, the television columnist for the New York Post, wrote, "Neither Danny Kaye nor his manager wants to phone chat about future TV plans, probably because there aren't any after Kaye's current, low-rated go-round."

But the series was again renewed. CBS tried to give it a boost by slotting the popular Dick Van Dyke Show just ahead of it, but that didn't keep the Armstrong Rubber Company from pulling out as a cosponsor. It was of little consolation that NBC rescheduled its network movies, for now the immensely popular I Spy was pitted opposite *The Danny Kaye Show*. It stumbled into a fourth season with ratings plummeting.

The attempts to promote the show turned pathetic. For instance, the actor George Hamilton was booked as a guest star because he was dating the president's daughter, Lynda Bird Johnson. Even the television critic Harriet Van Horne, admittedly "an old admirer of his towering talents," cited these Kaye shows for "inept and occasionally offensive writing." She complained about "boorish and unseemly passages" that she found "terribly unfunny and embarrassing." She was particularly incensed when,

> after a young and beautiful French singer named Mireille Mathieu finished a song, Kaye "translated" it in a jokey, gibberish translation, totally irrelevant and somehow faintly insulting to Mlle. Mathieu. Now and again she sang another eight bars [so] that Mr. Kaye might hurl another eight-bar joke at the audience. It was all terribly unfunny and embarrassing. One felt greatly relieved when nice, funny George Burns came on. His jokes are older than the old Palace but they're quick, neat and unbarbed.

Only a few months into the new season, in a rather sad display of public relations bravado, Kaye's agent, Ted Ashley, distributed copies of a message he had ostensibly wired to John Reynolds, the president of CBS-TV.

> As you know, your four-year contract with Danny Kaye, which expires at the end of this season, requires that we advise you by January 15 whether or not he elects to continue with a weekly TV series next season. In order to answer questions concerning Mr. Kaye's plans, we are taking this early opportunity to notify you that he will not appear on a weekly series during the 1967–1968 season.

In fact, *The Danny Kaye Show* had already been canceled, and it had been Perry Lafferty's responsibility, in his role as West Coast vice president for CBS Television, to deliver the news to Danny. He felt that in view of their history, he had to do this personally. It was doubly unpleasant, since they had not been communicating for two years.

He went over to the house on San Ysidro. "There was no screaming," he remembered. "Danny was cold, very quiet, very sotto voce. I tried to explain: 'These things happen.' I reminded him that for the last two years of the show I'd warned him that some of the things he was doing weren't exactly right."

Kaye sat in the chair and gazed icily at Lafferty.

"The curtain came down—I'm talking to the wall."

Thus concluded the first unsuccessful episode of Kaye's career, and the blame for it was to be found at home. For he had not been undone by television's exposure of his personal character, as Melvin Frank had predicted. Nor had he been undone by his agent, Ted Ashley, who had guided him to work where the money was best for Danny Kaye but not the conditions.

He had been undone by the elimination of Sylvia Fine from her managerial role. She had always said she knew his gifts and his abilities and what was right for him, and it was true.

All eras end. Ended now was the one of live entertainers and great stars; of humans singing, dancing, or telling jokes, alone on the stage, in the spotlight. That era, having been short-circuited by radio, was now dead of television, which simulated the performer with phosphors on a cathode-ray tube, finally making him an electronic replica, live on tape.

And so Danny Kaye was a relic. Who was to know what magic he had made, what greatness had been his?

In the *World-Journal-Tribune*, Frank Farrell reported, "Danny Kaye tells friends he is totally fed up with television and will concentrate on movies again as soon as he completes six weeks on stage in England's Chichester Theatre Festival."

Now that was news. It was also an interesting idea. Kaye had always shown potential as an actor and sometimes came close to fulfilling it. Surely he had spoken with Laurence Olivier about acting and the possibility of his attempting something on the stage.

In 1962, Olivier had been asked to start a summer drama festival in the village of Chichester, just outside of Portsmouth. A theater was built to his specifications, and its first seasons were filled with great English actors doing the Western world's best plays. But when Olivier became, as well, the director of the National Theatre of Great Britain, he found that he could not manage the Chichester Theatre Festival, too. Yet it remained a place of history and sentiment for him, and he was very proud of it ("the first time I had actually started a theatre").

At Olivier's urging, Danny agreed to appear at Chichester from

August 1 to September 16, 1967, receiving the common salary of sixteen pounds (seventy-five dollars) per week. The play that he was to do under the direction of Peter Coe was Carlo Goldoni's *Servant of Two Masters*. Written in 1745 and an acknowledged model of its genre, it is a work in the tradition of commedia dell'arte. Thus, it incorporates improvisation as well as classic elements of balletic movement and mime. Kaye's role, the leading part, of course, was Truffaldino, a Harlequin character. No work of the standard dramatic literature could have been better tailored to suit Danny Kaye, if he wanted to do a classic.

"I'm not worried about doing the play," he told an interviewer, pointing out that he would never do Shakespeare. "It's not my racket." But the Goldoni, he quite correctly explained and as Olivier had probably pointed out, "is a prototype of burlesque, which is my kind of humor."

But in June, barely two months before the engagement was supposed to start, he canceled his appearance. The reason he gave was the Six-Day War between Israel and the Arab countries. It was more important, he said, that he entertain the Israeli troops.

It seemed to touch a chord of betrayal that enraged all of England. The Chichester Theatre Festival had made Kaye the centerpiece of its season and had based its promotions on his appearance. Every seat had been sold for every performance of *A Servant of Two Masters*. In the *Sunday Times* in London, drama critic Harold Hobson wrote that Kaye's cancellation had "staggered" the Chichester management. In the *New York Times*, critic Walter Kerr wrote:

> If the British have been a bit testy about Danny Kaye's failure to appear as scheduled . . . it is probably because they suspect that . . . apprehension, rather than an urgent date in Israel, was the real cause of his defection. Mr. Kaye's business in Israel may well have been bona fide . . . there is some feeling in British theatrical circles, however, that the star grew timorous: tackling unfamiliar materials, he might not be Palladium-strong, or Samuel Goldwyn-great.

Finally, in the *New York Post*, columnist Sheilah Graham wrote,

> The onetime glorious friendship between Laurence Olivier and Danny Kaye has dimmed. It was Sir Larry who had

persuaded Danny to make the plunge at the Chichester Festival. When Danny canceled to go to Israel, Sir Larry couldn't and never will understand the breach of the show business rule that the show must go on.

In fact, there is not anyone or anything to suggest that Olivier and Kaye ever spoke to each other again.

25

*Tell Danny they are waiting for him in Israel like they are
waiting for the* "meschiach" [*the messiah*].

—Lillian Lux

SOME YEARS EARLIER, LILLIAN LUX, AN OLD GIRLFRIEND OF KAYE'S
FROM THE CATSKILLS, AND HER HUSBAND, PESACH BURSTYN, HAD
toured Israel with their Yiddish theater company. They brought
their teenage twins along, Susan and Michael—he as a member of
the company.

Michael Burstyn was so smitten with the new nation that he
stayed. After learning to speak Hebrew, he continued to act, and
when he landed the lead role in *Kuni Leml* ("the first Israeli musical
movie in CinemaScope"), he became one of Israel's first movie stars.

But movie star or no, in 1967, like most every other twenty-two-
year-old Israeli, Mike Burstyn was in the army and fighting in the
Six-Day War. His rank was *turai* (private), and after the hostilities,
he was assigned to an entertainment unit.

There he was informed by his commanding officer that "Danny
Kaye is coming, and since you are an Israeli and an American, we
would like you to travel along with him and be his host." That was
how it happened, by coincidence and chance, that Lillian Lux's son
became Danny Kaye's official guide on his first extended visit to
Israel (and his first visit at all since the *See It Now* show).

Young Burstyn's monthlong assignment involved not only being Kaye's tour guide and interpreter; he was also to act as the host of Danny's troop shows, introducing him to the soldiers. That meant "traveling with him throughout the country," Burstyn remembered, "and being with him twenty-four hours a day, from getting up in the morning to going to sleep late at night."

Show business being show business—even on a battlefront in Israel—young Burstyn had heard the gossip about Kaye and *A Servant of Two Masters*. "Rumor had it," the young actor remembered, "that he wanted to get out of that—he wasn't really happy with it. And so this was perhaps an excuse to break his agreement with Chichester."

That certainly was the consensus opinion, for Kaye could have just as easily gone to entertain the Israeli soldiers after Chichester. But he was no longer young enough to dare anything. He now had a reputation to protect, a career established, and so instead of trying something as new as classical acting at the age of fifty-four, he opted to sing "Minnie the Moocher" for the troops.

Landing at David Ben-Gurion Airport in Tel Aviv, he was greeted as an international star with a UN connection. He stepped out of the airplane wearing what had become his everyday way of dressing, a striped alpaca sweater, denim pants, a shapeless rain hat, and space shoes. Behind him stood his little entourage—his personal manager, Herb Bonis, and his accompanist, Sammy Prager. It was definitely safer than Chichester.

They were taken to the King David Hotel, where Danny dressed for an air force dinner to celebrate the flamboyant and smashing Israeli victory, the six-day miracle. For Kaye, all the good things about being Jewish may have seemed wrapped up in the warmth and exhilaration of this fabulous victory and its demonstration that Jews could fight. And if there was a single moment during the monthlong visit that captured this mood, it might have come at the air force dinner that first night. Something happened there that he would talk about with rapture ever after.

A lieutenant was called to the dais, hailed for having shot down four Russian-built Arab jets. But by mistake this young officer was introduced to the audience as a captain.

The ballroomful of airmen began to chant, "Make him a captain! Make him a captain!"

In the exultation of the moment, the hero was promoted from

lieutenant to captain, and the next morning, Kaye was still savoring the memory. "He had a year to go for captain, but . . . they promoted him on the spot!

"Now in what other army in the world would you see something like that?"

It had inspired him to tell a story. Invited as an honored guest, almost a dignitary, he was not expected to entertain. In other circumstances, he might have relished the prestige of not being a performer, but this was a victory celebration in Israel, and he was caught up in the joy of the moment. And so he told a funny story, albeit one recast to reflect his lofty status. Otherwise, it was just a variation on the dialect routines he had been doing on television for years. Just as they were about four foreign chefs, four foreign golfers, or some such, in this version the men from the four different countries were diplomats who had been invited to his home for dinner. Having established, for the benefit of the assembled airmen and local politicians, that Danny Kaye has diplomats to his home, he then played out the anecdote.

Each of the diplomats is asked to describe his notion of happiness. The audience hushed. This was *Danny Kaye*.

The French diplomat, he said, defined happiness by saying, "Well, monsieur, 'eppiness for me, you know, ees vairy sehmple—a good buddle of wine, you know, a leetle bit of l'amour, you know, a good piece of sheeze. Theese, for me, constitutes complit 'eppiness."

Then, Kaye said, he turned to the Englishman. " 'And tell me, George, what is *your* idea of happiness?'

"And George said to me, 'You know, old chap. I don't know really. Well, uh, I suppose if I were hard-pressed, I should say that happiness for me is sitting at home with the *Financial Times*, you know. A good cup of tea, Yorkshire pudding, you know. That would be happiness for me.' "

Kaye waited while the audience finished chuckling over his British dialect.

"The next fellow I asked," he continued, "was Fritz, the German. 'Vell, heppiness for me iss any-zing I can put in my belly. Sauerbraten, Wiener schnitzel, a goot frenkfooter, wurst. Zat, for me, iss heppiness.' "

The fourth diplomat to be asked, Kaye concluded, was the Russian. " 'And you, Ivan,' I said. 'What is your idea of happiness?' And Ivan said to all of us, 'Well, gentlemyen, cheppiness for me iss very zimple. I em sitting alone in my apartment in Moscow wit my leedle boy Boris on my lap and me reading to Boris editorial from *Pravda*. All of a sodden, knock on door.

" 'I go open door. In door stands secret police. Secret police say to me, "Are you Ivan Ivanovich?" I say, "No, Ivan Ivanovich live upstairs."

" 'That is my idea of happiness.' "

The audience roared, and Mike Burstyn, who had translated it into Hebrew for them, roared, too.

The next morning, Kaye was taken on a tour of the city. Once again, he wore the denim pants with a sweater and, of course, the space shoes. His official companion was Teddy Kollek, the mayor of Jerusalem, who had come to Tel Aviv for the victory celebration. Along the way, they picked up Fred Pomerantz, an American who was a major fund-raiser for Israel.

As Kollek stepped out of the car to let Pomerantz in, the man proudly announced, "I just raised five million dollars for you in New York."

Climbing back into the car, the mayor replied, "Just tell them it's for a good cause." So it was now the three of them squeezed into the backseat.

Kaye did not seem interested in the fund-raising, or else he didn't like being off the center of attention. "I hope I'm not being forward," he said coldly to Pomerantz, "but would you mind getting off my foot?"

The embarrassed American said, "Look, this is the first time I ever had to sit in the middle." But it was a bad start.

Kollek changed subjects. "You don't know what problems we have here," he said to the visitors. "The Jordanians emptied the prisons before they pulled out. We've got three hundred convicts running around loose, with fifteen murderers among them."

But the moment was covered with ice.

That evening, young Burstyn was appearing in a club named Omar Khyyam. The little cabaret was in the Old Jaffa section just outside of Tel Aviv, and Mike invited Kaye, Bonis, and Prager to come as his guests and watch him perform. The manager and the accompanist accepted, but Kaye begged off with jet lag, which naturally disappointed the young performer. Nevertheless, after his songs and anecdotes, Burstyn quieted the audience and explained that he had been working with the great Danny Kaye. Introducing Bonis and Prager at their table, he added, "Since Danny couldn't come, as a tribute to him, let me tell you a story that I heard him tell just the other night.

"This," he said, "is Danny Kaye's story," and he proceeded to tell the anecdote about the four diplomats—exactly as Kaye had told it at the air force gala. The next morning, the government driver brought him around to Danny's hotel for the day's round of troop shows. Kaye came out with Prager and Bonis. He got into the car's front seat, alongside the driver. The manager and the accompanist slid into the back with Burstyn.

"Danny didn't even turn around to look at me," the actor remembered. "It was like the cold wind from Siberia just came in."

They went from one hospital to the next, and at each one Burstyn introduced Kaye to the wounded soldiers. But between the shows and all through the morning, Kaye didn't talk to his young interpreter. "I had no idea what was going on," Burstyn said, "but the man ignored me totally—and this went on for an entire day."

In early evening, when they got back to the hotel, Danny stepped out of the car and walked briskly into the hotel. Prager hurried along behind him. Burstyn, sitting in the car with Herb Bonis, asked the manager, "What did I do wrong? Because Danny has been ignoring me all day."

Bonis replied, "It seems that when I told him at breakfast this morning how much we enjoyed your show and what you did and that you told his story—well, that didn't go down very well.

"Matter of fact, he was furious."

Kaye was so furious that he did not speak to Burstyn for a week. "Finally," the young actor remembered, "he gave me a dressing-down. He said I was like a son to him [he would later tell Burstyn's mother, "Mike *could* have been our son"], and he wanted to give me a moral lesson.

"*You do not steal other people's material.*"

So there that was again.

HOME IN LOS ANGELES, KAYE HAD BARELY UNPACKED WHEN HE LEFT —again to entertain soldiers, this time Americans, on the USO Pacific hospital circuit. He visited hospitals in Okinawa, Guam, the Philippines, and Hawaii. There could no longer be any mistaking these trips for anything but flights from depression. The question now was whether the depressions were being exacerbated by a career in decline. And the signs of that slide were unmistakable, whether in the suspension of moviemaking, the cancellation of the television series, or the Chichester fiasco. Moreover, at only fifty-five, Danny Kaye was beginning to look old. Unlike most show people, who pamper their looks and become peculiarly sleek, Kaye had taken on a gray pallor. It made his occasional moments of whimsy all the more incongruous.

By the time he left for Nice, he looked like an old man.

It was just after Dena's twenty-first birthday. She was in her senior year at Stanford and had come to New York on Christmas holiday. On that big day, December 14, 1967, Danny and Sylvia took her to dinner at Luchow's, a fashionable German restaurant on Fourteenth Street. Two other couples were invited along, which didn't make it a very personal birthday party. The guests were the cardiologist Izzy Rosenfeld and his stunning wife, Camilla, along with the new head of Unicef, Paul Hoffman, with his wife, Anna.

Dena was quiet at the table, which was hardly surprising. She was the only young person there, and her parents' friends were successful, confident, and assertive people.

She was looking ever more like Sylvia, and like her mother, she was bright and talented. In a few years she would be working for a magazine as a travel writer. But there was also a Danny side to her, and becoming a *travel* writer reflected it, for she also needed flight. Alan King once found her alone on the casino floor of the Sands Hotel in Las Vegas. That was not where she was supposed to be. She was supposed to be at school in Palo Alto, California. King asked whether her parents knew she was there. She responded evasively and then disappeared into the crowd.

IT WAS IN NICE THAT KAYE'S FIRST PICTURE IN FIVE YEARS WAS TO BE filmed, and it was vastly different from any other movie he had yet made, for it marked the first time that he was not the leading player. Rather, he was to join an all-star cast in a deluxe, international version of the Jean Giraudoux play *The Madwoman of Chaillot*. Katharine Hepburn had the title role, and Kaye was cast as a Chaplinesque character, "the Rag Picker." Others in this considerable company were Charles Boyer, Irene Papas, Yul Brynner, Donald Pleasance, Margaret Leighton, Giulietta Masina, Richard

Chamberlain, Paul Henreid, Oscar Homolka, and Michael Wilding. With direction by John Huston, the project had prestige to squander. It promised to be Kaye's remedy for the Chichester abortion.

By the time they all gathered in Nice, Huston had quit the project, his place taken by Bryan Forbes, and it was Forbes who greeted the company, "practically a who's who of the cinema."

He was a youthful Englishman, civilized, cultured, educated, witty, and well spoken. His most recent film, *King Rat*, had been lavishly praised; in fact, he was better equipped than Huston for so literary a project as the Giraudoux play.

Forbes had met Kaye previously, at the Frank Sinatra–Mia Farrow engagement party. But long before that, along with everyone else in the world, he had been a fan of Danny's early movies. It was the old git-gat-giddle. "As a young boy I was entranced when he first hit the screen and did that frenetic sort of talk." Later, Forbes had been caught up in the Palladium excitement. "I'd always seen his performances when he was the toast of London in his heyday."

Heyday. The slide could be so precipitous, but, it appeared to Forbes, "he seemed to make himself old. The joy had gone out of him."

That memory, in this beautiful place and amid the celebrated actors, made Kaye appear even grayer. How sad, for as production began, the general mood was jovial, and the conditions charming. "It is very civilized working in France," Forbes said. "You start work at twelve, go on until seven. It is so lunatic elsewhere . . . acting at half-past eight in the morning." Moreover, as they convened each morning on the set of a beautiful French town square (so beautiful that François Truffaut would use it in his movie about moviemaking, *Day for Night*), there would be fresh croissants waiting, and baguettes of bread, and, Forbes remembered, "lovely French coffee."

A frightened Danny Kaye greeted the director with a plea. "Please release me, I don't think I can do this." He seemed to be suffering another Chichester panic, and Forbes's impression was, "His bottle had gone."

It is a cockney expression. It means one's confidence has been lost. Forbes talked him out of his fears, "wisely or not."

The director, himself an actor, was proud of being sensitive to the acting sensibility. "You'll be very good," he assured Kaye. "I'll help you through it. I know it's difficult for you—it's a difficult role, but don't be intimidated. I'm an actor's director, and I will make sure that you are good.

"I will take care of you."

In Bryan Forbes's experience, actors who were suffering like Kaye needed such talk. "The only person they're playing to is the director, and they've got to trust the director's taste." Forbes preferred a sympathetic approach to an abusive one. "Some directors," he said, "will cry, 'Cut!' and when the actor asks why, they'll say, 'Just go again!' The actor doesn't know if the director wants it faster or funnier or what. Then the actor goes downhill.

"You've got nothing to gain by humiliating them. If it's a man, he gets uptight; if it's a woman they burst into tears, and their makeup is ruined. I say to an actor, 'Try and trust me, because the only thing I want you to be is as good as possible. I'll never tell you to do something which is to your detriment.' "

Kaye wasn't the only one on the set to be intimidated by the lofty source material and the prestigious cast. The great Greek tragedian Irene Papas also asked to be released, and that wish was granted. Dame Edith Evans took her place.

The company was housed in villas or at the luxurious Hôtel Cap d'Or. They were a sociable group, sometimes even rowdy. ("Imagine all that lot sitting at the table," Forbes said with a chuckle. "We would clear the hotel.") Margaret Leighton got drunk regularly and tooted around singing opera arias. Her best pal was Michael Wilding, who had a thick Midlands English accent that nobody could understand. There were recurring laughs about his incomprehensibility. Somehow and unaccountably, Giulietta Masina, who spoke no English at all, was the only one on the set who could understand him.

When Danny was in a cheerful mood—not very often—he and Masina would take over the hotel kitchen and cook pasta. More often, he was one of the company loners, like Richard Chamberlain. As for Hepburn, she did not get on with Kaye at all and in fact was generally short-tempered—understandably so, considering the recent death of Spencer Tracy.

The most impressive actor in the group, for Forbes, was Charles Boyer, because of his life story. The actor's son had committed suicide at twenty-one. His wife never left the house after that. She would die four days after *Madwoman* was finished.

As rehearsals began, the director found Kaye a "very humble man" to work with and responsive to all suggestions. "Once he got going and had got a bit of confidence, he was magnificent." But "at the end of the day," as Forbes put it, he could not shake a feeling of Danny's being "vulnerable and sad, and very lonely. All comedians have a dark side," the director believed, but that was not enough to justify Danny Kaye's behavior with the costume designer, Rosie de la Marre. One morning, she tapped on his dressing-room door. She had come for a costume fitting.

As she marked the adjustments, Kaye unzipped his fly. Then he exposed himself.

When she told Forbes about it, the director asked how she had responded.

She said she told Kaye, "Oh, put it away. I've seen better."

This was a curious new development.

FORBES SAW HIM ONLY ONCE AFTER WORK ON *MADWOMAN* ENDED. IT was at the house on San Ysidro, and Danny was cleaning the pool. "There he was," the director remembered, "this great comedian, wearing those strange health shoes—with a net, taking leaves out of the obviously unused pool. I felt the epitome of the loneliness of his life. It had a sort of *Sunset Boulevard* flavor about it."

26

I'm not doing this for the money. Because for one concert, I could make . . . no, it's not for money or keeping busy. I've done that. I've done it all.

ONE EVENING, AT A TIME WHEN THE TELEVISION SERIES WAS STILL RUNNING, A COUPLE OF CBS VANS PULLED INTO THE KAYE DRIVEWAY. A team of workmen piled out and began ripping out the patio. A week later, it was gone, and in its place was an extension to the house. It was a second kitchen, a "Chinese kitchen," restaurant-grade in every respect and built to Danny's specifications.

The equipment included a custom-made series of three Chinese stoves, designed to generate what the food critic Craig Claiborne would describe as "77,000 BTUs of volcanic heat." Each of the stoves was fitted with an oversized wok, fired by mammoth gas jets whose lever controls were set at knee level. That way, the cook could manipulate them with his hands full.

Opposite was yet another stove, a professional range for cooking Peking duck. Above it were racks for drying the ducks and, alongside, a restaurant-size refrigerator that was fitted with three giant drawers. The room was also equipped with a special ventilating system to cope with the savage heat.

The kitchen was especially fitted for storing the equipment unique to Chinese cooking—the woks, a chopping block, steamers, cleavers, assorted implements for cutting, crunching, and pounding, spatulas, wok spoons and scoops, ladles and chopsticks. As for work tables, the whole place was geared for mixing, cooking, and sampling.

When construction was finished, Kaye stocked the pantry with such staples as licorice root, water-chestnut powder, Chinese nutmeg, yellow-rice wine, Szechuan peppercorns, cottonseed oil, and anise-flavored sauce as well as the more familiar soy sauce and Chinese mustard.

It was functional, a workplace. Unlike the decorated rest of the house, this place was spartan and even corny, amused only by a group of Chinese lanterns and a sign that read "Don't look at it. Eat it." There was also a sign in hand-painted Chinese calligraphy— Danny Kaye, Skilled Hands—that had been given him by a chef at Johnny Kan's restaurant on Grant Avenue in San Francisco after he had paid a visit to the kitchen and tried his hand there.

Nearby was a small bookcase, its shelves filled with French and Italian as well as Chinese cookbooks. In fact, Kaye had first developed a knack for Italian and American cooking. His efforts at Chinese cuisine began with sweet-and-sour pork, progressing to chicken hoisin, lobster or shrimp with black bean sauce, and chicken Szechuan. In time, he concluded that the spicy Szechuan style was not as refined as Mandarin cuisine, and he went on to specialize in batter-fried scallops, stir-fried oysters, and "lion's head" pork— meatballs, spinach, and chestnuts.

He didn't entirely sacrifice his sense of humor to this expertise and was capable of announcing a main course of "Empress Chicken with Devoted Eunuch Vegetables." But his cooking was obviously a serious business, and at the heart of it lay a blend of artistry, sensual awareness, and philosophy. "At the sound of raw food hitting hot oil," he told Craig Claiborne, "all your senses are drawn into play. . . . Cooking is an expression of one's being, that minute." There was a certain naïveté in rhapsodizing this way, especially to a professional like Claiborne, but naïveté makes the difference between a detached professional and an involved enthusiast. Kaye added, with plain sincerity, "If you're not cooking with joy and love and happiness, you're not cooking well."

A performance does not exist without an audience to see it, and cooking makes no sense without the food being eaten. So his new kitchen included a dining area with a round table that was also specifically designed for Chinese food. Fitted into its center was an oversized lazy Susan, and on that revolving tray was a grouping of porcelain serving dishes. That is how food is traditionally served in Chinese homes, and there were eight chairs around the table.

Watching the construction of all this, the neighbors were not only startled by the speed of the renovation and the use of CBS facilities and employees to accomplish it; they were also mystified by Kaye's flouting of Beverly Hills building ordinances, for the new kitchen actually abutted the next-door driveway. But the neighbors were not inclined to complain about Danny Kaye; in fact, Sylvia had managed to get a variance for the extension.

Now Kaye was ready to cook for guests, something he would do three or four nights a week, although those were more like food events than dinner parties. On the mornings of those evenings, he would shop for provisions either in Chinatown or the Los Angeles farmers' market on Third Street and Fairfax. For company he would bring along one of his "cookers"—a group of Los Angeles friends that included Linda Ashley, the wife of his agent; Olive Behrens, a Los Angeles decorator; Kenny Shapiro, a former cue-card boy for the Kaye television show; and Steve Wallace, a Phil Silvers look-alike who owned the fancy Wally's Wines and Liquors on Westwood Boulevard. (On the eternally vexing question of what wine to serve with Chinese food, Wallace found that "Danny never resolved the issue." He was never a serious oenophile and would say, "If this is what I'm cooking, you bring something that's going to work." Wallace concluded, "Chenin Blancs and the lighter wines seem to work.")

Accompanied by one or another of the cookers while moving through the meat and vegetable stalls, Kaye made his selections with a chef's eye. "He would always buy his quail eggs or meat there," Linda Ashley remembered. "The butcher would even take him into the meat locker, and he'd get to pick out his own meat." Then he would poke, browse, and schmooze in his rain hat, sweat suit, and space shoes.

He would be recognized, of course, but Linda had noticed that while the public had a "sense of accessibility" toward television stars, "there is a certain respectful distance with a movie star, especially one in Danny's category."

He tended to be amiable with his public, although one of the cookers recalled that when asked for autographs, "he just didn't want to put down his shopping." Instead, he would peer through his sunglasses at the fan and say, "I know what you think—you think I'm Danny Kaye, but I'm not. Everybody thinks I look like him. I know I look like him, but I'm not!"

Then he would spend the afternoon preparing the dinner. When the guests arrived—always eight people—drinks would be served in the "music room," as Sylvia called his den. There was no spread of hors d'oeuvres, just a plate of nuts, and he did not join the group. But those who cared to help in the kitchen were welcome to slice, chop, and stir.

At the precise moment of readiness, he called everyone to the table. He didn't join them but sat on a bar stool off to the side and from that vantage point watched them eat, insisting that they begin each dish precisely as it was served by his cooking assistant, a woman named Ming Lo Chin.

Conversation was discouraged. "Did you come here to eat or to talk?" he would snap. "Eat it while it's perfect. It's still cooking on your plate."

And while everyone ate, he scanned the faces for reactions. As for latecomers, he did not dote on them. As cooker Steve Wallace put it, "If you came late to dinner at Danny's, you were in deep shit." He came late himself one evening and found a locked door and a note that read "You're late. Fuck you."

"It was not," Wallace said, "a social occasion. It was a dining occasion. Sometimes, if you were driving there and you knew you were going to be four minutes late, your stomach would start churning." And he wasn't the only cooker who would mention anxieties about going to Danny's for dinner.

"It wasn't fun sometimes," he said.

There was no logic to the guest lists, no attempt to orchestrate the tables. Local celebrities like Peter O'Malley—the owner of the Dodgers—or the radio talk-show host Michael Jackson might sit with Shirley MacLaine, who lived a few houses down the street on San Ysidro Drive. Henry Kissinger and Zubin Mehta could be joined at dinner by Fishel Goldfarb and the queen of Holland. Whoever the guest, the dress code was informal. When the king of Sweden arrived in black tie, Danny told him, "Your Majesty, when I ate in your palace, I dressed the way you dressed. In this house we don't dress the way you are." While the Swedish foreign minister and the ambassador gaped, the king removed his coat and tie, even his shoes.

Danny himself wore the usual sweatpants and space shoes beneath his long white apron.

When royalty was involved, security personnel sometimes came with them, but not to the table. Danny's neighbor remembered that when Princess Margaret was there, "The secret fucking service was all over my garden!"

If anyone from Unicef was in town, they might be invited, or Itzhak Perlman, Lillian Lux, Tommy Lasorda, Jascha Heifetz. The name of each dinner guest, famous or not, was entered in a log on the kitchen counter, along with a notation of exactly what had been served. The most elaborate of these entries, unsurprisingly, involved three of France's greatest chefs—Paul Bocuse, whose restaurant in Lyon bore his own name; Roger Verge, chef-patron of the Hostellerie du Moulin de Mougins; and Jean Troisgros, of Freres Restaurant in Roanne. For these master chefs, Kaye cooked an eight-course Chinese banquet that included cucumber soup, beef with onion rings, "banjo" duck, deep-fried squab, sweet-and-sour deep-fried scallops, and one of his specialties, stir-fried shrimp with oysters.

The only one who never seemed to show up at the round table in the Chinese kitchen was Sylvia, a fact that found its way into a Sheilah Graham gossip column. Describing an evening when the guests included Shirley MacLaine and her date, Michael Caine, the Cary Grants and Prince Philip, Graham wrote, "Danny had six different Chinese specialties. . . . All very informal with everyone taking off their shoes and loosening ties. Even royalty has to relax sometimes. . . . Why wasn't Mrs. Danny Kaye at the Chinese dinner? . . . She would have enjoyed the feast."

But Sylvia would not be at that table even on the unique occasion when she was in the house at the same time as Danny. The reason, he would tell anyone naive enough to ask, was that his wife didn't like Chinese food. Yet, on at least one occasion, he was overheard telling Ming Lo Chin to send some of the leftovers upstairs to Sylvia.

Another time, his guests were startled to learn that while they were eating, his wife was giving her own dinner party elsewhere in the house. Sylvia was even handing out bronze replicas of the little bust of Danny that she had commissioned from a local sculptor. This gift provided, if not Danny Kaye, at least a memento of a wife's devotion.

She gave one of the busts to Izzy Rosenfeld. He was now commuting to Los Angeles once a week to do his medical spot on the *CBS Morning News*, and more often than not, he stayed with Danny. He used Dena's old room, and, of course, he was invited to the dinners. While Danny was cooking, he would greet the guests.

"Yes?" he said to a fellow he perceived as "nondescript looking."

The young man in jeans asked, "Is Mr. Kaye in?"

"What's your name?"

"John Denver," the fellow said.

The cardiologist had never heard of him.

"Just a minute," he said. Then he turned and called out, "Danny—a John Denver here wants to see you."

Later, Kaye took him aside. "Do me a favor," he said. "Never answer the door or phone in my house again."

But during dinner Rosenfeld asked Denver, "What do you do?"

"*Please*, Izzy," Kaye whispered to him. "Don't ask them any questions."

But any star can go unrecognized sometimes. Rosenfeld asked Danny if he might invite the Greek shipping magnate Stavros Niarchos, who was his patient. Niarchos, as Rosenfeld put it, "had the wealth of Croesus—billions of dollars."

After that dinner, Danny himself offered to drive Niarchos back to the Beverly Hills Hotel. Along the way, the fabulously rich Greek enthused about the meal he had just been served. It was so marvelous, he said, that thinking his companion the cook/driver, he offered Danny Kaye a job as his personal chef in Los Angeles.

As Kaye told Rosenfeld the next morning, he asked Niarchos exactly what the job would entail.

"You cook the meals," the shipping tycoon said, "and you drive the car."

"How much do I get paid?"

"Twenty-five thousand dollars a year," which was a nice salary in 1969.

"I have my own room?"

He certainly would.

And Kaye innocently asked, "Do I get my own color TV?"

That could be arranged.

"Well," Kaye said, "right now my employers pay me fifty thousand dollars a year."

That was not a problem, said the Greek billionaire. He could even double it.

It was only then that Kaye identified himself. Moreover, he already had a job. He was going to star in a new Broadway musical. It was called *Two by Two*, and the songs were to be provided by the great Richard Rodgers, with words by the youthful lyricist Martin Charnin. The libretto was being written by Peter Stone, who had just won a Tony Award for *1776*, and the director was Joe Layton, an experienced Broadway hand who had staged Rodgers's earlier success *No Strings*.

"Kaye was not actively interested in returning to Broadway," Layton remembered, but he did agree to hear an outline of the show. He and Sylvia went to the Rodgers apartment, which was in the Hotel Pierre, just a block down from their own place in the Sherry-Netherland. "He came in humble, timid, crazy," Charnin remembered. "He was, well, Danny Kaye."

Peter Stone explained the show, which dealt with a Noah as old as six hundred and as young as ninety; the composer played some of the songs. When they were finished, Danny closed the script and set it on his lap. It was a Yiddish-flavored retelling of the story of Noah and the Ark—a strangely appropriate project for Danny Kaye, who had so complex a relationship to his Jewishness. The source was *The Flowering Peach*, a 1954 play by Clifford Odets—which was, as Jerry Tallmer of the *New York Post* put it, "Odets coming to grips with Jewishness as he had not even done in *Awake and Sing*."

But the way Danny said he saw it, the story was about the generation gap, and everyone nodded, including Richard Rodgers, who was another de-ethnicized Jew. Danny turned to Sylvia. "If I do this," he said, "it's not going to be a concert, with me flitting about the stage." Again, she nodded, and again, everyone else nodded.

Then Sylvia offered to write special material for the show. After all, Cole Porter had let her write two songs for *Let's Face It!* However, Richard Rodgers's ego was not as secure as Cole Porter's. Besides, special material for Danny Kaye would have distorted a musical about Noah. Rodgers thanked her for the offer.

Danny stood up, they all rose, and he said he would think about it.

"After he left," Layton remembered, "everyone made the sign of the cross. We were scared to death that he would do it—he had become this egomaniac from living in Hollywood and being the master star."

But within a week he accepted the part, and Ted Ashley negotiated a contract to equal the richest on Broadway. It guaranteed the same $14,000 a week that Katharine Hepburn had been paid for *Coco* and Lauren Bacall for *Applause*. They all could make more money elsewhere, but there was something special about doing a Broadway musical. And there was something special about getting Danny Kaye to do one, even as the authors watched with worried fascination while, right in front of them, he went from insecurity ("Will it be right for me? Will it be good for me?") to assurance ("I know how to play this thing").

"It was an enormous casting coup," Charnin thought, and he was right. Kaye might have been on the way out in Hollywood and television, but Broadway was more loyal, and his name still meant a million-dollar advance sale at the box office.

With him in place, the rest of the show was cast, and plans were made for tryouts in New Haven and Boston and for a New York opening in early November 1970. Kaye moved into his Sherry-Netherland apartment for the duration and the show-making process began.

It began with discussions about how Jewish *Two by Two* was going to be. In the Odets original, Danny's part had been played by Menasha Skulnik, a star of the Yiddish stage. He played Noah with a rich and unashamed Yiddishness. The watering-down process began when Rodgers expressed concern that Christian audiences might feel alienated from too Jewish flavored a show. It was a somewhat tenuous argument considering that *Fiddler on the Roof* was then in its sixth year on Broadway, but Rodgers was the kind of Jew who claimed to have "forgotten" what his real family name was. "Dick would admit he was Jewish," Charnin said, "only by telling his rehearsal pianist [Trude Rittmann] to 'put in that diminished chord—whatever it is that makes it sound Jewish.' "

Kaye presumed to moderate, telling the composer, "I'll find a way to make it more acceptable to the non-Jewish audience and still," he assured the other authors, "make the Jewish audience feel they aren't being cheated."

For a time Charnin believed it as he listened, enthralled, to "the Danny Kaye who allowed himself to sing with that plaintive little kvetch in his voice that made you come apart at the seams.

"That was the Danny Kaye we knew was Jewish, the tummler from the Catskills."

But Kaye, who had himself told interviewers that he had "forgotten" the correct spelling of his own name, Kaminski; Kaye, with a history of ambivalence about his Jewishness that ranged from deploring "Jew comics" to turning down the original lead in *Fiddler on the Roof*; elegant Danny Kaye, whose most successful dialect was the unaccented one he had invented for himself, was not likely to play Jewish onstage now. As Charnin put it, "Stone and I were two Jews, and Rodgers and Kaye were two closet Jews. They were pushing for this white bread approach to Jewishness."

The tall, rangy, and rather shy Joe Layton (real name, incidentally, Joseph Lichtman) was caught in the middle, but on Broadway allegiances tend to lie where the clout is, and Richard Rodgers was not only Richard Rodgers; he was also producing the show.

While Layton continued to work with Rodgers and Charnin and Stone, Kaye went to Washington, D.C., to appear at a state of Israel fund-raising dinner. He was more comfortable with political Jewishness than the personal kind. The dinner was at the Shoreham Hotel, and he sat on the dais next to an opera singer, the tall (five feet eleven), slender, blonde, brainy, and quite beautiful Joanna Simon.

Between speeches, he asked if she would join him for a drink afterward, and she agreed.

Joanna Simon had grown up in sophisticated New York circles. Her father was the founder of the prestigious and, of course, still magnificent publishing house Simon and Schuster. Her sisters were a popular singing team, Carly and Lucy Simon. But Joanna's sophistication notwithstanding, she was awed by Danny Kaye.

He put her at ease. "Within the first ten minutes," she remembered, "all of that awe vanished, and we were equals.

"And he didn't make a pass."

He was fifty-seven, she was twenty-eight, and he took her telephone number, promising to call after they returned to New York.

On the first day of rehearsal at the Imperial Theatre, he stood up in the stage-left box and cried out, "Where is he? Where's the boy who's going to play my son?"

Kaye had the contractual right to approve that actor as well as the actress who would be playing his wife.

"This is Walter Willison here," director Layton said, indicating the actor who was playing Japheth.

Kaye stepped to the front of the box and looked the young fellow over. Then he came down, walked up to the twenty-one-year-old, leaned sidewise, and, tilting a head and turning a cheek, said, "Kiss your papa."

The bewildered actor could only comply, and with that, a ritual was begun. At the end of every rehearsal day, Kaye would say, "Come on—kiss me good night."

The show had a small cast for a Broadway musical, and in that respect at least, it was adventurous. The company included Madeline Kahn, Harry Goz, Tricia O'Neill, Marilyn Cooper, and as Noah's wife, Joan Copeland.

Because the set for the ark was going to be a complicated one, they rehearsed in the Bronx scenic studio where it was being built. At the end of each day, the director would turn to the authors and sigh. "I know—more Jewish." But as they all shipped out to New Haven for the start of the tryout tour, the Old Testament story remained nondenominational.

The tryout reviews were typical for a musical at this point. *Variety* said there was "enough material for a show and a half," while the *New Haven Journal* reviewed it as "moving and magical . . . the magic supplied by Danny Kaye." Two weeks later, they moved to Boston to continue the tune-up. Anticipation began to build on Broadway, and interviewers started coming up from New York. One of them asked Danny whether the show was going to deal with the Jewishness in *The Flowering Peach*. He replied:

> Actually, when you talk about Noah, there really were no religions then. It's really about a universal group, not any one ethnic thing.

On the Boston opening night, Walter Willison remembered, "Danny was more scared than I was," and one of his fears was peculiar. He was afraid the audience wouldn't recognize him. "With the 'old' makeup on," he pouted to the young actor, "I won't get any entrance applause."

That, as Willison put it, was absurd. "How could you be Danny Kaye, be playing Noah, be the star of the show, have your picture in front of the theater, have star billing, and really think you won't get entrance applause because nobody will recognize you?"

The principal Boston critics were Elliot Norton of the *Sunday Advertiser* and Kevin Kelly of the *Globe*. Norton tended to recognize that the shows were in Boston as works in progress and saw his role as a constructive one. Starting gently by praising *Two by Two* as "fine entertainment," he warned that in the second act "Danny begins to play the comic instead of the character." He suggested that director Layton had "much to do."

Kelly saw his role in more traditional terms and wrote as a representative of the audience rather than of the theater. "While there's nothing particularly wrong," he criticized, "with a musical about Noah and his ark, there's nothing especially right about *Two by Two*. Kaye," he added, "has charm but . . . he seems slighted most of the evening."

Danny was steady through this and professional, responding with hard work. All the authors agreed about that. He could act the star, and he could pout, but while Charnin analyzed his personality as "passive-aggressive," he also thought Kaye "deserved credit for doing everything possible to make the show work."

On November 10, 1970, *Two by Two* opened in New York at the Imperial Theatre. The daily press gave Danny better reviews than the show. In the all-powerful *New York Times*, Clive Barnes wrote, "Mr. Kaye is so warm and lovable an entertainer, such a totally ingratiating actor, that for me at least, he can do no wrong." The paper's Sunday man, Walter Kerr, managed a critical waffle, suggesting that the show "works in spite of all that is wrong with it." Rodgers and Kaye, said the critic, were "two champions in fine form."

But Jack Kroll was not so forgiving in *Newsweek*. "Its badness is total," he wrote, in regret that "the greatest of all tummlers, Danny Kaye, is given . . . cretinous old man things to do." And the notice in *Time* was not much better.

But *Two by Two* was in no danger of closing, given Kaye's box-office clout and the Richard Rodgers imprimatur. The only question was whether it would run long enough to earn back its cost.

"If anything," Charnin later said, "the second night should have been where Danny called everybody together and said, 'We're in it, we're going to make it, we've got theater parties, let's continue.'

"Instead, he became one of the most singularly selfish human beings I've ever confronted in my entire life."

27

He was world weary when I met him. He didn't have that
exuberant quality he had when he was a performer. He was
cynical about the world of showbiz, and he was tired. He was
only interested in cooking and traveling.

—Joanna Simon

WITH THE SHOW RUNNING, DANNY STARTED SEEING JOANNA
SIMON, THE OPERA SINGER HE HAD MET IN WASHINGTON. SINCE HE
was on stage six nights a week, they spent most of their time together
during the day. He only had one night off, and that was Sunday. He
usually went to Los Angeles that morning, or Miami Beach or Seattle, and didn't come back until the Monday night show, so they had
lots of lunches. These might be at Brownie's, his preferred health-
food restaurant, or in Chinatown. Sylvia had gone back to California, but Joanna still sensed her touch in the Sherry-Netherland
apartment, "beautifully decorated and filled with memorabilia." Actually, it was the touch of a Los Angeles decorator named Laura
Mako, but no decorator could take a one-bedroom apartment, not
even one as spacious as this, and make it big enough for Danny and
Sylvia to live there at the same time.

Inevitably, Joanna talked with Danny about the marriage. He
was still bothered by the old line "a Fine head on his shoulders" and
insisted that "she did not create me." Rather, he said to Joanna, "she
was a complete partner."

"Have you ever thought about divorce?"

"I did with Eve Arden," Danny admitted. "I broke her heart. But I would never divorce Sylvia now. I owe her too much," he said quietly.

Joanna Simon would never fall "madly" in love with Kaye. "I didn't have time for it," she remembered, but while she was evasive on the subject of sexual relations with him, she did concede, "I was very involved. It was a very special relationship in my life.

"But I was singing all over the world, and he was spending a lot of time performing."

Joanna appealed to his love of classical music, and they shared many friends in the concert world. He claimed to be interested in books and politics, too, but his favorite subject seemed to be psychology; personal relations and feelings.

"He would advise me about life," Joanna remembered. "Who to trust and who not to."

It was a time when she needed to talk, which made this new friendship especially appealing, yet it was a strangely difficult time for someone as sophisticated as she. For despite her worldliness, she was depressed because her younger sister was getting married before she did. Her sister—and roommate—Carly was marrying the singer James Taylor.

Joanna told Kaye she wasn't sure which depressed her more, Carly getting married first or Carly moving out. She would call him late at night to talk about it.

"Maybe," she told him, "I'm just afraid of living alone."

"Honey," he said, "living alone is hard until you get used to it. I wouldn't live any other way. You'll like it, you'll see."

She wasn't so sure at all.

"Maybe," she morosely speculated, "I should move into a smaller apartment."

"It'll be gloomy for a while," Danny said, "and lonely. For the first six months it's going to be rough. But after six months it won't be."

She was dubious.

"And then you'll like it. You'll never want to live with anybody ever again."

She still wasn't convinced.

"I swear to you," he said, "I really like being alone. That's why I never spend the night sleeping in the same bed with anybody. I don't believe in it."

Joanna could see that performing was not giving Danny much pleasure anymore, and the *Two by Two* schedule of eight performances a week was a grueling one. "He was tired of being an entertainer," she said. "He became terribly bored."

But audiences were responding, and the musical was popular. He was even named "Entertainer of the Year" by *Cue* magazine. The award was to be presented at the Tavern on the Green restaurant in Central Park, and Sylvia flew in for it, even writing a song for the occasion. It was to be sung by Walter Willison and Madeline Kahn, of the *Two by Two* cast, and they performed it that evening for a surprised Kaye.

"It was a charming piece of special material," Willison remembered, "about six minutes long and very Sylvia Fine."

It was so Sylvia Fine that it even included a gesundheit joke. When Madeline Kahn noticed it in the lyrics, she told Willison, "I get it. Gesundheit is a cue, and these are the *Cue* magazine awards." But Sylvia explained it when she taught them the number.

"In every show I ever wrote with Danny," she said, "I always put in a gesundheit joke. That's my little thing with him."

During the party, she sat next to Danny and beamed as—directly in front of their table—Willison and Kahn sang the number. Sylvia was wearing expensive designer clothes, but she had never learned anything about style. Even now, having completed plastic surgery to reduce her breasts and minimize her nose, she still wasn't attractive. And, it seemed to cast members, "she was treated like the Chinese wife—she didn't walk beside him but behind him."

When the song was done, Danny turned to her and said, "That was just brilliant, wasn't it?" Then he looked to the rest of the table. "Who wrote that? Marty [Charnin]?"

It was a painful moment, a deliberate jab at Sylvia, and the actors knew it, sensitive as they are to any pinprick of rejection. Young Willison was "shocked" and felt "Danny had to know that she wrote it. How could he not? Gesundheit was a recurring bit of theirs. I knew it had to be killing her. He was just taking the knife and sticking it."

AT THE FEBRUARY 5, 1971, PERFORMANCE, KAYE WAS DOING HIS LITtle dance to the "Two by Two" title song when his lips twitched and his face turned white with pain. Lurching, he froze in his tracks.

He had twisted his leg, and he whispered to Willison, "Let's just sit down here." Then, instead of leading the others in the dance, he just watched.

Joan Copeland, who was playing his wife, Esther, shifted over and asked under her breath, "What's going on?"

"I've hurt myself," he whispered. "They're going to have to bring down the curtain."

In fact, his foot was trembling. Copeland edged to the wings and turned to the stage manager, who was standing at his desk, turning script pages and calling out scenery and lighting cues.

"Bring down the curtain," she said. "Danny's hurt."

And at the end of the number, it came down.

He was helped back to his dressing room. It was obvious that he could not finish the performance. His understudy, Harry Goz, got into costume while Kaye was taken to Lenox Hill Hospital on the Upper East Side. There his injury was diagnosed as torn ligaments, with a possible hairline fracture.

He was hospitalized for four days, and performances were suspended. The actors telephoned each other with rumors that the producers were talking to Milton Berle, Alan King, or Art Carney as replacements. Two weeks later, with his foot in a plastic cast, Danny was out of bed. He had not wanted to resume the show, but the authors knew that it would close without him. The librettist, Peter Stone, improvised a plot development involving gout to explain a Noah who is confined to a wheelchair at six hundred and walking on crutches at ninety. Then they all talked Kaye into returning.

While the new version was being rehearsed, he resurrected the changes that he had not been able to effect the first time around. Now he would say, "I can't do that," or "My foot hurts," and finally, director Layton told the company, "If the show is going to continue, everyone is going to have to let Danny do what he wants to do."

The reopening of *Two by Two* made the front page of the *New York Times*. When the curtain went up and he made his entrance, popping his head out of the ark, he ad-libbed, "Well, I finally showed up."

The audience roared.

"That laughter," Willison remembered, "was like turning a maniac loose."

For as the performance proceeded, Kaye made remarks about his leg, his cast, his wheelchair. In performances that followed, he made jokes about *No, No, Nanette*, which was playing next door; he greeted friends in the audience. ("Hi, Izzy. Enjoying the show, Doc?") When he wasn't onstage, he would go into the orchestra pit and try to make the actors laugh. An irritated Willison made him pout—"The only thing I'm sad about is my son doesn't love me anymore"—because the actor had stopped kissing his cheek. He even had his manager complain to Willison's agent (who said, "You must be nice to Danny. He thinks you don't love him anymore.") But that stopped when his plastic cast caught on the back of a prop and he accidentally slipped, almost falling backward. As Willison caught him, Danny jammed the injured foot.

"Let go of me," he cried aloud, "you fucking asshole!"

The audience gasped. The actors gaped. Kaye hobbled offstage, and the incident was reported in some of the press.

After the cursing out, the young actor avoided the star entirely. "I never spoke to him again except onstage."

There, Danny's antics were worsening. He stuck his crutch between Harry Goz's legs and jerked it upward and after the show told the actor, "Next time I do that, respond in falsetto." When Goz did, Danny cried, "I used to have three sons. Now I have two sons and a daughter!"

Charnin saw that "everyone was afraid except Willison." Some complained to the stage manager, but Kaye simply told Goz, "The next time I do that bit with the crutch, break up more."

He did not spare Joan Copeland. While singing a duet, "Who Is Always in My Corner?," he reached behind her back and unzipped her dress, revealing her bra to the audience and baring her back from the neck to the buttocks. The laughter guaranteed that the actress would have to endure this embarrassment at every ensuing performance. She joined the rest of the company in refusing to speak to Kaye, but it did not spare her. At another performance, in the middle of the same duet, he cried, "Wait a minute! Whoa! Stop the music!

"You know," he said to the audience while Copeland stood nonplussed beside him, "when Al Jolson did Broadway, he used to just stop the show and have the cast sit back and he'd sing you some of his songs. Now Jay Blackton, our conductor, doesn't have my orchestrations, so he can't play my numbers, or I'd sing some of my old songs for you right now."

Copeland started for the wings.

"Wait!" Danny cried. "Esther, where are you going?"

As she walked offstage, he followed her and brought her out to finish the number. After the show, he asked, "What were you doing, walking offstage on me like that?"

"I just figured, you'd do whatever you wanted to do, and then you would call me back out again, and we'd finish the number."

Some nights, Danny would make a little speech after the curtain calls. "I'm glad you're here," he would tell the audience, "but I'm glad the authors aren't." When an article about this behavior was being prepared by *Variety*, Kaye told the reporter, "Since I hurt my leg . . . we have been forced to turn it into an entertainment . . . People like it better than they did before." Richard Rodgers told the newspaper, "I have no objections," but later (in his autobiography, *Musical Stages*), he said that the show "left a sour taste in my mouth . . . because of Danny's behavior."

The Tony Award committee agreed. When its nominations for the best leading actor in a musical were announced in March, Kaye was not among them—and it was a weak field, with only two of the four nominees legitimate, Bobby Van of *No, No, Nanette* and Hal Linden of *The Rothschilds*. The others were fill-ins—Larry Kert, who had not been in the original cast of *Company*, and David Burns, who was not even the leading man in *Lovely Ladies, Kind Gentlemen*. Danny's omission was a public slap in the face, but one of the nominators—Radie Harris of the *Hollywood Reporter*—explained, "The award is for excellence in the theater, and part of that is maintaining performance. We see a show in the beginning and he's brilliant; we see the show now and he's doing vaudeville jokes and debasing the property."

Charnin said, "Not getting that nomination broke his spirit." After the snub, Kaye began to sulk through the show, and to make matters worse, Walter Willison *was* nominated—for the best supporting actor in a musical.

Now Danny began to do onstage dirty tricks, such as moving on Willison's lines or starting to talk in the middle of his applause. The *New York Times* printed letters to the editors complaining about the star's antics:

> My husband and I saw "Two by Two" with a sense of indignation amounting to outrage at the exhibition put on by Danny Kaye. . . . The producers should be required to make refunds and apologies to all playgoers who went to see a musical and found themselves at a burlesque show.

And another:

> He used his wheelchair, his crutches, and his encased leg
> to terrorize the cast into "breaking up" at every available
> opportunity. . . . With the single exception of the actor who
> played the youngest son (who absolutely refused to get out
> of character), the others at times could barely read their lines
> audibly.

"If it was ever bad before," Willison remembered, "now it was
frightening, not knowing what you were going to be doing onstage,
knowing that you may be humiliated at any time."

The Kaye-Willison relationship in some ways resembled the one
between Kaye and Farley Granger during the making of *Hans Christian Andersen*. Paternal, it could be benign or punitive. Kaye's "father-son thing" was bewildering to the young actor, with its good-
night-kiss requests. "Gay people," the actor said, "were positive he
was homosexual—but that he had grown up in a time when it was
unacceptable." Then the actor came close to the nub of it. "He was
very covered, but maybe he wasn't homosexual, or even bisexual.
Maybe he never expressed that part of his sexuality. Maybe he was
just hung up about it."

That would explain his surprising Benay Venuta in her kitchen
during a dinner party. "He came late, after a performance of *Two by
Two*. He grabbed me," she remembered, "and stuck his tongue halfway down my throat."

She told him to "stop acting like a child" and added, "You know,
Danny, if I took you up on it, I bet you would run." And that was
the end of it.

Joanna Simon, while acknowledging that Danny "was an impossibly difficult person to work with," defended his stage antics. She
thought the actors should have been grateful. "They wouldn't have
had a job if Danny Kaye wasn't playing the lead." But she also tended
to see the theater as less disciplined than opera. "You can't possibly
ad-lib in an opera," she said, because every syllable is sung, and the
orchestra doesn't stop. She perhaps did not realize that the script of
a stage work is as inviolate to a professional actor as the notes in an
opera are to a singer.

Kaye performed in the plastic cast for nine months, and from
day to day the company of actors never knew what was going to
happen while they were onstage. Since Rodgers was himself the

principal investor in the show and an old friend of Kaye's, there is no way of knowing the extent to which he tolerated the misbehavior for personal or financial reasons. The closing was announced only after his investment was recouped. By then, the actors had been so demoralized that most of them had accepted other assignments anyway.

Following the 343rd and final performance, Kaye took off his costume for the last time and slipped out of his dressing room. He was always the first one to leave, since he didn't wear stage makeup. The auditorium was already darkened. He stepped into the glare of the single, unshaded stage lamp. He hardly limped as he walked on the cast. Willison watched from the wings. Kaye stood at center stage. Then he moved to the edge of it.

Bending over, he pulled off the plastic cast and held it in his hand for a moment. Then he tossed it high above the seats, up and out and into the darkened auditorium.

There was a dull thud as it landed.

He went over to the side of the stage and leaped down. Then he strode up the aisle and out the front of the house, avoiding the crowd waiting at the stage door.

28

A jester unemployed is nobody's fool.

—Sylvia Fine, *The Maladjusted Jester*

N OT SURPRISINGLY, THE FIRST THING HE DID UPON HIS RELEASE FROM *TWO BY TWO* WAS TO FLEE. HE FLEW BACK TO LOS ANGELES and then fled to Europe. That was flight, and it was mighty flight, piloting a giant commercial jet airliner—across the country, over the Atlantic, and then flying it from Europe to the Middle East.

As an aviator, Kaye's accomplishments were remarkable: jet certification, commercial licensing. The only thing to compare, in its utterly and almost comically different way, was his competence with Chinese cuisine. These, quite literally, were fields of endeavor rather than mere hobbies or avocations. They were disciplines, one scientific, the other artistic, both in apposition to his own gifts for entertainment and self-expression and each developed to the level of mastery. He flew airplanes and cooked Chinese food as well as an amateur could, and of course in his own field he had been supreme.

By any measure, it was extraordinary to have learned to do so many things so well.

His copilot in the instrument-crammed cockpit of the DC-10 was Jack McGowan, the president of the McDonnell Douglas Corp. They had become friendly through Danny's interest in aviation, and now McGowan needed help. His company, already in bankruptcy, had made a huge investment in a new aircraft, the DC-10. The plane was a key to its financial recovery, but although this jumbo jet had a major flight category to itself, being desirably smaller than the new Boeing 747, it was suffering gestation problems. Several midair incidents of blown doors, although nonfatal, had hurt its safety image, which was, of course, crucial to commercial success. Even at attractive fares, many passengers seemed to prefer leaving an airplane after it has landed.

McGowan's overseas trip with Kaye, then, was image-conscious, a public relations effort as well as a sales promotion for the foreign market. That was why they flew to Athens, picking up Aristotle Onassis and taking the owner of Olympic Airlines for a personal joyride with Danny Kaye at the wheel.

He came home with a picture to show for it, a photograph of himself in the cockpit of the DC-10. It was framed and hung on the wall of his den, alongside the picture of him scrubbed up for surgery in Dr. Michael Ellis De Bakey's operating room. Two real-life Walter Mittys.

His career was essentially over. His appearances—his appearance—betrayed a loss of interest. Turning sixty, he looked old and tired, certainly tired of entertaining. "I don't look back now," he said, "except to think, Christ, I haven't been one place for any length of time for thirty years."

He agreed to appear in a series of television specials that would be created through "animated action"—clay figures that seem to move. This is an effect accomplished through a process of stop-motion photography. Like animation (cartoons), animated action is aimed at youngsters. The producers who approached Danny—Arthur Rankin and Jules Bass—had previously made *Rudolph, the Red Nosed Reindeer* and *Frosty the Snowman*. It was his viability in the children's market that prompted this new proposal.

The first, and ultimately the only, production of the series was going to be *The Enchanted World of Danny Kaye*, subtitled "The Emperor's New Clothes." It was Hans Christian Andersen yet again. The notion was for Danny to introduce the show on-camera and then provide the voice for a conjurer in the story. The introductory sequences were to be videotaped on location in Århus, the Danish village where Andersen had been born. Restored and made into a national landmark, the little town was now a tourist attraction that coproducer Arthur Rankin described as "the Williamsburg of Denmark."

He did not find it to be the after-hours capital of Denmark, and in the evenings, he and Danny would go back to the inn where they were staying and drink *gobbledansk*. In the process they became friends, the former zany in his casual clothes and floppy hat and the slender, blue-blazered, sandy-haired Rankin, still youthful at fifty—and, as a personal type, very similar to Perry Lafferty.

They moved on to Japan, where the animated action was to be created through the "Animagic" process, as the Rankin-Bass team called their technique. The artists had already begun modeling the clay figures that would be based on Danny and the other actors providing the voices (Imogene Coca, Cyril Ritchard). Now they had to incorporate Kaye's personality, making the model move like him, capturing his facial expressions and gestures. That was accomplished by filming him "with his shtick," Rankin said. "His walk, his grimaces, and all that." The final version of the doll's face was then shaped, and the features were manipulated into expressions that replicated his own. The laborious stop-and-change-and-go photography could then begin; later, the actors would dub the voices and the songs.

Rankin suggested that on the way home they make a stop in Hong Kong. As a Bermudan, he seemed to know people in high places throughout the British Empire. Kaye knew Hong Kong, too, not only from his youthful adventures but also because he had visited Phil Goldfarb there. The senior Catskills tummler was now retired, but he had conducted much of his novelties business in Hong Kong and still spent a great deal of time in the British colony.

Arthur Rankin watched Danny seem to turn young again with Fishel. The old mentor's hair was white now—he was seventy—but the man was still wiry, athletic, and a dapper dresser, and he led them all over a Hong Kong that was new to Rankin. "Fishel seemed to have employed half the city," the producer remembered. "He and Danny were great together. They joked and quarreled and yelled at each other and then told each other, 'Oh, shut up!' "

Pals to the end, they laughed and argued, punching each other in the arm as a sign of affection.

"They fought like twelve-year-old kids."

Then, at evening, Kaye and Rankin took the Star Ferry back across the harbor to the Kowloon side of the city, where they were sharing a suite in the old and elegant Peninsula Hotel. There was a dinner party to dress for. The Asian movie mogul, Sir Run Run Shaw, had invited Rankin, telling him to bring Kaye along.

The dinner was at the home of the new American consul general, and it was a formal evening, with four tables and six places at each. Rankin was seated with the hostess, who promptly asked what he was doing in Hong Kong.

It was an inclination of Danny's to learn about personal idiosyncrasies, and one of the first things he had learned about Arthur Rankin was that the producer did not like to be asked what he did. In fact, Arthur said, "I tended to go blank when asked that."

Danny, seated at the adjacent table, overheard that very question being asked.

He was bored, anyway (he later told Rankin), by the diplomatic types and the stuffy conversation. Turning around, he whispered to the hostess, "Don't ask him what he does. Please don't ask him. He won't be able to tell you."

She looked querulously at Kaye.

"Please," he repeated. "Don't pursue that."

"What do you mean?" she whispered back.

"He's a very eminent brain surgeon."

Overhearing, Rankin thought, God, this is the oldest joke on earth.

But the consul general's wife kept whispering to Danny. Finally, she returned her attention to the guest at her table.

"Mr. Rankin," she said. "I know what you do, and I think I know what you're doing. I'll just bet you are going from here to Indonesia."

Now he was really uncomfortable.

"That's right," he said, hoping to cut the conversation short.

She excused herself and went to her husband's table. She whispered, as Rankin later learned, that he was a brain surgeon on his way to Djakarta to operate on President Suharto.

Hong Kong was a city where Arthur was known, and he would see these people again. At evening's end, when he thanked his hosts, he made sure that Danny, the troublemaker, was beside him, and he took the opportunity to straighten out the consul general.

"No matter what your wife has told you," he said, glaring at Kaye, "I want to tell you the facts. And the facts are, I am an animator. I work in Tokyo filming in animation."

The consul general stared at him, broke into a beaming smile, and said, "And you expect me to believe that?"

Danny, as Rankin remembered, "was in tears of laughter."

The next morning, they packed to leave, Rankin for New York and Kaye for Los Angeles. While Arthur was waiting for his plane, the maids came to clean the suite. Danny had left several items behind, including a sweater that had been worn through at the elbows and a pair of corduroy trousers that Rankin could see "were too shabby to ever be worn again." He told the maid to throw them out.

Two weeks later, Danny called him in New York.

"Did you get my pants?"

It took the producer a moment to realize what pants. Then he was positive that this was "a real joke."

"Your pants? No, I threw them out."

Now it was Kaye who thought that Rankin was kidding.

"I'll be in New York next week. I'll come and get them."

"No, really," Arthur said. "I threw them out."

Kaye hung up on him. "And just because I'd thrown out this old pair of pants. Stretch corduroys that he loved. He was sore because I hadn't paid enough attention to know that he loved those pants."

The incident was forgotten, or at least forgiven, when Rankin and his partner, Jules Bass, came to Los Angeles to complete the voice dubbing for the show. Sylvia invited them to a dinner party celebrating Danny's sixtieth birthday, and since it was her party, dinner was prepared in the regular Kaye kitchen, which was impressive in its own right. A professional Garland stove had been installed along with a large cooking island in the center. It seemed to be Sylvia's final Los Angeles statement, for the closing of *Two by Two* meant that Danny was basically moving to California. And that meant Sylvia would be moving to New York. In anticipation of the transfer, she was trying to sell Yale University on a musical-comedy lecture series. She was also taking steps, in a sad and hopelessly one-sided gesture, to have Danny's special Chinese kitchen duplicated in the Sherry-Netherland apartment.

But as Linda Palmer, freshly divorced from Ted Ashley, said, "It used to be a joke that they got together for state occasions." And so, although they were seldom together, the arrangement was not inviolate. But separation was so much a part of their life that they were apart even when together; in fact, Sylvia had her own wing in the California house.

They were hardly even awake at the same time. Her nocturnal life had become ingrained, staying up all night, smoking, and playing the piano. She seldom went to sleep before five or rose before dusk. Her meals were usually served in her bedroom, even while Danny might at the same time be downstairs in his kitchen, serving high-cuisine Chinese food to his friends.

His friends and acquaintances multiplied, one bringing another to the dinners. One evening, Danny's executive secretary, Connie Griffin, brought along Bronya Galef, a young woman whose spirit, wit, and beauty evidently charmed him instantly, because he began inviting her to the dinners as well. And one of the first things she noticed was the sheer number of people who passed through. "He had hundreds of friends and acquaintances," she said.

She, of course, noticed that his wife was not among them. "Sylvia had a hold on him," Bronya recognized, "but she was entirely alone in the relationship."

They seemed to have only one friend in common, a Los Angeles decorator named Olive Behrens, tall, lithe, and elegant, described by Bronya as "looking like a greyhound in full motion. She kept the peace for them; she was the referee."

If the air itself seemed barbed when Danny and Sylvia were in the same room, the barbs occasionally softened. At that sixtieth birthday party, for instance, the atmosphere was even cozy. Perhaps it was because of the weather. "It was dark and stormy," Arthur Rankin remembered, and the rain was pounding on the roof.

Suddenly, there was a loud knocking at the door. When the maid opened it, Jack Warner strode in, drenched but smiling.

Stretching out his hand, the famed producer cried, "Happy birthday, Danny!"

Rankin was "impressed that a powerful movie producer would surprise someone on a night like that," but Sylvia was not so impressed. She took one look at Warner, turned on her heel, and left the room, going upstairs.

Warner did not seem to take notice of it. He and Danny were soon telling Hollywood stories, "doing a lot of comedy," Rankin said, "and we were all enjoying ourselves."

Only after Warner had gone did Sylvia reappear.

"How could you let that man into the house?" she said to Danny.

"Oh, come on," he said lightly. "That's all water under the bridge."

"You don't forget about something like that."

"But he came all this way in the rain," Danny said, shrugging the subject off and changing it.

The water under the bridge, Rankin later learned, was Warner's conservative politics, his role in the McCarthyism of the 1950s, and the unpleasant business dealings involving *The Inspector General*. Sylvia had not forgotten any of it, and she was not about to forgive it by socializing with Jack Warner now. That was Sylvia, too.

DANNY'S MOODS WERE GROWING DARKER, DEPRESSION FESTERING into anger. Offers of work were fewer and not so fancy, and he seemed to choose them greedily, a hunger without taste. His one remaining career option seemed to be his credibility as an entertainer of children. Everything he did now was child-related and becoming vaguely second-rate. He made a one-hour *Peter Cottontail* television special. He costarred in a couple of inferior television musicals, *Peter Pan*, with Mia Farrow, and *Pinocchio*, with Sandy Duncan. Neither was worthy of a major star.

While taping *Pinocchio*, he ran into his old television producer Perry Lafferty in a Hollywood restaurant. Perry was with Dinah Shore, and Danny came up to the table, kissed her—a pal since the making of *Up in Arms*—and shook Perry's hand for the first time in eleven years.

Lafferty mentioned that he had resigned from CBS. Suddenly ("like you had turned on a light switch"), Danny was his friend again. "From that second on, I'm invited to his house for dinner two or three nights; then he wants me to come with Dena Productions. It was like the old days."

Lafferty turned down the offer ("Dena Productions wasn't really that active") in favor of one from a movie company. When he made that decision, "the light switch went off, and that's where it stayed for the rest of his life."

He was especially difficult during the London production of *Peter Pan*. His part as Captain Hook was considerably smaller than Mia Farrow's in the title role, and perhaps that was why he was being so irritable. He was so unpleasant during production, in fact, that Farrow got herself a spray gun, and whenever she finished a scene with him, she would spray the space he had occupied.

She even made a label for the spray gun. The label read, "Bull-shit Spray."

Bronya Galef happened to be in London at the time and stopped by for lunch. Waiting on the set, Danny sat alone. The producers (Dwight Hemion and Gary Smith) were not talking to him. The crew and cast had already left.

"What the hell is going on here?" she asked.

But he was not inclined to talk about it. Instead, he suggested, "Let's go eat in the commissary." Over lunch she told him that she was getting married and was looking for a house in Los Angeles. Danny said, "The one next door to me is for sale," and that was where Bronya moved, 1105 San Ysidro Drive.

Whether it was *Peter Pan* or *Pinocchio*, the time was being filled but not well packed. He occupied the loose spots with institutional work, conducting orchestras and even doing a comedy lecture at the Metropolitan Opera. He became a regular member of a San Francisco cooking class that was actually called "Mme. Chiang's Salon de Cuisine."

Then the Unicef public information office issued a brief but ominous press release. Danny Kaye was going to embark on his fourth Unicef Trick or Treat promotion in ten years. He was going to visit sixty-five cities in five days.

It sounded like a joke—thirteen cities a day—and the Unicef information officer conceded that it was "probably ridiculous," as he would have no more than fifteen minutes at each stop. But Trick or Treat for Unicef was faltering after twenty-five years as the organization's fund-raising centerpiece, and $4 million was needed immediately.

The reason for the sixty-five cities seemed to be the sixty-five takeoffs and landings. Kaye hadn't flown in six months, and he needed the practice. He also needed to log air mileage to keep current on his license. Anyway, without the flying, he said, "I'd be bored to death." And so the organization chartered a Lear jet (at a cost of $22,000) for the seventeen-thousand-mile trip—a journey across forty states and three Canadian provinces, made in 120 hours.

The organization assigned C. Lloyd Bailey, the executive director of the U.S. Committee for Unicef, to accompany Danny and to arrange the logistics. Volunteers had to be found in every location, mainly to ferry children to the airports—where, in most cases, they would see him for just a few minutes. For that, they had to be rehearsed and, in some cases, told who he was. According to a memo written by Judy Kessler, a reporter who went along on assignment for *People* magazine, C. Lloyd Bailey himself "was a nervous wreck" as the trip began. In fact, Ms. Kessler later wrote to her editors, Bill Ewald and Dick Stolley, that Bailey "has worked with Danny for years, and knows he can be difficult. His hands shook throughout the day and if the slightest thing went wrong, Kaye would yell at him."

The journey started at eight in the morning, with a Gene Shalit interview on the *Today* show. Waiting, meanwhile, in front of the NBC entrance near Rockefeller Center was a limousine to take Kaye to La Guardia Airport's Marine Terminal. There the small jet sat fueled and checked out, freshly painted white with blue lettering: Unicef One. The body had even been stenciled with the organization's insignia.

Danny climbed the mobile stairway, dressed casually as usual, now in gray flannel trousers and a wool sweater, with a porkpie hat. Having quit cigarettes, he had a pipe in his mouth and, of course, space shoes on his feet. He was followed by C. Lloyd Bailey and the *People* magazine team, as well as Clay Lacy, the copilot who had succeeded Bob Dorn.

When Allen Green, the *People* photographer, asked jokingly if the space shoes were for flying, Kaye snapped, "No, they're just for fucking."

Not every such special moment would be reported in the magazine.

Kaye and Lacy made their way into the cockpit, where a sign had been posted: Captain Danny Kaye and Clay Lacy. Checking out the switches and gauges, Danny folded himself and his long legs into the cramped seat. When he had the jet engines humming, he eased the craft into the service lane, then moved out toward ground traffic. Soon he had the craft lifting up over Jamaica Bay and into the overcast sky, banking south toward Philadelphia. It was going to be a hectic day, and he was expected for dinner in Ottawa as the guest of Prime Minister Pierre Trudeau. Over his shoulder, he warned Unicef's Bailey that despite the flight schedule, he had to be at that dinner on time.

In Philadelphia, the children were waiting at the airport, costumed for Halloween and holding signs: Hooray for Danny Kaye. We Love Danny Kaye. Welcome Danny. Thanks Danny. Taxiing the plane to the corner of the airfield where the youngsters had been herded, he stepped to the door and then smiled at the top of the ramp and came halfway down the stairs. "Now what," he cried, "will you say when you go trick or treating for Unicef?" They shouted all over each other. Quieting them, he said, "This is a chance to reach out over boundaries and colors and races and creeds and help other children. I've seen what this money can do."

He raised his arms like a conductor's and led them in a round of "Happy Birthday, Dear Unicef." Then he explained that he had sixty-four more stops to make in the next five days, went back up the stairs, and was on his way to Baltimore.

There he seemed to be elated by a wonderfully terrible school band that greeted them at the airport. When a newspaper photographer asked for a picture, he said, "Yeah, let me get a light one," meaning a small child to pick up, but he seemed to make sure that it was one with red hair. The magazine people noticed that he favored redheads.

At Logan Airport in Boston, the children weren't allowed on the tarmac, and so Danny's appearance took place in the terminal. His friend from the Boston Symphony Orchestra, Harry Ellis Dickson, was waiting in the midst of the orange-and-black Unicef collection-box costumes that the kids were wearing. Dickson boarded the plane for the stretch through Montreal, and they moved on to Providence, Rhode Island, where Kaye again mentioned his hectic schedule. "If you blink a lot," he said to the kids, "you're going to miss me.

"I've done this for twenty-two years," he added, "and I keep getting happier."

In Montreal they were joined by Gail Smith, the director of the Unicef Canadian Halloween Committee. Judy Kessler of *People* magazine noted that this handsome blond woman in her forties "was very nervous and excited about meeting Kaye, her idol."

He promptly embraced her and insisted that she kiss him. "Now, don't turn your cheek, Mrs. Smith," he said. "Kiss me on the lips."

But she did turn her cheek.

"I bet"—he grinned—"you're one of those women who hugs with her ass sticking out." This was printed in *People*, with "butt" replacing "ass."

Mrs. Smith, according to Judy Kessler's memo, was "too dumbfounded to reply," but the romantic moment was doomed to brevity, since the limousine Mrs. Smith had engaged was waiting to whisk them off. She made nervous small talk as they walked to the car, telling Danny that, believe it or not, the driver's name was "Richard Burton." When she began to give this fellow driving directions, Kaye interrupted.

"You must be having an affair with this guy," he said. "That's why you're calling him 'Mr. Burton.' It's the way people cover up."

She lit a cigarette, the match trembling. According to the eventual article, "she doesn't smoke but goes through a pack of borrowed cigarettes." The picture being drawn of Danny Kaye, even in the magazine's expurgated version of Kessler's story, was very different from Kaye's lifetime of press protection. It had been a mistake allowing the journalist along without a public relations man around.

The hour in Montreal passed without further incident, so hectic that by the time they landed in Ottawa, Kaye still hadn't scrubbed off his makeup from the *Today* show, but they were only thirty minutes behind schedule, and when he was finally checked into the big suite at the Château Laurier, he had ample time to clean up and dress for the Trudeau dinner.

At the prime minister's home, he romped with the children— three-and-a-half-year-old Justin and little Sacha, who was almost two. The youngsters were costumed as leopards for Halloween, and Kaye played the lion with them, roaring and leaping until they became hysterical with laughter. Mrs. Trudeau mentioned that both children had been born on Christmas Day, which was fortunate, she said, because that was the prime minister's only day off. Danny countered her with a vaguely disrespectful remark that in that case they should have been born in September.

He stayed through dinner, having asked the *People* team to fetch both him and Mrs. Smith at a quarter to ten. As the car pulled up to his hotel, he said to Judy and Allen, "Now why don't you put away those fucking cameras and come in and have a drink?" They accepted, later telling their editor, "We had no alternative," feeling sympathetic with Mrs. Smith. Perhaps their presence would shield this woman "whose mission in life was only to have everything in Canada perfect for Kaye."

When they were all in his hotel suite, he asked Mrs. Smith what kind of white wine she preferred. Before she could answer, he said, "I like a Chilean wine that comes from Hungary."

Ignoring the clumsy and mean-spirited joke, she picked up the telephone to order wine from room service.

"No, Mrs. Smith," Danny said, altering his seductive approach. "Order a pussyfuissé."

It was another line that was unprintable in *People*, and this time she blushed.

"Let's also get a bottle of gin, too," he said, "and a bottle of scotch and a bottle of vodka. Plus the wine."

She dialed room service again, pale and trembling.

He smiled at the journalists. "You'll have plenty left over to drink on the plane." He filled Mrs. Smith's glass to the brim with scotch.

"What's her room number?" he whispered to Judy. That comment was excluded from her story, too, along with the reporter's observation that "by the end of the evening, [Kaye's] image had been demolished, and hopefully she didn't have a nervous breakdown."

Kessler didn't give him Gail Smith's room number, but when she left, the forlorn woman said, "I guess this is a small price to pay for getting Danny to do this for us."

29

The other afternoon I went to a reception for Danny Kaye. On hand were only Mr. Kaye, his three French hosts, his American public relations man, one American film critic, two bartenders, and several dozen glasses. I had been told this would be a small reception, but this was more intimate than I had expected.

—Vincent Canby, the *New York Times*

THE ARTICLE THAT APPEARED IN THE NOVEMBER 17, 1975, ISSUE OF *PEOPLE* MAGAZINE, EVEN AS SANITIZED, WAS A CONTEMPTUOUS depiction of Danny Kaye's behavior on the Unicef trip. A letter from C. Lloyd Bailey of Unicef was printed in the next issue:

> Judy Kessler's recent "report" on Danny Kaye's 65 city tour for Unicef seemed intent on playing down the significance of his Herculean effort and its humanitarian purpose. Mr. Kaye's trip was designed to increase the consciousness of both adults and children across the country of the urgent needs of millions of hungry, sick and seriously deprived children in the developing world.

Kaye never undertook another Trick or Treat tour for Unicef. Other stars would associate themselves with the organization, including Marlon Brando, John Denver, George Harrison, Muhammad Ali, and most prominently, Audrey Hepburn. Commendable as their work was, none of them became so identified with Unicef or with the worldwide cause of needy children as Danny Kaye. Perhaps, in the end, this association was tainted by a certain cynicism, but there is also the altruism of his earlier work for Unicef, and that was by far the greater share of it.

There should be no doubt of that. His travel for Unicef had been crucial to the organization and beneficial, even, to the United Nations itself. As for children, he had become their saint, and in his best moments, that was nearly the truth.

> Most children I deal with don't speak my language—and I don't speak theirs. Their culture is different, their environment is different. The only way I communicate with them is on an emotional level . . . not on a language level. Kids have a built-in radar—they are basically the same all over the world. They can tell if one is truly interested in them . . . or just pretending to be.

Now even that was gone. Without Unicef to work for, he no longer was Danny Kaye—the performer—except for the occasional pension-fund concert. Rather, he was the man who had been Danny Kaye. Like many lives at the start of older age, his present increasingly became based on his past, a fund on which to draw for credit.

He certainly seemed to have all the money he needed, and he needed a fair amount. The house in Los Angeles and the co-op in the Sherry-Netherland were paid for, but as the writer Larry Gelbart said, "People in Hollywood would wonder, 'How the hell does this guy keep going without working?' He has all these expensive hobbies. I remember him telling me that it cost $75,000 [just] to run the line in for the special gas to fuel his woks."

And he had bought himself a newer, bigger airplane, a million-dollar Jet Commander.

Gelbart suspected, "He must have done something smart very early. He probably made some very good investments." The television producer Perry Lafferty felt the same way. "He lived very lavishly, had lawyers surrounding him, and I had the impression he was a very wealthy man because of good business advisers."

He'd had thirty years of brilliant management, which Sylvia had supervised from the outset. Between his Northwest radio-station holdings, his earnings from Dena Productions and its role in several of his movies as well as his television series, and his extensive stock portfolio, he would never have to worry about money. Moreover, he now joined with five partners in buying a major league baseball expansion franchise for what would prove a bargain price of

$5.5 million. "It's a Walter Mitty dream come true," he said, but the Seattle Mariners notwithstanding, he was a Dodger fan forever. He would arrive at Dodger Stadium two hours before game time and head for the locker room to pal around with the ball players and give tactical advice to the team's manager, Tommy Lasorda. Then he would move up to owner Peter O'Malley's box, bringing along his own kosher hotdogs from Nate and Al's, the Beverly Hills of Jewish delicatessens. To wash them down, he mixed what his cooker friend Steve Wallace called "his famous lethal margaritas."

Wallace not only went to the ball games with Danny and to the house for Chinese dinners; he and the other cookers became Danny's inner circle, and any project might be cause for summoning them. He didn't concern himself with their other responsibilities. He would call Steve Wallace at his shop, Kenny Shapiro at Dick Clark Productions, Olive Behrens at her decorating office, or Linda Palmer at Tri-Star Productions. One morning, he convened a half dozen of them for a baking lesson. When Bronya Galef came over from next door, she still didn't know what the purpose was.

"We're going to learn how to make pretzels."

"Sounds fabulous," said the amiably sarcastic neighbor. "How do you do that?"

She joined the others who were already in Kaye's kitchen (the regular one), "waiting," she said, "in their cooking outfits. Then in walks this buxom milkmaid type."

Danny had brought the woman all the way from Milwaukee and now introduced her as "the world's best pretzel maker. She's going to teach us how to make them."

She got to work with a rolling pin, flattening, slapping, pounding, and then showing everyone how to shape the dough while Kaye delivered a brief lecture on the history of pretzel making. He traced the delicacy to a German monastery in the fifteenth century. The original purpose, he had learned, was to encourage peasants to go to church, as symbolized by the traditional three-ring shape, for the Holy Trinity.

As he was concluding this talk, the pretzel lady reached into the shopping bag she had brought, and Bronya was stunned with what came out of it.

"That's a plumbing supply!" she muttered. "It's lye."

The woman opened the can and poured some of its contents into a bowl, adding water and stirring.

"We all stand there," Bronya remembered, "with our eyes like saucers. And she then proceeds to take these pretzels which we've carefully twisted—*and dips them in the lye!*"

In a thick German accent, the woman said, "This is the only way you can brown a pretzel."

"Wait a minute!" one of the cookers cried. "We've been eating lye?"

"There is no other way to brown pretzels," she said. "They are all browned in lye."

Danny beamed. It was educational, it was funny, it was perfect.

Bronya came home with three pretzels. "They were fairly bleached out looking," she recalled, having taken it easy on the lye.

HE WAS CALLING BRONYA A LOT. SHE WAS ALWAYS HOME IN THE morning.

"What are you doing, kid?"

"Not a whole lot."

"Want to go for a drive?"

"Why?" she asked, knowing why. She had seen him depressed —seen him "sit in the music room and stare at the wall."

Bronya would usually go for the drive, and she did this time. He had just taken delivery of a second Mercedes, the top of the line, and they went for a test roar up Mulholland Drive. "Every road he took," she remembered, "was a racetrack," and Mulholland is a curving, steep, mountainside road. He coasted to a stop at its crest and pulled over. Drawing off his leather driving gloves, he sat and looked through the windshield as he talked about people who find life difficult.

"It's not me," he would say, "but I always say to people when they have this problem—"

"What problem, Danny?"

He would not specify the problem, and yet it would emerge, for the depressions weren't because of a problem. The problem was the depressions.

"Terrible," she described them, the faceless anxieties. "He had a lot of demons. I mean, really a lot of demons."

He told her that he had been in and out of analysis for years. She feared that the only thing he got out of it was "a lot of psychobabble, a lot of pat answers to complicated questions. You could read it in any self-help book. It kept him away from his own demons.

"He was a tormented man," she said. "Nothing was ever going

to sit easy for Danny." The nub of it, she felt, was that "he was always going to tear himself up on some level. The Danny that he presented to the world and the Danny he was—the two personalities —it was practically schizoid. And he just could never reconcile them."

Her conclusion was that he was not insecure but unsure. "He never knew how wonderful he was," she said with love and sorrow. "If he'd had some self-confidence, his whole world would have been different."

That analysis was strikingly similar to Dr. Rosenfeld's reading of Kaye's depressions. ("He was successful—he was worshiped—but I don't think he ever felt he deserved it.")

Such perceptions make depression understandable and grievous. It is possible that with greater emotional confidence Kaye could even have divorced Sylvia, but as others had observed, she had a grip on him. She had helped create his dependency on her. That was her last line of defense.

That was why it seemed to Bronya that "Sylvia had him but she never had him."

He finally did make a pass, embracing her and trying to kiss her on the mouth. She averted her lips. "Uh-uh," she said, offering a cheek. "This is fine."

She didn't find him romantically attractive. "Anyhow, I was married to somebody I adored. But I was glad he tried and would have been sort of upset if he hadn't."

Bronya believed that she was "one of the few women he knew really well that he didn't have a rip-roaring affair with." But so many of his woman friends thought that. He didn't seem to have rip-roaring affairs with any of them, and that may well have included Bronya's pal, Joanna Simon.

It had been almost two years since Danny had seen her. When he read that she was singing with the New York Philharmonic in a performance of Gustav Mahler's *Resurrection* Symphony, he showed up. After the concert, he sought out the "green room," as all backstage lounges are called.

As usual, at Lincoln Center or anywhere, he wore sweatpants, a zipper jacket, space shoes, and a hat, and he threw his arms around her. He held her, he almost held on to her, "for over a minute," she remembered. They hugged that way, with a silent, dear, and unidentified grief, and then he went away. She would never see him again.

He was in a grim mood the day he fired his accompanist of twenty-six years, Sammy Prager. That was prompted by an overheard remark about Prager having an "old-fashioned" playing style.

And he was in one of the dark moods on a night when Anthony Newley and Leslie Bricusse came for Chinese dinner. The team had written the songs for the Broadway hit *Stop The World—I Want to Get Off* as well as for Danny's television musical *Peter Pan*. Newley found himself with a Danny Kaye who was displeased with the way the cooking was going. He seemed to be blaming his assistant and was in a "foul mood." In Newley's word, it made everyone "mournful" as Kaye escalated "from irascible to terrifying."

Scarcely concealing his annoyance, he invited his guests to bring their drinks into the Chinese kitchen and see its special features. It occurred to Newley "that we were there to watch and applaud Danny's cooking skills."

If that was an accurate insight, perhaps fearing the food wasn't good enough for applause was another clue to the depressions; perhaps they were related, somehow, to whatever it was that had driven him to perform in the first place. Perhaps not being good enough for applause—a failure to please an audience—is read as not being good enough as a human being. It is noteworthy that Newley's was the observation of someone who was himself a performer.

After the food was served and eaten, they were herded into the music room for an after-dinner entertainment. This, figuratively and literally, was the connection between Danny's cooking and his performing.

A 16-mm film projector was brought out while Kaye unfurled a movie screen, pulling it down like a window shade. He loaded a large film reel onto the projecting machine, started it, and then pulled off his black space shoes, the low ones with the straps, the kind that he had been wearing for decades. He cared for his feet as if they had hurt for a lifetime, and liked having them rubbed. Turning to the prettiest woman among the guests, he asked if she would massage his toes and the balls of his feet.

Sitting sideways on the sofa, he rested them in the woman's lap, and as she kneaded and massaged, with his image clowning across the screen, "he sat rapt," Newley remembered. "He pointed out details, telling us why things worked and didn't work. He was the epitome of what the funnyman becomes . . . that terror to make laughter. And he was terrified, too, that the kinescope wouldn't come off."

But his moods were by no means exclusively low and with-drawn. Sometimes he could be emotionally provocative. For in-stance, at Elaine's Restaurant in Manhattan, Alan King was having dinner with his wife and some friends when Danny "suddenly loomed up at the table."

By then, King was one of the top comedians in America. Even still, he saved a special respect for Kaye. ("He was masterful at what he did. He took it to another level. He was one of the giants.") And so he was startled to unexpectedly see Danny looking at him, stand-ing at his table in the crowded celebrity restaurant. King was always a meticulous dresser, favoring sleek, elegant, and expensive Italian suits. Kaye was wearing his floppy hat and a Los Angeles Dodgers zipper jacket.

"I've got to talk to you," Danny said, as if an edict were being issued. He turned and went back to his table. King excused himself to his guests and followed.

Kaye nodded toward an empty chair at his table and King sat.

"You never liked me," Danny said, "did you?"

This was not the first time that Alan King had run into Danny Kaye in the thirty years since that painful incident in a Philadelphia nightclub. Once, they had thrilled an uproarious audience, ex-changing wisecracks across a hotel ballroom during a gala birthday party for Zubin Mehta. This, though, was the first time that any-thing personal was being exchanged between them, and Kaye's re-mark, "You never liked me," was certainly confrontational.

King "was speechless for a minute."

Finally, he replied. "No, Danny. I always respected you. You know that. But I never liked you, it's true."

Danny looked at him for a while. "Why?"

Slowly, still painfully, King recalled the time at the Latin Casino in Philadelphia when he was eager for Kaye's reaction to his work and was instead disparaged as a "Jew comic."

Kaye looked dumbfounded until he finally said, "It never hap-pened."

King replied, "Danny, I want to tell you something. When you're just a kid and your hero Danny Kaye comes in to see you and says something like that—well—not only do I remember it verbatim. It's something that never—never ever—leaves your mind. It doesn't get exaggerated. It stays."

With that, he stood up, turned, and walked away.

30

Danny would sometimes hang out while I had my hair cut in
a barbershop. He had nothing else to do.

—Steve Wallace

A NEW WOMAN CAME INTO DANNY'S LIFE, OFFERING HIS LAST CHANCE FOR A RELATIONSHIP OF INTIMACY. HER NAME WAS MARLENE Sorosky, and she had nothing to do with show business. She wasn't sophisticated or tough or competitive. She was a middle-class woman, warm, traditional, kind, maternal, and Jewish. She was also a very fancy cook.

She was of medium height (five feet five) and slender, with big brown eyes and close-cropped dark hair, and she dressed with a neat elegance. At thirty-eight, she was some twenty-seven years younger than Danny, and she was married. She lived in Encino with her four young children. All in all she looked, Linda Palmer thought, "like a pretty version of Sylvia," but generally, if Marlene Sorosky was like anyone in Danny's life, it was Rosie Kaye. Marlene was a young Rosie.

She was a respected food professional, a writer and lecturer, and had just opened Marlene Sorosky's Cooking Center in Tarzana, but the day Danny called, he reached her at home. He had gotten the telephone number from James Beard, the food authority.

"Hi, I'm Danny Kaye."

She wasn't awed. "I grew up in Beverly Hills," she would remember. "I was used to stars."

"What are you doing?" Kaye asked.

"I'm just getting my family dinner."

"Well, stop everything and come on over and see my Chinese kitchen."

"I really can't," she said. "My husband's coming home any minute."

"Aren't you ever spontaneous? Don't you ever do anything that your husband wouldn't expect?"

She told him she would come the next night.

"And be sure," Danny said, "to bring me a book, and don't forget to autograph it."

Marlene brought one of her cookbooks and two friends as well, her cooking-school manager and the celebrated chef Jacques Pepin, who had once worked for Charles de Gaulle. But after dinner, as they were all starting down the driveway, Danny called out for her to come back.

She got out of the car and walked back to the house. He stood and chatted with her for a moment. Then he took her into his arms and kissed her. So, she remembered, it all began—"through food."

They became close almost at once, and she joined his little circle of intimates, the cookers. For theirs was no undercover romance. Steve Wallace, Linda Palmer, Kenny Shapiro, and Bronya Galef all met and liked Marlene, and it became plain to them how deeply in love she was falling with Danny. Linda said: "She thought they'd get married." And Bronya declared: "That was the only relationship that moved him."

Kaye apparently opened up to Marlene in a way that was unprecedented for him, even though she, too, found him secretive. He never talked about his family, his past, or his previous romances. "Secretive, yes," she would say, "but never dishonest. I never, ever, caught him in a lie, and if you asked him to keep a confidence, nobody could wring it out of him."

He talked to her about why he had stopped performing, sounding like a professional athlete. "I don't want to end up doing something I'd be sorry for," he said. "I don't want to do anything I'm too old for." He had seen too many stars make fools of themselves. He had no sense of himself having performed past his prime.

He talked about his black moods and about his icy reactions to autograph seekers.

"They expect Danny Kaye," he said. It was only Danny Kaye the performer that the autograph hounds wanted. "I'm not that person."

One strange time they were with a group of people in a restaurant when a man came to the table and asked for his autograph. Kaye looked up and snatched the piece of paper out of the fellow's hand. Then, turning scarlet with rage, he rose, rolled the paper into a ball, and threw it at the man.

"It was just an inch away from a fight," Marlene remembered. "Everyone was stunned."

Driving home, she asked, "What happened in there? Why did you do that?"

"The guy was anti-Semitic," Kaye replied.

"What? Where did that come from?"

"I could tell," Danny said.

That was strange, but just as strangely, she believed him. She believed he could sense it, that he had not been paranoid.

"He believed he knew," Marlene would say, "and I believe it, too."

He also talked to her about Sylvia. The women among the cookers agreed that if he were ever going to leave her, it would be for Marlene, but Danny insisted that he owed Sylvia too much to leave her.

"I would not have been what I was without her," he told Marlene. "I know I had the talent, but I didn't have the discipline. I was all over the place. I didn't know what direction to go in. Sylvia gave me direction; she took over. I owe her for that."

Marlene agreed that he owed her for that, "but," she said, "do you owe her your whole life?"

He must have thought so.

"She had a hold on him," Marlene concluded. "He didn't want to be around her, but he couldn't leave.

"It was very sad," she said, "and very strange. I don't think he knew whether he loved her. It was part of his demon. He couldn't get away. It was a love-hate relationship if you ever saw one," and she certainly saw it. Danny would even invite her to dinner with Sylvia there, although Marlene sensed that "Sylvia was insanely jealous of me."

The Kayes were vicious with each other—Marlene surely had

been invited as part of the viciousness. And "it was painful to watch them," she said. "They would stick it to each other with people around. It was like a duel with words. It was awful, you didn't want to be there, and she was better with words than Danny, so she would usually win."

That was assuming there ever was a winner in such a situation.

He also talked to Marlene about living alone in much the same terms as he had spoken with Joanna Simon. And Marlene found out for herself that he could never spend a night sleeping with a woman —"after having sex with them," as he put it.

As for homosexuality, he said—without being asked—"I've never had a homosexual experience in my life. I've never had any kind of gay relationship. I've had opportunities, but I never did anything about them."

That, Marlene believed, was not for lack of daring. She knew him for "a real free spirit. It would go along with his personality that he would do anything." But if he had said that to her, unprompted, then she believed it. As for his heterosexuality with her, "I know he was very sexual. I was definitely in love with him."

Indeed, her friends believed that she left her husband for him. In that traumatic period, she nearly broke down. "I do not believe I would have survived without Danny. He was without a doubt the best thing that happened in my life. Especially at that time. It was more than just emotional. He practically picked me up and carried me into the hospital."

She was not the only friend to talk about his dependability in a crunch. Both Steve Wallace and the talk-show host Michael Jackson were profoundly moved by Kaye's help in a crisis, but Marlene was the most eloquent. "If you needed Danny," she said, "he simply was the best friend in the whole world. He loved to be needed. That was his strong point. If you were sick, he wanted to get you to the best doctors. If you were hurting, he wanted to do anything to take away the pain."

But it was getting late for him and for last chances with her. He was on schedule for testimonials, honors, awards, and the first stages of eulogy. It was time for retrospective and for illness. Bronya Galef said, "He was getting older, and he didn't take it very well." For that matter, Sylvia was not doing so well herself. A lifetime of cigarette smoking had rewarded her with cancer, the removal of a lung, and a serious case of emphysema. Still, she remained as industrious as a schoolgirl. She sold the Prudential Life Insurance Company on funding *Musical Comedy Tonight* for PBS broadcast. Based on the lecture series that she had been delivering at Yale, with Broadway performers providing entertainment examples, it was aired on October 1, 1979.

She gave interviews to promote it, clinging to the myth of "a Fine head on Danny's shoulders." The notion had long soured their life, an irony that escaped her. It now seemed ludicrous for her to say, "I guess I may have been overshadowed [by Danny] to a certain extent."

One might wonder who she thought she was. Then again, who *did* she think she was? If Sylvia was a songwriter, she was a songwriter only because of Danny Kaye. Nobody else ever sang a song of Sylvia Fine's. Instead, she clung to a partnership in his accomplishments, a joint persona, that childhood fantasy of a perfect marriage. Thus, she felt that she was being overshadowed in her half of Danny Kaye. This was a gloomy madness.

She made an uncomfortable hostess for *Musical Comedy Tonight*, and in that respect she had not changed since childhood. She never had been a performer and still was shy despite decades of life in international circles. The marks of her background were beyond cosmetic surgery and remained to identify her. However bright she was, however vital and productive, she looked and talked like a middle-class matron from Brooklyn.

But she was Sylvia Fine, smart and persuasive, and she even sold Alan King on singing "Sue Me," from *Guys and Dolls*. It was harder convincing Danny to appear on her show, but she managed that, too, on a sequel produced on February 11, 1981. He sang "Tschaikowsky," the number that had started his career. It was an unfortunate choice that Sylvia surely promoted because of the significance of *Lady in the Dark* in the American musical theater. But Danny would have been shown to better effect doing "Melody in Four F," because in playing the introductory scene to "Tschaikowsky," he had a grotesque take on the effeminate character. By current standards, this parody of stereotypical homosexual mannerisms was not only inane but tasteless and unpleasant. As played by a mincing, aging Danny Kaye, it was nasty. When he finished this business and finally got around to singing "Tschaikowsky," he made its bravura seem as lifeless as his dyed hair, as mean as his dead eyes. Thus, the death of the inspired young performer who had once sprung to vibrant life with this number.

He had one last role to play, the comedian as Hamlet, a holocaust survivor on a television movie called *Skokie.* Broadcast by CBS on November 17, 1981, it was a two-and-a-half-hour dramatization of the confrontations in suburban Chicago between neo-Nazi demonstrators and Jews who had survived the concentration camps. The issue was compelling, a test of the emotional limits of free speech, and Kaye was pleased. His reviews were excellent. "He was hugely proud of it," according to Bronya. "He took that deeply seriously," she said. "It helped to finally reconcile him with his Jewishness."

He was honored at the 1982 Academy Awards with the Jean Hersholt Humanitarian Award and, the following year in Denmark, with the Knight's Cross of the First Class of the Order of Danneborg. But he also found himself in hospitals. In 1982 it was to correct a hernia, and at the start of 1983, it was for a seemingly insignificant "leg condition." Three weeks later, he developed chest pains, and an examination revealed an irregular heart rhythm. At Cedars-Sinai Medical Center in Los Angeles, a team of specialists performed a battery of heart tests and diagnosed his condition as "a mild angina." They recommended "preventive" quadruple bypass heart surgery.

A panicky Sylvia telephoned Dr. Rosenfeld in New York. "Listen, Izzy," she said. "Danny's in big trouble. I don't understand what the doctors here are saying. Would you come out to see him?"

Within hours, the cardiologist was flying west, and by afternoon, he was studying the tests. He told Danny, Sylvia, and Dena that in his opinion bypass surgery would be premature at this point. Despite the counsel, Kaye, according to Rosenfeld, "intellectually couldn't stand anything less than perfect, and he was unwilling, in my view, to live with a coronary circulation that wasn't a hundred percent. So he decided to have the surgery."

The chief of cardiac surgery at Cedars-Sinai was Dr. Hyman Engelberg, and as the operation began, he was supervising a three-man operating team. Suddenly, there was trouble. As Rosenfeld described it, while a catheter was being inserted in Kaye's bladder, an artery ruptured and began to hemorrhage. While the spurting blood was clamped down, the operation proceeded. The rest was successful, but massive blood transfusions were required for the blood loss. As they continued, Rosenfeld visited a very shaken Danny Kaye.

"What's going on, Izzy?"

The doctor knew how scared his friend was. "Danny was a very sophisticated guy, and he knew this wasn't par for the course. He was worried. He was anxious."

He was right, but he didn't know why yet. For the duration, he became "withdrawn and less effusive," which meant even more withdrawn and even less effusive. Rosenfeld considered this "a normal reaction to serious illness," but across the country, in the *New York Post*, it was reported that "sources close to the performer described his condition as 'low' despite hospital assurances that he was improving."

He didn't improve enough. Several weeks after being discharged, he learned that he had contracted hepatitis C, presumably from an infected blood transfusion.

"It was amazing to me," Rosenfeld said a few years later, "that he didn't get AIDS, because in those days we didn't screen blood for the AIDS virus.

"There are people," the cardiologist stressed, "who said he had AIDS, but he didn't. He had hepatitis C."

Kaye became irritable as the liver condition worsened, and that mood might have been one of the effects of the hepatitis itself. Everything else seemed to be affected by it, from his general state of physical ill-being to the kind of salt-free food he could and could not eat—which had to be aggravating to this gourmet. At the same time, his physical weakness brought Sylvia's ultimate domination. Danny's cooker friend Steve Wallace felt that "Sylvia and Dena tried to keep him to themselves. They wanted to deny the part of his life that went on with the cookers. They wanted their own Danny."

He slumped into a foul and fearful mood, which must have affected Sylvia, too, because they met with lawyers to draw up a strange and terrifying document.

The item about it appeared in an out-of-the-way newspaper, the *Houston Chronicle*. The date was December 11, 1983.

> Danny Kaye and his wife Sylvia Fine have been very upset by the recent rash of books by the children of stars, one example being the Christina Crawford book about her mother, Joan Crawford. They've warned their daughter, travel writer Dena Kaye, that if she ever writes about them she'll be disinherited in their will and this is now a matter of legal record. The Kayes are worth a fortune, so Dena knows she'll be better off writing travel articles than washing the family's dirty laundry.

It is difficult to comprehend what "dirty laundry" Danny and Sylvia so feared might be hung out to dry. The only explanation for this extraordinary legal agreement is that it was drawn to preserve the fraud they had made of their lives. Sylvia Fine and Danny Kaye were *not* America's marriage fantasy; Sylvia's gift of her brains, her industriousness, herself, to make the funny-face Red Kaminski into the brilliant entertainer Danny Kaye had not been rewarded as expected. Times had changed since the fairy tales, and instead of getting her frog prince, what she got for her gift was a Strindberg marriage in a Freudian age; not blazingly hellish but neurotic and insidious, a marriage enduring because of manipulation and need.

It was a wan and frail but at least unhospitalized Danny Kaye who now returned to his cooking. He even offered to go into Benay Venuta's kitchen and make an Italian meal for her and her new husband, the actor Fred Clark. This time, he came with Sylvia.

They had a practiced way of behaving together in public. The way Danny's friend Linda Palmer described it, "Sylvia was always warm to him . . . and he behaved to her like somebody's wife to whom he was being polite. There was not a trace of warmth in it."

In fact, he was warmer, in some ways, to his old friend Benay as he mixed and stirred the foodstuffs in her kitchen. He began with a clear soup. The pasta course was his own creation, a gorgonzola pasta. The main course was fegato (liver) Veneziano. For dessert, he delicately contrived a coffee soufflé. He wouldn't let the maid serve that, spooning it out himself "because," Venuta said, "you must take it out of the soufflé dish carefully so that you get a little of that crust on the edge."

But the specialty had been his own recipe for gorgonzola cheese sauce, poured gently over the pasta, which he had made using his own pasta machine. While he was working it through, he had said, "Sylvia, I've got to go to Genoa next week."

They were all standing around in the kitchen, sipping wine and keeping him company while he cooked.

"Why," Benay asked, "are you going to Genoa?"

"Because, Benoo, I've got to get another pasta machine."

"Danny," Benay said (with a waggle of her finger because Sylvia was the only one allowed to call her Benoo), "that's such bullshit. Can't you just buy one here?"

"No," he said. "I've got to go to a certain store in Genoa to get it."

It seemed so strange, going when he had been so ill. He looked haggard, and his hair—once so red he had been called "Red," so red it had colored his life—that wavy pompadour now was like string, all the thinner for being dyed. But he was serious about going to Genoa, and his cooker-pal Steve Wallace understood that. Invited to come along on the shopping excursion, Wallace suggested that they make a culinary expedition of it. They both knew an importer named Darryl Corti, who ran the fine Corti Brothers food stores in Sacramento. Corti and Kaye agreed on a two-week trip through France, Switzerland, and Italy, and they were off.

The importer set up the itinerary and arranged the appointments, contacting producers of pasta, vinegar, olive oil, and cheese. He arranged for visits with the chefs of the great Swiss, French, and Italian restaurants. He even managed invitations to private homes for special meals.

But three days after their arrival in France, he blew a whistle and demanded a conference because Danny had immediately taken charge, arranging for dinners at restaurants he knew (Roger Verge's Moulin de Mougins, Paul Bocuse's Restaurant Bocuse). Steve Wallace could appreciate Corti's irritation. "Darryl knew a lot more than Danny." And Corti told Wallace, "I have to make something clear to him."

They sat down over lunch. Corti looked Kaye in the eye. This was serious business, and he said, "Remember, you're with me. I'm not with you."

That did not exactly sit beautifully with Danny Kaye. As Izzy Rosenfeld once conceded, "Danny expected a certain amount of deference and ass kissing." He wasn't going to get that from Darryl Corti, who, according to Steve Wallace, "knew more about food and wine than anyone you'd ever meet." And so it was touch and go for the next couple of days while, Steve remembered, "they went their separate ways.

"Then, after a couple of days, Danny got back together with Darryl, and after that he called him 'the Professor.'"

In Switzerland, they were the guests of Fredy Girardet, whose Girardet restaurant in Crissier, Switzerland, was, Wallace and Corti agreed, "the best restaurant in the world." Still, it was because of Danny's celebrity, not Corti's expertise, that they were invited on a tour of that kitchen.

Italy was Corti's strength. He had contacts at all levels. They watched parmesan cheese being made in Parma. They were shown the refining of six-hundred-year-old balsamic vinegar. They also just wandered, poking their noses into anything that smelled like food. Corti had taken them to a little Italian fishing village to visit a family-owned olive-oil business. Afterward, they stood on the waterfront, watching the fishing nets being repaired. Then, as they strolled on, Corti peeked into an open door on an unmarked building. He turned and gestured for them to follow.

It was dark inside, and men were at work, wearing long-sleeved underwear shirts, oil-stained pants, and sandals. "The first guy we watched," Wallace remembered, "had salt and fish all over him. He was in the back, packing either anchovies or sardines into jars. Then he filled them over with olive oil."

He continued to work, taking no notice of the three Americans who were watching. Unshaved, his beard a stubble, he packed and poured in the sunless room. "That was what he did for a living," Wallace remembered, thinking that the scene was as simple and as far away from California as anything could be. "And it's dark and we're watching this guy and we don't say anything in English and he doesn't say anything in Italian."

But the man obviously had noticed something. Without looking up and without interrupting his work, Wallace remembered, "he doesn't say anything, but he starts singing 'Thumbelina' from *Hans Christian Andersen*. Then he shot Danny a fast look out of the corner of his eye."

That movie had without question created an international impact for Kaye, but too often great lives are remembered for minor details rather than the overall arc and genius at the core. Not long afterward, Gerald Nachman wrote in the *San Francisco Chronicle*:

> If you didn't see Danny Kaye in his prime, it is hard to imagine how good he was at everything, because nobody today comes close. . . . Kaye in person was a man inspired, which you miss when you watch the clips of his simpler side singing "Thumbelina."

There is no answer to the question of whether it is more difficult and more admirable to please the sophisticated few or the broader masses. Certainly it was the popular Danny Kaye, the git-gat-giddle man, the Walter Mitty, and the cheerful purveyor of "Thumbelina" for whom praises were now being sung. It was on that Danny Kaye that a 1984 Kennedy Center honor was conferred along with Lena Horne, Isaac Stern, Gian Carlo Menotti, and Arthur Miller.

President Reagan cited Danny's work for Unicef as well as two movies in particular, naturally *The Secret Life of Walter Mitty* and *Hans Christian Andersen*. With that, a chorus of children filed on stage, students from the United Nations School in New York, hailing Kaye in song.

> You are a clown
> And when you smile the world becomes
> An apple pie
> Long live Danny Kaye

He was in pain as they serenaded him, in pain throughout the ceremony. In the preceding months, he had found it increasingly difficult to walk and even had trouble getting out of a chair. He was suffering from what the doctors called "a degenerative arthritic condition" and in fact had postponed a scheduled hip-replacement operation so that he could be present at the Kennedy Center honors. He entered the hospital soon afterward, and the hip replacement was performed without incident.

Marlene Sorosky was one of the first to visit him in the hospital, slipped in by Steve Wallace despite Sylvia's efforts to screen his visitors. Another who came by to see him was Arthur Rankin, the television producer of "The Emperor's New Clothes." As they were talking, there was a tap at the door. Another man entered, a man Danny introduced as the president of the Burlington Mills Company. Rankin felt that it was appropriate to excuse himself.

"I'll be back tonight," he said, but as he started down the hall, the second visitor followed.

"I only had a minute," the Burlington man said to him as they strolled toward the elevators. "Tell me, do you know Danny well?"

"I think so," Rankin replied.

"He's very curious, isn't he?"

"I suppose everybody is," Rankin said.

"Well, he found me last year, through mutual business friends, and telephoned. And he's been calling regularly—ever since he read that we're about to introduce a new product. We call it stretch corduroy."

Rankin laughed out loud. "Here it was, ten years later," he marveled, "and Danny was still looking for those corduroy pants that

I had thrown out in Hong Kong. He never let me forget it. He wanted that guy in the hospital room when I came to visit him."

Then, not as good as new, Danny was back in Los Angeles and still unable to shake the hepatitis. It had already knocked him for a tremendous loss. It had made him impotent.

"They broke my dickie."

That was what he told Linda Palmer, and infantile as such phrasing might seem, she felt, "It wasn't said in a baby talk way. It was a way to deal with the pain of it. Danny tried to distance himself from the things that hurt the worst . . . as if, if he said it, then it would go away."

Perhaps he had never been sexually hot. As Lovelady Powell . had colorfully put it, the flag did not always go up. But this was clinical impotence, and it would never go away. He referred to the "broken dickie" on several occasions, telling Linda that it was "impossible for him to make love in any conventional way."

That was when he broke off with Marlene. The relationship had endured for four years. "He hurt the lady very much," Linda believed, and Marlene, with girlish sensuality, dedicated her new book *Marlene Sorosky's Year-Round Holiday Cookbook* (Harper & Row, 1982)

> to Danny Kaye, who is not a professional cook, but who is truly the most professional nonprofessional I know. His philosophies of life and mankind are enthusiastically poured into his cooking and his creativity has overflowed into mine.

Age, illness, and infirmity can sometimes re-unite alienated couples simply out of physical need and emotional exhaustion. Danny's hip operation seemed to give Sylvia hope for that because she found a bigger apartment in New York. It was in their own building, the Sherry-Netherland Hotel, and even though the monthly maintenance was a steep $6,500, money still was no problem.

She asked her friend Laura Mako, the Beverly Hills decorator, to do it up as a clone of the house in Los Angeles. One of the high points was to be a replica of Danny's den—the music room—a room she was planning as "Danny's room," presumably because it assured him that he could continue sleeping alone. It was to be walled with bookshelves and equipped with a giant projection television screen.

Even more important in the planning of the new apartment

was the duplication of his Chinese kitchen, which Sylvia had once projected for the old apartment. It made more sense in this new setting, and now there could be little doubt of it. Such plans were being hatched for a future together, a reunion for what had never been a union and yet was indivisible.

31

Sylvia was competitive to the end. She wanted to own him.

—Bronya Galef

THE DANNY KAYE WHO SHUFFLED THROUGH SYLVIA'S WORK-IN-PROGRESS, THE NEW APARTMENT IN NEW YORK, WAS BUT A RELIC OF the once-dazzling young man. The renovation was becoming surreal, a project for the years, the pyramids of interior decoration. The replicating of Danny's Chinese kitchen was in itself a massive undertaking. The oversized components were fabricated in Los Angeles. The mammoth three-unit stove, with its triple giant woks, had to be trundled across the country. Monstrous to deliver, it was a feat of engineering to install. When that was managed, its scalding heat required a tearing out of walls to accommodate elaborate new ventilating shafts. There was no telling when the place was going to be finished.

And the hepatitis would not go away. It was a punishment without parole, draining his energy, sucking the life out of him. He went to Florida and visited Rosie. It was always miraculous to board a plane in the bone chill of a New York winter and emerge a few hours later into the blushing comfort of a Florida sun. To Rosie, an ashen Danny Kaye seemed to stir as she greeted him at the Fort Lauderdale International Airport.

It wasn't like the old days, when he used to come down with Fishel Goldfarb. Fishel was back in New York and flat on his back with a stroke, staring into space and unable to speak.

Rosie drove Danny to her condominium. She had come across some pictures of the whole gang at White Roe, and they reminisced over Fishel, Nat Lichtman, and Danny's boyhood partner, Lou Eisen, from the Red and Blackie team, and the beautiful dancers Kathleen Young and Dave Mack. Then they walked back to the car, and as Danny was gingerly easing himself into the passenger seat, one of Rosie's neighbors happened by. The woman stopped to stare.

"It isn't."

"It is," said Rosie.

"It is?"

Danny smiled weakly. "It is."

And they drove to the baseball park, because he loved so much to watch the Dodgers practice in spring training. But it had been exhausting for him to travel and then, immediately on his return to California, foolish to conduct a Musicians Fund benefit at the Hollywood Bowl. It was plain to Bronya Galef that "he couldn't get up the energy for it. He didn't feel like being funny, he didn't feel well, he wasn't feeling connected to what he was doing. He was in a major depression and he shouldn't have gone on."

Near the end of 1986, the hepatitis hospitalized him yet again, and this time it brought him to the brink of death. That was when Sylvia moved back to Los Angeles permanently. She had him. She commandeered his hospital room. None of Danny's friends were allowed to visit, and none could get through on the telephone. The answer was always the same: Danny was too weak to talk. "He was like a prisoner," Marlene Sorosky said, "until he was well enough to make calls on his own."

"Everything was a secret," Steve Wallace said. "They wanted that control."

"Sylvia was really a watchdog," Bronya remembered, although once, Danny did pick up the telephone. His voice was a faint groan.

"It sucks," she said, "doesn't it?"

"Yeah," he croaked. "It really sucks."

But there were some nights when both Sylvia and Dena needed to sleep, and then the overnight vigil was kept by Danny's public relations man, Warren Cowan. On those nights, he would call friends—Steve, Linda, Bronya—and give them the grim reports on Danny's worsening condition. And Steve would call Marlene.

On the night of March 2, 1987, a radio newscast described Danny's condition as critical. He was being moved into the intensive care unit. Steve Wallace drove over and simply walked into Cedars-Sinai Hospital, his mind set on seeing his friend.

Sylvia and Dena were sitting in the hall as he approached. "They sort of looked at me," he remembered, "and Dena said, 'Do you want to see him?' "

Not bothering to answer, he walked into the room and found Danny "hooked up to the machines and bottles." His eyes were closed. At three fifty-eight in the morning, two months after his seventy-fourth birthday, the pied piper died of "a heart attack brought on by internal bleeding and post-transfusion hepatitis." The amateur doctor had been done in by a medical accident.

THERE WAS NO FUNERAL. THE COOKERS TRIED TO ORGANIZE A MEMO-rial service, but, Marlene remembered, "Sylvia had a fit." She now transcended his life to take possession of him in death. Bronya said, "Sylvia wouldn't tell anybody where he was buried." Even at Sylvia's own death, several years later, she would leave instructions that nobody was to know where he was buried.

Danny's friends were profoundly offended. "It was such a cruel thing to do," Bronya said. "To him and to the people who loved him. A number of us feel very incomplete because we were never able to go and say good-bye to him."

Marlene Sorosky, then writing a food column for the *Los Angeles Times*, wrote a tribute to Danny couched in references to his cooking. She cited several of his favorite recipes, which he had demonstrated at her school. Days later, she and her editor received letters from Sylvia's attorney "saying basically that I had used Danny's recipes without permission and that she owned them now. If I ever did anything like this again, they were going to press charges."

This was an obsessive possession, and Sylvia took extraordinary, perhaps bizarre, measures to keep her husband's remains to herself. His body had in fact been taken from Cedars-Sinai Hospital to Hillside Memorial Park on Centinela Avenue in Los Angeles. But it was not buried there. According to the cemetery officials, he was there "for a minute," a technicality for the sake of a misleading death certificate. Kaye's body was immediately removed from the cemetery to a crematorium, and Sylvia took the ashes to New York.

T HE SPRAWLING NEW APARTMENT NOW CAME TO A FINISH, AND S YLVIA put up the house on San Ysidro Drive for sale. She moved permanently to New York, into the place with Danny's room and Danny's Chinese kitchen, neither of which he ever saw. For herself, she had her ebony-finish Steinway "B" concert grand piano shipped from California and set in the spacious living room overlooking Central Park.

One of her first acts, in fact, just months after Danny's death, was a gift of $1 million toward the renovation of the Hunter College Playhouse, painted (its programs would state) in "the same shade of red as Sylvia Kaye's favorite lipstick." As a Hunter student she once dreamed of writing for the musical theater. Now she had a theater of her own there. Thus, she publicly and symbolically joined with Danny. She did not dedicate the theater to him. She had once announced a memoir, to be called *Fine and Danny*, but now she dropped even the pose of a separate identity and stopped writing the book. The Hunter gift stipulated that the new playhouse be renamed not for Sylvia Fine and Danny Kaye but as the Sylvia and Danny Kaye Playhouse.

That was the last word, ensuring her equal share in his existence.

She began to entertain, even though emphysema had made a rattle of her breathing and she was forced to keep within tube distance of intravenous medication. That did not stop her from giving dinner parties. The steel pole and the glass bottle and the rubber tube became her regular dinner partner.

At one of these dinners she included Colin Romoff, who had been the musical director for a television show of Danny's. Such invitations, as the tall, slender, and rather elegant Romoff well understood, implied semi–guest status. The invitation meant yes, he was invited for dinner, but yes, he was expected to entertain, and Romoff was one of the smoothest pianists in New York.

After the last guests had gone, with only Dena remaining, Sylvia asked him to stay and play four-hands piano with her. There were still hours to go until her dawn bedtime. And so it was just herself, Romoff, and Dena in the big, quiet, hushed apartment.

Sylvia and her wheelchair and the pole with the intravenous fluid and the tube were set at the Steinway. Romoff sat on the black tufted leather piano bench beside her.

Dena nestled on the sofa. She was forty-one. She had not married and probably never would.

Sylvia placed her hands on the keyboard. She was not a facile pianist. As Romoff said, "She didn't play piano-piano-piano. She played enough to make her ideas set."

He was momentarily distracted by the clicking mechanism of her intravenous equipment. Then they began to play a Cole Porter song, and as they played into the night, Romoff remembered, "The machine was going *pocketa-pocketa.*

"Like *The Secret Life of Walter Mitty.*"

Index